WESTERN CIVILIZATION

VOLUME I

Pre-History Through the Reformation

Third Edition

EDITOR

William Hughes

Essex Community College

William Hughes is a professor of history at Essex Community College, in Baltimore County, Maryland. He received his A.B. from Franklin and Marshall College and his M.A. from the Pennsylvania State University. In addition he continued graduate studies at the American University and the Pennsylvania State University. Professor Hughes is interested in audio-visual media in historical research and education. He has written several articles, essays, and reviews for *The Journal of American History, The New Republic, The Nation,* and *Film and History.*

Annual Editions
A Library of Information from the Public Press

Cover illustration by Mike Eagle

The Dushkin Publishing Group, Inc.
Sluice Dock, Guilford, Connecticut 06437

The Annual Editions Series

Annual Editions is a series of over thirty-five volumes designed to provide the reader with convenient, low-cost access to a wide range of current, carefully selected articles from some of the most important magazines, newspapers, and journals published today. Annual Editions are updated on a regular basis through a continuous monitoring of over 200 periodical sources. All Annual Editions have a number of features designed to make them particularly useful, including topic guides, annotated tables of contents, unit overviews, and indexes. For the teacher using Annual Editions in the classroom, an Instructor's Resource Guide with test questions is available for each volume.

PUBLISHED

Africa
Aging
American Government
American History, Pre-Civil War
American History, Post-Civil War
Anthropology
Biology
Business
China
Comparative Politics
Computers in Education
Criminal Justice
Early Childhood Education
Economics
Educating Exceptional Children
Education
Educational Psychology
Environment
Global Issues

Health
Human Development
Human Sexuality
Latin America
Macroeconomics
Marketing
Marriage and Family
Personal Growth and Behavior
Psychology
Social Problems
Social Psychology
Sociology
State and Local Government
Urban Society
Western Civilization, Pre-Reformation
Western Civilization, Post-Reformation
World Politics

FUTURE VOLUMES

Abnormal Psychology
Death and Dying
Drugs, Society and Behavior
Computers in Business
Computers in Society
Congress
Energy
Ethnic Studies
Foreign Policy
Geography
Judiciary
Middle East and the Islamic World
Nutrition

Parenting
Philosophy
Political Science
Presidency
Religion
South Asia
Soviet Union and Eastern Europe
Twentieth Century American History
Western Europe
Women's Studies
World History

Library of Congress Cataloging in Publication Data.
Main entry under title: Annual editions: Western civilization, vol. I: Pre-history through the Reformation.
1. Civilization—Addresses, essays, lectures—Periodicals. 2. World history—Addresses, essays, lectures—Periodicals. Title: Western civilization, vol. I: Pre-history through the Reformation.
901.9′05   82-645823   ISBN 0-87967-586-1

Third Edition

Manufactured by The Banta Company, Menasha, Wisconsin 54952

Editors/ Advisory Board

To The Reader

In publishing ANNUAL EDITIONS we recognize the enormous role played by the magazines, newspapers, and journals of the *public press* in providing current, first-rate educational information in a broad spectrum of interest areas. Within the articles, the best scientists, practitioners, researchers, and commentators draw issues into new perspective as accepted theories and viewpoints are called into account by new events, recent discoveries change old facts, and fresh debate breaks out over important controversies.

Many of the articles resulting from this enormous editorial effort are appropriate for students, researchers, and professionals seeking accurate, current material to help bridge the gap between principles and theories and the real world. These articles, however, become more useful for study when those of lasting value are carefully *collected, organized, indexed,* and *reproduced* in a *low-cost format,* which provides easy and permanent access when the material is needed. That is the role played by *Annual Editions.* Under the direction of each volume's *Editor,* who is an expert in the subject area, and with the guidance of an *Advisory Board,* we seek each year to provide in each *ANNUAL EDITION* a current, well-balanced, carefully selected collection of the best of the public press for your study and enjoyment. We think you'll find this volume useful, and we hope you'll take a moment to let us know what you think.

What exactly are we attempting to do when we set out to study Western Civilization? The traditional course in Western Civilization is a chronological survey of sequential stages in the development of European institutions and ideas, with a cursory look at Near Eastern antecedents and a side glance at the Americas and other places where westernization has occurred. So we move from the Greeks to the Romans to the medieval period and on to the modern era, itemizing the distinctive characteristics of each stage, as well as each period's relation to preceding and succeeding developments. Of course in a survey so broad (usually moving from Adam to the Atom in two brief semesters) a certain superficiality seems inevitable. Key events whiz by as if viewed in a cyclorama; often there is little opportunity to absorb and digest the complex ideas that have shaped our culture. It is tempting to excuse these shortcomings as unavoidable. But to present a course on Western Civilization that leaves students with only a jumble of events, names, dates, and places is to miss a marvelous opportunity. For the great promise of such a broad course of study is that by examining the great turning points or shifts in the evolution of our culture we can understand the dynamics of continuity and change over time. The course at best can provide a coherent view of our traditions and offer the opportunity for reflection about everything from the forms of authority to the nature of mankind to the meaning of progress.

One way to bring coherence to the study of our civilization is to focus on what is distinctly "western" about Western Civilization. Much has been written about the subject. Vera M. Dean, for example, has argued that "There is no real differential between West and non-West except that created by the West's chronologically earlier acquisition of technology." She concludes that industrialization will shortly obliterate all differences between East and West.

Not all western observers are so monolithic in their views. Arnold Toynbee, Herbert Muller, and F.S.C. Northrop, to mention just a few, have written with pride of the unique qualities of the West, while urging our civlization to learn from the East.

And what about the eastern perspective? The West, writes Zen philosopher D.T. Suzuki, is "analytical, discriminative, differential, individualistic, intellectual, objective, scientific, generalizing, conceptual, schematic, impersonal, legalistic, organizing, powerwielding, self-assertive, disposed to impose its will upon others." The East is "synthetic, totalizing, integrative, non-discriminative, deductive, non-systematic, intuitive, subjective, spiritually individualistic, and socially group-minded."

As students become attuned to the distinctive traits of the West they develop a sense of the dynamism of history—the interplay of the forces of continuity and change. They begin to understand how ideas relate to social structures and social forces. They come to appreciate the nature and significance of conceptual innovation and recognize the way values infuse inquiry. More specifically, they develop an understanding of the evolution of western ideas about nature, humankind, authority, and the gods, i.e., they learn *how* the West became distinctly western.

Of course the articles collected in this volume can't deal with all these matters, but by providing an alternative to the synthetic summaries of most textbooks, they can help students acquire a fuller understanding of the dynamics of Western Civilization and a clear sense of its unique components. This book is like our history—unfinished, always in process. It will be revised biennially. We welcome comments and criticism from all who use this book. To that end the publisher has included a postpaid article rating form at the end of the book. In addition, we would like to know of any articles you think could improve the next edition. With your assistance we will continue to improve this anthology.

William Hughes,

Editor

Contents

The concepts in italics are developed in the article. For further expansion please refer to the Topic Guide and the Index.

Unit 3

The Judeo-Christian Heritage

Five articles examine the impact that Jesus, St. Peter,
politics, and clashing cultures had on the Judeo-
Christian heritage.

The concepts in italics are developed in the article. For further expansion please refer to the Topic Guide and the Index.

Unit 4

Moslems and Byzantines

Three selections discuss what effects the Hellenic and Christian cultures had on the development of the Moslem and Byzantine world.

Unit 5

The Medieval Period

Eight selections examine the Medieval world. The topics include the role of women, trade, exploration, crime, technology, warfare, and culture.

The concepts in italics are developed in the article. For further expansion please refer to the Topic Guide and the Index.

Unit 6

Renaissance and Reformation

Nine articles discuss the Renaissance and Reformation periods. The importance of trade and commerce on the development of the modern state, the effects of exploration, the role of art in the Renaissance society, and the emergence of religion are discussed.

The concepts in italics are developed in the article. For further expansion please refer to the Topic Guide and the Index.

Topic Guide

This topic guide suggests how the selections in this book relate to topics of traditional concern to western civilization students and professionals. It is very useful in locating articles which relate to each other for reading and research. The guide is arranged alphabetically according to topic. Articles may, of course, treat topics that do not appear in the topic guide. In turn, entries in the topic guide do not necessarily constitute a comprehensive listing of all the contents of each selection.

TOPIC AREA	TREATED AS AN ISSUE IN:	TOPIC AREA	TREATED AS AN ISSUE IN:
Agriculture	2. How Man Invented Cities	**Greek Society**	6. The First Olympics
Art and Architecture	20. The Byzantine Greeks' Heritage from the Hellenic Greeks		7. Love and Death in Ancient Greece
	36. Our Man from Arezzo		8. Life with Father, Life with Socrates
			9. The Two Thousand Years' War
Christianity	16. New Finds Cast Fresh Light on the Bible		10. Charting the Unknown
	17. Who Was Jesus?	**Hunting and Gathering**	2. How Man Invented Cities
	18. Who Was St. Peter?	**Industrial Revolution**	30. Medieval Roots of the Industrial Revolution
	19. The Contest for Men's Souls		
	22. Understanding Islam	**Islam**	21. The World of Islam
	26. Wandering for the Love of God		22. Understanding Islam
			34. To Mecca in Disguise
City-States	3. Potlatch Politics and Kings' Castles		
	4. Where Nations Began	**Jews/Judaism**	15. Jews and Judaism in the Ancient World
Commerce	11. Maritime Trade in Antiquity		16. New Finds Cast Fresh Light on the Bible
	24. The Viking Saga		
	31. How Jacques Coeur Made His Fortune	**Justice**	7. Love and Death in Ancient Greece
	32. Bruges		27. Murder and Justice, Medieval Style
	33. In Place of Strife	**Medieval Society**	23. The Natural History of Medieval Women
Crime	7. Love and Death in Ancient Greece		25. Student Power in the Middle Ages
	8. Life with Father, Life with Socrates		26. Wandering for the Love of God
	27. Murder and Justice		27. Murder and Justice, Medieval Style
	28. Robin Hood Revisited		28. Robin Hood Revisited
Culture	1. The Cosmic Calendar		29. The Social Influence of the Motte-and-Bailey Castle
	2. How Man Invented Cities		30. Medieval Roots of the Industrial Revolution
	3. Potlatch Politics and Kings' Castles		31. How Jacques Coeur Made His Fortune
	15. Jews and Judaism in the Ancient World		32. Bruges
	34. To Mecca in Disguise		33. In Place of Strife
	35. The Enigma of Aztec Sacrifice	**Modern Society**	31. How Jacques Coeur Made His Fortune
Economics	5. War and Man's Past		
	24. The Viking Saga	**Moslems**	21. The World of Islam
	32. Bruges		22. Understanding Islam
	33. In Place of Strife	**Nation-States**	4. Where Nations Began
Exploration	10. Charting the Unknown		
	11. Maritime Trade in Antiquity		
	24. The Viking Saga		
	34. To Mecca in Disguise		
	35. The Enigma of Aztec Sacrifice		

TOPIC AREA	TREATED AS AN ISSUE IN:	TOPIC AREA	TREATED AS AN ISSUE IN:
Philosophy	8. Life with Father, Life with Socrates 20. The Byzantine Greeks' Heritage from the Hellenic Greeks 37. Machiavelli 38. Luther: Giant of His Time and Ours	**Roman Society**	12. The Silent Women of Rome 13. Nero, Unmaligned 14. Murderous Games
Pilgrimages	26. Wandering for the Love of God	**Social Organization**	2. How Man Invented Cities 3. Potlatch Politics and Kings' Castles 4. Where Nations Began 5. War and Man's Past
Politics	3. Potlatch Politics and Kings' Castles 4. Where Nations Began 13. Nero, Unmaligned 14. Murderous Games 15. Jews and Judaism in the Ancient World 21. The World of Islam 33. In Place of Strife 37. Machiavelli 38. Luther: Giant of His Time and Ours	**Society**	5. War and Man's Past 36. Our Man from Arezzo 39. Heartland of the Witchcraze
		Sports (games)	6. The First Olympics 14. Murderous Games
		Technology	5. War and Man's Past 29. The Social Influence of the Motte-and-Bailey Castle 30. Medieval Roots of the Industrial Revolution
Population	5. War and Man's Past		
Pre-civilized Cultures	2. How Man Invented Cities 3. Potlatch Politics and Kings' Castles 4. Where Nations Began	**Trade**	11. Maritime Trade in Antiquity 24. The Viking Saga 31. How Jacques Coeur Made His Fortune 32. Bruges 33. In Place of Strife
Religion	6. The First Olympics 15. Jews and Judaism in the Ancient World 16. New Finds Cast Fresh Light on the Bible 17. Who Was Jesus? 18. Who Was St. Peter? 19. The Contest for Men's Souls 20. The Byzantine Greeks' Heritage from the Hellenic Greeks 21. The World of Islam 22. Understanding Islam 26. Wandering for the Love of God 38. Luther: Giant of His Time and Ours 39. Heartland of the Witchcraze	**Vikings**	24. The Viking Saga
		War	5. War and Man's Past 9. The Two Thousand Years' War 14. Murderous Games 29. The Social Influence of the Motte-and-Bailey Castle
		Witchcraft	39. Heartland of the Witchcraze
Renaissance	33. In Place of Strife 36. Our Man from Arezzo 37. Machiavelli 38. Luther: Giant of His Time and Ours 39. Heartland of the Witchcraze	**Women**	7. Love and Death in Ancient Greece 12. The Silent Women of Rome 23. The Natural History of Medieval Women 39. Heartland of the Witchcraze

Pre-History and the Earliest Civilizations

Civilization is a relatively recent phenomenon in the human experience, as Carl Sagan demonstrates in "The Cosmic Calendar." But what exactly is civilization? How did it begin? How do civilized people differ from those who aren't civilized? How is civilization transmitted?

Civilization, in its contemporary meaning, denotes a condition of human society marked by an advanced stage of artistic and technological development and by corresponding social and political complexity. Thus civilized societies have developed formal institutions for commerce, government, education, and religion—activities that are carried out informally by pre-civilized societies. In addition, civilized people make much more extensive use of symbols. The greater complexity of civilized life requires a greater degree of specialization.

Symbolization, specialization, and organization enable civilized societies to extend greater control over their environments. Because they are less dependent than pre-civilized societies upon a simple adaptation to a particular habitat, civilized societies are more dynamic. Indeed, civilization institutionalizes change.

In sum, civilization provides us with a wider range of concepts, techniques, and options to shape our collective destinies. Or, as popular historian Sprague de Camp puts it, civilized men "are organized in larger masses and possess technical skills beyond those of uncivilized men."

In the West the necessary preconditions for civilization first emerged in the great river valleys of Mesopotamia and Egypt with the development of irrigation techniques, new staple crops, the introduction of the plow, the invention of the wheel, more widespread use of beasts of burden, improved sailing vessels, and copper metallurgy. These developments revolutionized society. Population increased, became more concentrated and more complex. The emergence of cities—"the urban revolution"—marked the beginning of civilization. John Pfeiffer explains this process in "How Man Invented Cities."

Civilization combines complex social, economic, and political structures with a corresponding network of ideas and values. The Sumerians organized themselves in city-states headed by kings who acted in the name of the local patron deity. The Egyptians developed a more centralized and authoritarian system. Aspects of the earliest state structures are explored in "Where Nations Began." These early civilizations allowed for very little individualism or freedom of expression. As Nels M. Bailkey notes, "Their

thought remained closely tied to religion and found expression predominantly in religious forms." Elaborate myths recounted the deeds of heroes, defined relations between mankind and the gods, and generally justified the prevailing order of things. Myths, therefore, invite careful study because they reveal something of the relationship between values and the social order in ancient civilizations.

We are inclined nowadays to make much of the limitations of such systems of thought and authority. Yet the record of the Mesopotamians and Egyptians demonstrates, from the very beginning, civilization's potential for innovation and collective accomplishment. They developed writing and mathematics, monumental architecture, laws, astronomy, art and literature rich with diversity and imagination, and a sense of righteousness and justice.

For a time the great river valleys remained islands of civilization in a sea of barbarism. The spread of civilization to rain-watered lands required that outlying areas find means to produce a food surplus and develop the social mechanisms for transferring the surplus from farmers to specialists. The first condition was met by the diffusion of plow agriculture, the second by culture contacts that came about through conquest, trade, and migration. Several of these satellite-civilizations evolved into great empires, which further enhanced cultural exchange between diverse and dispersed societies. The problem of governing scattered and often hostile subjects required that conquerors create new patterns of authority. Empires like those of the Assyrians and Persians were not mere acts of conquest, they were innovations in government and administration. John Keegan discusses ancient warfare in the concluding selection.

Looking Ahead: Challenge Questions

Relatively speaking, how recent a development is civilization?

How did cities begin?

What price has mankind paid for civilization?

What was the function of religion in ancient societies?

Was the Hebrew notion of God truly original or did it derive from Mesopotamian antecedents?

What do primitive cultures and ancient civilizations reveal about the origins and nature of warfare?

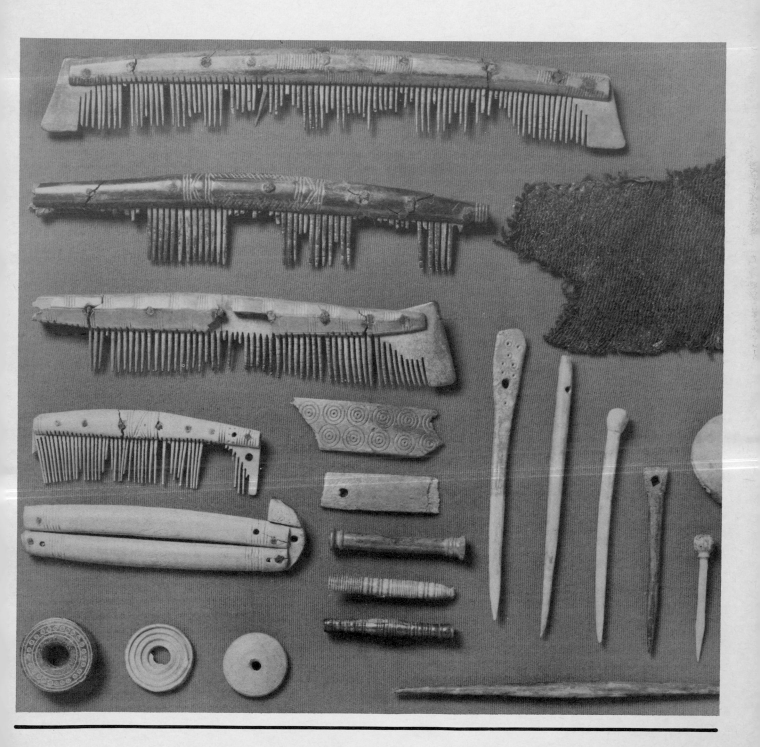

THE COSMIC CALENDAR

Carl Sagan

How a Pulitzer Prize-winning scientist-author visualizes cosmic history—from the Big Bang creation of the universe up to present-day time on Earth. His "calendar" may stagger your imagination.

PRE-DECEMBER DATES	
January 1	Big Bang
May 1	Origin of the Milky Way galaxy
September 9	Origin of the solar system
September 14	Formation of the Earth
September 25	Origin of life on Earth
October 2	Formation of the oldest rocks known on Earth
October 9	Date of oldest fossils (bacteria and blue-green algae)
November 1	Invention of sex (by microorganisms)
November 12	Oldest fossil photosynthetic plants
November 15	Eucaryptes (first cells with nuclei) flourish

The world is very old, and human beings are very young. Significant events in our personal lives are measured in years or less; our lifetimes, in decades; our family genealogies, in centuries; and all of recorded history, in millennia. But we have been preceded by an awesome vista of time, extending for prodigious periods into the past, about which we know little—both because there are no written records and because we have real difficulty in grasping the immensity of the intervals involved.

Yet we are able to date events in the remote past. Geological stratification and radioactive dating provide information on archaeological, paleontological, and geological events; and astrophysical theory provides data on the ages of planetary surfaces, stars, and the Milky Way galaxy, as well as an estimate of the time that has elapsed since that extraordinary event called the Big Bang—an explosion that involved all of the matter and energy in the present universe. The Big Bang may be the beginning of the universe, or it may be a discontinuity in which information about the earlier history of the universe was destroyed. But it is certainly the earliest event about which we have any record.

The most instructive way I know to express this cosmic chronology is to imagine the 15-billion-year lifetime of the universe (or at least its present incarnation since the Big Bang) compressed into the span of a single year. Then every billion years of Earth history would correspond to about 24 days of our cosmic year, and 1 second of that year to 475 real revolutions of the Earth about the sun. I present the cosmic chronology in three forms: a list of some representative pre-December dates; a calendar for the month of December; and a closer look at the late evening of New Year's Eve. On this scale, the events of our history books—even books that make significant efforts to deprovincialize the present—are so compressed that it is necessary to give a second-by-second recounting of the last seconds of the cosmic year. Even then, we find events listed as contemporary that we have been taught to consider as widely separated in time. In the history of life, an equally rich tapestry must have been woven in other periods—for example, between 10:02 and 10:03 on the morning of April 6th or September 16th. But we have detailed records only for the very end of the cosmic year.

The chronology corresponds to the best evidence now available. But some of it is rather shaky. No one would be astounded if, for example, it turns out that plants colonized the land in the Ordovician rather than the Silurian period; or that segmented worms appeared earlier in the Precambrian period than indicated. Also, in the chronology of the last 10 seconds of the cosmic year, it was obviously impossible for me to include all

DECEMBER

SUNDAY	MONDAY	TUESDAY	WEDNESDAY	THURSDAY	FRIDAY	SATURDAY
	1 Significant oxygen atmosphere begins to develop on Earth.	**2**	**3**	**4**	**5** Extensive vulcanism and channel formation on Mars.	**6**
7	**8**	**9**	**10**	**11**	**12**	**13**
14	**15**	**16** First worms.	**17** Precambrian ends. Paleozoic era and Cambrian period begin. Invertebrates flourish.	**18** First oceanic plankton. Trilobites flourish.	**19** Ordovician period. First fish, first vertebrates.	**20** Silurian period. First vascular plants. Plants begin colonization of land.
21 Devonian period begins. First insects. Animals begin colonization of land.	**22** First amphibians. First winged insects.	**23** Carboniferous period. First trees. First reptiles.	**24** Permian period begins. First dinosaurs.	**25** Paleozoic era ends. Mesozoic era begins.	**26** Triassic period. First mammals.	**27** Jurassic period. First birds.
28 Cretaceous period. First flowers. Dinosaurs become extinct.	**29** Mesozoic era ends. Cenozoic era and Tertiary period begin. First cetaceans. First primates.	**30** Early evolution of frontal lobes in the brains of primates. First hominids. Giant mammals flourish.	**31** End of the Pliocene period. Quaternary (Pleistocene and Holocene) period. First humans.			

significant events; I hope I may be excused for not having explicitly mentioned advances in art, music, and literature, or the historically significant American, French, Russian, and Chinese revolutions.

The construction of such tables and calendars is inevitably humbling. It is disconcerting to find that in such a cosmic year the Earth does not condense out of interstellar matter until early September; dinosaurs emerge on Christmas Eve; flowers arise on December 28th; and men and women originate at 10:30 p.m. on New Year's Eve. All of recorded history occupies the last 10 seconds of December 31; and the time from the waning of the Middle Ages to the present occupies little more than 1 second. But because I have arranged it that way, the first cosmic year has just ended. And despite the insignificance of the instant we have so far occupied in cosmic time, it is clear that what happens on and near Earth at the beginning of the second cosmic year will depend very much on the scientific wisdom and the distinctly human sensitivity of mankind.

1. PRE-HISTORY AND THE EARLIEST CIVILIZATIONS

DECEMBER 31

1:30 p.m.	Origin of *Proconsul* and *Ramapithecus*, probable ancestors of apes and men
10:30 p.m.	First humans
11:00 p.m.	Widespread use of stone tools
11:46 p.m.	Domestication of fire by Peking man
11:56 p.m.	Beginning of most recent glacial period
11:58 p.m.	Seafarers settle Australia
11:59 p.m.	Extensive cave painting in Europe
11:59:20 p.m.	Invention of agriculture
11:59:35 p.m.	Neolithic civilization; first cities
11:59:50 p.m.	First dynasties in Sumer, Ebla, and Egypt; development of astronomy
11:59:51 p.m.	Invention of the alphabet; Akkadian Empire
11:59:52 p.m.	Hammurabic legal codes in Babylon; Middle Kingdom in Egypt
11:59:53 p.m.	Bronze metallurgy; Mycenaean culture; Trojan War; Olmec culture; invention of the compass
11:59:54 p.m.	Iron metallurgy; First Assyrian Empire; Kingdom of Israel; founding of Carthage by Phoenicia
11:59:55 p.m.	Asokan India; Ch'in Dynasty China; Periclean Athens; birth of Buddha
11:59:56 p.m.	Euclidean geometry; Archimedean physics; Ptolemaic astronomy; Roman Empire; birth of Christ
11:59:57 p.m.	Zero and decimals invented in Indian arithmetic; Rome falls; Moslem conquests
11:59:58 p.m.	Mayan civilization; Sung Dynasty China; Byzantine empire; Mongol invasion; Crusades
11:59:59 p.m.	Renaissance in Europe; voyages of discovery from Europe and from Ming Dynasty China; emergence of the experimental method in science
Now: The first second of New Year's Day	Widespread development of science and technology; emergence of a global culture; acquisition of the means for self-destruction of the human species; first steps in spacecraft planetary exploration and the search for extraterrestrial intelligence

How Man Invented Cities

John Pfeiffer

The most striking mark of man's genius as a species, as the most adaptable of animals, has been his ability to live in cities. From the perspective of all we know about human evolution, nothing could be more unnatural. For over fifteen million years, from the period when members of the family of man first appeared on earth until relatively recent times, our ancestors were nomadic, small-group, wide-open-spaces creatures. They lived on the move among other moving animals in isolated little bands of a few families, roaming across wildernesses that extended like oceans to the horizon and beyond.

Considering that heritage, the wonder is not that man has trouble getting along in cities but that he can do it at all—that he can learn to live in the same place year round, enclosed in sharp-cornered and brightly-lit rectangular spaces, among noises, most of which are made by machines, within shouting distance of hundreds of other people, most of them strangers. Furthermore, such conditions arose so swiftly, practically overnight on the evolutionary time scale, that he has hardly had a

chance to get used to them. The transition from a world without cities to our present situation took a mere five or six millenniums.

It is precisely because we are so close to our origins that what happened in prehistory bears directly on current problems. In fact, the expectation is that new studies of pre-cities and early cities will contribute as significantly to an understanding of today's urban complexes as studies of infancy and early childhood have to an understanding of adolescence. Cities are signs, symptoms if you will, of an accelerating and intensive phase of human evolution, a process that we are only beginning to investigate scientifically.

The first stages of the process may be traced back some fifteen thousand years to a rather less hectic era. Homo sapiens, that new breed of restless and intelligent primate, had reached a high point in his career as a hunter-gatherer subsisting predominantly on wild plants and animals. He had developed special tools, special tactics and strategies, for dealing with a wide variety of environments, from savannas and semideserts to tundras and tropical rain forests and

mountain regions. Having learned to exploit practically every type of environment, he seemed at last to have found his natural place in the scheme of things—as a hunter living in balance with other species, and with all the world as his hunting ground.

But forces were already at work that would bring an end to this state of equilibrium and ultimately give rise to cities and the state of continuing instability that we are trying to cope with today. New theories, a harder look at the old theories, and an even harder look at our own tendencies to think small have radically changed our ideas about what happened and why.

We used to believe, in effect, that people abandoned hunting and gathering as soon as a reasonable alternative became available to them. It was hardly a safe or reliable way of life. Our ancestors faced sudden death and injury from predators and from prey that fought back, disease from exposure to the elements and from always being on the move, and hunger because the chances were excellent of coming back empty-

"How Man Invented Cities," by John Pfeiffer, *Horizon*, Autumn 1972. Reprinted with the permission of the author.

7

1. PRE-HISTORY AND THE EARLIEST CIVILIZATIONS

handed from the hunt. Survival was a full-time struggle. Leisure came only after the invention of agriculture, which brought food surpluses, rising populations, and cities. Such was the accepted picture.

The fact of the matter, supported by studies of living hunter-gatherers as well as by the archaeological record, is that the traditional view is largely melodrama and science fiction. Our preagricultural ancestors were quite healthy, quite safe, and regularly obtained all the food they needed. And they did it with time to burn. As a rule, the job of collecting food, animal and vegetable, required no more than a three-hour day, or a twenty-one-hour week. During that time, collectors brought in enough food for the entire group, which included an appreciable proportion (perhaps 30 per cent or more) of dependents, old persons and children who did little or no work. Leisure is basically a phenomenon of hunting-gathering times, and people have been trying to recover it ever since.

Another assumption ripe for discarding is that civilization first arose in the valleys of the Tigris, Euphrates, and Nile rivers and spread from there to the rest of the world. Accumulating evidence fails to support this notion that civilization is an exclusive product of these regions. To be sure, agriculture and cities may have appeared first in the Near East, but there are powerful arguments for completely independent origins in at least two other widely separated regions, Mesoamerica and Southeast Asia.

In all cases, circumstances forced hunter-gatherers to evolve new ways of surviving. With the decline of the ancient life style, nomadism, problems began piling up. If only people had kept on moving about like sane and respectable primates, life would be a great deal simpler. Instead, they settled down in increasing numbers over wider areas, and society started changing with a vengeance. Although the causes of this settling down remain a mystery, the fact of independent origins calls for an explanation based on worldwide developments.

An important factor, emphasized recently by Lewis Binford of the University of New Mexico, may have been the melting of mile-high glaciers, which was well under way fifteen thousand years ago, and which released enough water to raise the world's oceans 250 to 500 feet, to flood previously exposed coastal plains, and to create shallow bays and estuaries and marshlands. Vast numbers of fish and wild fowl made use of the new environments, and the extra resources permitted people to obtain food without migrating seasonally. In other words, people expended less energy, and life became that much easier, in the beginning anyway.

Yet this sensible and seemingly innocent change was to get mankind into all sorts of difficulties. According to a recent theory, it triggered a chain of events that made cities possible if not inevitable. Apparently, keeping on the move had always served as a natural birth-control mechanism, in part, perhaps, by causing a relatively high incidence of miscarriages. But the population brakes were off as soon as people began settling down.

One clue to what may have happened is provided by contemporary studies of a number of primitive tribes, such as the Bushmen of Africa's Kalahari Desert. Women living in nomadic bands, bands that pick up and move half a dozen or more times a year, have an average of one baby every four years or so, as compared with one baby every two and a half years for Bushman women living in settled communities—an increase of five to eight babies per mother during a twenty-year reproductive period.

The archaeological record suggests that in some places at least, a comparable phenomenon accompanied the melting of glaciers during the last ice age. People settled down and multiplied in the Les Eyzies region of southern France, one of the richest and most-studied centers of prehistory. Great limestone cliffs dominate the countryside, and at the foot of the cliffs are natural shelters, caves and rocky overhangs where people built fires, made tools out of flint and bone and ivory, and planned the next day's hunt. On special occasions artists equipped with torches went deep into certain caves like Lascaux and covered the walls with magnificent images of the animals they hunted.

In some places the cliffs and the shelters extend for hundreds of yards; in other places there are good living sites close to one another on the opposite slopes of river valleys. People in the Les Eyzies region were living not in isolated bands but in full-fledged communities, and populations seem to have been on the rise. During the period from seven thousand to twelve thousand years ago, the total number of sites doubled, and an appreciable proportion of them probably represent year-round settlements located in small river valleys. An analysis of excavated animal remains reveals an increasing dietary reliance on migratory birds and fish (chiefly salmon).

People were also settling down at about the same time in the Near East —for example, not far from the Mediterranean shoreline of Israel and on the border between the coastal plain and the hills to the east. Ofer Bar-Yosef, of the Institute of Archaeology of Hebrew University in Jerusalem, points out that since they were able to exploit both these areas, they did not have to wander widely in search of food. There were herds of deer and gazelle, wild boar, fish and wild fowl, wild cereals and other plants, and limestone caves and shelters like those in the Les Eyzies region. Somewhat later, however, a new land-use pattern emerged. Coastal villages continued to flourish, but in addition to them, new sites began appearing further inland— and in areas that were drier and less abundant.

Only under special pressure will men abandon a good thing, and in this case it was very likely the pressure of rising populations. The evidence suggests that the best coastal lands were supporting about all the hunter-gatherers they could support; and as living space decreased there was a "budding off," an overflow of surplus population into the second-best back country where game was scarcer. These people depended more and more on plants, particularly on wild cereals, as indicated by the larger numbers of flint sickle blades, mortars and pestles, and storage pits found at their sites (and also by an increased wear and pitting of teeth, presumably caused by chewing more coarse and gritty plant foods).

Another sign of the times was the appearance of stone buildings, often with impressively high and massive walls. The structures served a number of purposes. For one thing, they included storage bins where surplus grain could be kept in reserve for bad times, when there was a shortage of game and wild plants. They also imply danger abroad in the countryside, new kinds of violence, and a mounting need for defenses to protect stored goods from the raids of people who had not settled down.

Above all, the walls convey a feeling of increasing permanence, an increasing commitment to places. Although man was still mainly a hunter-gatherer living on wild species, some of the old options no longer existed for him. In the beginning, settling down may have involved a measure of choice, but now man was no longer quite so free to change locales when the land became less fruitful. Even in those days frontiers were vanishing. Man's problem was to develop new options, new ways of working the land more intensively so that it would provide the food that migration had always provided in more mobile times.

The all-important transition to agriculture came in small steps, establishing itself almost before anyone realized what was going on. Settlers in marginal lands took early measures to get more food out of less abundant environments—roughing up the soil a bit with scraping or digging sticks, sowing wheat and barley seeds, weeding, and generally doing their best to promote growth. To start with at least, it was simply a matter of supplementing regular diets of wild foods with some domesticated species, animals as well as plants, and people probably regarded themselves as hunter-gatherers working hard to maintain their way of life rather than as the revolutionaries they were. They were trying to preserve the old self-sufficiency, but it was a losing effort.

The wilderness way of life became more and more remote, more and more nearly irretrievable. Practically every advance in the technology of agriculture committed people to an increasing dependence on domesticated species and on the activities of other people living nearby. Kent Flannery of the University of Michigan emphasizes this point in a study of one part of Greater Mesopotamia, prehistoric Iran, during the period between twelve thousand and six thousand years ago. For the hunter-gatherer, an estimated one-third of the country's total land area was good territory, consisting of grassy plains and high mountain valleys where wild species were abundant; the rest of the land was desert and semidesert.

The coming of agriculture meant that people used a smaller proportion of the countryside. Early farming took advantage of naturally distributed water; the best terrain for that, namely terrain with a high water table and marshy areas, amounted to about a tenth of the land area. But only a tenth of that tenth was suitable for the next major development, irrigation. Meanwhile, food yields were soaring spectacularly, and so was the population of Iran, which increased more than fiftyfold; in other words, fifty times the original population was being supported by food produced on one-hundredth of the land.

A detailed picture of the steps involved in this massing of people is coming from studies of one part of southwest Iran, an 880-square-mile region between the Zagros Mountains and the Iraqi border. The Susiana Plain is mostly flat, sandy semidesert, the only notable features being man-made mounds that loom on the horizon like islands, places where people built in successively high levels on the ruins of their ancestors. During the past decade or so, hundreds of mounds have been mapped and dated (mainly through pottery styles) by Robert Adams of the University of Chicago, Jean Perrot of the French Archaeological Mission in Iran, and Henry Wright and Gregory Johnson of the University of Michigan. Their work provides a general idea of when the mounds were occupied, how they varied in size at different periods and how a city may be born.

2. How Man Invented Cities

Imagine a time-lapse motion picture of the early settling of the Susiana Plain, starting about 6500 B.C., each minute of film representing a century. At first the plain is empty, as it has been since the beginning of time. Then the pioneers arrive; half a dozen families move in and build a cluster of mud-brick homes near a river. Soon another cluster appears and another, until, after about five minutes (it is now 6000 B.C.), there are ten settlements, each covering an area of 1 to 3 hectares (1 hectare = 2.47 acres). Five minutes more (5500 B.C.) and we see the start of irrigation, on a small scale, as people dig little ditches to carry water from rivers and tributaries to lands along the banks. Crop yields increase and so do populations, and there are now thirty settlements, all about the same size as the original ten.

This is but a prelude to the main event. Things become really complicated during the next fifteen minutes or so (5500 to 4000 B.C.). Irrigation systems, constructed and maintained by family groups of varying sizes, become more complex. The number of settlements shows a modest increase, from thirty to forty, but a more significant change takes place—the appearance of a hierarchy. Instead of settlements all about the same size, there are now levels of settlements and a kind of ranking: one town (7 hectares), ten large villages (3 to 4 hectares), and twenty-nine smaller villages of less than 3 hectares. During this period large residential and ceremonial structures appear at Susa, a town on the western edge of the Susiana Plain.

Strange happenings can be observed not long after the middle of this period (about 4600 B.C.). For reasons unknown, the number of settlements decreases rapidly. It is not known whether the population of the area decreased simultaneously. Time passes, and the number of settlements increases to about the same level as before, but great changes have occurred. Three cities have appeared with monumental public buildings, elaborate residential architecture, large workshops, major storage and market facilities, and certainly with administrators and bureaucrats. The settlement hierarchy is more

1. PRE-HISTORY AND THE EARLIEST CIVILIZATIONS

complex, and settlements are no longer located to take advantage solely of good agricultural opportunities. Their location is also influenced by the cities and the services and opportunities available there. By the end of our hypothetical time-lapse film, by the early part of the third millennium B.C., the largest settlement of all is the city of Susa, which covers some thirty hectares and will cover up to a square kilometer (100 hectares) of territory before it collapses in historical times.

All Mesopotamia underwent major transformations during this period. Another city was taking shape 150 miles northwest of Susa in the heartland of Sumer. Within a millennium the site of Uruk near the Euphrates River grew from village dimensions to a city enclosing within its defense walls more than thirty thousand people, four hundred hectares, and at the center a temple built on top of a huge brick platform. Archaeological surveys reveal that this period also saw a massive immigration into the region from places and for reasons as yet undetermined, resulting in a tenfold increase in settlements and in the formation of several new cities.

Similar surveys, requiring months and thousands of miles of walking, are completed or under way in many parts of the world. Little more than a millennium after the establishment of Uruk and Susa, cities began making an independent appearance in northern China not far from the conflux of the Wei and Yellow rivers, in an area that also saw the beginnings of agriculture. Still later, and also independently as far as we can tell, intensive settlement and land use developed in the New World.

The valley of Oaxaca in Mexico, where Flannery and his associates are working currently, provides another example of a city in the process of being formed. Around 500 B.C., or perhaps a bit earlier, buildings were erected for the first time on the tops of hills. Some of the hills were small, no more than twenty-five or thirty feet high, and the buildings were correspondingly small; they overlooked a few terraces and a river and probably a hamlet or two. Larger structures appeared on higher hills overlooking many villages. About 400 B.C. the most elaborate set-

tlement began to appear on the highest land, 1,500-foot Monte Albán, with a panoramic view of the valley's three arms; and within two centuries it had developed into an urban center including hundreds of terraces, an irrigation system, a great plaza, ceremonial buildings and residences, and an astronomical observatory.

At about the same time, the New World's largest city, Teotihuacán, was evolving some 225 miles to the northwest in the central highlands of Mexico. Starting as a scattering of villages and hamlets, it covered nearly eight square miles at its height (around A.D. 100 to 200) and probably contained some 125,000 people. Archaeologists are now reconstructing the life and times of this great urban center. William Sanders of Pennsylvania State University is concentrating on an analysis of settlement patterns in the area, while Rene Millon of the University of Rochester and his associates have prepared detailed section-by-section maps of the city as a step toward further extensive excavations. Set in a narrow valley among mountains and with its own man-made mountains, the Pyramid of the Sun and the Pyramid of the Moon, the city flourished on a grand scale. It housed local dignitaries and priests, delegations from other parts of Mesoamerica, and workshop neighborhoods where specialists in the manufacture of textiles, pottery, obsidian blades, and other products lived together in early-style apartments.

The biggest center in what is now the United States probably reached its peak about a millennium after Teotihuacán. But it has not been reconstructed, and archaeologists are just beginning to appreciate the scale of what happened there. Known as Cahokia and located east of the Mississippi near St. Louis, it consists of a cluster of some 125 mounds (including a central mound 100 feet high and covering 15 acres) as well as a line of mounds extending six miles to the west.

So surveys and excavations continue, furnishing the sort of data needed to disprove or prove our theories. Emerging patterns patterns involving the specific locations of different kinds of communities and of buildings and other artifacts within communities

can yield information about the forces that shaped and are still shaping cities and the behavior of people in cities. But one trend stands out above all others: the world was becoming more and more stratified. Every development seemed to favor social distinctions, social classes and elites, and to work against the old hunter-gatherer ways.

Among hunter-gatherers all people are equal. Individuals are recognized as exceptional hunters, healers, or storytellers, and they all have the chance to shine upon appropriate occasions. But it would be unthinkable for one of them, for any one man, to take over as full-time leader. That ethic passed when the nomadic life passed. In fact, a literal explosion of differences accompanied the coming of communities where people lived close together in permanent dwellings and under conditions where moving away was not easy.

The change is reflected clearly in observed changes of settlement patterns. Hierarchies of settlements imply hierarchies of people. Emerging social levels are indicated by the appearance of villages and towns and cities where only villages had existed before, by different levels of complexity culminating in such centers as Susa and Monte Albán and Cahokia. Circumstances practically drove people to establish class societies. In Mesopotamia, for instance, increasingly sophisticated agricultural systems and intensive concentrations of populations brought about enormous and irreversible changes within a short period. People were clamped in a demographic vise, more and more of them living and depending on less and less land—an ideal setting for the rapid rise of status differences.

Large-scale irrigation was a highly effective centralizing force, calling for new duties and new regularities and new levels of discipline. People still depended on the seasons; but in addition, canals had to be dug and maintained, and periodic cleaning was required to prevent the artificial waterways from filling up with silt and assorted litter. Workers had to be brought together, assigned tasks, and fed, which meant schedules and storehouses and rationing stations and mass-produced pottery to serve as food containers. It took time to organize such activities efficiently. There were undoubtedly many false starts, many attempts by local people to work things out among themselves and their neighbors at a community or village level. Many small centers, budding institutions, were undoubtedly formed and many collapsed, and we may yet detect traces of them in future excavations and analyses of settlement patterns.

The ultimate outcome was inevitable. Survival demanded organization on a regional rather than a local basis. It also demanded high-level administrators and managers, and most of them had to be educated people, mainly because of the need to prepare detailed records of supplies and transactions. Record-keeping has a long prehistory, perhaps dating back to certain abstract designs engraved on cave walls and bone twenty-five thousand or more years ago. But in Mesopotamia after 4000 B.C. there was a spurt in the art of inventing and utilizing special marks and symbols.

The trend is shown in the stamp and cylinder seals used by officials to place their "signatures" on clay tags and tablets, man's first documents. At first the designs on the stamp seals were uncomplicated, consisting for the most part of single animals or simple geometric motifs. Later, however, there were bigger stamp seals with more elaborate scenes depicting several objects or people or animals. Finally the cylinder seals appeared, which could be rolled to repeat a complex design. These seals indicate the existence of more and more different signatures and more and more officials and record keepers. Similar trends are evident in potters' marks and other symbols. All these developments precede pictographic writing, which appears around 3200 B.C.

Wherever record keepers and populations were on the rise, in the Near East or Mexico or China, we can be reasonably sure that the need for a police force or the prehistoric equivalent thereof was on the increase, too. Conflict, including everything from fisticuffs to homicide, increases sharply with group size, and people have

known this for a long time. The Bushmen have a strong feeling about avoiding crowds: "We like to get together, but we fear fights." They are most comfortable in bands of about twenty-five persons and when they have to assemble in larger groups which happens for a total of only a few months a year, mainly to conduct initiations, arrange marriages, and be near the few permanent water holes during dry seasons they form separate small groups of about twenty-five, as if they were still living on their own.

Incidentally, twenty-five has been called a "magic number," because it hints at what may be a universal law of group behavior. There have been many counts of hunter-gatherer bands, not only in the Kalahari Desert, but also in such diverse places as the forests of Thailand, the Canadian Northwest, and northern India. Although individual bands may vary from fifteen to seventy-five members, the tendency is to cluster around twenty-five, and in all cases a major reason for keeping groups small is the desire to avoid violence. In other words, the association between large groups and conflict has deep roots and very likely presented law-and-order problems during the early days of cities and pre-cities, as it has ever since.

Along with managers and record keepers and keepers of the peace, there were also specialists in trade. A number of factors besides population growth and intensive land use were involved in the origin of cities, and local and long-distance trade was among the most important. Prehistoric centers in the process of becoming urban were almost always trade centers. They typically occupied favored places, strategic points in developing trade networks, along major waterways and caravan routes or close to supplies of critical raw materials.

Archaeologists are making a renewed attempt to learn more about such developments. Wright's current work in southwest Iran, for example, includes preliminary studies to detect and measure changes in the flow of trade. One site about sixty-five miles from Susa lies close to tar pits, which in prehistoric times served as a source of natural asphalt for fastening stone

blades to handles and waterproofing baskets and roofs. By saving all the waste bits of this important raw material preserved in different excavated levels, Wright was able to estimate fluctuations in its production over a period of time. In one level, for example, he found that the amounts of asphalt produced increased far beyond local requirements; in fact, a quantitative analysis indicates that asphalt exports doubled at this time. The material was probably being traded for such things as high-quality flint obtained from quarries more than one hundred miles away, since counts of material recovered at the site indicate that imports of the flint doubled during the same period.

In other words, the site was taking its place in an expanding trade network, and similar evidence from other sites can be used to indicate the extent and structure of that network. Then the problem will be to find out what other things were happening at the same time, such as significant changes in cylinder-seal designs and in agricultural and religious practices. This is the sort of evidence that may be expected to spell out just how the evolution of trade was related to the evolution of cities.

Another central problem is gaining a fresh understanding of the role of religion. Something connected with enormous concentrations of people, with population pressures and tensions of many kinds that started building up five thousand or more years ago, transformed religion from a matter of simple rituals carried out at village shrines to the great systems of temples and priesthoods invariably associated with early cities. Sacred as well as profane institutions arose to keep society from splitting apart.

Strong divisive tendencies had to be counteracted, and the reason may involve yet another magic number, another intriguing regularity that has been observed in hunter-gatherer societies in different parts of the world. The average size of a tribe, defined as a group of bands all speaking the same dialect, turns out to be about five hundred persons, a figure that depends to some extent on the limits of human memory. A tribe is a community of people who can identify closely with one another and engage in repeated face-to-face encounters and recognitions; and it happens that five hundred may represent about the number of persons a hunter-gatherer can remember well enough to approach on what would amount to a first-name basis in our society. Beyond that number the level of familiarity declines, and there is an increasing tendency to regard individuals as "they" rather than "we," which is when trouble usually starts. (Architects recommend that an elementary school should not exceed five hundred pupils if the principal is to maintain personal contact with all of them, and the headmaster of one prominent prep school recently used this argument to keep his student body at or below the five-hundred mark.)

Religion of the sort that evolved with the first cities may have helped to "beat" the magic number five hundred. Certainly there was an urgent need to establish feelings of solidarity among many thousands of persons rather than a few hundred. Creating allegiances wider than those provided by direct kinship and person-to-person ties became a most important problem, a task for full-time professionals. In this connection Paul Wheatley of the University of Chicago suggests that "specialized priests were among the first persons to be released from the daily round of subsistence labor." Their role was partly to exhort other workers concerned with the building of monuments and temples, workers who probably exerted greater efforts in the belief that they were doing it not for mere men but for the glory of individuals highborn and close to the gods.

The city evolved to meet the needs of societies under pressure. People were being swept up in a process that had been set in motion by their own activities and that they could never have predicted, for the simple reason that they had no insight into what they were doing in the first place. For example, they did not know, and had no way of knowing, that settling down could lead to population explosions.

There is nothing strange about this state of affairs, to be sure. It is the essence of the human condition and involves us just as intensely today. Then as now, people responded by the sheer instinct of survival to forces that they understood vaguely at best—and worked together as well as they could to organize themselves, to preserve order in the face of accelerating change and complexity and the threat of chaos. They could never know that they were creating what we, its beneficiaries and its victims, call civilization.

Potlatch Politics and Kings' Castles

*Hunting and gathering tribes have never made the leap
into the struggle for power and prestige*

Marvin Harris

*Columnist Marvin Harris teaches anthropology at
Columbia University.*

Some of the most puzzling life-styles on exhibit in
the museum of world ethnography bear the imprint of a
drive for prestige. Many people seem to hunger for
approval. Occasionally their craving becomes so
powerful that they compete with each other for status
as others compete for land, food, or sex. At times this
competition is so fierce that it becomes an obsession,
wholly divorced from, and even directly opposed to,
material costs.

Americans spend their entire lives trying to climb
further up the social pyramid in order to impress each
other. We seem to be more interested in being admired
for the wealth we accumulate than in the actual wealth
itself, which often consists of chromium baubles or
other useless objects. Thorstein Veblen's mordant
phrases "conspicuous consumption" and "conspicuous
waste" convey a sense of the intense desire to "keep
up with the Joneses" that lies behind the ceaseless
cosmetic alterations in the automotive, appliance, and
clothing industries.

Early in the present century, anthropologists were
surprised to discover that certain "primitive" tribes
engaged in conspicuous consumption and conspicuous
waste to a degree unmatched by the most wasteful of
modern consumer economies. Ambitious, status-hungry
men competed with each other by giving huge feasts
and judged each other by the amount of food that was
provided. A feast was a success only if the guests ate
until they were stupefied, staggered into the bush,
vomited, and came back for more.

The most bizarre instance of status seeking was
discovered among the American Indians who formerly
inhabited the Pacific Northwest. Here the chiefs
practiced *potlatch;* their object was to give away or
destroy more wealth than their rivals. In an attempt to
shame his rivals and gain everlasting admiration from
his followers, a powerful chief might destroy food,
clothing, money, and sometimes, even burn down his
own house.

Potlatch was made famous by Ruth Benedict in her
book *Patterns of Culture,* which describes how the
custom operated among the Kwakiutl, the aboriginal
inhabitants of Vancouver Island. Benedict thought that
potlatch was part of a megalomaniacal life-style
characteristic of the Kwakiutl. Ever since, potlatch has
been a monument to the belief that cultures are the
creations of inscrutable forces and deranged person-
alities.

But the Kwakiutl potlatch was not the result of
maniacal whims; it was caused by definite economic
and ecological conditions. In the absence of these
conditions, the need to be admired and the drive for
prestige express themselves in completely different
ways. Inconspicuous consumption replaces conspicuous
consumption; conspicuous waste is forbidden; and
there are no competitive status seekers.

The Kwakiutl lived in villages close to the shore.
They fished and hunted along the island-studded
sounds and fjords in dugout canoes. Eager to attract
traders, they made their villages conspicuous by
erecting on the beach the carved tree trunks we
erroneously call "totem poles." The carvings on these
poles symbolized the ancestral titles to which the
village chiefs laid claim.

A Kwakiutl chief was never content with the degree

From *Natural History,* May 1984, pp. 10-12, 14, 16-19. From COWS, PIGS, WARS, AND WITCHES, by Marvin Harris. Copyright
©1984 by Marvin Harris. Reprinted by permission of Random House, Inc.

of respect he received from his followers and from neighboring chiefs. Always insecure about his status, each chief felt the obligation to justify and validate his chiefly pretensions. The prescribed manner for doing this was through a potlatch, which was given by a host chief and his followers to a guest chief and his followers. The object was to show that the host chief was truly entitled to chiefly status and was more exalted than the guest chief. To prove this point, the host chief gave his guests quantities of valuable gifts. The guests, in turn, would belittle what they received and vow to hold a return potlatch at which their chief would prove that he was greater than the present host by giving even larger quantities of more valuable gifts.

Preparations for a potlatch required the accumulation of fresh and dried fish, fish oil, berries, animal skins, blankets, and other valuables. On the appointed day, the guests paddled up to the host village in their dugout canoes and went into the chief's house. There they gorged themselves while dancers, masked as beaver gods and thunderbirds, entertained them.

The host chief and his followers neatly piled up the wealth that was to be given away. As the host pranced up and down, boasting about how much he was about to give them, the visitors stared sullenly. Counting out the boxes of fish oil, baskets of berries, and piles of blankets, the host commented derisively on the poverty of his rivals. Laden with gifts, the guests finally returned to their village, where, stung to the quick, the guest chief vowed to get even. This could only be achieved by holding a return potlatch and obliging his rivals to accept even more valuables than they had given away. Considering all the Kwakiutl villages as a single unit, potlatch stimulated a ceaseless flow of prestige and valuables moving in opposite directions.

An ambitious chief and his followers had potlatch rivals in several different villages at once. Specialists in counting property kept track of what each village had to do to even the score. If a chief managed to best his rivals in one place, he still had to confront them in another.

At some potlatches, valuables were not given away but were destroyed. Successful potlatch chiefs sometimes decided to hold "grease feasts" at which boxes of candlefish oil were poured on the fire in the center of the house. As the flames roared, the guests sat impassively or even complained about the chill in the air. At some grease feasts the flames ignited the roof, and the entire house would become a potlatch offering, causing the greatest shame to the guests and much rejoicing among the hosts.

According to Ruth Benedict, potlatching was a result of the obsessive status hunger of the Kwakiutl chiefs. "Judged by the standards of other cultures the speeches of their chiefs are unabashed megalomania," she wrote. "The object of all Kwakiutl enterprises was to show oneself superior to one's rivals." In her opinion, the whole aboriginal economic system of the

Pacific Northwest was "bent to the service of this obsession."

I think that Benedict was mistaken. The economic system of the Kwakiutl was not bent to the service of status rivalry; rather, status rivalry was bent to the service of the economic system.

All of the basic ingredients of the Kwakiutl giveaways, except for their destructive aspects, are present in other societies dispersed over different parts of the globe. Stripped down to its elementary core, the potlatch is a competitive feast, a nearly universal mechanism for assuring the production and distribution of wealth among peoples who have not yet fully acquired a ruling class.

Melanesia and New Guinea present the best opportunity to study competitive feasting under relatively pristine conditions. Throughout this region, so-called big men owe their superior status to the large number of feasts that each has sponsored. Each feast is preceded by an intensive effort by an aspiring big man to accumulate the necessary wealth.

Among the Kaoka-speaking people of the Solomon Islands, the status-hungry individual begins his career by making his wife and children plant larger yam gardens. As described by the Australian anthropologist Ian Hogbin, the aspiring big man then has his kinsmen and age-mates help him fish. Later he begs sows from his friends to increase his pig herd. As the litters are born, he boards additional animals with his neighbors. Soon his relatives and friends feel that the young man is going to be a success; seeing his gardens and pig herd, they redouble their work efforts. When he does become a big man, they want him to remember that they helped him.

Finally, they all build a fine house in which, as in the case of potlatch, the wealth is stacked in neat piles and displayed for the guests to count and admire.

At one feast given by a young man named Atana, Hogbin counted 250 pounds of dried fish, 3,000 yam and coconut cakes, 11 large bowls of yam pudding, and 8 pigs. In this instance, some of the guests themselves brought presents to be added to the giveaway. Their contributions raised the total to 300 pounds of fish, 5,000 cakes, 19 bowls of pudding, and 13 pigs.

Atana proceeded to divide this wealth into 257 portions, one for everyone who had helped him or who had brought gifts, rewarding some more than others. "Only the remnants were left for Atana himself," notes Hogbin. Status seekers in Guadalcanal always say: "The giver of the feast takes the bones and the stale cakes; the meat and the fat go to the others."

The feast-giving days of the big man, like those of the potlatch chiefs, are never over. On threat of being reduced to the status of a commoner, each big man prepares for the next feast. Since there are several big men per village and community, these plans and preparations often lead to complex competitive maneuvering for the allegiance of relatives and neighbors.

The big men work harder, worry more, and consume less than anybody else. Prestige is their only reward. They may be megolomaniacal, but they render an important service to society by increasing production. As a result of the big man's craving for status, more people work to produce more food and other valuables.

Under conditions where everyone has equal access to the means of subsistence, competitive feasting serves the function of preventing the labor force from falling back to levels of productivity that offer no safety margin in crises such as war and crop failures. In the absence of formal political institutions that can integrate independent villages into a common economic framework, competitive feasting creates a network of intervillage economic expectations. It promotes the sharing of food and resources among people who live in different villages. Finally, competitive feasting by big men acts as an equalizer of annual fluctuations in productivity among villages occupying different micro-environments—seacoast, lagoon, or upland habitats. Automatically, the biggest feasts in any given year will be given by villages that have enjoyed conditions favorable to production.

All of these points applied to the Kwakiutl. The Kwakiutl chiefs were like Melanesian big men except that they operated with a much more productive technology in a richer environment. Like big men, they competed with each other to attract men and women to their villages. The greatest chiefs were the best providers and gave the biggest potlatches. The chief's followers shared vicariously in his prestige and helped him to achieve more exalted honors. The totem poles were grandiose advertisements proclaiming that a village had a mighty chief.

Thus, despite the overt competitive thrust of potlatch, it functioned to transfer food and other valuables from centers of high productivity to less fortunate villages. Since fish runs, wild fruit, and vegetable harvests fluctuated unpredictably, intervillage potlatching was advantageous from the standpoint of the regional population as a whole. When the fish spawned in nearby streams and the berries ripened close at hand, last year's guests became this year's hosts. To eat, all a poor village had to do was admit that the rival chief was a great man.

Why did the practical basis of potlatch escape the attention of Ruth Benedict? Anthropologists began to study potlatch only after the Pacific Northwest aborigines had entered into commercial and wage-labor relations with Russian, English, Canadian, and American merchants and settlers. This contact gave rise to epidemics of smallpox and other European diseases that killed off a large part of the native population. The Kwakiutl population fell from 23,000 in 1836 to 2,000 in 1886, a decline that intensified the competition for manpower.

At the same time, wages paid by the Europeans pumped unprecedented amounts of wealth into the potlatch network. The Kwakiutl received thousands of blankets from the Hudson's Bay Company in exchange for animal skins. These blankets replaced food as the most important item given away at the great potlatches. The dwindling population soon found itself with more valuables than it could consume. Yet the need to attract followers was greater than ever due to the labor shortage. So the potlatch chiefs ordered the destruction of property in the vain hope that such spectacular demonstrations of wealth would bring the people back to the empty villages. But these were the practices of a dying culture struggling to adapt to a new set of political and economic conditions; they bore little resemblance to the potlatch of aboriginal times.

To the participants, competitive feasting is a manifestation of an insatiable craving for prestige. But from the point of view outlined in this article the insatiable craving for prestige is a manifestation of competitive feasting. Every society makes use of the need for approval, but not every society links prestige to success in competitive feasting.

Competitive feasting as a source of prestige must be seen in evolutionary perspective to be properly understood. Big men like Atana or the Kwakiutl chiefs carry out a form of economic exchange known as redistribution. That is, they gather together the results of the productive effort of many individuals and then redistribute the aggregated wealth in different quantities to a different set of people. As I have said, the Kaoka big man works harder, worries more, and consumes less than anybody else in the village. This was not true of the Kwakiutl chiefs, however. The great potlatch chiefs performed the entrepreneurial and managerial functions required for a big potlatch, but they left the hardest work to their followers. The greatest potlatch chiefs even had a few war captives working for them as slaves. The Kwakiutl chiefs had begun to reverse the Kaoka formula and were keeping some of the "meat and fat" for themselves, leaving most of the "bones and stale cakes" for their followers.

If we follow the evolutionary line leading from Atana, the impoverished big man, to the semi-hereditary Kwakiutl chiefs, we eventually find societies ruled by hereditary kings, who perform no industrial or agricultural labor and who keep the best of everything for themselves. Exalted divine-right rulers maintain their prestige by building conspicuous palaces, temples, and monuments; they validate their right to hereditary privileges, not by potlatch, but by force.

Reversing direction, we can go from kings to potlatch chiefs to big men, ending up with egalitarian societies in which competitive displays and conspicuous consumption by individuals disappear, and where anyone foolish enough to boast about his greatness is accused of witchcraft and is stoned to death.

In the truly egalitarian societies that have survived

long enough to be studied by anthropologists, the mode of exchange known as reciprocity predominates. Reciprocity is the technical term for an economic exchange between two individuals in which neither specifies precisely what is expected in return or when they expect it. Attitudes of reciprocity are similar to those we take when we exchange goods or services with our close relatives or friends.

Everything about reciprocity is opposed to the precise counting and reckoning of one person's debts to another. In fact, the idea is to deny that anybody really owes anything. One can tell whether a life-style is based on reciprocity if people do not say thank you. In truly egalitarian societies, it is rude to be openly grateful for the receipt of material goods or services. The Semai of central Malaya never express gratitude for the meat that a hunter gives away in exactly equal portions to his companions. Robert Dentan, who has lived with the Semai, found that to say thank you was rude because it suggested that you were either calculating the size of the piece of meat you had been given or that you were surprised by the success and generosity of the hunter.

In contrast to the conspicuous displays of Kaoka big men, the boasting of potlatch chiefs, and our own flaunting of status symbols, the Semai follow a life-style in which those who are most successful must be the least conspicuous. Status seeking through rivalrous redistribution, conspicuous consumption, or waste is unthinkable to them.

After Richard Lee of the University of Toronto had studied the Bushmen of the Kalahari Desert, he wanted to show his gratitude. As Christmas approached he learned that the Bushmen were likely to camp at the edge of the desert near villages where they sometimes obtained meat through trade. Intending to give them an ox for a Christmas present, he located a fat animal of monstrous proportions in a remote village. Returning to camp, Lee told the Bushmen one by one that he had bought the largest ox he had ever seen.

The first man to hear the news became alarmed. He asked Lee where he had bought the ox, what color it was, and what size its horns were, and then he shook his head. "I know that ox," he said. "Why, it is nothing but skin and bones!"

Lee confided in several other Bushmen, but continued to meet with the same reaction. When Christmas came the ox was slaughtered. It was covered with a thick layer of fat and was devoured with gusto.

Lee insisted upon an explanation. "Yes, of course we knew all along what the ox was really like," one hunter admitted. "But when a young man kills much meat he comes to think of himself as a chief or big man, and he thinks of the rest of us as his servants or inferiors. We cannot accept this." He went on, "We refuse one who boasts, for someday his pride will make him kill somebody. So we always speak of his meat as worthless. This way we cool his heart and make him gentle."

The Eskimo fear of generous gift givers is expressed by their proverb "Gifts make slaves just as whips make dogs." And that is exactly what happened. In evolutionary perspective, ambitious status seekers gave gifts that came from their own extra work; soon others found themselves working harder to reciprocate, which permitted the gift givers to give more gifts. Eventually the gift givers became so powerful that they disobeyed the rules of reciprocity. They could force people to pay taxes and to work for them without redistributing what was in their storehouses and palaces. Of course, as assorted modern big men and politicians sometimes recognize, "slaves" work better if given an occasional big feast instead of constant whippings.

If people like the Eskimo, Bushmen, and Semai understood the dangers of gift giving, why did others permit it to flourish? And why were big men permitted to get so puffed up that they could enslave the people whose work made their glory possible? Permit me to make a few suggestions.

Reciprocity is a form of economic exchange that is primarily adapted to conditions in which overproduction would have an adverse effect upon group survival. These conditions are found among certain hunters and gatherers, who, if they killed more animals and uprooted more plants than they needed, would risk permanent impairment of their food supply.

Lee found that the Bushmen worked for only ten to fifteen hours a week. "Primitive" hunters and gatherers work less than we do—without benefit of a single labor union—because their ecosystems cannot tolerate weeks and months of intensive extra effort. If an aspiring Bushman got his followers to work like the Kaoka for a month, every game animal for miles around would be killed or scared off and the people would starve to death.

Competitive feasting and other redistributive forms overwhelmed reciprocity when domesticated plants and animals were substituted for wild plants and animals. This raised the habitat's carrying capacity. Now the greater the effort, the more food produced. Prestige-hungry individuals could work harder and give away more to everyone's benefit. The only hitch was that this generosity had to be reciprocated. So people began to work harder in order to reciprocate the generosity of the few overzealous producers. As the reciprocal exchanges became unbalanced, they became gifts. As the gifts piled up, the gift givers were rewarded with prestige and counter gifts. Soon redistribution predominated over reciprocity, and prestige went to the most calculating gift givers, who shamed everybody into working harder than the Bushmen ever dreamed possible.

Conditions appropriate for the development of competitive feasting and redistribution sometimes also occurred among nonagricultural populations. Among the coastal peoples of the Pacific Northwest, annual runs of salmon, other migratory fish, and sea mammals provided the ecological analogue of agricultural harvests. The salmon or candlefish ran in such vast numbers that if the Kwakiutl worked harder, they would catch more fish. The main function of the potlatch, therefore, was not to award prestige, but to increase food production.

Stepping away for the moment from reciprocal and redistributive prestige systems, we can surmise that every major type of political and economic system uses prestige in a distinctive manner. For example, with the appearance of capitalism in Western Europe, acquisition of wealth once more became the criterion for big-man status. Only in this case, the big men tried to take away each other's wealth, and highest prestige and power went to the individual who managed to accumulate and hold on to the greatest fortune. After they became secure, the capitalist upper class resorted to grand-scale conspicuous consumption and conspicuous wast in order to impress their rivals. They built mansions, adorned themselves with jewels, and spoke contemptuously of the impoverished masses.

Eventually, the rich were threatened by taxation aimed at redistributing their wealth. Conspicuous consumption in the grand manner became dangerous, so highest prestige now once again goes to those who have most but show least. With the upper class no longer flaunting its wealth, some of the pressure on the middle class to engage in conspicuous consumption has also been removed. This suggests to me that torn jeans and the rejection of overt consumerism among middle-class youth of late has more to do with aping upper-class trends than with any so-called cultural revolution.

One final point. You might wish to question the sanity of the process by which mankind was tricked into working harder in order to feed more people. The answer I see is that many primitive societies did refuse to expand their productive effort. But the fate of these peoples was sealed as soon as any one of them, no matter how remotely situated, crossed the threshold to redistribution and the full-scale stratification of classes that lay beyond. Virtually all of the reciprocity-type hunters and gatherers were destroyed or forced into remote areas by bigger and more powerful societies that maximized production and population. At bottom, this replacement was essentially a matter of the ability of larger, denser, and better-organized societies to defeat simple hunters and gatherers in armed conflict. It was either work hard or perish.

Where Nations Began

Excavations on the Nile suggest how a powerful elite welded prehistoric villages into the world's first nation-state.

Michael Allen Hoffman

Michael Allen Hoffman, an archeologist at the University of South Carolina's Earth Sciences and Resources Institute, returned to Egypt in January 1983 for his seventh season. He is the author of Egypt Before the Pharaohs.

He was called Catfish, or Narmer in the language of the ancient Egyptians, and in his day, 5,100 years ago, he was probably the most politically powerful man in the world. For it was he who founded humanity's first nation-state, a political empire far bigger and more complex than any city-state. Known by the legendary name of Menes in later times, Narmer was Egypt's first pharaoh, founder of the First Dynasty and first ruler of a new form of political organization that would last nearly 3,000 years. In 1898 English archeologists found a large, carved slate palette, inscribed with Narmer's name and carved on both sides with scenes of the king vanquishing his foes in battle. On one side Narmer wears the white crown of Upper Egypt while on the other he sports the red crown of Lower Egypt. Together the crowns symbolize the monarchy's early role as unifier of all Egypt.

The unification of separate regions under a single ruler was a catalytic event, climaxing nearly a thousand years of Predynastic development and triggering a flowering of art and architecture, of writing and religion that has seldom, if ever, been matched.

The achievements of ancient Egypt, however, could hardly have arisen *de novo,* nor could they have been the work of one man. Cultures and new forms of social organization don't just happen; they grow out of what came before. The question that fascinates me, as an archeologist specializing in Egypt, is the origin of the political structure we call the nation-state. What was happening in Predynastic Egypt that made it possible for Narmer to take the decisive step, portrayed so graphically on his palette, of unifying the disparate entities in Upper and Lower Egypt? How, in other words, did our species make the first transition from scattered, politically independent towns and chiefdoms into a unified nation administered by a central government?

After several seasons of digging in the ruins of an ancient Egyptian town called Hierakonpolis, I believe our research team is close to an answer. Two things led us to Hierakonpolis: previous discoveries, including the Narmer palette, and ancient Egyptian legends. The English archeologists, Quibell and Green, had found, in addition to the palette, a giant decorated macehead belonging to a predecessor of Narmer by the name of Scorpion and an even earlier painted tomb, probably of a local Predynastic king. Also, a whole succession of expeditions had shown that the early historic town of Hierakonpolis—or Nekhen, as the ancient Egyptians called it—was surrounded by the largest Predynastic settlement complex in all of Egypt. The final link to the site's importance came from Egyptian legends that traced the ancestry of the pharaohs to the "Divine Souls of Nekhen" and to the "Followers of Horus," the falcon-headed god. Hierakonpolis, which means City of the Falcon, is the name the Greeks later applied to Nekhen.

Though many of the settlements and tombs we excavated at Hierakonpolis had long since been rifled, enough scraps of evidence remained for us to piece together the story of what was happening in the Nile Valley in the centuries just preceeding Narmer's rise.

The process appears to have begun at Hierakonpolis about 3800 B.C., 700 years before Narmer was born. In those days, according to staff archeological surveyor Fred Harlan of Washington University in St. Louis and geologist-chemist Hany Hamroush of Cairo University and the University of Virginia, Hierakonpolis was situated on a protected embayment of the Nile floodplain. There it enjoyed light seasonal rainfall and easy access to the river, the fertile floodplain, and the wooded grasslands that covered what is now the barren Western Desert.

Two centers of settlement dominated the landscape from 3800 B.C. to 3500 B.C. Each included zones for habitation, industry, and trash disposal. Around these were smaller farming hamlets, herders' camps, cemeteries, and other holy places. Dwellings ranged from small, circular huts in seasonal camps to more substantial, rectangular houses of mudbrick and wattle-and-daub in the towns. The wattle-and-daub houses, in which mud was plastered over a wovenwood and reed framework, often had floors dug below ground level.

Houses were sometimes bunched closely together and sometimes surrounded by spacious, fenced enclosures. These dwellings and the different, often specialized objects found in them, reflect underlying economic and social differences in the community that allowed the eventual emergence of a politically powerful elite.

The area covered by the housing sites—some 100 acres—suggests that during this period, called the Amratian, or Naqada I, the regional population of Hierakonpolis had soared from perhaps several hundred people to several thousand—between 2,300 and 10,500. Such large populations were necessary for state development.

Although the evidence from settlements suggested that Amratian society was big enough and complex enough to support elite groups, clear proof of their existence eluded us until we began digging in a cemetery on the banks of a dry stream bed, or wadi, called Abu Suffian. Carter Lupton of the Milwaukee Public Museum and Barbara Adams of the Petrie Museum, University College, London, cleared some sand-filled graves and came upon the largest Amratian tombs ever found.

The large tombs were arranged in curving rows and confined to one area apparently reserved for the elite members of the society. Although hardly spectacular by later Egyptian standards, the tombs were impressive for their time, consisting of rectangular holes cut into the hard wadi terrace. One grave, for example, was more than eight feet long, five feet wide, and almost six feet deep. It had been looted in ancient times but still contained several beautiful black-topped clay jars of the type called Plum Red Ware, well known from other Amratian and Gerzean sites. We also found the remains of baskets, braided leather rope, painted reed arrow shafts, flint arrowheads, grass matting, and even pieces of a wooden bier.

In the neighboring tomb we found painted scraps of a paper-like material from a plant related to papyrus. This, along with some complex graffiti scratched onto some of the pots, suggests that the origins of Egyptian writing may be much older than previously suspected. Clearly we were dealing with the remains of a people more advanced than Egyptologists used to think.

Finally, under a heap of broken furniture and small bones, we found a beautiful, disc-shaped macehead made of polished green and white porphyry, a key piece of evidence for the development of a political elite. Maceheads have long been recognized as symbols of political authority. Unfinished examples have been found in our village sites, showing they were produced locally. This one must have been a forerunner of the much larger limestone macehead found at Hierakonpolis 85 years ago. This pear-shaped macehead showed Narmer's predecessor, Scorpion.

Our porphyry macehead, predating Scorpion by about 500 years, tells us that the process of political centralization was already well underway at Hierakonpolis. Whoever wielded that macehead was hardly a pharaoh, but he was clearly someone with considerable wealth and political power. As such, he is one of the earliest candidates for the "Divine Souls of Nekhen," the semi-mythical rulers of Hierakonpolis in the remote times before Narmer.

Several other Amratian sites have produced maceheads, suggesting they too had chiefs. Still Hierakonpolis must have had some advantage that allowed its leaders ultimately to prevail. How could it afford the biggest tombs in the first place, and how was it able to prosper and grow through the succeeding centuries? One factor was the large population. Another was its ideal environment. Our excavations point to one other outstanding advantage at Hierakonpolis. In Amratian times it appears to have been the center of a huge pottery industry, one that would have given its proprietors enormous economic power. Even today an estimated 50 million pieces of broken bowls, jars, and other vessels litter the desert, and we have identified and mapped at least 15 Amratian pottery kilns in the area. The largest were massive, industrial-scale installations covering more than 1,200 square yards.

The pottery barons profited from the belief in an afterlife.

Around each ruined kiln were scraps of pottery representing one of two distinctive types—a coarse, Straw-tempered Ware and a fine, untempered Plum Red Ware. Most of the coarse pots were used for everyday household or industrial purposes, but the finer pots were usually used as grave offerings.

All the kilns used to make the high-quality Red Ware were situated high in desert cliffs, in natural wind tunnels overlooking the elite Amratian tombs. There the prevailing breezes could fan the hotter flames needed to fire the better pots. In studying vessels fired at these kilns, student Jeremy Geller found that each kiln specialized in certain types and quantities of pots. Together all the kilns appeared to be part of one well-organized industrial complex. The volume of production appears to have been far greater than needed to meet the local demand. Most likely, pottery, along with other locally made prestige goods such as maceheads and beads, was not only supplied for the elaborate burials in local cemeteries but also traded up and down the Nile.

Here was the key to the power of Hierakonpolis. By providing prized offerings for the deceased, the pottery barons encouraged and profited from the pervasive Egyptian belief that the dead could take their wealth with them into an afterlife. By successfully managing the production, transport, and exchange of their goods, the local "big men" gained leadership experience, acquired clients, and forged useful trading contacts with other population centers.

Eventually, however, their flourishing industrial center collapsed. Just after 3500 B.C. the fragile desert-savannah ecosystem suddenly became more arid, and the far desert settlements, along with their pottery kilns, were abandoned as people moved into more thickly settled villages along the wetter Nile floodplain. This traditionally marks the end of the Amratian period of the Egyptian Predynastic era and the beginning of what is called the Gerzean, or, as some authorities prefer, Naqada II, which lasted from about 3500 B.C. until the century preceding the founding of the nation-state and the First Dynasty in 3100 B.C.

The cause of the ecological shift is not known for certain, but the pottery industry may have been a major factor. Botanist Nabil El Hadidi, keeper of the Herbarium at Cairo University, in studying the ashes at the kilns, has identified large amounts of burned acacia and tamarisk wood. These were the principal trees in the savannah ecosystem, and it looks as if the forests along the wadi were cut down to feed the kiln fires. Zoologist John McArdle of the Humane Society of America points also to the hundreds of sheep and goat bones found in Amratian settlements as evidence of heavy grazing. Finally, indirect evidence suggests the local rains ended about this time.

The collapse of the pottery industry and the migration of the population closer to the Nile Valley must have presented the pottery barons of Hierakonpolis with both a problem and an opportunity. Either they reinvested their wealthy or they lost it. Studies elsewhere suggest the situation was typical of many societies on the threshold of statehood. In some cases they returned to more egalitarian ways, but at Hierakonpolis the elite tightened its grip by aggressively reinvesting the "capital" it held in the form of valuable objects and real estate. As the new villages grew, the elite class used its wealth to build town walls, temples, palaces, and bigger tombs and to help develop and support the irrigation canals that some prehistorians believe originated at this time. Irrigation rendered the Nile floodplain more attractive because it led to bigger and more reliable harvests, but it also encouraged more centralized water management and greater reliance on stored grain surpluses. With each step more power was concentrated in the hands of the elite class and its leaders.

Signs of wealth, power, contacts with Eastern civilizations, and armed conflict all increase in the archeological record of the late Gerzean period. In the iconography of the time one finds symbols such as crowns that are later associated with the kingship. Regional kingdoms were appearing throughout the Nile valley from northern Sudan to the apex of the delta near modern Cairo at sites such as Abydos, Naqada, Qustul, and, of course, Hierakonpolis.

Sometime around 3200 B.C., Predynastic society achieved critical mass and regional power struggles became a way of life. For a century battles flared, and pieces of territory shifted from one local king to another, each trying to establish a permanent hold on adjacent kingdoms. Among the contesting kings, it was Narmer who succeeded, extending his conquests and the process of political unification to the entire Egyptian Nile valley.

During these troubled times, the ambitious rulers of Hierakonpolis—the predecessors of Scorpion and Narmer—returned to the long abandoned desert cemetery of their Amratian ancestors. As if to recall their links with the past, they built their tombs near those of their pottery baron predecessors.

Their new cemetery formed an idealized map—a model in miniature—of the new state, spelling out the ideal relationships among a divine king, the geographical regions of Upper and Lower Egypt, the diverse provinces or "nomes" that had been absorbed by political alliance or military conquest, and a multitude of regional gods.

Tombs in the cemetery appear to have been arranged to symbolize the unification of northern and southern Egypt. The idea that Egypt was actually two regions that became one remained prominent throughout Dynastic times. In fact, the ancient Egyptians called their country Tawy, the "Two Lands." They are usually referred to as Upper Egypt—the land upstream on the Nile, toward

Sudan—and Lower Egypt—the land downstream, toward the Mediterranean. Because the Nile flows northward, Upper Egypt is south of Lower Egypt. These same orientations were symbolized in the desert cemetery, where the Wadi Abu Suffian represented the Nile.

The tombs occupied by the Protodynastic rulers of Hierakonpolis were built of mudbricks, in the style of Lower Egypt (at that time probably not the Delta, but simply a kingdom downstream from Hierakonpolis) and, accordingly, are situated in the lower, or downstream, part of the cemetery. They were built in groups of threes, fours, and fives, suggesting that rulers were buried with close members of their families or courts. In size and splendor, these tombs exceed those of the preceeding Gerzean period like the Painted Tomb. One was a chamber about 16 feet long and eight feet wide with a central, L-shaped burial pit. It has given us our first glimpse of the paraphernalia of a prehistoric court.

The most surprising find was a fragmented wooden bed. No longer the simple bier of the earlier tombs, this was a finely carved and joined work of art. Two legs, carved from sycamore wood to resemble a bull's legs, are the direct ancestors of the furniture found in Tutankhamon's tomb.

The largest mudbrick tomb in the cemetery (number 1 in our site numbering system) stands on the downstream, or Lower Egyptian, border of the site. It is about 21 feet long and 11½ feet wide. Its style, location, pottery, and one radiocarbon date indicate that it was probably the last tomb built before Narmer and may well have belonged to his ancestor Scorpion.

Careful excavation of this and other tombs, using trowels and brushes instead of the more common mattocks and picks, has allowed us to solve one of the mysteries of Egyptian archeology. Although everyone knows that great monumental buildings covered the tombs of later pharaohs, until our work in the Hierakonpolis cemetery there was no clear evidence of anything over the graves of Predynastic rulers.

Now we have found the remains of extensive wooden structures that once capped the tombs. The evidence survives in the form of circular, brown discolorations in the soil around the borders of tomb pits. They are rotted posts—postmolds in archeological jargon—and they clearly outline ancient buildings and their fenced enclosures. In plan these closely resemble temples and palaces depicted on stone cylinder seals and ivory and wooden labels of this period from Hierakonpolis and Abydos.

In its heyday the cemetery was a veritable city of the dead—a necropolis—with wooden and reed shrines or model palaces surrounded by low reed fences. Some of these same structures and architectural motifs were imitated 500 years later in stone when King Djoser built Egypt's first pyramid at Saqqara, near modern Cairo. For example, stone chapels at Saqqara were built to look as though they were made of bundled reeds with wooden picket fences along the base of their walls,

apparently honoring a tradition established at the Hierakonpolis cemetery.

Our desert necropolis, like the Saqqara complex, seems to have been deliberately planned. There is a posthole cut into the rock atop a cliff overlooking Tomb 1, the possible Scorpion tomb. We had no idea what its function might have been until a staff architect suggested it provided an excellent view of our excavations at Tomb 1. After clearing the remains of the wooden structure and fence over the tomb, we discovered a row of postmolds marking the centerline of the wooden structure. They were perfectly in line with the posthole atop the cliff. In ancient times the hole must have held a post used by a surveyor to align the tomb. We now believe that much of the necropolis was similarly surveyed.

Tomb 1's mudbrick lining represented the architecture of Lower Egypt but at the opposite end of the cemetery—upstream with respect to the wadi—is a stone tomb, in the architectural style of Upper Egypt during the Protodynastic period between 3200 and 3100 B.C. It is a long, narrow trench with an L-shaped hole in the middle of the floor. From one side a burial chamber reaches under the rock.

The political implications are obvious—the joining of Upper and Lower Egypt in one royal cemetery just at the time Egypt was undergoing the struggles that would lead to her unification under Narmer and his successors.

One curious feature of the cemetery is an animal precinct surrounding the stone tomb at the Upper Egyptian end. It was a veritable zoo that included the remains of elephant, hippopotamus, crocodile, and baboon in addition to the more prosaic cattle, sheep, goat, and dogs. These burials must have had religious significance and at least some animals were mummified. Bits of resin and molded dung still cling to some of the bones. In one animal tomb were three cattle—a bull, a cow, and a calf. We believe the three represent one of the "family triads" common in ancient Egyptian religion.

The animal tombs seem to be another way of mixing religion with politics as only the ancient Egyptians could do—symbolically involving the various gods and provinces in the new royal mortuary cult. It is already known that the Egyptians of this period used various animals as godlike symbols of the different provinces, or "nomes," of Egypt. Some of the nome symbols can be seen on the Narmer palette, displayed atop standards. But animal gods could possess other attributes. For example, in keeping with the symbolic directional orientation of the necropolis, the easternmost animal tomb contained the remains of six baboons, animals the ancient Egyptians associated with the rising sun.

If our interpretation is correct, Narmer's forefathers, the descendents of the pottery barons, combined symbols of all the key elements of the new nation-state in the cemetery at Hierakonpolis. There they devised an extraordinary royal death cult that would define the political order of pharaonic Egypt for thousands of

1. PRE-HISTORY AND THE EARLIEST CIVILIZATIONS

1. PRE-HISTORY AND THE EARLIEST CIVILIZATIONS

years to come. The cemetery on the banks of Wadi Abu Suffian lies at the wellsprings of that cult. It immediately became the prototype for the royal necropolis of the First Dynasty at Abydos and of its successors for the next 2,500 years.

The desert graveyard played a critical role in developing the symbols and relationships that gave the Egyptian state its distinctive style: extreme centralization under a divine king, the use of a royal mortuary cult and cemetery as symbols of national social integration, the division of the state into the ritualized geographic halves of Upper and Lower Egypt, and the practice of incorporating the gods and peoples of earlier political units into the new state through a complex but pragmatic religious-familial hierarchy. These principles could be readily accepted because throughout Predynastic times an active trade along the Nile diffused and homogenized everything from material goods such as pottery to religious beliefs and political ideology. The Predynastic

merchants who controlled that trade had begun to unify Egypt culturally long before their descendents did it politically.

In contrast to other early states in the Middle East and Southwest Asia, Egyptian symbols of political integration were less deeply rooted in great walled towns than in royal cemeteries and temple complexes. By developing a concept of political authority not tied to any particular city or town, Egypt (like China 1,500 years later) anticipated the great, centralized "super urban" states of the modern world rather than the overgrown city-states of Mesopotamia, Greece, or Rome.

Through a combination of favorable climate and environment, mercantile acumen, a dense population and archeological imponderables like individual genius and the lust for power, the wealthy elite of Hierakonpolis evolved from successful pottery merchants to divine kings like Narmer who established the world's first and most enduring nation-state.

WAR AND MAN'S PAST

John Keegan

'War, far from being an exact science, is a terrible and impassioned drama' wrote Baron de Jomini in 1862. It is this drama that military historians must confront in their probe into man's past.

MILITARY HISTORIANS NOTORIOUSLY suffer from an identity anxiety. So, too, it is said, do economic, social and cultural historians, suspecting that general historians tacitly and patronisingly regard them as partial and peripheral practitioners of the craft. Military historians conceal the affliction in a more acute form, however, since they know that war is not a 'nice' subject, like culture, nor a rigorous or 'significant' system of study, which is what economic and social historians claim for their work. War, they are made to feel, is an aberrant activity, which distorts and disrupts the proper rhythms of man's life and would not happen in a world run by people with the right training – say in general history, or even in its cultural, economic and social dependencies.

It does not help that military historians have to travel in pretty mixed company. Other specialists are encumbered by hangers-on: by genteel biographers of dead lady novelists, by enthusiasts for obsolete railway engines and abandoned tin mines, and by prurient excavators of the archaeology of sex. But usually they can be disowned, when they do not disbar themselves by incompetence or obsessiveness. 'Military history' is, however, a garment loose and ample enough to be thrown over the most heterogeneous range of subjects and activities: the study of uniforms, buttons and badges, the 're-enactment' of historic battles, the collection of antique firearms, and such arcane matters as the height of Frederick the Great's guardsmen and the survival of the heliograph. Academic military historians

(Top) The ferocious appearance of these Papuan warriors is belied by the low lethality of their style of warfare.

From *History Today*, January 1983, pp. 27-32. Reproduced by kind permission of History Today, Ltd., 83-84 Berwick Street, London W1V 3PJ England.

shrink from association with such vulgarities and inanities; by convulsive reaction, many have come to insist that they themselves are not historians of war at all, but of institutions, administration or ideas – armies, conscription, strategic thought.

Such claustral purity is all very well in its way; it does produce work which is unarguably historical. But, of course, the more it is what it says it is – institutional or administrative – the less is it *military* history. For military institutions exist and are administered – unless they have become wholly fossilised survivals, like the Gentlemen-at-Arms or the Swiss Guard – in order to fight; and unless historians will look at what they do, they cannot understand what they are. Nor can historians explore to any depth their relationships with competing institutions or with society at large, for the heavy exactions which military institutions make on the time, liberty and wealth of peoples must have their rationale in the performance of some essential function. There is, in short, no getting away from fighting, and military historians must force themselves to examine what fighting is like if they are to understand what it is for and why it generates the institutions it does.

History Today recently confronted me with just such a set of issues in their bald form when it invited me to address its new television series on the question, 'Why War?' I wriggled, squirmed and expostulated, but in the end agreed to look for a way into the subject. The answer seemed to start where historical answers should: at the beginning. For there is still to be found in the world an activity, better known to anthropologists than historians, which is called 'primitive warfare'. It in almost no way resembles the exchange of violence between organised states which is called war today, but, through its very dissimilarity, may provide the sort of insight which is an opening to understanding.

Primitive warfare is characterised by its endemic nature, its high level of 'military participation', its low level of lethality and its lack of results, at least as the civilised understand the term. Until the expansion of the great European empires, and outside the historic empires of China, Central America, India and the Middle East, it was the form of warfare most commonly practised in the world. Its nature varied with the prevailing level of culture – the more

The lack of body armour indicates that battle, for these Egyptian Middle Kingdom spearmen, was not yet too serious a business.

developed the concept of chieftainship, for example, the greater the likelihood of the existence of a separate warrior class – but in its essentials it was distinguishable throughout the globe. We can still study it in practice in the highlands of New Guinea where tribes like the Kapauku are continuously at war. All fit adult males among the Kapauku are warriors and they devote most of their time either to raiding neighbouring villages or to fighting the occasional pitched battles which such raids provoke. The motive of the raids is revenge, ultimately for some act of material wrong, of which wife-stealing is the most common, but more immediately to repay a killing. Killing, however, is rarely multiple, and, when the pitched battles occur, a single death, or even a serious wounding, is normally enough to satisfy honour and lead to a truce between the warring parties. Anthropologists observe that over long periods – a twenty-year cycle has been

suggested – such warring results in a redistribution of territory, from villages which have shrunk in numbers to those which have grown; but it seems very unlikely that the perceived motivation is territorial, or even that the participants draw a connection between cause and effect.

Population density and pressure on land is, in any case, low in such areas, and villages are separated by wide no man's lands. Where life is harder, for seasonal or hydraulic reasons, such no man's lands have historically been eroded fairly quickly. Evidence of organised warfare – fortifications, standardised weapons, depictions of armies – are found from an early date in the historic centres of intensive agriculture, particularly where it depended upon large-scale irrigation, as within the boundaries of the Sumerian cities from about 3000 BC. There incessant warfare over narrowly drawn boundaries, together with the need to keep barbarians from the infertile zone at a distance, encouraged the rise of alliances and eventually of an imperial authority which could command the largest army possible and wage warfare at the highest level contemporary technology made feasible.

Military necessity tends to concentrate authority, until it resides in the hands of a single family or single man, whose power may be reinforced by religious beliefs about his relationship with the life-giving elements, particularly the sun, as in Pharaonic Egypt. But where the religious status of the ruler becomes exaggerated, and particularly if he is venerated as divine, his effectiveness as a military commander almost inevitably suffers. Divinity requires worship, worship encourages large-scale building, and the object of worship all too easily becomes a fixture within his temple-palace. Field command must then pass to trusted subordinates, whose

(Below) Roman Legionary versus Gallic swordsman, first century BC: discipline overcomes ferocity.

(Above) This Mongol harrier of civilisation is fifteenth-century AD: steed and weapons had probably altered little over 2,000 years.

(Below) The tomb in Salisbury Cathedral of William Longespée, c. 1230: epitome of what iron and heavy horse did for the warrior.

1. PRE-HISTORY AND THE EARLIEST CIVILIZATIONS

A German mercenary (*circa* 1515) winds his crossbow: machinery begins its victory over warrior muscle. Detail of a painting by Hans Holbein the Elder, 1515-17.

Geometry challenges artillery: Vauban's *Neuf Brisach,* begun in 1698, represents a temporary stay to the inexorable triumph of explosives.

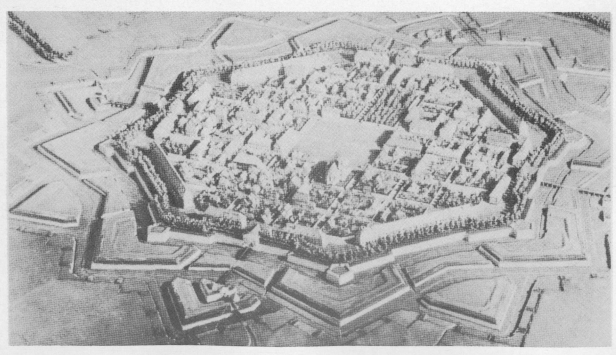

discovery of their real power eventually becomes a standing invitation to betray that trust. Pharaonic Egypt was almost blessedly immune from the fissiparous consequences of such mechanisms, owing, it has been suggested, to the ease with which power could be exercised through control of the Nile. But the Mesopotamian kingdoms suffered from chronic instability, most probably the result of incessant rebellion by provincial garrisons.

Mesopotamian civilisation was also prone, as desert-girdled Egypt was not, to attack by barbarians from Asia Minor and the inner Asian Steppe. Ironically such attacks may in part have been prompted by excursions made from the civilised regions by their own most adventurous inhabitants. William McNeill, the world historian, has advanced the most developed version of this theory in his recent book, *The Pursuit of Power.* It depends on the observation that organised warfare puts a premium on superior weapon technology, but that the necessary resources may have widely separated points of supply. The comparatively rare tin, for example, is not often found near the commoner copper with which it makes bronze, best of the early weapon metals.

Trade into the barbarian regions was the obvious expedient, but trade goods served not merely as a means of exchange. They also served to advertise the riches which civilisation offered. It was but a short step for barbarians to grasp that the riches were there for the taking, and to mount campaigns of conquest out of their hunting ground and grazing lands into the fields and plantations along the rivers.

A distinctive difference between the first civilisations, which were probably theocratic in character, and the barbarian societies which assailed, and in many cases supplanted, them towards the end of the second millennium, was the appearance and consolidation of a military class. The fighting power of peoples from 'marginal lands' continues to be valued into our own time: the Gurkha mountaineers whom the British army recruits today are the generic descendants of alien military bands whom civilisation has known first as conquerors, then as mercenaries for much of the last three thousand years. But when they first appeared they introduced a new principle into political organisation, that of the equality and solidarity of men who were better at fighting than their fellows and united by a bond of common military prowess. Such heroic societies in the earliest form were probably narrowly aristocratic, since they were based on the use of chariots and bronze, both scarce resources. With the discovery of iron, and the adaptation of the horse to cavalry use, towards the beginning of the first millennium BC, the military class could become larger and provide the basis of a new and distinctive polity. It was to underlie the rise of new organised states in China, India, Persia, and Greece and along the southern Mediterranean shore.

Agriculture and the cavalry principle are antipathetic. Cavalry armies require either preserved forage in enormous quantities, which only the most developed cultivation can provide (forage for the five cavalry divisions and the draught horses of the British Expeditionary Force of 1914-18 made the largest charge on its cross-Channel shipping space) or the free use of wide pasture. As long as the barbarians remained merely raiders, they could treat agricultural land as grazing ground. But when for whatever reason – harsher barbarian pressure behind them, or the glimmer-

Soldiers as automata: the seventeenth-century invention of drill transformed European battlecraft. Painting by George Stubbs, *circa* 1780.

ing of political wisdom – they forsook raiding for settlement, an accommodation had to be made with indigenous farmers. The result, extended no doubt over centuries, was the appearance of a warrior class which shared in the agricultural process and fought on foot. Two representatives of such societies were the Greek descendants of the Myceneans, originally a chariot people, and the Celts, later incursors into Western Europe on horseback.

It is here that we must presuppose the appearance of a new institution in warfare, the pitched battle. Ritual battles, as we have seen, are an ingredient of primitive warfare. Chariot warfare no doubt culminated in battles, but we have no clear view of their nature, while mounted battle is always an amorphous and inchoate business. Fighting on foot for the protection of cultivated land requires strict organisation. Attack can be expected when the ripening of the crop makes the farming community most vulnerable; defence of the cultivated area is most desirable at its borders; preservation of food surpluses urges that warriors be in the field for as short a time as possible; agricultural rhythms require the minimum of interruption. The warrior societies of the Greeks and later the Romans therefore derived their political character from a

class which could mobilise and assemble quickly, act in concert in the face of the enemy and inflict such casualties on him at one place and time that he would not return for the rest of that season.

There is, of course, an alternative to living *toujours en vedette*: to fortify the frontiers with barriers which will repel invaders with the minimum of human participation. It was a solution which appealed strongly to the warrior class in China, and the Romans were also to incorporate it into their military system. But fortification requires wealth, or power, or both, on an enormous scale, and by the time the Romans had become rich enough to fortify extensively they had used their wealth in another way as well: to devolve the warrior function onto paid professionals. In its heyday the professional Roman army was without peer. But the dissociation of military from political functions proved, as we know, fatal to Roman government. The army became a political force, neglected its duty, was reinvigorated by the recruitment of barbarians always anxious for an invitation to immigrate, but eventually succumbed to barbarian pressure of relentless intensity.

The collapse of the western Roman empire has been variously represented: in terms of a general manpower shortage, agricultural as well as military; and

in terms of a military revolution – the rise of heavy cavalry – manifested at Adrianople (378), when the Gothic horsemen destroyed the Roman field army and killed the Emperor Valens.

The two are not incompatible with each other, or with alternative explanations. Lamentation over the disappearance of the warrior-farmer was a familiar theme in Roman writing, while the military survival of the empire in Byzantium was closely associated with the creation of the 'theme' system, which was one of agricultural garrisons. We may choose to regard the consolidation of the barbarian warrior states in the West, and their gradual feudalisation, as a similar response to recurrent attack from the Steppe horsemen and their seaborne equivalents, the Norsemen.

But we must also take account of another factor: the beginning of a series of technical revolutions in warfare which have not ended to this day. Improvements in metal-working, the basis of military technology, had hitherto been circumscribed by the weight-carrying capacity of the human body and the unbred horse. The appearance of the heavy horse, the product of selective breeding, and the introduction of the Steppe warrior's stirrup, both probably in the eighth century, allowed the mounted warrior to wear armour of unprecedented weight and so to transform himself into an agent of shock-force irresistible on the battlefield. From

Weapons assault the environment: the Somme valley in the fourth month of the battle, 1916.

the ninth to the fourteenth century, a period during which the construction of armour was progressively refined, the knight was the dominant element, politically as well as militarily, in European society.

The success of the armoured horseman in holding at bay warrior-invaders from the Steppe and the desert was the underlying cause of European economic revival in the later middle ages. But economic revival brought with it developments which were hostile to the

Nagasaki, 1945: man glimpses his new-found power to end civilisation.

knightly class. Some were technical, like the introduction of the crossbow (perhaps a mechanical adaptation of the composite bow which was concurrently improving the military value of the Steppe horseman). Some were financial, putting into the hands of cities and sovereigns the power to buy military force rather than support it by agricultural effort. Mercenaries are an ancient military phenomenon. They were certainly known to the states of the Hellenistic world, and probably much earlier. But their rise in the late medieval world, even when they were intermingled in armies with feudal contingents, anticipated the military and political transformation of Europe. The introduction of gunpower made that transformation inescapable. It would only be a matter of time before the most efficient money-rising authorities could buy both the loyalty of soldiers and the weapons which spelt the extinction of those who opposed the centralising power. Those authorities were the kings of the emergent European dynastic states.

The subsequent history of those states – 'modern history' – is conventionally pursued through their political, social and economic development. But it is as essential as it is infrequently done to put those developments into their military context. Europe remained vulnerable to assault from the east, by armies which drew their fighting strength from inner Asia, until the seventeenth century.

There then began that great counter-offensive by Habsburgs and Romanovs which would culminate in the repossession of the Balkans from the Turks and the extension of the Russian empire to the Pacific and the Himalayas. The warrior states of Western Europe meanwhile turned seaward. There had already been one major exportation of their military energies, in the Mediterranean crusades. From the sixteenth to the nineteenth centuries the techniques and the psychological hardening which two millennia of incessant warfare had developed in Europeans worked for the overthrow and subjection of less militant societies at the end of every sea-route on the world's surface. Even the Red Indians of North America, a by-word for ferocity, found that the European style of fighting was 'too furious and slays too many men'. It was only when the Europeans were at last brought face-to-face with the centralised power of the Chinese, hardened by the same experience of incessant irruption, that their powers of conquest faltered.

It was warrior qualities, rather than superior technology, which explained the triumph of European colonialism; the ships with which the early voyagers opened up the sea routes to Asia were rarely larger or more seaworthy than those maintained by the Ottomans in the Indian Ocean or by the Chinese in the South China Sea. The rise of technology nevertheless explains the last and most paradoxical twist in the story of Europe's mastery of the art of war: fuelled first by the need to make the warrior the victor against the intruder, then by the desire to make him the subject of his sovereign, the armourer's art ended by empowering the sovereigns of the developed world with the means to obliterate each other's populations. Primitive warfare, with its careful bloodlettings and rhythmic pauses for diplomacy and peacemaking, has come to look in our own age less a starting-place for progress than a desirable destination for a return journey.

Greece and Rome: The Classical Tradition

For the West civilization began in Mesopotamia, but it was in Greece that civilization became distinctly Western. The Greek ideals of order, proportion, harmony, balance, and structure—so pervasive in classical thought and art—inspired Western culture for centuries, even into the modern era. Their humanism, which made man the measure of all things, not only liberated Greek citizens from the despotic collectivism of the Near East, but also encouraged them, and us, to attain new levels of creativity and excellence. Lionel Casson explores the Greeks' commitment to excellence in "The First Olympics." Though the Greeks did not entirely escape from the ancient traditions of miracle, mystery, and authority, they nevertheless elevated reason and science to new levels of importance in human affairs. There is evidence of this in "Life with Father, Life with Socrates." It was the Greeks' unique social-political system, the polis, that provided scope and incentive for the great achievements of Greek culture. Although the civil order rested on slavery, and excluded women from the political process ("Love and Death in Ancient Greece"), each polis was an experiment in local self-government.

Yet, for all its greatness and originality, classical Greek civilization flowered only briefly. The weaknesses of the polis system surfaced in the Peloponnesian Wars. Walter Karp compares this conflict to America's cold war with Russia in "The Two Thousand Years' War." Thereafter the polis ceased to fulfill the lives of its citizens as it had in the past. But it was not the war alone that undermined the civic order. The Greek way of life depended upon unique and transitory circumstances—trust, smallness, simplicity, and a williness to subordinate private interests to public concerns. The postwar period saw the spread of disruptive forms of individualism and the privatization of life. Above all, as H.D.F. Kitto has forcefully argued, the polis ideal, with its emphasis on public participation and the wholeness of life, eschewed specialization. "If one man in his time is to play all the parts," Kitto writes, "these parts must not be too difficult for the ordinary man to learn. And this is where the polis broke down. Occidental man, beginning with the Greeks, has never been able to leave things alone. He must inquire, improve, progress; and Progress broke the polis."

Eventually, Alexander's conquests and the geographical unity of the Mediterranean enabled the non-Greek world to share Greek civilization. Indeed, a distinctive stage of Western civilization emerged from the fusion of Greek and oriental elements. It is called the Hellenistic age. At best it was a time when new cities were built on the Greek model—a time of intellectual ferment and cultural exchange, travel and exploration, scholarship and research. At worst it was an era of amoral opportunism in politics and derivative styles in the arts. The Greeks' interest in the world around them is documented in "Charting the Unknown."

Later the Greek ideal survived Rome's domination of the Mediterranean. "Conquered Greece took her savage conqueror, and introduced the arts into rustic Latium," as a Latin poet put it. Modern scholars continue that theme, depicting Roman culture as nothing more than the practical application of Greek ideals to Roman life. Yet the Romans were not merely soulless imitators of the Greeks. They were creative borrowers, borrowing from the Etruscans as well as the Greeks. Furthermore, they invented a marvelous system of imperial government and a unique conception of law. They bequeathed their language and disseminated Greek thought and values to Europe. Greek culture provided the basis for the cultural unity of the Mediterranean. The Romans provided the political unity. Between them they forged and preserved the standards and assumptions upon which our tradition of civilization is built—the classical ideal.

Looking Ahead: Challenge Questions

How do the modern Olympic Games differ from the original Greek Olympics?

What restrictions did Greek women have to contend with?

Why was Socrates a truly dangerous man?

What analogies are there between the Peloponnesian War and America's rivalry with Russia?

Why did the Greeks and Romans fail to see the practical uses of water and steam power?

Explain the historical "silence" of the women of ancient Rome.

How has Nero been misjudged by history?

The first Olympics: competing 'for the greater glory of Zeus'

There was bribing, boasting and jeering of losers, and only first place mattered, but judges kept almost no statistics at all

Lionel Casson

Lionel Casson is a classics professor at New York University. His new book, Ancient Trade and Society, *was just published by Wayne State University Press.*

One midsummer day in the year we calculate to have been 776 B.C., a 200-meter dash was run in a rural backwater in southwestern Greece, and a young local named Coroebus won it. It was an obscure event in an obscure spot but it earned him immortality: he is the first Olympic victor on record.

It came about this way. Not far from his hometown, in the place called Olympia, was a primitive sanctuary to the Greeks' chief god, Zeus. Festivals for the deity had been going on there for centuries. For some reason the people in charge decided to embellish what was traditionally done: they would offer up, in addition to the customary sacrificial victims and prayers, the honor of an outstanding athletic performance. So they organized a race, the race Coroebus won.

The next embellished festival was scheduled for 772 B.C.—and from then on, every four years, it took place more or less without a break for more than a millennium, right up to A.D. 261. And what began as a simple neighborhood affair soon burgeoned into a celebrated spectacle, boasting a dozen or so different events that pulled in contestants and viewers from all over. They came from the whole ancient world, from as far away as what are now France and Syria. There were other religious festivals, some very important, whose programs included sports, too, but none ever attained the prestige of the Olympics. Then as now, a victory there was the be-all and end-all for all truly serious athletes.

Despite the growing renown of the Olympics, despite the fact that it attracted tens of thousands of people, the time and place were constant: everybody had to make the long and arduous pilgrimage to the out-of-the-way sanctuary. And when there, everybody,

Uffizi Gallery, Florence

Two pancratiasts battled until one gave up. In regular wrestling, winner got the first three falls.

right up to champions of the highest repute and backers who sometimes were heads of state, had to submit to the arrangements, rules and regulations enforced by a local committee—about ten worthy citizens of Elis, the chief town of the area.

That was the way things were at the beginning and that is how the ancient games continued to be: for the greater glory of Zeus, not to improve the political image of any particular state or leader, as is sometimes the case today. And there was little fine talk of promoting international goodwill or anything like that. At the time the festival was launched and for four centuries afterward, the Greeks were organized into a multitude of little independent states, and one or more of these was always at war with another. When the date of the festival drew near, heralds were sent out to announce a sacred truce so that those who wanted to attend could make their way through the battle lines to get to Olympia. After a while, the truce was length-

Boxers wrapped their fists in leather thongs, fought without a break until one was knocked out or gave up.

ened to three months or so because travel time increased as spectators and contestants flocked in from farther and farther away.

For some centuries there were no athletic facilities whatsoever at Olympia, just an open space in which a running track would be paced off, areas for the discus and javelin throw laid out, and so on. Finally, by about 500 B.C., a few amenities had come into existence: a stadium for the runners and a hippodrome for the horse and chariot races (but no stands with seats for the spectators, just a sloping embankment to sprawl on), a bathhouse for the athletes, a headquarters building for the Olympic committee, and, of course, a temple to Zeus. Progress was slow because funding depended upon contributions.

Los Angeles, site of the 1984 summer Olympic Games, is better off than Elis was, for it at least can collect gate receipts; in ancient times, since the games were part of a religious ceremony, no admission could be charged. As it happens, Elis was not poor, but it was in no position all by itself to undertake a building program of the size needed. It was able to start work on Zeus' temple only when a successful war against a neighbor provided enough booty for the labor and materials. Many of the other improvements came, if at all, from generous wealthy states or individuals.

There was not even a gymnasium until sometime after 200 B.C.; the athletes worked out wherever they

could. Though eventually there was the equivalent of a VIP hotel, there were never any facilities at all for ordinary spectators. They arrived hot and tired and stayed that way during the five days the festival lasted. The rich were not too badly off: they slept in tents that their retinue of slaves put up. Most, however, slept in the open and munched on bread, cheese and olives, and drank wine they had brought along or bought from itinerant vendors. Sanitation was rudimentary or nonexistent and water, from springs and cisterns, was always in short supply. It was not until the second century A.D., after the games had been going on for about 900 years, that Herodes Atticus of Athens, at the time probably the richest Greek in the world, finally gave the place an aqueduct and a proper water system. In addition to all this, there was the heat and dust of a Greek summer and the flies—so bad that it is said the citizens of Elis used to offer up a special sacrifice to Zeus to keep them away from Olympia. The story goes that all a master had to do to make a sulky slave turn angelic was to threaten to take him along to the games.

"Aren't you all jammed in together?" asked the Greek philosopher Epictetus of would-be spectators. "Isn't it hard to get a bath? Don't you get drenched when it rains? Don't you get fed up with the din and the shouting and the other annoyances?" The answer in every case was a resounding Yes!—but this did not stop people from coming in droves. After all, the Olympics gave them, as ours do us, the one chance in four years to see many of the world's very best athletes in action. And there were other rewards. They could attend the sacrifices and services—which, now that the festival had gained such fame, were impressive ceremonies. They could get a look at some of Greece's finest works of art: a gigantic statue of Zeus in his temple was one of the Seven Wonders of the Ancient World, and all over the sanctuary grounds were statues of

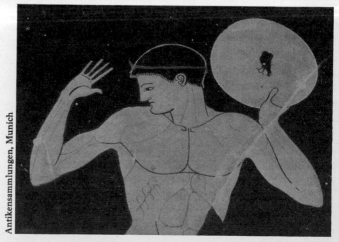

Poised competitor, from fifth century B.C., wields discus with owl, which was symbol of the goddess Athena.

other deities and of winning athletes. Imagine today's Olympics being held, say, in Rome during Easter Week and you get some idea of why so many made the long journey and put up with all the discomforts.

Like a number of key features of Greek life, the games were for males only. With the exception of a special priestess, married women were barred from entrance—and on pain of death, no less. Since the assemblage of spectators was joined by the kinds of people who lived off crowds—pickpockets, beggars, con men, pimps, prostitutes—it was no place for respectable unmarried women. (Other festivals eventually ran events for women athletes, but never the early Olympics.) On one occasion a matron from a great sporting family, who could not bear not seeing her son compete, sneaked in dressed as a trainer; when he was victorious, she enthusiastically vaulted the barrier that marked off the trainers' section and, in so doing, revealed her sex. Out of respect for the family's long line of winners she was spared execution, but a ruling was passed stating that trainers, like athletes, were to go around naked.

Shortly after 500 B.C. the program of sports reached its more or less final form—three days of major competition given over to about a dozen different events. It most likely started with the most spectacular, the chariot race. The number of entrants varied each year; at a comparable festival, the Pythian Games held in Delphi, there were as many as 41. The competitors lined up, each standing in a two-wheeled chariot that was light, like a modern trotter's gig, but pulled by a team of four horses that would be driven at the fastest gallop they could generate. They made 12 laps around the course—about nine kilometers—with 180-degree turns at each end. As at our Indianapolis 500, viewers enjoyed not only the excitement of a race but the titillation that comes from the constant presence of danger: as the teams thundered around the turns, or one chariot tried to cut over from the outside to the inside, crashes and collisions were common and doubtless often fatal. In one celebrated race at the Pythian Games, competition was so lethal that only one competitor out of several dozen managed to finish!

Next came the horse race, and it, too, offered the spice of danger because jockeys rode bareback on earth just churned up by the chariots. Both of these events were strictly for the very rich; owning a racehorse in ancient times was like owning a Rolls-Royce today, and owning a chariot and team was like owning a fleet of four of them. In the very beginning the owners may have done their own driving and riding, but they soon turned these jobs over to professionals. The prize, however, went only to the owners. Once, for example, a famous mare named Αὔρα (Breeze) threw her rider at the very beginning of the race, but being well trained, covered the course in perfect style and came in first; the judges awarded her owner the prize. Women owners, who could not even get inside the grounds to

Metropolitan Museum of Art, New York

A local athlete is honored. Proud hometowns sometimes gave Olympic winners a special purse.

watch, could yet win a prize this way, and there are the names of some in the lists of Olympic victors.

The chariot and horse races were the showiest events. But the crowd's favorites tended to be the body-contact sports—wrestling, boxing and the pancratium (a combination of the two)—which the arrangers of the program shrewdly scheduled for the fourth day, the latest possible. Wrestling was the mildest of the three. Unlike today's wrestling, the contestants were on their feet most of the time, since three falls ended a match and even touching the ground with the knees constituted a fall. Ancient wrestlers, like our TV mammoths, ran to size and beef. A certain Milo, who lived around 500 B.C., was so mighty a man that a whole series of fabulous stories grew up about him: that every day he packed away seven and a half kilos each of meat and bread, washing it down with seven and a half liters of wine; that he once carried a full-grown bull around the stadium, then cooked and ate it; that he could tie a band around his head and snap it by swelling his veins.

Fight crowds in any age like to see blood, and ancient boxing supplied plenty. The men fought with their hands wrapped in tough leather thongs, they fought continuously with no rounds and they fought till one was knocked out or gave up. It was a rare boxer who, after several years in the sport, still had uncauliflowered ears and all his teeth; boxers' battered physiognomies became a favorite butt of contemporary satirists, whose humor was crueler than ours.

The bloodiest and most popular event was the pancratium, or "all-powerful contest," a modified free-for-all. The contestants punched, slapped, kicked or wrestled, and the bout was over when one was knocked out, gave up or—as happened every now and then—died. No holds were barred, not even the stranglehold, and much of the time, as with today's wrestlers, the contestants were thrashing about on the ground, since a fall did not matter. One pancratiast actually developed a technique in which he would throw himself on his back with his opponent on top and work from there;

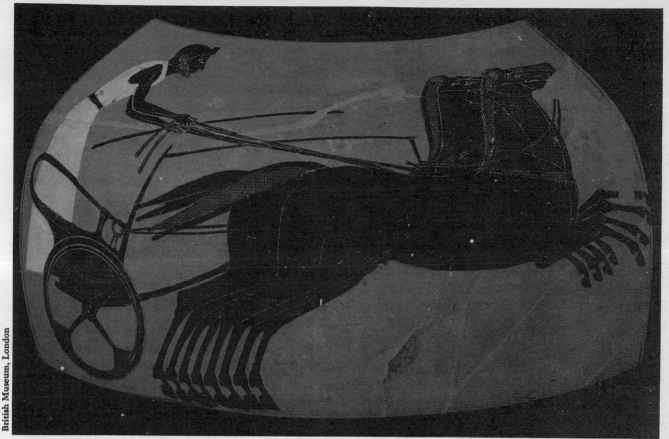

British Museum, London

Greek charioteer reins in rampaging team; racing was Olympics' most spectacular (and dangerous) event.

Dozens competed, but during the nine-kilometer race, many chariots smashed up taking 180-degree turns.

he was never beaten. There was also biting and gouging, though these were theoretically illegal. The end usually came when one man got such a hold that the other quit to avert a broken bone or dislocated joint.

The first Olympic event to be recorded, Coroebus' race, was a straight run the length of the course, in effect a 200-meter dash. Soon a second race was introduced: down the course and back, a 400-meter dash. A long-distance run was added of nearly 4,800 meters, and then even a dash in which contestants ran in armor. These were the only track events; the marathon in today's games is a modern idea. The field events were three: broad jump, discus throw, javelin throw. They were never independent contests but always part of a curious mix called the "pentathlon," the "five-contest": the jump, discus and javelin followed by a 200-meter dash and a wrestling match. If a man took three of the five he was the winner.

It is hard to see how any one athlete could develop high skill in so many different sports. Yet the pentathlon was one of the earliest items in the Olympic program. It was sandwiched in between the spectacular horse events of the second day and popular body-contact bouts of the fourth. The modern Olympics, begun in 1896, made things easier by deleting the wrestling. After 1924, the men's pentathlon was dropped entirely,

although the Olympics had already instituted a quite different competition, known as the "modern pentathlon," involving, among other things, horsemanship and pistol shooting. This year's games are going to include, at least for women, a version that goes the ancient pentathlon two better: a heptathlon—a seven-part contest, all track and field.

The fifth and last day was devoted to prize giving. Winners formed a procession and marched to the Temple of Zeus. It was an ancient version of the ticker-tape parade, since bystanders along the route showered them with leaves and flowers. At the temple, each was handed what ancient athletes considered the most precious object in the world, the victor's olive wreath. Its intrinsic value may have been nil, but it was worth a fortune to the man who walked away with it. An Olympic victory, as it happens, was just as great an honor for a winner's fellow townspeople as for himself, and they sometimes showed their gratitude by voting him a cash bonus—sometimes even a pension for life—as well as other perquisites. Moreover, Olympic champions were welcomed as contestants at festivals where bountiful cash prizes were awarded.

All such benefits were for winners only. Vince Lombardi would have been right at home in the ancient Olympics. Winning was everything; there were no

Metropolitan Museum of Art, New York

Runners, like these shown c. 530 B.C., contested in only four distances at Olympia: 200- and 400-meter dash and a 4,800-meter Greek "mile," as well as a cumbersome sprint that had to be run in armor.

seconds or thirds, no Greek equivalents of silver or bronze medals. And modesty in victory was not required. It was expected that a winner would savor his triumph to the full, would publicly exult in it. The Greeks did not go in for our ceremonious "sportsmanship," the generous congratulations of the vanquished. Far from it: losers were jeered and, hiding their heads in shame, slunk away. Even their mothers treated them with scorn. "The wreath or death" was the motto.

Greek record keeping, too, was very different. Almost no records were kept of the actual distance a winner jumped, or threw the discus or javelin, or the exact time it took to win any of the races. In ancient Greek, there isn't even a way to say "set a record" or "break a record." What interested people were "firsts."

In the beginning, Olympic athletes tended to be aristocrats. Only they had enough free time to go in for the extended work needed to train a man up to championship standard, as well as the free time and the money to travel to the festival every four years. Besides, most aristocrats had a good head start since wrestling, running and other sports were the way Greece's gilded youth spent its leisure. As the years passed, though, lesser folk managed to enter the competition, and in increasing numbers. Perhaps this was what prompted

a famous crack by Alexander the Great, a very fine runner, when he was urged to enter the dash: "Only if the contestants are kings." One reason that common folk came to compete more was that hometowns took as much pride in a victory as did the victor himself. When a promising lad turned up, they would subsidize him; they did for their athletes what American corporations today do for ours. And once the lad had racked up a win, between bonuses and prize money at other cash-paying festivals, he was set for life. One ancient Olympic victor was offered 30,000 drachmas—the 1984 equivalent of at least half a million dollars in purchasing power—just to take part in some local festival; our barnstorming tennis stars do not do much better. Then as now, the popularity of a man's sport made a difference. Where cash prizes were given, the reward for a win in the pancratium could be six times that for a win in the pentathlon.

There was a price to be paid for getting into the charmed circle of Olympic winners, the same price paid today: endless, grueling training under the iron rule of the best coaches to be found. These had their special techniques, some of which make sense, some of which do not. Runners, for example, were probably paced by men on horseback. Boxers shadowboxed and worked out with the punching bag. Wrestlers worked out with partners called "statues" in the Greek sports jargon. Pancratiasts worked out with a punching bag heavier than the boxer's type, and they not only practiced punching it but kicking it as well. They also let it bash them on the head, presumably to accustom that member to a bash from a fist.

Trainers had their hang-ups about food, then as now. When it came to fish, to eat or not to eat depended on the kind of seaweed the fish fed on. As for meat, pork from pigs pastured along the shore was taboo, since the chances were they had fed on the sea garlic that flourished there. One trainer refused to let his charges go to dinner parties on the grounds that intelligent conversation would cause headaches.

All entrants were eventually compelled by the rules to train continuously for the ten months prior to opening day. The last month of training was conducted at Elis under the gimlet eyes of the judges. This procedure immeasurably impressed the competition since any who saw themselves clearly outclassed would quietly take off to avoid the shame of defeat.

The word "judges," when applied to the ancient Olympic committee, is a misnomer. Although the Greeks called them that, judging was only a small part of their duties. They checked the credentials of the competitors, supervised their training at Elis, served as referees and umpires, heard complaints of fouls and bribery. They were chosen by lot from a list of wealthy locals likely known as generous contributors.

If chosen, a man got the chance to be an absolute autocrat within the area of his competence and to display his importance by strutting about in a special purple robe and carrying a whip, followed by whip-carrying flunkeys. For the judges could punish athletes who had broken training—or committed fouls or accepted bribes—not only by fines or expulsion from the games but also by scourging, a most unusual procedure since Greek practice was never to lay a whip on a freeman (this was something reserved for slaves). Money from the fines went to erect statues of Zeus in-

scribed with appropriate sentiments, e.g.: "Show that you win at Olympia with the speed of your feet and the strength in your body, and not with money." The bribes seem not to have come from gamblers or betting combines but from fellow athletes who wanted a victory desperately enough to try buying it. Hometowns were so fervently behind their boys that even bribery did not faze them. When an Athenian pentathlete was fined for trying to bribe his way to a win, the Athenians sent out a top advocate to plead for him; when that failed, they paid the fine themselves.

The original Olympic Games endured for so long because they were part of a religious festival, an offering to the great god Zeus. Ironically, what kept them going was also what brought them to an end. As more and more of the ancient world turned to Christianity, Zeus was gradually forced to abdicate his throne. The Olympics were held, regularly as clockwork, down to A. D. 261, when a threatened invasion of barbarians, the Herulians, interrupted the long sequence. The games were quickly resumed and continued—whether unbroken or not we do not know—until 393, the year in which the Roman Emperor Theodosius I, a fervent Christian, ordered the closing of all pagan centers. The site was abandoned. Over the centuries it was devastated by invaders, battered by earthquakes and gradually covered by silt from floodwaters of a nearby river. All this, together with endless years of neglect, left it buried until a British traveler found it in 1766. In 1875 the first of a number of German archaeological teams set about a systematic excavation.

Soon afterward, a French aristocrat, Baron Pierre de Coubertin, was passionately promoting the cause of athletics in general and a revival of the Olympic Games in particular. Resurrection of the site spurred him to even greater efforts, and in 1896 he finally achieved his dream: the first modern international Olympic Games. But they were held in urban Athens, not rural Olympia—the modern spectator took a dim view of sleeping alfresco, or even under a tent.

Love and Death in Ancient Greece

Catching him in the act, an obscure citizen of Athens slew his wife's lover. But was it a crime of passion—or premeditated murder?

Kenneth Cavander

Euphiletos was tired. He had been out in the country all day attending to business, and now he was home trying to get some sleep, and the baby was crying. His house was on two floors; the baby slept with a maid on the first floor; above, there was a combined living-dining-sleeping area for him and his wife. Euphiletos told his wife to go downstairs and nurse the baby. She protested that she wanted to be with him; she'd missed him while he was in the country—or did he just want to get rid of her so that he could make a pass at the maid, as he had the time he got drunk? Euphiletos laughed at that and at last his wife agreed to go downstairs and hush the child, but she insisted on locking the door to their room. Euphiletos turned over and went back to sleep. It never occurred to him to ask why his wife had gone through the charade of keeping him away from the maid, or why she had spent the rest of the night downstairs. But a few days later something happened that made him ask these questions, and by the end of the month a man was dead, killed in full view of a crowd of neighbors and friends.

This drama took place nearly two thousand five hundred years ago in ancient Athens. The characters were none of the brilliant and celebrated figures of the times—Socrates, Plato, Euripides, Aristophanes, Alcibiades—but members of the Athenian lower-middle class, obscure people who receded into the shadows of history. Their story is a soap opera compared to the grander tragedies being played out at the festivals of Dionysos in the theatre cut into the slopes of the Acropolis.

By a quirk of fate and an accident of politics the speech written for the murder trial that climaxes this story was the work of a man named Lysias. As a boy, Lysias sat in the company of Plato and Socrates, who often visited his father's house. As an adult, he was active in politics, and when a coup by the opposition party sent his family into exile, his property was confiscated and he narrowly escaped with his life. But a countercoup soon allowed him to return to Athens, and Lysias, now without a livelihood, had to find a profession.

He found one in the Athenian legal system. Athenian law was complex and attorneys were unknown; every citizen had to prosecute or defend himself in person. As a result, a class of professional legal advisers emerged that made a living supplying litigants with cogent, legally sound briefs. In time, Lysias became one of the most sought-after of these speech writers and several examples of his elegant and literate Greek style have been preserved, including the speech written for the defendant in this case.

Euphiletos, like many Athenians of modest means, lived in a small house in the city and commuted to the country to attend to his farm or market garden. He cannot have been well-off, for his house had the minimum number of slaves—one. Even a sausage seller or baker had at least one slave. Euphiletos had recently married and he was a trusting husband, so he said, giving his wife anything she asked for, never questioning her movements, trying to please her in every possible way. The most exciting event in the marriage was the birth of their child, whom his wife nursed herself. But the most significant event was the death of his mother: the whole family attended the funeral and, although Euphiletos did not know it at the time, his marriage was laid to rest that day along with his mother.

After the birth of their child Euphiletos and his wife had rearranged their living quarters. It was too dangerous to carry the baby up and down the steep ladder to the upper floor every time the child needed to be washed or changed, so the family was split up. Euphiletos and his wife moved into the upper part of the house, while the baby, with the slave girl to look after it, stayed downstairs.

The arrangement worked well, and Euphiletos's wife often went down in the middle of the night to be with the baby when it was cranky. But on the evening of the day Euphiletos came back tired from the country, two things in addition to the little drama of the locked door struck him as unusual. One was his wife's makeup: it was only a month since her brother had died—yet he noticed that she had put powder on her face. And there were noises in the night that sounded like a hinge creaking. When his wife awakened him by unlocking the bedroom door the next morning, Euphiletos asked her about these sounds. She said she had gone next door to a neighbor's house to borrow some oil for the baby's night light, which had gone out. As for the makeup, when Euphiletos thought about it he remembered his wife saying how much she had missed him and how

"Love and Death in Ancient Greece," by Kenneth Cavander, *Horizon*, Spring 1974.

reluctantly she had left him to go down and take care of the baby. Reassured, he dismissed the whole episode from his mind and thought no more about it—until something happened to shatter this comforting domestic picture and rearrange all the pieces of the puzzle in quite a different way.

One morning, a few days later, Euphiletos was leaving his house when he was stopped in the street by an old woman. She apologized for taking his time. "I'm not trying to make trouble," she said, "but we have an enemy in common." The old woman was a slave. Her mistress, she said, had been having an affair, but her lover had grown tired of her and left her for another woman. The other woman was Euphiletos's wife.

"The man is called Eratosthenes," said the old slave. "Ask your maid about him. He's seduced several women. He's got it down to a fine art."

In the midst of his shock and anger Euphiletos revealed a streak of something methodical, almost detached, in his character. Instead of going straight to his wife or her lover, he proceeded like an accountant investigating an error in the books.

He retraced his steps to his house and ordered the maidservant to come with him to the market. His wife would see nothing unusual in this, for respectable married women did not go out shopping in fifth-century Athens. That was left to the men and the slaves. Halfway to the market Euphiletos turned aside and marched the girl to the house of a friend, where he confronted her with the old woman's story. The girl denied it. Euphiletos threatened to beat her. She told him to go ahead and do what he liked. He talked of prison. She still denied it. Then Euphiletos mentioned Eratosthenes' name, and she broke down. In return for a promise that she would not be harmed, she told Euphiletos everything.

Her story was bizarre as well as comic and macabre. It began at the funeral of Euphiletos's mother. Eratosthenes had seen Euphiletos's wife among the mourners and had taken a fancy to her. He got in touch with the maid and persuaded her to act as go-between. Whether it was a difficult or an easy seduction we don't know; but, as the old woman had said, Eratosthenes was a practiced hand.

This love affair, first planned at a funeral and then set in motion by proxy, was carried on mostly at Euphiletos's house when he was away in the country. On one occasion his wife may have contrived to meet her lover away from the house, for she had gone with Eratosthenes' mother to the festival of the Thesmophoria, one of several festivals celebrated in honor of feminine deities. During these festivals a woman could leave the seclusion of her own house without arousing suspicious comment.

The slave girl also told Euphiletos that on the night he came back tired from the country, her mistress had told her to pinch the baby to make it cry, which gave her an excuse to go downstairs. His wife's parade of jealousy, Euphiletos now realized, was an act, designed to provide her with a reason to lock the door on him. So while he was a temporary prisoner in his own bedroom, his wife was downstairs in the nursery with her lover, and the maid was keeping the baby quiet somewhere else.

In a crisis, a person will often revert to archetypal behavior. For the Greeks of the fifth century B.C. the Homeric poems provided a mythological blueprint for almost any life situation, and it is interesting to see how Euphiletos's next move re-created a scene out of the legends. In *The Odyssey* Homer tells the story of what happened when Hephaistos, the god of fire, found out that his wife, Aphrodite, had been sleeping with the war god, Ares. Hephaistos decided not to face Aphrodite with her infidelity; instead, he wove a magical net that was sprung by the two lovers when they climbed into bed together. Then, as they lay there trapped, Hephaistos invited the other Olympians to come and view the guilty pair, "and the unquenchable laughter of the gods rose into the sky." In his own mundane way, but without the magic net, Euphiletos would follow the example of Hephaistos. He made his slave promise to keep everything she had told him a secret; then, pretending to his wife that he suspected nothing, he went about his business as usual and waited for a chance to spring his trap.

The part of cuckold is a mortifying one to play, and it was particularly so in ancient Athens where the relative status of men and women was so unequal. A freeborn Athenian woman was free in little more than name. She could not vote, make contracts, or conduct any business involving more than a certain sum of money; legally she was little more than a medium for the transmission of property from grandfather to grandchildren through the dowry she brought with her to her husband. Her husband, of course, was invariably chosen for her by her father or by the nearest male relative if her father was dead. Almost the only thing she could call her own was her reputation, which depended on good behavior, an unassertive demeanor, a life spent dutifully spinning, weaving, dyeing clothes, cooking, bearing and raising children, and, above all, on not interfering in the serious business of life as conducted by the men. In a famous speech in praise of the Athenian men who died during the Peloponnesian War, Pericles makes only one reference to women: according to Thucydides, who reports the speech in his history of the war, Pericles said that women should never give rise to any comment by a man, favorable or unfavorable. In the tragic dramas, moreover, women who offer their opinions unasked or who go about alone in public usually feel they have to apologize for behaving in such a brazen and immodest way.

Such was the official status of women. Unofficially, the women of ancient Athens found ways, as their

2. GREECE AND ROME

sisters have done in every age and culture, to undermine the barriers of male prejudice. In Euripides' play *Iphigeneia at Aulis* (written within a year or two of Euphiletos's marriage), Agamemnon tries to assert his authority over his wife, Clytemnestra, in order to get her out of the way while he sacrifices his own daughter, Iphigeneia, to Artemis. Clytemnestra, with a show of wifely stubbornness that surely came out of the playwright's contemporary observation, refuses to be dismissed and finally cuts the conversation short by sending her husband about his business. In another play by Euripides, *Hippolytos,* there are some lines that might have been written specifically for Euphiletos himself to speak. Hippolytos, told that his stepmother, Phaidra, is in love with him, remarks scathingly: "I would have no servants near a woman, just beasts with teeth and no voice, [for] servants are the agents in the world outside for the wickedness women do."

Drink and sex are the traditional outlets for the oppressed. The comedies of Aristophanes are studded with snide references to the excessive drinking habits of women. According to Aristophanes, festivals such as the Thesmophoria were excuses for massive alcoholic sprees. More likely, these mystery cults were the safety valve for pent-up emotions, a chance to transcend the cruelly narrow boundaries imposed on women by their roles in a rigidly male society.

As for sex, women were the weaker vessel when it came to this human urge. In *Lysistrata* Aristophanes has the women wondering whether they can hold out long enough to bring the men to their knees. And in the legends that canonized popular wisdom on the subject there is a story about Zeus and Hera squabbling over who gets the greater pleasure out of sex—the man or the woman. When they finally appeal to Teiresias, the blind seer and prophet, who, as part man and part woman, ought to be able to settle the question for them, he duly reports that in the sexual act the woman, in fact, gets nine-tenths of the pleasure, and the man only one-tenth.

These scraps of myth and folklore, however, filtered through male fantasy as they are, reveal a sense of unease about women. In the Orestes myth, for instance, it is Clytemnestra who takes over the reins of government in the absence of Agamemnon, then murders him when he returns; and it is her daughter Electra who pushes a faltering Orestes into taking revenge for the slain king. A whole army of formidable heroines—Electra, Clytemnestra, Antigone, Hecuba, Andromache, Medea—marches through the pages of Greek drama. The Fates, the Muses, and the Furies are all women. None of these female figures is anything like the meek and passive drudge that the Greek woman of the fifth century was expected to be.

But were they real types, these mythological heroines, or were they phantom projections of male fears and desires, mother imagoes, castration anxieties dressed up as gods, embodiments of the part of a man he most wants to repress—his own irrational and emotional side, his moon-bound, lunatic aspects—thrust onto women because he dare not admit them in himself?

It is possible. Every mythologized figure embodies inner and outer worlds. We see what we wish to see, and the picture we perceive turns into a mirror. Were there actual women in Athens capable of organizing a fully functioning communistic state and pushing it through the assembly, like the Praxagora of Aristophanes' play *Ekklesiazousai?* Were there Electras and Clytemnestras and Medeas? If there were, they never reached the pages of the history books. We hear of Aspasia, Pericles' "companion" (the Greek word is *hetaira,* meaning "woman friend"), for whom he divorced his legal wife. But Aspasia was a member of the demimonde of "liberated" women who lived outside the social order, not necessarily slaves, but not full citizens either. They were often prostitutes, but some of them were cultured and educated, better traveled and more interesting to Athenian men than their own wives. Custom permitted one or more relationships with *hetairai* outside the marriage, but a *hetaira* had no legal claim on a man, and he could sell her or dispose of her any time he liked. Meanwhile, for the trueborn Athenian woman who wanted a more varied life than the one prescribed by convention, what was there? Gossip with the neighbors. The bottle. A festival now and then. A clandestine love affair.

Four or five days passed while Euphiletos brooded over the wrong done to him. Suppose a child was born from this liaison: who could tell whether it was his or Eratosthenes'? All kinds of complications might follow. But whatever he was feeling, Euphiletos managed to hide it from his wife. She never suspected that he knew anything at all.

Euphiletos had a good friend named Sostratos. Less than a week after his interview with the maid Euphiletos met Sostratos coming home from the country, and since it was late Euphiletos invited his friend to his house for supper. This casual meeting was to become important later at the trial. The two men went upstairs, ate and drank well, and had a pleasant evening together. By custom Euphiletos's wife was not present. After Sostratos had gone home Euphiletos went to sleep.

Some time in the middle of the night there was a knock on his door. It was the maid. Eratosthenes had arrived.

Leaving the maid to keep watch, Euphiletos slipped out a back way and went around the neighborhood waking up his friends. Some of them were out of town, but he managed to collect a small group who went to a nearby store and bought torches. Then they all trooped off to Euphiletos's house where they stood outside in the street holding the lighted torches while Euphiletos tapped on the door. Quietly the maid let him into the courtyard. He pushed past her into the room where his wife was supposed to be asleep with the baby. A few of Euphiletos's friends managed to crowd in behind him.

For a split second the scene must have been like a tableau out of Homer: Eratosthenes naked in bed, Euphiletos's wife in his arms, the two lovers trapped in the light of torches held by the neighbors.

Then Eratosthenes, still naked, sprang up. Euphiletos shouted at him, "What are you doing in my house?" and knocked him off the bed, pulled his wrists behind his back, and tied them.

Eratosthenes offered to pay Euphiletos any sum he named. Euphiletos had a choice: he could accept the bribe, or he could take a form of revenge allowed by law—brutalizing and humiliating Eratosthenes by such methods as the insertion of tough thistles up his rectum. There was also a third option open to him under the circumstances: since he had caught Eratosthenes in the act, and there were witnesses present, Euphiletos could kill him.

Euphiletos interrupted the other man's pleas. "I won't kill you," he said, and then, in the kind of logical twist the Greeks loved, he added, "but the law will."

And in the name of the law he killed Eratosthenes.

Athenian homicide law required the dead man's family, not the state, to bring charges of murder. Eratosthenes' family undertook the task, and approximately three months later Euphiletos found himself facing a jury of fifty-one Athenians in the court known as the Delphinion, located in the southeast corner of Athens, where cases of justifiable homicide were tried. Eratosthenes' family charged Euphiletos with premeditated murder on the grounds that he had sent his maid to lure Eratosthenes to the house; they may also have tried to prove that Eratosthenes was dragged into the building by force, or took refuge at the hearth before he was killed. In the speech he writes for Euphiletos, Lysias sets out to rebut all these charges.

Lysias puts into Euphiletos's mouth some ingenious legal arguments. The law (of which a copy is read to the court) says that a seducer caught in the act may be killed. "If you make it a crime to kill a seducer in this way," he argues, "you will have a situation in which a thief, caught burglarizing your house, will pretend that he is an adulterer in order to get away with a lesser crime." Lysias also refers the jury to the law on rape. Rape carries a lower penalty than seduction. Why? Because, theorizes Lysias, the rapist simply takes the woman's body, while the seducer steals her soul.

Nevertheless, in spite of Lysias's able and sophisticated defense, there is a flaw in Euphiletos's argument. His defense rests on the assumption that his action was unpremeditated, committed in the heat of the moment, under the shock and stress of finding his wife in bed with another man. That is surely the intent of the law, and Euphiletos goes to great lengths to prove he had not planned the encounter. He cites the dinner invitation to Sostratos, which, he says, is not the behavior of a man planning murder. But the rest of his story contradicts this. The signals by which the maid warned him that Eratosthenes had arrived and by which he let her know

that he was waiting at the front door; the rounding up of friends to act as witnesses; the presence of the murder weapon on his person—all point to prior preparation. Euphiletos may prove to the jury's satisfaction that he did not lure Eratosthenes deliberately to his house that night, but he fails to prove that he was taken totally by surprise or that he tried to do anything to stop the affair before it reached that point. His action looks suspiciously like cold-blooded revenge executed under color of a law that forgives even violent crimes if they are committed in the heat of passion.

Neither the speech for the prosecution nor the testimony of witnesses has survived, so we do not know if the wife or the maid gave evidence. Though women were not allowed to appear as witnesses in court cases, the rules for murder trials may have been different. A slave could not testify at all, but a deposition could have been taken from her under torture and read to the court. On the other hand, Euphiletos may have wanted to avoid bringing the women into it: after all, they had been in league against him throughout the whole unhappy affair.

There is something touching in the alliance between the slave, an object without rights or status, and the wife, legally a free citizen but in reality a kind of slave too. The maidservant probably accepted a bribe from Eratosthenes, but all the same she had a moment of heroism when, threatened with a beating and prison, she refused to incriminate her mistress. Afterward, when she became Euphiletos's accomplice, there is an eerie reversal of the situation: the slave admits her master to the house in the same stealthy way that she had opened the door for her mistress's lover a few minutes earlier. But still, there was a moment when Euphiletos was the outsider, barred from his own house and his wife's arms, with only his rage and his group of male friends for company.

Finally there is the wife herself, the center of the drama and its most shadowy character. Apart from his grudging admission that she was thrifty and capable and a good housekeeper, Euphiletos tells us little about her. From what we know of Athenian marriage customs, we can guess that she was probably married at fourteen or fifteen to a virtual stranger and expected to keep house for this man who spent much of his time away from home on business. Was she satisfied with the trinkets that Euphiletos says he let her buy, and with all of the household duties and her young baby?

A small fragment survives from a lost play by Aristophanes in which a character says, "A woman needs a lover the way a dinner needs dessert." Euphiletos's wife was no Lysistrata, able to express her frustration and rebellion in some dramatic act of revolutionary will, but she did find a way to rebel all the same. It cost her dear. By Athenian law, if a man discovered that his wife had been raped or seduced, he was expected to divorce her. And from what we know of Euphiletos's character, we can be sure that he obeyed the law.

Life with Father, Life with Socrates

Virginia Wetherbee

My father was opinionated, argumentative, over-bearing, irreverent, brilliant, and an optimist. That is, he thought I was amenable, or would be, or should be. But, since I was very like him (without, I regret to say, the brilliance), we frequently ran at each other full tilt, clashing noisily, always with the same result. I was unseated.

Movie magazines were a common casus belli. I loved them. He detested them. At school, I would eat an Eskimo Pie for lunch and save the rest of my food allowance for buying *Photoplay.* Inevitably, he caught me reading it and confiscated it forthwith. I took to hiding it under my mattress and reading in bed under the covers by flashlight. One night, uninvited, he came into my room, took in the situation at a glance, disinterred me, snatched the magazine, and stormed out. I ran after him down the stairs into the living room where, with a furious gesture, he tore the magazine in half and threw the pieces into the fireplace. I stood sadly watching them burn (more Eskimo Pies ahead) and then went back up to my room. A few minutes later, Father strode in again and threw a book onto the bed. "You're not going to read that trash, do you hear me? Read this instead! And to make sure you do," he added menacingly, "I will test you on it next week."

The book was *Plato: The Collected Dialogues.* The ribbon marker had been placed in the *Lysis.*

Had I been prescient, I might have said, echoing Thomas Huxley when Bishop Wilberforce made a grievous error in their debate on Darwin's theory of evolution, "The Lord hath delivered him into my hands." In truth, Father delivered himself. Up until then, I had been defending myself in our arguments with, so to speak, a stick. Father handed me a sword.

It took me awhile to see that. In the meantime, dutifully, I read the *Lysis.*

I was walking straight from the Academy to the Lyceum, by the road which skirts the outside of the walls, and had reached the little gate where is the source of the Panops, when I fell in with Hippothales, the son of Hieronymus, Ctessipus the Paeanian, and some more young men, standing together in a group.

Hippothales, seeing me approach, called out, Ha, Socrates, whither and whence?

The young men, among them Lysis, a beautiful young man with whom Hippothales is infatuated, persuade him to join their conversation, which becomes, with Socrates' guidance, a search for the meaning of "friendship." The more they talk, the more elusive the meaning becomes, so that when the party finally breaks up, Socrates comments, "Well . . . we have made ourselves rather ridiculous today, I, an old man, and you children. For our hearers here will carry away the report that though we conceive ourselves to be friends with each other—you see I class myself with you—we have not as yet been able to discover what we mean by a friend."

What did Father expect me to learn from all this?

Not, surely, a lesson on homosexuality in ancient Greece. In testing me on this and subsequent dialogues, he did not mention the subject. And, having never heard of word or deed, neither did I.

Not, surely, an understanding of "friendship." Like the young men, I knew less about it when I finished reading the dialogue than when I started.

Did he think to wean me from *Photoplay?* Not likely. I was addicted. And, ironically, Father had only himself to blame.

Reprinted from THE AMERICAN SCHOLAR, Volume 52, Number 4, Autumn, 1983, pp. 497-510. Copyright ©1983 by Virginia Wetherbee. By permission of the publishers, the United Chapters of Phi Beta Kappa.

My mother had died when I was a year old and my brother was three. Father's family rallied to help him through the first difficult years but, inevitably, all went on about their own lives and he had to depend for our care on housekeepers. None of them stayed long. One, at the end of her first day, was waiting for Father on the front porch, suitcase in hand. Father, perhaps *pour encourager les autres,* began taking my brother and me with him to his office. A young doctor with a growing practice, he had an office on the second floor of a two-story building on Main Street in the center of town. Beneath the office was a small theater, the Garden. Father bought tickets for us, ushered us into seats, and told us to stay there until he came back to get us. At the end of the first showing, the lights would come on and the theater would empty except for my brother and me and the local derelicts from the Mission around the corner. The two of us regularly sat through two shows, sometimes three. Those were halcyon days, for us and for Hollywood: wonderful Westerns (with Tom Mix, Hoot Gibson), before they were ruined by the singing cowboy, and Harold Lloyd comedies. In our Garden of Eden, we sat entranced through a double feature every day plus a serial on Saturdays. To my knowledge, Father censored only one movie, which featured Theda Bara, after he found me in the little lobby staring at voluptuous ads for coming attractions.

So, what did I, then an eighth grader whose favorite reading included *Photoplay, The Girl of the Limberlost,* and *Tom Swift,* learn from my penance of Plato?

To be more circumspect. Father never caught me out again.

That love doesn't imply license. The parents of Lysis love him *very* dearly, he concedes, and wish him to be as happy as possible. Nevertheless, far from indulging his every wish, they are keeping a firm grip on him until he is old enough to rule himself.

A little discipline, I suppose. I did not stop reading *Photoplay,* but I obediently read Plato.

Whatever Father had in mind—and I'm not sure even he knew in the heat of the moment—one overriding thing I did learn: Anytus, Meletus, and Lycon were right—Socrates was a dangerous man. In 399 B.C. they accused him of believing in gods of his own invention instead of those sanctioned by the state and of corrupting the minds of the young. Of his heresy, I can't judge. Of his influence on the young, I can: more than two thousand years after Socrates was brought before the Athenian court to answer to these charges, found guilty, sentenced to death and executed, I fell under his spell, for better or worse, for once and for all.

In an age whose sculptors gave the Western world an enduring ideal of physical beauty, Socrates was, by his own admission and the testimony of statues portraying him, ugly. Heavy-faced with bulging eyes, a broad, snub nose whose nostrils spread wide, a large, thick-lipped mouth partly hidden by an untidy beard, balding, a paunchy body carelessly wrapped in a coarse cloak,

barefoot—in appearance, a satyr. Perhaps it is just as well. The looks of a Greek god would have confused the issue of his fascination for young men.

Born in Athens in 469 B.C., the son of an artisan-sculptor and a midwife, Socrates grew up in the Golden Age of Pericles that followed the Greeks' successful conclusion of the Persian Wars. During these momentous years, Socrates fought with great courage and stamina as a hoplite (a heavily armed soldier) in the infantry during several important battles— at Potidaea, which began the Peloponnesian War, at Delium, at Amphipolis. He served on the City Council, singularizing himself as the only one of fifty councillors to vote against a politically popular but illegal resolution. When not fulfilling his civic duties, he was, by profession, a stonecutter, by avocation, or mission, so he believed, the gadfly of Athens.

> It seems to me that God has attached me to this city to perform the office of such a fly, and all day long I never cease to settle here, there, and everywhere, rousing, persuading, reproving every one of you. . . . I spend all my time going about trying to persuade you, young and old, to make your first and chief concern not for your bodies, nor for your possessions, but for the highest welfare of your souls, proclaiming as I go, "Wealth does not bring goodness, but goodness brings wealth and every other blessing, both to the individual and to the state."

From the marketplace to the gymnasia, from morning to night, Socrates walked the streets of Athens, arguing with anyone and everyone (men, women, politicians, soldiers, foreigners) about the meaning of justice, friendship, the good life, piety, immortality. Young men in particular gathered eagerly around him to listen, to argue, perchance, to learn.

The *Lysis* illustrates clearly Socrates' unique method of teaching. The boys, guided by him, seek the meaning of "friendship" by question and answer. As usual in these dialogues, they all become, Socrates confesses, "quite dizzied by the entanglement of the subject." That is the way he leaves them, intentionally, for his aim is not to reach a final definition but to awaken their minds, to rouse them to think, question their beliefs, and eliminate their false assumptions, examining themselves in the process, for "the unexamined life is not worth living."

I was quite dizzied myself by Socrates. For awhile, he took over my life. I read everything I could find about him and fifth-century Athens in Father's extensive library (which included that font of information the *Encyclopaedia Britannica*).

The time came when I interrupted my father, who was pontificating about something, to say, "That's sophistry, Father, and you know it." He was speechless, briefly. Then, he began to laugh, the proverbial laugh of the little boy caught with his hand in the cookie jar. From then on, whenever Father was pleading a shaky case (as Stephen Leacock pointed out, "A half-truth in argument, like a half-brick, carries better"), he would catch my eye and start to laugh.

As, with his help, I plodded my way through the dialogues—with a modest percentage of comprehension—I became aware of Father's joy in our reading. Plato was his bible. I began to think of him as a latter-day Athenian. Like Socrates, he was not a Greek god. Rather short, heavy-bodied (an eighteen-inch collar), he always looked slightly rumpled even in tailor-made suits. His head was large, his nose big, his vision poor, requiring strong glasses, and his hearing worse. He took advantage of his deafness in our arguments. I had to shout, which made subtlety difficult, humor impossible, mistakes humiliating. Eventually, he wore an earphone, and when he thought I was winning, he turned it off.

Like Socrates, he attracted followers. Dynamic, a fascinating conversationalist, with enormous enthusiasms and ever-increasing financial success, he offered excitement (*never* a dull moment), infinite variety, and, very important, jobs. With his younger brother, an ear, eye, nose, and throat specialist and a kind, docile man, he had started a small hospital and, after a time, moved his office there. So my brother and I hung around the hospital, which was almost as entertaining as the Garden and far more educational, sometimes deplorably so. Through our small house in the suburbs (and, later, our very large house on the street next to the hospital), there now moved a steady procession of resident boarders who worked at the hospital: relatives, friends, nurses, technicians, cooks, maids. In both neighborhoods, needless to say, the households attracted attention and gossip, which, like philosophy, was part analytical and part speculative.

But Socrates and Father parted company on some basic issues.

Fee for service. Socrates adamantly refused to accept fees for his teaching. Since, in pursuit of his mission day and night, he was too busy to work at his profession, his service to God, he admitted, had reduced him to extreme poverty. (Xanthippe, Socrates' wife, was, by reputation, a shrew. Inasmuch as she was waiting at home with three small sons to feed, while he was happily walking and talking his way around Athens, nagging seems sensible.) Father subscribed to the sentiment Samuel Johnson expressed in his remark, "No man but a blockhead ever wrote except for money."

The good life. For Socrates, the good life was to be found in the quest for virtue and knowledge. Knowledge produces right conduct; right conduct produces happy, just, useful, good citizens. Father's idea of the good life was thick, juicy steaks, charcoal-broiled rare, a Packard touring car (my brother and I happily claimed the jump seats), trips to Europe, largesse distributed throughout his small, bustling kingdom.

Despite these lapses, Father practiced, to the limit of his patience, the Socratic method of seeking knowledge about a subject by question and answer (preferably someone else's question, his answer), but without the Socratic irony. Even for the sake of taking advantage of an opponent in debate, he couldn't profess ignorance.

Life with Father was one long course in rhetoric. Mealtimes were particularly instructive and noisy. We ate in the first shift in the hospital dining room, and there was no telling who would be eating with us. A relative or two, a local politician, a visiting doctor, a traveling drug salesman, one of Father's boccie partners. (He had had an alley built in the hospital's side yard so he could get in some play between patients.) Once, for months, a mysterious, elderly German refugee from something appeared and ate dinner with us. Father had decided to learn German. Characteristically, he whipped through a grammar book and now needed conversation practice, so the discussions went bewilderingly back and forth between English and garbled German.

In later years, after I had started college and friends of mine, male and female, would come to visit, those dinners became a test of our friendship. One young man, shaken by the experience (he thought we were fighting), never came back. We weren't fighting. We were arguing. About what? Philosophy—an argument without end. Our motto could have been "Philosophia Biou Kubernētēs"—philosophy, the guide of life (or, equally well, like that of McGeorge Bundy's family, "don't talk while I'm interrupting").

As a discipline, philosophy in the Western world began, appropriately, with a question. Not, up until then, the usual "Who made the world?" with, for possible answers, a wide choice of local gods, but "What is the world made of?" asked by Thales of Miletus, a seventh-century B.C. Ionian Greek. For the next two centuries, the nature philosophers—Thales, Anaximander, Anaximenes, Pythagoras, Heraclitus, Democritus—sought to determine the original "stuff" of the universe. Then, in the fifth century B.C., attention turned away from the heavens to man. "Man is the measure of all things," declared Protagoras, the first to call himself a Sophist. A wise man, later a teacher of wisdom, the Sophist, for a fee, taught the humanities: language, literature, history, grammar, rhetoric. The pejorative sense of the title came when their teaching of rhetoric, the art of persuasion, had developed into a kind of Dale Carnegie course in how to outsmart one's opponents by quibbling.

Unfortunately for him at his trial, Socrates was identified with the Sophists. Like them, he had no interest in natural science. Like them, he taught, but with a different goal—the moral improvement of mankind. He saw himself as a midwife, like his mother, bringing forth "just men."

In pursuit of that goal, Socrates' genius was to ask new questions. What is virtue? courage? friendship? the good life? and why should one pursue it? With the ideas of definition, of value, a whole world of fresh questions opened up.

"The history of systematic thought," Sir Isaiah Berlin explains, "is largely a sustained effort to formulate all the questions that occur to mankind in such a way that the answers to them will fall into one or other of two great baskets: the empirical, i.e. questions whose answers depend, in the end, on the data of observation; and the formal, i.e. questions whose answers depend on pure calculation untrammelled by factual knowledge." Those that do so become part of a recognized science. However, "between the two original baskets, the empirical and the formal, there is at least one intermediate basket, in which all those questions live which cannot easily be fitted into the other two. . . . The only common characteristic which all these questions appear to have is that they cannot be answered either by observation or calculation, either by inductive methods or deductive; and, as a crucial corollary of this, that those who ask them are faced with a perplexity from the very beginning—they do not know where to look for the answers. . . . Such questions tend to be called philosophical."

There is a famous scene in Aristophanes' *Clouds:*

At Socrates' school or thinking-house, Strepsiades, a simple, old peasant, and a student are gazing overhead at a figure suspended in a basket.

STREPSIADES: Hallo! Who's that? that fellow in the basket?
STUDENT: That's HE.
STREPSIADES: Who's HE?
STUDENT: Socrates.
STREPSIADES: Socrates!
    You sir, call out to him as loud as you can.
STUDENT: Call him yourself: I have not leisure now.
STREPSIADES: Socrates! Socrates! Sweet Socrates!
SOCRATES: Mortal! why call'st thou me?
STREPSIADES: O, first of all, please tell me what you are doing.
SOCRATES: I walk on air and contemplate the Sun.
STREPSIADES: O then from a basket you contemn the Gods, And not from the earth, at any rate.
SOCRATES: Most true.
    I could not have searched out celestial matters
    Without suspending judgement, and infusing
    My subtle spirit with the kindred air.
    If from the ground I were to seek these things,
    I could not find: so surely doth the earth
    Draw to herself the essence of our thought.
    The same too is the case with watercress.
STREPSIADES: Hillo! what's that?
    Thought draws the essence into watercress?
    Come down, sweet Socrates, more near my level,
    And teach the lessons which I come to learn.

Aristophanes, the great Athenian playwright, in this brilliant comedy produced in 423 B.C., is holding up Socrates and his notions to ridicule. Twenty-four years later, in Socrates' speech to the jury at his trial, he acknowledges the lasting damage to his reputation from this satirical attack. Aristophanes must surely bear a share of responsibility for the severity of the jury's sentence.

The tragic consequences aside (though not forgotten or forgiven), there is a lovely symbolism in the image of Socrates up in the air in that third great basket of philosophical questions. A full basket, "for," Berlin points out, "no matter how many questions can be so transformed as to be capable of empirical or formal treatment, the number of questions that seem incapable of being so treated does not appear to grow less."

So, we never ran out of topics for discussion. A word, a phrase, a name—equality, the big bang, Darwin, Rousseau, Mrs. Roosevelt (Father's bete noire)—was enough to set us off.

It would be fair to say that I went off to college with an unusual background for a seventeen-year-old girl. (Mount Holyoke prides itself on its interest in the "uncommon woman," but my experience there suggests they are disconcerted by the real thing.) Life with Father had left me with a questionable attitude toward authority and a disdain for ex cathedra pronouncements, for which my professors did not give high marks. I was too young and intolerant to hide my want of faith. Even if I said nothing, as Father irritably noted, my eyes gave me away. But skepticism, like virtue, has its own reward. At that time, on college campuses, communism was intellectually fashionable, and some students, cutting conscience to fit fashion, joined the Communist party or became fellow travelers (to their later discomfort). Because of Father and Socrates, I had no trouble resisting Marxist catechism disguised as dialectic.

After graduation, I married a young man whose interest in me had survived dinner with my family. Perhaps he thought distance the better part of valor, for I shortly found myself living in a small town in the Mississippi Delta. I was just twenty-one, having been married on my birthday, old enough at last to drink and vote, away for the first time from home where, by and large, I had proposed and Father disposed. Samuel Johnson had it right: "The transition from the protection of others to our own conduct is a very awful point of human existence."

Well, like the French abbé who, when asked what he had done during the Reign of Terror, replied, "J'ai vécu," I survived. Thanks, I believe now, to Socrates, with a fond wave to Father and *Photoplay.*

Keats has a phrase: "*negative capability,* that is, when a man is capable of being in uncertainties, mysteries, doubts. . . ." Negative capability, it seems to me in retrospect, is the lasting lesson I learned from all those hours of tagging along in my imagination behind the gadfly of ancient Athens—to ask questions and, like Lysis and his friends, to find no certain answers. ("When you know all the answers, you haven't asked all the questions.") To live, that is, in ambiguity.

Chaerephon, a friend and admirer of Socrates,

2. GREECE AND ROME

asked the oracle at Delphi, "Is there anyone wiser than Socrates?" The priestess, medium for the message from Apollo, replied, "No one." Baffled by the god's answer, Socrates set out to check the truth of it by examining men with great reputations for wisdom. He came away from the interviews at last understanding Apollo's meaning: the wisest man is he who knows his own ignorance.

One thing I did know: this issue had no limits of time or place. In 399 B.C. it had led to Socrates' death sentence. "Socrates is guilty of corrupting the minds of the young and believing in deities of his own invention instead of the gods recognized by the state."

The gods recognized by the state were Homer's Olympians: Zeus, the patriarch; Hera, his wife; Apollo, his son; Athena, his daughter and the protecting deity of Athens; Poseidon and Hades, his brothers; and the extended family. The temples and statuary of the Acropolis in Athens are their enduring monument. But the search of the early Greek philosophers for natural explanations for the existence of things presented a challenge not only to their power but to their existence. "Concerning the gods," wrote Protagoras, "I am not able to know whether they exist or do not exist."

In about 430 B.C., Sophocles took up the challenge in *Oedipus Rex,* a murder mystery with the hero as detective. The origins of the crime are in the past. Laius, king of Thebes, has been told by an oracle that he will be killed by his own son. To prevent this, he has the feet of his newborn son pinned together and the child left to die on Mt. Cithaeron. However, the baby, called Oedipus (the name means "swollen foot"), is rescued, taken to Corinth, and raised as the son of King Polybus. When the oracle tells Oedipus that he will kill his father and marry his mother, he flees from Corinth. On his way to Thebes, at a crossroad, he quarrels with another traveler, an old man, over the right-of-way and in anger kills him (King Laius). Continuing on his way, he meets the celebrated Sphinx, solves her riddle, and receives as his reward the kingdom of Thebes and its queen, Jocasta (his mother), in marriage. As the play opens, plague has struck Thebes. The oracle is consulted and declares that the city is being polluted by the presence of the murderer of the former king, Laius. Oedipus vows to find the murderer.

The chorus, representing the people's point of view, watches the tragedy unfold before them. Seeing the danger in Oedipus's and Jocasta's contempt for the oracles, they appeal to Apollo to make his prophecy come true, lest the gods and religion seem meaningless.

The answer is prompt. The awful truth is revealed: the prophecy *has* been fulfilled. The gods *do* exist. They *do* know the future and man's destiny from which there is no escape. Man *is* subordinate in the universal scheme of things. The lesson displayed for all doubters to *see,* Oedipus and Jocasta rush offstage to kill themselves. That's that.

Or should be. The play should be over. Jocasta has

hanged herself. But Oedipus has chosen not to kill himself. Instead, in his despair, he has gouged out his own eyes. ("No more, no more shall my eyes see the horrors of my life—what I have done, what I have suffered!") The play ends with Oedipus, in the care of his daughter Antigone, wandering off into exile.

In Oedipus's choice is Sophocles' answer to the challenge of his times—a reconciliation of the traditional beliefs with the new ideas. Oedipus is courageous, intelligent, a good ruler, if hotheaded at times. His only crime is ignorance. The remedy for ignorance is knowledge, and he is free to search for it. Oedipus chooses to do so. But knowledge has its price. When he discovers the truth, too horrible to face, he blinds himself. That, too, is choice. ("It was my hand, mine, that struck the blow!") And his choice to go on living. ("You would be better dead," the chorus tells him.) The reward for his search for the truth is self-knowledge. He knows now who he is, accepts his place in the universe, and chooses to live with that truth and its consequences.

This is very like what Socrates is saying, day after day, walking the streets of Athens, looking for someone to talk with. "Where do you come from, Phaedrus my friend, and where are you going?" As they stroll into the countryside to find a shady tree to sit under and talk, Phaedrus brings up the new scientific ideas. Socrates has "no time for the business," he says, "and I'll tell you why, my friend. I can't as yet 'know myself' as the inscription at Delphi enjoins; and so long as that ignorance remains, it seems to me ridiculous to inquire into extraneous matters." Ignorance is shameful. Knowledge is the greatest good, for if man *knows* what is good, he will *do* it. And through knowledge, man can to some degree influence his destiny.

Sophocles and Socrates were speaking many years apart, however. When *Oedipus Rex* was produced in 430 B.C., one could still say: bliss was it in that Golden Age to be alive, but to be Greek and a citizen of Athens (the world's first democracy) was very heaven! The Sophists' and the rhetoricians' love affair with words had enveloped the city in a golden glow of talk as heady as wine. It was in that glowing freedom that Sophocles (the "quintessential Greek," Edith Hamilton calls him, "direct, lucid, simple, reasonable") chose to probe the awesome relationship between the gods and men.

But the days of glory were running out. The Peloponnesian War had begun in 431, and the Spartan army invaded Attica. In 430, perhaps because of the overcrowding of the city by refugees fleeing to within the protection of the walls, plague broke out in Athens. It would last three years and kill a great number of the population, including Pericles. From then on, the Athenians seem to have been their own worst enemy. The democracy was overthrown and restored. Disastrous campaigns were undertaken and lost. Finally, in 404, not surprisingly, the Spartans were victorious. The democracy was again overthrown and again restored in 403, but the ravages of the plague, the long years of wartime suffering, and the humiliating defeat by Sparta had left the Athenians dispirited, fearful, disillusioned. Belief in the gods and traditional morality was waning, especially among young men. As Edith Hamilton says, "No pupil of Socrates could take seriously Homer's gods, still the state religion."

The loss of faith is ominous. "It is, I think, important to realize," Gilbert Murray stresses, "that the normal reason for consulting an oracle was not to ask questions of fact. It was that some emergency had arisen in which men simply wanted to know how they ought to behave." If the gods do not exist, then, as the saying has it, everything is permitted.

This is the atmosphere in which Socrates is walking and talking his way around Athens, fulfilling his God-given mission. And he will continue to do so, he tells the jury at his trial, despite fair warning that, as Anytus declares, "I must be put to death, because if I once escaped, your sons would all immediately become utterly demoralized by putting the teaching of Socrates into practice."

(Xenophon claims that Anytus was angry because his young son, after listening to Socrates, rejected his father's authority and his father's profession, tanner, for which he had been prepared. The boy later turned to wine, Xenophon adds, and "in the end he became worthless to his state, his friends and to himself.")

What *was* Socrates teaching to the sons of Athens? Micheline Sauvage (in *Socrates and the Human Conscience*) says it clearly: "Even in his most trivial discussions, Socrates aims at getting his interlocutor to face himself, so as to substitute a considered, autonomous conduct for an automatic, tacitly accepted conduct which is bound to deteriorate, for it is the fate of traditions and habits to be lost, of beliefs to be shaken, of obediences to be refused, sooner or later."

The transition from the protection of others—fathers, gods, and oracles—is a very awful point of human existence. Socrates' mission as midwife is to deliver men from the protective womb of the gods into a world where self-reliance, self-government, and goodness will bring every blessing to the individual and the state. In those declining years of the Athenian city-state, the gods themselves—exhorting suppliants: "Know thyself," "Nothing in excess"—could only hope for safe deliverance.

Knowledge is all, Socrates says over and over. No one pursues evil except through ignorance. If a man *knows* what is good, he will *do* it. But some of Socrates' young followers, notably Critias and Alcibiades, prove the uncertainty principle in human conduct is always with us.

Critias was one of the Thirty Tyrants chosen by the Spartans to rule Athens after the defeat of 404, a rule of terror, it turned out. Critias, according to Xenophon, so resented Socrates' criticism of the injustices of the Thirty that, knowing firsthand Socrates' persuasive powers, he had a law enacted forbidding the teaching of the art of argument. To make sure that Socrates understood that the law applied to him, Critias and another of the Thirty summoned him and spelled it out: "You must not hold discussions with the young." Socrates was lucky. Before democracy was restored the following year, many citizens—fifteen hundred or more—were put to death.

Alcibiades, perhaps Socrates' favorite pupil, was from the same wealthy family as Pericles. He was a golden youth, charming, witty, handsome, brilliant, and thoroughly spoiled and irresponsible. Everything in excess, gifts and vices, describes him. But he did know himself. Staggering in, drunk and uninvited, to a dinner party where Socrates is one of the guests, he is persuaded to give a eulogy of Socrates. In his rambling, drunken speech, he confesses, "And there's one thing I've never felt with anybody else—not the kind of thing you'd expect to find in me, either—and that is a sense of shame. Socrates is the only man in the world that can make me feel ashamed. Because there's no getting away from it, I know I ought to do the things he tells me to, and yet the moment I'm out of his sight I don't care what I do to keep in with the mob. So I dash off like a runaway slave, and keep out of his way as long as I can, and then next time I meet him I remember all that I had to admit the time before, and naturally I feel ashamed. There are times when I'd honestly be glad to hear that he was dead, and yet I know that if he did die, I'd be more upset than ever—so I ask you, what is a man to do?" Shame was not enough. All that bright promise ended in treason, banishment, and an early, violent death.

The jury trying Socrates ("cleaners, shoemakers, carpenters, blacksmiths, farmers, merchants") would have been thinking of Critias, Alcibiades, Anytus's son . . .

Socrates' speech in his own defense is prickly and unsatisfactory. He dismisses the charges against him of disbelief in the gods as "pure flippancy" and of his corrupting the young by pointing to many of his followers (including Plato) and their families present in the courtroom who, if he had been giving them bad advice all this time should then "be coming forward to denounce and punish me." He identifies correctly the basis of the charges—hostility toward him built up over many years by distortion of his ideas by so many people, "it is impossible for me even to know and tell you their names, unless one of them happens to be a playwright." He avoids any mention of the real issue involved in his teaching: the bill of rights of the autonomous individual includes the freedom to make mistakes, the freedom to fail. Socrates' trial, by a nice irony, illustrates the danger of his teaching. A man should not make emotional appeals to the jury, Socrates tells them, parading before them his parents and relatives and sons. Instead, "he ought to inform them of the facts and convince them by argument . . . where justice lies." He lost that argument as he had with Critias and Alcibiades.

To add insult to injury, Socrates suggests that since he has done nothing wrong, he does not deserve punishment but, indeed, a reward. "Well, what is appropriate for a poor man who is a public benefactor and who requires leisure for giving you moral encouragement?" A man who has neglected his family all these years while he is going about the city urging its citizens to think on goodness? Well, "... if I am to suggest an appropriate penalty which is strictly in accord with justice, I suggest free maintenance by the state."

Xanthippe would have agreed with that sentence for, unquestionably, the point about Socrates' neglecting his family was well-taken. At the celebrated dinner party that Alcibiades staggered into, the guests spent the evening drinking enormous quantities of wine. Other revelers arrived to join the party; some left; others fell asleep until only Agathon, the host, Aristophanes (the playwright), and Socrates were still awake, still drinking, and Socrates, still arguing. "The gist of it was that Socrates was forcing them to admit that the same man might be capable of writing both comedy and tragedy—that the tragic poet might be comedian as well. But he clinched the argument, which the other two were scarcely in a state to follow, they began to nod, and first Aristophanes fell off to sleep and then Agathon, as day was breaking. Whereupon Socrates tucked them up comfortably and went away.... And after calling at the Lyceum for a bath, he spent the rest of the day as usual, and then, toward evening, made his way home to rest."

Perhaps this was the evening the hard-pressed Xanthippe met him at the door complaining that their eldest son, Lamprocles, had been disrespectful to her. Xenophon recounts Socrates' little examination with Lamprocles of "filial duty." There is none of this "Certainly, Socrates, certainly," after each point in the dialogues. Lamprocles argues right back, defending himself stoutly when his father lists all his mother has done for him, "But even if she has done all this and much more than this, no one could stand her bad temper." The argument, I think it fair to say, ends in a draw.

It has the ring of truth, a familiar ring. I remember similar little examinations. My husband's mother was intensely competitive. She would have made a fine gambler, had her religious scruples permitted it—cool, skillful, and *lucky*. In the small Mississippi town in which she lived, her talents were narrowly confined, but whatever she did (playing bridge was one outlet), she always won. It was exasperating, especially to her grandchildren when she played their favorite card game, slapjack, with them. No matter how hard she tried (and how many times I suggested it), she could not bring herself to lose. Games invariably ended in tears, tantrums, and harsh words. My elenchus on grandfilial duty was no more persuasive than Socrates'.

Ved Mehta tells of a wonderful encounter with Bertrand Russell, who said, "When I was an undergraduate, there were many boys cleverer than I, but I surpassed them, because, while they were *dégagé*, I had passion and fed on controversy. I still thrive on opposition. My grandmother was a woman of caustic and biting wit. When she was eighty-three, she became kind and gentle. I had never found her so reasonable. She noticed the change in herself, and, reading the handwriting on the wall, she said to me, 'Bertie, I'll soon be dead.' And she soon was."

If I had been a gentle, obedient daughter, Father would not have caught me with *Photoplay* and, in reprisal, thrown *Plato: The Collected Dialogues* at me. Of course, Socrates was waiting for me all along in Father's library and I might have found him on my own. I did meet him in college, fleetingly, in a philosophy course. But I would not have come upon him so young. And Father did have some reason for optimism because, while I was not amenable, I was malleable, and who better to mold the long, long thoughts of youth than one of the greatest teachers who ever lived?

THE TWO THOUSAND YEARS' WAR

Walter Karp

AROUND THE TIME Republicans were vowing to "roll back Communism," a wise old college professor of mine suggested that his Humanities 1 class might get more out of Thucydides if it compared the Peloponnesian War to the ongoing struggle between America and Russia, then only recently named the Cold War. This, he assured us (quite needlessly), would not do violence to the great Athenian historian, since Thucydides himself believed that "human nature being what it is, events now past will recur in similar or analogous forms." Of the profundity of that remark Humanities 1 had not the slightest inkling. Nonetheless, analogies fell at our feet like ripe apples.

The combatants we identified readily. Authoritarian Sparta, ruling over a mass of terrified helots, was plainly the Soviet Union. Democratic Athens was America, of course. There were even neat correspondences between the two sets of foes. Sparta, as Thucydides tells us, was an insulated, agricultural, and sluggish state, rather like Russia. Athens, like America, was commercial, fast-moving, and far-ranging. "They are never at home," complained a Corinthian envoy to the Spartans, "and you are never away from it." In Athens and America, commerce and democracy seemed, 2,300 years apart, to have nurtured the very same kind of citizen. "I doubt if the world can produce a man," said great Pericles, "who, where he has only himself to depend upon, is equal to so many emergencies and graced by so happy a versatility as the Athenian." What the Athenians possessed, concluded Humanities 1, was Yankee ingenuity.

More striking than the analogies between past and present combatants were the resemblances between the two conflicts. In neither struggle do the enemies fight alone. Like America and the Soviet Union, Athens and Sparta are leaders of great confederations of inferior and subordinate allies. Similarly, they represent hostile political principles, Athens championing democracy, Sparta a traditional oligarchy. In the Peloponnesian War, as in the Cold War, the enemies are "ideological" foes. And neither is physically capable of winning. Sparta, with its invincible infantry, is so superior by land that Athens avoids pitched battles at all costs. Athens is so superior by sea that Spartan ships flee her peerless navy on sight. As a result, the Peloponnesian War, like the Cold War, is fought indirectly, peripherally, and spasmodically.

That was about as far as Humanities 1 got in its hunt for analogies between the ancient struggle for supremacy in Hellas and the ongoing struggle for supremacy in the modern world. Youth and ignorance doubtless limited our inquiry, but a greater handicap was the fact that the Peloponnesian War lasted twenty-seven years while the Cold War had not yet survived six.

THAT WAS NEARLY three decades ago, decades in which the struggle for supremacy between America and Russia did not cease for a single day. When I decided to reread Thucydides, the struggle was about to enter a new and more vigorous phase, under a newly elected president and a political faction that Thucydides would have unhesitatingly described as the war party. Two things struck me as I read: that the Cold War, now so long protracted, had come to resemble the Peloponnesian War more than ever and that in this resemblance lay a wholly unexpected vindication of political history, created by Thucydides, despised by the modern *eruditi,* and barely kept alive today by Grub Street hacks and doting amateurs.

The grounds for vindication are clear enough. Ancient Hellas and the modern world have nothing in common technologically, economically, or socially, none of those "factors" so dear to the hearts of the modern historian. If the ancient war and the modern war bear strong and essential resemblances, only political causes could have produced them; precisely those political causes that Thucydides' titanic genius found operating in the Peloponnesian War.

"Of the gods we believe, and of men we know," an Athenian envoy tells an ally of Sparta's, "that by a necessary law of their nature they rule wherever they can." Our nature as *political* beings is what Thucydides describes. Nothing compels men to enter the bright, dangerous arena of political action, but what lures them there—love of fame, power, glory, fortune, distinction—makes it fairly certain, a "law," that they will strive to rule over others. According to Pericles, Athenians, out of a love of splendid deeds and for the glory of their city, "forced every sea and land to be the highway of [their] daring." In doing so they also forged a far-flung empire, which they had to struggle continuously to maintain; for if men strive for dominion, others strive to resist it. "You risk so much to retain your empire," the Athenian envoy is told, "and your subjects so much to get rid of it."

In the striving to gain dominion and in the inevitable struggle to maintain it, men produce one thing with certainty—they "make" history. Such was Thucydides' great discovery. History is the story woven by men's deeds, and the political nature of man provides a completely intelligible account of the story. That is why the great Athenian dared to predict that the tragic events of the Peloponnesian War would one day recur in similar forms.

CONSIDER THE ORIGINS of the Peloponnesian War. Thucydides describes the petty squabbles that poison relations between certain allies of mighty Sparta and those of upstart Athens. The squabbles set in motion the great train of events, but, like Soviet–American squabbles over the Yalta accords, they are not, says Thucydides, the "real cause" of the war. "The growth of the power of Athens and the alarm which this inspired in Lacedaemon [Sparta] made war inevitable."

In 432 B.C. the Hellenic world reached a political condition that the modern world was to duplicate in 1945 A.D.— and with much the same result. Two superpowers, Athens and Sparta, have so completely absorbed all the available power in Hellas that any further gain by one appears a menacing loss to the other. Under such conditions no real peace is possible. Of course if men and states accepted the diminution of their power there would have been no Peloponnesian War (and precious little human history), but that is just what men and states do not accept.

War with Sparta is unavoidable, Pericles tells the Athenian assembly (it is pondering whether to accede to a Spartan fiat), because "we must attempt to hand down our power to our posterity unimpaired." Moral scruple has nothing to do with it. The Athenian empire "is, to speak somewhat plainly, a tyranny," says Pericles, referring to Athens' crushing subjugation of her nominal allies. "To take it [the empire] perhaps was wrong, but to let it

go is unsafe." With respect to its unwilling allies, Athens resembles the Soviet Union and, like it, must expend a great deal of her strength keeping her "allies" down.

Because such tyranny is inherently unstable, Pericles urges his countrymen to fight a strategically defensive war and seek no "fresh conquests" in the course of it. The result of the Periclean policy reveals the extraordinary, history-making dynamism released by merely trying to hang on to one's own. Framed by a statesman of the highest genius, the policy scores a brilliant success and then leads Athens to its ultimate ruin.

To the astonishment of the Hellenic world, the newfangled Athenian navy, as Pericles foresaw, proves tactically superior to Sparta's great infantry, which the Athenians, safely walled up in their city, can avoid with impunity. Facing a foe so swift, so daring, so immune to injury, Sparta, after seven years of war, becomes deeply unnerved. "Being new to the experience of adversity," observes Thucydides, "they had lost all confidence in themselves."

Buoyed up by their unexpected triumphs over the traditional leader of Hellas, however, the Athenians fall prey to the fateful temptation inherent in all political action—rashness. Success "made them confuse their strength with their hopes," says Thucydides, providing, at least, a definition of political rashness that cannot be improved upon. After a Spartan garrison surrenders without a fight, something unprecedented in Spartan history, the Athenians are ripe for any daring folly; just as President Truman, blinded by General MacArthur's sweeping victory at Inchon, rashly attempted to conquer North Korea; and just as President Kennedy, puffed up by his Cuban missile triumph, was ripe for the Vietnam war—a confusion of strength and hope that drained the country of both.

The Peloponnesian War, like the Cold War, brings civil war and revolution in its wake. The political causes are the same in both cases. When states are at peace, hostile factions and classes within countries are willing to rub along together. But when the great powers are desperately competing for allies, domestic rivals are no longer willing to preserve internal peace. Popular leaders can call on the opposing power to put their domestic enemies to

the sword; oligarchic factions, to set their own cities aflame.

Love of dominion, the desire for "the first place in the city" (never far from the surface in peacetime), convulses all Hellas in wartime. Men betray their own cities without scruple and cheer foreigners for killing their own countrymen. Political exiles, aided by foreign powers, wage ceaseless war against their own cities. The Peloponnesian War, which spawns a half dozen analogues of the Bay of Pigs and of Moscow-trained revolutionary brigades, blights the integrity of the city-state, just as the Cold War now erodes the integrity of the nation-state.

ATHENS IS by no means immune to the war's corrupting effects on domestic politics. At one point Athenians undergo a spasm of political paranoia that duplicates with remarkable fidelity the American McCarthy era. The causes here, too, are the same, as the sequence of events clearly shows. Shortly after the Spartan garrison's stunning surrender, Sparta humbly sues for peace, and the Athenians, a little out of breath themselves, reluctantly and ruefully accept. Thucydides regards the peace, which lasts six years, as a mere incident in a continuous war. It was, says Thucydides, "an unstable armistice [that] did not prevent either party doing the other the most effectual injury."

The chief reason for the instability is the emergence in Athens of a self-serving war party. Ten years have passed since the outbreak of war. Great Pericles is dead; new men have arisen with ambitions of their own, Pericles' own ward Alcibiades among them. The Periclean policy of deadlock, based on the determination to preserve past glories, does not content them. They want to win fresh glory for themselves, and with it, says Thucydides, "the undisturbed direction of the people." Their real complaint about the peace with Sparta is that it is an unambitious use of Athenian power (which is exactly what the American foes of détente believe).

Confusing strength with hope, the leaders of the war party think Athens can do far more than merely hold Sparta at bay; it can destroy Spartan pretensions forever. Like the Republicans of 1951–52, the war party will accept, in effect, "no substitute for victory." Like millions of Americans in 1951–52, the Athenian people, "persuaded that nothing could withstand them," find deadlock exasperating. Why must irresistible Athens suffer the endless tensions of the unstable armistice? Is it possible that there are oligarchy-loving pro-Spartans in their midst?

A shocking act of impiety, analogous to the Alger Hiss trial, turns baseless suspicion into angry conviction: "oligarchical and monarchical" Athenians are conspiring to subvert the democratic constitution. The enraged citizenry demands arrests; blatant perjurers supply the evidence; nonconformists, including Alcibiades, fall prey to the mania. At the war's outset Pericles had proudly noted the extraordinary personal freedom enjoyed by Athenians, who "do not feel called upon to be angry with our neighbor for doing what he likes." Now those who live differently from their neighbors fall under suspicion of treason. A war begun to safeguard the power of a democracy profoundly corrupts democracy.

Firmly in control of a rapidly degenerating polity, the war party launches its grandiose plan to tilt the balance of power once and for all against the Spartans. Beyond the little world of Hellas, across the Ionian Sea, lie the broad island of Sicily and a dozen Greek colonial city-states. The Athenians, as Thucydides icily remarks, do not even know Sicily's size; they are ignorantly contemptuous of the island's colonial "rabble." Nonetheless, the self-vaunting, overconfident Athenians intend to conquer it and use that huge accession of imperial power to throw down Sparta itself. When an opponent of the enterprise warns Athenians of the enormous costs and hazards of a war so far from home, enthusiasm for the expedition grows even warmer.

In the seventeenth year of the Peloponnesian War, "by far the most costly and splendid Hellenic force that had ever been sent out by a single city" sets sail for faraway Sicily. Vietnam is but a pale analogy to what fortune inflicts on the great armada. Thucydides' account of its hideous, heartbreaking fate—how its leaders blundered, how its strength drained away, how its dauntless Athenian oarsmen, the backbone of the democracy, lost their nerve and their courage—is one of the great feats of historical writing. On the hostile shores of a distant island, before the walls of an underestimated enemy, the power of Athens crumbles away forever.

Since the Cold War continues with no end in sight, its story remains incomplete. Still, it seems fairly certain even now that the same principle that makes the Peloponnesian War intelligible, 2,300 years after its end, will make the Cold War intelligible to posterity: "Of the gods we believe, and of men we know, that by a necessary law of their nature they rule wherever they can."

CHARTING THE UNKNOWN

JOHN NOBLE WILFORD

On the day before they made history by landing on the moon, the astronauts of Apollo 11 were far from Earth, 380,000 kilometers, orbiting the moon and adjusting their eyes and minds to a new world, blinking at how well reality compared with the maps in their own hands. Neil Armstrong, the commander, remarked over the air-to-ground radio: "The pictures and maps brought back by Apollos 8 and 10 give us a very good preview of what to look at here."

In a few minutes the Apollo 11 spaceship would move around behind the moon and out of radio contact, so astronaut Michael Collins asked Mission Control: "Could you give us a time of crossing the [moon's] 150 west meridian?"

This radio exchange between Apollo 11 and Mission Control at Houston on July 19, 1969, suggests the central role of cartography in the first human exploration of a world beyond Earth. Only a world that had been charted could be discussed in such language. Places had names. Their positions were located on a grid of latitude and longitude. There were landmarks the astronauts, with map in hand, could look for.

Explorers used to go to a remote place and then map it. But the reverse was true in the case of the moon. Through telescopy, photography and remote-sensing technology, cartography was able to precede lunar exploration.

Those who planned and flew the Apollos drew on three and a half centuries of lunar cartography, the story of which evokes a sense of déjà vu, for it was in many ways a rerun of what happened in Earth cartography. Myths and misconceptions had to be dispelled. A world represented on primitive maps of little value gradually came into focus through new technologies and voyages of exploration.

The origin of the map is lost to history. No one knows when or where or for what purpose someone got the first idea to draw a sketch to communicate a sense of place, some sense of *here* in relation to *there*. It must have been many millennia ago, probably before written language. It certainly was long before the human mind could conceive of the worlds beyond shore and horizon, beyond Earth itself, that would be embraced through mapping.

All the evidence suggests that the map evolved independently among many peoples in many separate parts of Earth. Before Europeans reached the Pacific, the Marshall Islanders were making stick charts. Sticks were lashed together with fibers to depict prevailing winds and wave patterns; shells or coral were inserted at the appropriate places to represent islands. The smaller stick charts were carried by the islanders in their outrigger canoes, while the larger ones were kept on land to be used for instruction. When a Tahitian communicated his knowledge of South Pacific geography to Captain Cook by drawing a map, it was clear that he and his people were quite familiar with the map idea.

Pre-Columbian maps in Mexico indicated roads by lines of footprints. Cortés traveled through Central America guided by a calico map provided by a local chief. It has also been discovered that centuries ago Eskimos carved accurate coastal maps in ivory, the Incas built elaborate relief maps of stone and clay, and early Europeans drew sketch maps on their cave walls.

Recent archeological excavations in the Hunan province of China uncovered two silk maps from the second century B.C. in the tomb of a prime minister's son. Although there are references to the use of maps in Chinese literature as far back as the seventh century B.C., these are the earliest maps found in China.

One of the maps, measuring 96 by 96 centimeters, depicts at a scale of between 1:170,000 and 1:190,000 (the ratio of distance on the map to actual distance) much of the topography of what is modern Hunan and regions as far south as the South China Sea. In some parts of the map the accuracy suggests that on-the-spot surveys were employed. Another hallmark of the map's sophistication is its use of standardized symbols and legends. The names of all provinces are placed in squares and cities and villages in circles.

The names of tributary rivers are written near their confluence with larger rivers. Irregular double wavy lines depict mountain ranges. Roads are drawn in rather thin lines. Thicker lines delineate the more than 30 rivers on the map, the thickness not only reflecting the importance of a river but also the direction in which it was flowing.

The second map, describing the defenses of the kingdom, is embellished with some color—blue rivers, red lines enclosing towns, as well as the basic black markings. Each military encampment is represented by a rectangle outlined in red and black, the size of which indicates its importance and number of troops; the commanding officer's name is inscribed inside each rectangle. Other symbols, usually assorted triangles, represent walled fortresses, supply dumps and observation towers. The map hints at a war: next to the name of some towns are written phrases such as "35 families, all moved away" or "108 families, none back" or "now nobody."

The earliest direct evidence of map-making comes from the Middle East, where archeologists have discovered several maps inscribed on clay tablets that are centuries older than the Chinese examples, though more primitive in execution. One of the earliest of these was found at Nuzi, in Iraq, and dated 2300 B.C. The Nuzi map specifies its orientation by naming three of the four cardinal points, each given by the appropriate wind: the west wind is at the bottom, the east at the top, the north on the left, but the south wind is missing. Ancient maps were oriented east (hence the expression orientation) presumably because that was the direction of sunrise; medieval Christian maps resumed the practice because east was supposed to be the direction to Paradise.

The city map seems to have been a prevalent type of cartography in ancient Mesopotamia. In the late nineteenth century an expedition from the University of Pennsylvania discovered a clay map of the city of Nippur, on the Euphrates, as it was in the second half of the second millennium B.C. Such a map is the answer to an archeologist's prayer for it shows the outlines of the entire city, including its foremost temples, the central park, the "canal in the heart of the city," the river, moats, walls and the city gates.

The Babylonians may have been the first to produce a map of the world—after a fashion, that is. The earliest extant world map is a Babylonian clay tablet from the sixth century B.C. on which Earth is shown as a circular disk surrounded by ocean and several mythical islands. This world is little more than the kingdom of Babylonia, schematically portrayed, with the city of Babylon shown as a long rectangle and with the Assyrians shown to the east and the Chaldeans to the southwest.

The Greeks were soon trying their hand at mapmaking, with about as much sophistication at first as the Babylonians. Herodotus tells a story of the use of one world map in political decision making. At the time of the Ionian Revolt of 499–494 B.C., Aristagoras of Miletus, the leader of the revolt, went to Greece to persuade Sparta, the dominant military power of the Hellenic world, to join the revolt and dispatch an army to fight against Persia. Aristagoras took with him a map of the world engraved on a bronze tablet. The tablet showed "the whole circuit of the earth, the seas and the rivers." According to Herodotus, he appealed to the greed of Cleomenes, the Spartan king, by pointing out on the map the Persian lands that could be his and then deliver-

ing the first documented map-illustrated discourse on economic geography.

Aristagoras pointed to the island of Cyprus, where the people paid annual tribute to the Persian king of 500 talents, and to the land of the Armenians, who had cattle in abundance. Farther east lay Cissia and the city of Susa, where the great king lived and kept his treasure. "Why," Aristagoras concluded, "if you take Susa, you need not hesitate to compete with God himself for riches."

Tempted, Cleomenes asked how long it would take to go from Ephesus to Susa following the route of the Persian royal road. At this point, Herodotus wrote, Aristagoras made his big mistake: he told the truth. When Cleomenes heard that the journey would take at least three months, he refused to commit any Spartan troops to the enterprise and ordered Aristagoras to leave the city before the sun set.

In the second century after Christ, when, as Gibbon wrote, "the Empire of Rome comprehended the fairest part of the Earth, and the most civilized portion of mankind," the foremost scholar at the great library in Alexandria was Claudius Ptolemy.

Ptolemy is best remembered for his rejection of Aristarchus's theory that the Earth revolves around the Sun. Ptolemy's geocentric, or Earth-centered, scheme of things was adapted from Aristotle and was made a premise of Ptolemy's princi-

pal book, which is generally known by its Arab title, *Almagest,* or The Greatest. Even now, Ptolemy's influence persists. Twentieth-century navies still find it more convenient to navigate by Ptolemaic astronomy, and every day we speak of the rising and setting of the Sun rather than the turning of the Earth.

As scholars have often pointed out, Ptolemy's original contributions to science were few; he compiled and systematized knowledge, usually improving upon the ideas of others but sometimes, inevitably, fostering their mistakes as well. In one such case, Ptolemy based his maps and descriptions of the world on a smaller estimate of Earth's circumference than the quite accurate one calculated by his predecessor Eratosthenes. As a result, Ptolemy's world was about three-fourths of the actual size. Moreover, he assumed that the known world in his day covered 180 degrees of longitude, from the Canary, or Fortunate, Isles in the west to the easternmost tip of Asia. This compound error—the smallness of the Earth's circumference and the exaggerated eastern extension of Asia—would someday embolden men like Columbus to risk the unknown seas.

Maps drawn with coordinates were fundamental to the scientific cartography of Ptolemy. He said that the coordinates should be established by careful astronomical observation. He had devised a scientific framework for maps, although he was often unable to say exactly where particular localities were situated.

Ptolemy's world consisted of three continents—Europe, Asia and Africa. The British islands, called Albion and Hibernia, are set off to the west, somewhat misplaced and quite misshapen. Scandinavia appears as Scandia, an island of moderate size. The northern coast of European and Asian Russia was beyond the realm of knowledge and therefore not shown.

Far to the east, Ptolemy places the Sinae—the Chinese. Ptolemy assumed that the land of the Sinae ran far to the south and then to the west until it joined the eastern coast of Africa, thus completely enclosing the Indian Ocean. Ptolemy's unknown land to the south of the Indian Ocean became the *terra incognita* which bemused and befuddled cartographers and explorers. As for Africa, Ptolemy knew almost nothing of its western coast or of the lands below the Equator. But he came remarkably close to the truth when he described the Nile as being formed by two rivers flowing from two lakes far to the south, a fact that was not proved until the nineteenth century.

More than a century after Ptolemy, Alexandria became a battleground of revolt, and the museum buildings, then over 500 years old, were destroyed. The temple housing the library survived until, in 391,

PTOLEMY'S WARNING

Even though his Earth-centered view of the cosmos proved totally wrong, it is unfair to remember Ptolemy only for his errors.

In his *Almagest,* he simplified the mathematics of the circle by abandoning the practice of expressing its divisions in awkward fractions. Instead, he introduced the minutes (') and seconds (") into which a degree of arc is now subdivided—a simple but invaluable concept.

Ptolemy lamented the casual approach to scale taken by his predecessors and contemporaries when they attempted to draw a map of the known world. They tended to sacrifice proportion in order to get everything on the map, stretching better-known areas of Europe and the Middle East to accommodate the many place names while shrinking Asia and Africa so as not to leave much of the map relatively blank. In his *Geography,* Ptolemy offers a practical solution: a

general map supplemented by 26 regional maps detailing more populous areas and drawn to a larger scale—the principle on which all modern atlases are based.

Ptolemy also advised mapmakers to "contemplate the extent of the entire Earth, as well as its shape and its position under the stars." In fact, many early mapmakers were astronomers, and progress in cartography often kept step with advances in astronomy. Ptolemy himself mentioned two devices then available for celestial angle-measurements to determine latitude: the gnomon (a type of sundial) and a brass astrolabe. But these instruments were too rarely used for north-south measurements. East-west distances in Ptolemy's time and for centuries thereafter were unreliable. They were based almost entirely on the accounts of travelers and, as Ptolemy warned, through "their love of boasting they magnify distances."

2. GREECE AND ROME

Christian mobs sacked it, burned the priceless contents and converted the shell into a church. It was a symbolic victory of faith over reason. The words of Claudius Ptolemy, among others, were lost to the Western world for more than a millennium and so too his ideas and ideals for a scientific cartography.

Western scholars who followed the eclipsed Ptolemy were cloistered souls who rejected scientific inquiry as possibly pagan and certainly irrelevant. They could not bother with the latitude of the next city when Paradise was out there waiting to be mapped in all its glory. If they speculated about alien worlds, it was usually out of fear, not curiosity.

In the absence of scientific inquiry, someone like Gaius Julius Solinus was bound to come along and win an enduring, uncritical audience. A Roman grammarian of the third century, Solinus was an engaging spinner of tall tales and quite a plagiarist. He borrowed shamelessly from Pliny the Elder, the first-century Roman scholar whose *Natural History* was the period's definitive encyclopedia of natural wonders. In the East, according to Solinus, there lived horse-footed men with ears so long that the flaps covered their entire bodies, making clothing unnecessary. There were one-eyed hunters and savages who quaffed mead from cups made of their parents' skulls. Farther out in Asia could be found gold and precious stones, but also griffons, vicious fowl that could tear an intruder to pieces. Some men in India were said to have only one leg each, though the foot was so large that it is often shown in medieval maps doubling as a parasol.

TALL TALES

In Germany, Solinus continued, the Hercynian birds had feathers that gave off light in the dark. An animal resembling the mule had such a long upper lip that it could feed only by walking backward. In Italy, he said, were lynxes whose urine congealed into the "hardness of a precious stone, having magnetic powers."

For Africa, the tales grew taller still. Solinus described hyenas whose shadows robbed dogs of their bark. He told of a beast in Libya, the cockatrice, that crept along the ground like a crocodile on its forequarters, while its hindquarters were suspended aloft by two lateral fins. The ants along the Niger River were as big as mastiffs, and the river itself boiled from the heat of the region.

The belief in African monsters continued into the eighteenth century, their existence being explained in the following notice accompanying the de Mornes map of 1761: "It is true that the center of the continent is filled with burning sands, savage beasts, and almost uninhabitable deserts. The scarcity of water forces the different animals to come together to the same place to drink. Finding themselves together at a time when they are in heat, they have intercourse with one another, without paying regard to the differences between species. Thus are produced those monsters which are to be found there in greater numbers than in any other part of the world."

Charles Raymond Beazley said of Solinus in his comprehensive *The Dawn of Modern Geography:* "No one ever influenced [medieval geography] more profoundly or more mischievously."

The mischief of Solinus was compounded by the scholars of "Christian topography," one of the first of whom was a sixth-century monk named Cosmas.

Whereas by observation and deduction the Greek sages had come to think of the Earth as spherical, Cosmas looked only to the Scriptures and found his guidance in the words of the Apostle Paul. In Hebrews 9, Paul described the tabernacle as "the worldly sanctuary," by which Cosmas decided Paul meant that the tabernacle of the "blessed Moses" was "a pattern of this visible world."

Invoking Scriptural authority, he went on to describe the world as a flat parallelogram twice as long as it was wide. In the center of his flat Earth, Cosmas placed Jerusalem, for it was written in Ezekiel 5:5, "I have set [Jerusalem] in the midst of the nations and the countries that are round about her." Beyond the ocean was another world, where man lived before the Flood, a world now uninhabited and inaccessible. Far to the north of the inhabited world stood a great mountain round which the Sun and the moon revolved, causing day and night. The sky consisted of four walls meeting in the dome of heaven, the ceiling of the great tabernacle.

The world map conceived by Cosmas seemed to bear the unmistakable imprint of an unscientific age. It was entirely devoid of practical information.

By November 1971, cartography had come a long way. Earth had been surveyed on foot and camel and horse, from ship and airplane and spacecraft, by camera and radar and laser beam. Earth's continents and ocean basins had all been mapped, if only lately and not always too well. Even Earth's moon had been charted and radar signals from Earth had penetrated the clouds of Venus and begun to probe the underlying topography, revealing in vague outline craters and canyons, basins and huge plateaus. And now cartography, in another act of audacity, had reached out millions of kilometers to embrace Mars.

The first surveying party reached Mars on November 13, 1971. It arrived in the form of the American spacecraft Mariner 9, an unmanned vehicle weighing less than a ton and shaped something like a flying windmill, a complex robot equipped with essential field tools for extraterrestrial mapping: television cameras, remote-sensing instruments for determining elevations and distances and a finely tuned communications system for transmitting its findings back to Earth.

7,000 TV PICTURES

From its vantage point, ranging between 1,350 and 19,000 kilometers above the surface, Mariner 9 conducted its historic survey for nearly a full year. The spacecraft took and transmitted more than 7,000 television pictures of Mars before its maneuvering rockets ran out of nitrogen in October 1972.

This was all the cartographers needed. Within a month after Mariner ceased operations, the cartographers produced from a mosaic of the photographs the first detailed map of the entire globe of another planet.

The character and technology of mapmaking may have changed over the centuries, as demonstrated by Mariner 9, but the potential of maps has not. Maps embody a perspective of that which is known and a perception of that which may be worth knowing.

Once, the mapmakers' range was quite limited. The only maps that could be trusted were confined to immediate surroundings. Those that essayed to describe distant lands and seas were, until the modern era, exercises in conjecture based on inadequate surveying, wishful thinking, theological dogma or sheer imagination. Such maps, where spaces that should have been left blank were adorned with imaginary continents and sea serpents or other fanciful creatures, inspired Jonathan Swift's well-known satirical verse:

So Geographers, in Afric-maps,
With savage-pictures fill their gaps;
And o'er unhabitable downs
Place elephants for want of towns.

But the very deficiencies of these old maps are valuable to historians. "The map," wrote Norman Thrower in *Maps and Man,* "is a sensitive indicator of the changing thought of man, and few of his works seem to be such an excellent mirror of culture and civilization."

Maritime Trade in Antiquity

LIONEL CASSON

"Bringing of forty ships filled with cedar logs." So runs an entry in the list of accomplishments of Snefru, pharaoh of Egypt in about 2650 or 2600 B.C. The Valley of the Nile nurtured few trees, so Egypt had to seek supplies of timber from outside her borders. Across the water to the north was Lebanon, home of renowned stands of cedar. It was from here that Snefru drew his 40 shiploads—and in the process left the first notice on record of a transaction in maritime commerce.

At Deir el-Bahari near Luxor in Upper Egypt stands the vast tomb monument of one of the earliest known queens in history, Hatshepsut, who ruled in about 1500 B.C. She chose to have part of the tomb decorated with pictures—carved in the low relief that Egyptian sculptors executed so skillfully—of a trade expedition to Punt, as Egyptians called what is today the northern part of the Somali Republic, to bring back a variety of products; above all the incense that burned on Egypt's multitudinous altars. We see her vessels arriving, mooring and being loaded by a line of stevedores who carry aboard live myrrh trees (with their roots carefully bagged in a ball), apes, cattle, ivory, exotic woods and other items. Inscriptions over the scenes inform us that, among the animals shipped, was a "panther alive, captured for her majesty."

Snefru's importing of timber and Hatshepsut's of Punt's products are the earliest direct proof of overseas trade in antiquity. But archaeology furnishes indirect proof that goes much further back. Tools made of a certain kind of obsidian have been excavated in Greece in levels as old as the seventh millennium B.C.; the obsidian came from deposits on the island of Melos in the middle of the Aegean Sea. And there are similar trails that attest to an active maritime commerce all through prehistoric times.

Unfortunately, information for these remote ages is haphazard and fragmentary. This is true even for Pharaonic Egypt and its contemporaries in the Near East. One has to descend to the fifth century B.C. to arrive at a period which offers the historian materials to reconstruct its maritime trade with any claim to completeness. At this time Athens was the commercial center of the eastern Mediterranean; her port, the Piraeus, was thronged with ships from as far west as Marseilles and as far east as the Black Sea. They brought a miscellany of imports but above all grain; as the city's political and economic importance increased, so did its population, to the point where it had to be fed almost wholly by supplies from overseas, chiefly the Ukraine, then as now an area of rich wheat fields. In exchange, Athens sent out some olive oil, honey, and masses of her famed ceramics which were in demand all over the ancient world. Many of the finest pieces that have survived, familiar to us from having been reproduced in book after book, were found in Italy in the tombs of well-to-do Etruscans. But the return from these exports did not add up to anything near what Athens spent for the grain she required. She had, to use current terminology, a balance of trade deficit. It did not upset her economy one bit: in the fifth century B.C. she was ruler of an empire of subject states and paid with tribute extracted from them; in the fourth century she paid with coin minted from her local silver mines or from the money that came her way by virtue of her position as a commercial and tourist center.

Grain was to the ancient world what oil is to ours.

The spectacular career of Alexander the Great (356-323 B.C.) changed all this. In the wake of his conquests Athens became a backwater, yielding her place to the powerful empires founded by his former generals. For the next two centuries, the third and second B.C., the major figure in maritime trade was Egypt. The country was ruled by the Ptolemies, monarchs with a keen eye for garnering profits who shrewdly promoted its commerce. Grain was to the ancient world what oil is to ours; very few places had a surplus for export, while very many, having outgrown what they could produce, had to import or go hungry. The Valley of the Nile yielded bountiful crops, and the Ptolemies turned Egypt into the grain supplier par excellence of the eastern Mediterranean; at times they sent shipments as far as Tunisia and Italy. But grain was only the biggest of their exports, by no means the only one. They furnished the whole Mediterranean world with its standard writing material, a form of paper made from the stalks of the papyrus plant; since the plant grew solely along the banks of the Nile, Egypt had an impregnable monopoly.

On top of this, the Ptolemies made Egypt into the middleman for the lucrative trade in exotic products from east Africa and India. From the third century B.C. on, these two areas gradually entered the commercial orbit of the west: Africa, as in the days of Hatshepsut, supplied incense, and India spices and silks, importing the latter from China. The precious cargoes were carried up the Red Sea to ports on the west coast opposite the point on the Nile where a great bend brought the river closest to the Red Sea. Here they were transferred to donkeys for the haul across the desert to Coptos, the town on the bend, put aboard Nile boats, and sailed downriver to Alexandria; from there Alexandrian merchants distributed them all over the Mediterranean world.

"I netted 10,000,000 sesterces on that one voyage."

"**I** built five ships, loaded them with wine—worth its weight in gold at the time—and sent them to Rome...Every one of my ships went down...Neptune swallowed up 30,000,000 sesterces in one day...I built others, bigger, better, luckier, loaded them with wine again, plus bacon, beans, perfume, slaves...When the gods are behind something, it happens quickly: I netted 10,000,000 sesterces on that one voyage." The time is the first century after Christ, and the speaker Trimalchio, the famous character in Petronius' *Satyricon* who rose from rags to riches. Petronius is, of course, exaggerating for comic effect but there is a solid core of fact behind his words: import-export was a flourishing business in those days, and many a shrewd dealer, like Trimalchio, was able to make his fortune in it. This was because the Roman Empire, founded by Augustus in the closing decades of the first century B.C., had not only taken over the commerce of its predecessors but, being vastly larger than any of them with domains that stretched from Spain to Syria and beyond, expanded it many times. The Mediterranean was now one Roman world, with trade routes crisscrossing it in every direction. The major ones all led to Rome itself, the capital of this mighty state, whose population, perhaps a million or even more, had its needs met almost totally from sources overseas. The emperors, we are told, kept the city's mob contented with "bread and circuses"; the bread was baked from fifteen million bushels of wheat imported annually, chiefly from North Africa and Egypt, and the games required shiploads of wild animals from Asia and Africa.

As for the wine and olive oil imported, there is a dramatic witness—the hill called Monte Testaccio on the east bank of the Tiber in the southern part of Rome. The name means "Mount Potsherd," and it derives from the fact that, as excavation has revealed, the hill is not nature's creation but a human one—it is made up, from base to tip, of hundreds of thousands of fragments of amphorae, the big jars—eight or so gallons was a common capacity—in which wine and oil were shipped. Like modern soft-drink bottles, they were disposable: after being emptied at the dockside, since they were too heavy and cheap to ship back for reuse, they were smashed and the pieces tossed to one side. So many of them were disposed of in this way that over the centuries their sherds piled up to form a hill where none had existed before.

To handle its shipments, particularly the huge cargoes of grain, the city of Rome boasted a fleet of sailing ships which was the largest and heaviest as a class that the world was to know until the eighteenth century. To handle what these brought in, the emperors built from scratch just north of the Tiber's mouth a huge port with long quays backed by lines of warehouses. A thriving town, Portus "The Port," sprang up about it to house and feed the army of required personnel—clerks, shipwrights, bargemen, ferrymen, stevedores, and so on.

Of the commodities that Roman merchants sent back and forth across the water, three bulked much larger than all others: grain, wine and olive oil. Egypt and North Africa were the key suppliers of grain, North Africa and Spain of oil, Spain, France and Italy of wine. Customers for these products were to be found all around the Mediterranean and beyond: Spain shipped its oil as far as Germany and Britain, Italy its wine as far as India. The single biggest customer for all three was the city of Rome. She had nothing at all to send out in return. Ships left Portus in ballast, and her balance of trade deficit would have been astronomical were it not that most of the necessities she imported cost her nothing since they came in as tribute levied upon the empire's overseas possessions.

After grain, wine and oil, but well below them in importance, were such commodities as dried fish, timber, copper, lead, and building stone. Masses of imported ornamental marbles were used by the emperors for the palaces, temples, monuments, and other structures they raised to adorn their capital. Trajan's Forum, for example, had columns of *cipollino,* a greenish marble from Greece; columns of *giallo antico,* a yellow marble from Tunisia; and floor slabs of *pavonazzetto,* a red or violet-veined marble from Asia Minor. Some of the stone pieces that arrived at Rome must have sorely taxed the dockside hoisting and transport equipment: the columns of the Pantheon, for instance, which are solid monoliths of granite from Egypt, each run 41 feet or 12 meters in height and 84 tons in weight.

The vessels into which these and other ponderous cargoes were loaded were necessarily of great size and strength. The average seagoing Roman merchantman had a capacity of some 300 tons, while those that hauled grain from Egypt were veritable super-freighters of their day, measuring 200 feet in length and having a capacity of over 1,000 tons. It was a ship from the Alexandria-Rome grain run that was pressed into service to bring from Egypt the obelisk now in front of St. Peter's in Rome. The total load was 1,300 tons: the obelisk with its base weighs 500, and since the 83-foot-long shaft had to be carried on deck, 800 tons of ballast was poured into the hold to ensure stability during the crossing. It was a ship on this run that the emperor Caligula (reigned A.D. 37-41) had in mind when he advised the Jewish prince Agrippa, who was departing for Palestine, to go by way of Egypt. "[They] are crack sailing craft," he explained, "and their skippers the most experienced there are; they drive their vessels like race horses on an unswerving course that goes straight as a die." Not only did they sail the shortest route, right over open water, but the ships' great size promised a fair degree of comfort to passengers.

Greek and Roman craft were exceptionally strong. This was because of the unique way in which they were constructed, a feature that has become known only in recent years, thanks to the discovery and investigation by underwater archaeologists of dozens of ancient wrecks. Indeed, an American diving team has raised and restored almost the complete hull of a small freighter measuring 47 feet or 14 meters in length of the fourth century B.C. that was found off the north coast of Cyprus. Their findings reveal that Greek and Roman shipwrights did not fasten a vessel's planks to a skeleton of ribs, as has been standard European practice for centuries, but to each other by means of close-set mortise and tenon joints, thereby forming a tight shell of wood. Then into this shell they inserted a complete set of ribs as stiffening. The result was a hull of formidable strength that needed little or no caulking.

Underwater archaeology has also provided for the first time specific details on how cargoes were packed and shipped. We know most about wine and oil cargoes for these commodities were put into amphorae, and amphorae, made of heavy, coarse clay, are well-nigh indestructible; a sure sign of the presence of an ancient wreck is a pile of them on the sea floor. Excavation has shown that they were stacked in the hold in tiers and wedged in tightly with brushwood and other dunnage, an essential precaution, for if any broke loose and began rolling around the results would be disastrous. Building stone was carried both on deck and in the hold, sometimes just roughed out blocks, sometimes partly finished pieces, sometimes totally finished pieces.

Investigation of ancient shipwrecks has made clear the wide range of products that traveled by sea, from the very cheapest clay rooftiles to the most precious works of art. Divers have had the great good luck of discovering the remains of at least two ships that were loaded with art. One, off Mahdia on the east coast of Tunisia, yielded enough statuary to fill half a dozen rooms in Tunis' Bardo Museum. The other, found near the islet of Anticythera off the southern coast of Greece, produced some splendid bronze statues and perfectly preserved glassware.

We have talked so far of Rome's trade within the Mediterranean. One long finger reached out far beyond it toward the Far East, bringing India and, indirectly, China into the orbit. In essence, Roman merchants carried on and expanded what the Ptolemies had started. They sent ships along the east coast of Africa, not only to the incense lands where Hatshepsut's and other Egyptian skippers had gone, but as far south as Zanzibar to pick up ivory and tortoise shell. More important, they sent ships across the open sea to India to bring back pepper, spikenard, ginger, ivory, cotton fabrics, as well as silks and cinnamon which India itself imported from China. At first they went only to India's west coast but as time passed they learned to sail round the tip of the peninsula and enter the Bay of Bengal to trade with the east coast. They even made their way to the Malay Peninsula—but this was as far as they got; as the author of a geography written in the fourth century after Christ put it, "Cattigara [Hanoi? Canton? Hangchow?], the leading port of the *Sinai*, [is] the end of the known and inhabited land in the regions of the south...There are no witnesses to point out the course beyond...unless it be some god who knows." Rome had very little to give the Far East in exchange. The costly imports were almost all paid for in hard cash. "There is not a year in which merchandise from India does not drain our empire of fifty million sesterces," declared Rome's savant Pliny the Elder (A.D. 23-79).

Such, in brief outline, is the story of ancient maritime trade. Its beginnings go back to earliest prehistory. By the middle of the third millennium B.C., it was already being conducted in organized fashion under government auspices. In the days of classical Athens during the fifth and fourth centuries B.C., a network of trade stretched from Italy to the eastern shores of the Mediterranean. Under the efficient and widespread Roman Empire it attained in the first to the third centuries after Christ an embrace that covered half the globe and a volume that would not be matched until just a few centuries ago.

FOR FURTHER READING on ancient maritime trade: L. Casson, *The Ancient Mariners* (Macmillan, New York 1959), for a general survey; George Bass, editor, *A History of Seafaring Based on Underwater Archaeology* (Thames and Hudson, New York 1972), for the achievements of underwater archaeology.

On ancient ships: L. Casson, *Ships and Seamanship in the Ancient World* (Princeton University Press, Princeton 1971) and *Travel in the Ancient World* (Allen and Unwin, London and Toronto 1974).

THE SILENT WOMEN OF ROME

M. I. Finley

The most famous woman in Roman history was not even a Roman—Cleopatra was queen of Egypt, the last ruler of a Macedonian dynasty that had been established on the Nile three centuries earlier by Ptolemy, one of the generals of Alexander the Great. Otherwise what names come to mind? A few flamboyant, ruthless and vicious women of the imperial family, such as Messalina, great-grandniece of Augustus and wife of her cousin once removed, the emperor Claudius; or the latter's next wife, his niece Agrippina, who was Nero's mother and, contemporary tradition insists, also for a time his mistress. One or two names in love poetry, like the Lesbia of Catullus. And some legendary women from Rome's earliest days, such as Lucretia, who gained immortality by being raped. Even in legend the greatest of them was likewise not a Roman but Dido, queen of Carthage, who loved and failed to hold Aeneas.

Such a short and one-sided list can be very misleading. The Roman world was not the only one in history in which women remained in the background in politics and business, or in which catching the eye and the pen of the scandalmonger was the most likely way to achieve notice and perhaps lasting fame. However, it is not easy to think of another great civilized state without a single really important woman writer or poet, with no truly regal queen, no Deborah, no Joan of Arc, no Florence Nightingale, no patron of the arts. The women of mid-Victorian England were equally rightless, equally victims of a double standard of sexual morality, equally exposed to risk and ruin when they stepped outside the home and the church. Yet the profound difference is obvious.

More correctly, it would be obvious if we could be sure what we may legitimately believe about women in Rome. Legend apart, they speak to us in five ways: through the erotic and satirical poetry of the late Republic and early Empire, all written by men; through the historians and biographers, all men and most of them unable to resist the salacious and the scandalous; through the letter writers and philosophers, all men; through painting and sculpture, chiefly portrait statues, inscribed tombstones, and religious monuments of all kinds; and through innumerable legal texts. These different voices naturally talk at cross-purposes. (One would hardly expect to find quotations from Ovid's *Art of Love* or the pornographic frescoes from the brothel in Pompeii on funeral monuments.) Each tells its portion of a complicated, ambiguous story. One ought to be able to add the pieces together, but unfortunately there will always be one vital piece missing—what the women would have said had they been allowed to speak for themselves.

> Friend, I have not much to say; stop and read it. This tomb, which is not fair, is for a fair woman. Her parents gave her the name Claudia. She loved her husband in her heart. She bore two sons, one of whom she left on earth, the other beneath it. She was pleasant to talk with, and she walked with grace. She kept the house and worked in wool. That is all. You may go.

Of course it wasn't Claudia who selected and set up this verse epitaph (the translation is Richmond Lattimore's) in the city of Rome in the second century B.C., but her husband or some other kinsman. And it is easy to make cynical remarks not only in this particular instance but in the hundreds of others recording domestic devotion, commonly including the phrase in one variation or another that husband and wife lived together X number of years *sine ulla querella,* "without a single quarrel". Yet there is much to be learned from the very monotony with which such sentiments are repeated century after century, at least about the ideal woman—an ideal formulated and imposed by middle- and upper-class Roman males.

To begin with, until fairly late in Roman history, women lacked individual names in the proper sense. Claudia, Julia, Cornelia, Lucretia, are merely family names with a feminine ending. Sisters had the same name and could be distinguished only by the addition of 'the elder' or 'the younger', 'the first' or 'the second', and so on. In the not uncommon case of marriage between paternal cousins, mother and daughter would have the same name, too. No doubt this was very confusing: a welcome confusion, one is tempted to suggest, since nothing could have been easier to eliminate. No great genius was needed to think up the idea of giving every girl a personal name, as was done with boys. It is as if the Romans wished to suggest very pointedly that women were not, or ought not to be, genuine individuals but only fractions of a family.

Anonymous and passive fractions at that, for the virtues which were stressed were decorum, chastity, gracefulness, even temper and childbearing. They loved their husbands, to be sure—though we need not believe everything that husbands said when their wives were dead—but as one loves an overlord who is free to seek his pleasures elsewhere and to put an end to the relationship altogether when and if he so chooses.

'Family' comes from the Latin, but the Romans actually had no word for 'family' in our commonest sense, as in the sentence, 'I am taking my family to the seashore for the summer.' In different contexts *familia* meant all persons under the authority of the head of a household, or all the descendants from a common ancestor, or all one's property, or merely all one's servants—never our intimate family. This does not mean that the latter did not exist in Rome, but that the stress was on a power structure rather than on biology or intimacy. A Roman *paterfamilias* need not even be a father: the term was a legal one and applied to any head of a household. His illegitimate children were often excluded, even when his paternity was openly acknowledged, and at the same time his son and heir could be an outsider whom he had adopted by the correct legal formalities. Theoretically his power—over his wife, over his sons and daughters and his sons' wives and children, over his slaves and his property—was absolute and uncontrolled, ending only with his death or by his voluntary act of 'emancipating' his sons beforehand. As late as the fourth century A.D. an edict of Constantine, the first Christian emperor, still defined that power as the "right of life and death". He was exaggerating, but around a hard core of reality.

Save for relatively minor exceptions, a woman was always in the power of some man—of her *paterfamilias* or of her husband or of a guardian. In early times every marriage involved a formal ceremony in which the bride was surrendered to her husband by the *paterfamilias*: he 'gave her away' in the literal sense. Then, when so-called 'free' marriages became increasingly common—free from the ancient formalities, that is, not free in the sense that the wife or her husband had made a free choice of partner—she remained legally in the power of her *paterfamilias*. Divorce and widowhood and remarriage introduced more complications and required more rules. Where did property rights in dowry and inheritance rest? In the next generation, too, if there were children? The Roman legislators and lawbooks gave much space to these matters. From the state's point of view it was essential to get the power and property relations right, since the *familia* was the basic social unit. But there was more to it than that: marriage meant children, and children by any means, for as Rome extended her empire to the Atlantic and the Middle East, the bulk of the population within her borders were either slaves or free noncitizens. Obviously the political rights and status of the children were the state's concern and could not be left to uncontrolled private decision. So the state laid down strict rules prohibiting certain kinds of marriage: for example, between a Roman citizen and a noncitizen, regardless of rank or wealth; or between a member of the senatorial class and a citizen who had risen from the class of freedmen (ex-slaves). Within the permitted limits, then, the right to choose and decide rested with the heads of families. They negotiated marriages for their children. And they were allowed to proceed, and to have the marriage consummated, as soon as a girl reached the age of twelve.

The story is told that at a male dinner-party early in the second century B.C., the general Scipio Africanus agreed to marry his daughter Cornelia to his friend Tiberius Gracchus, and that his wife was very angry that he should have done so without having consulted her. The story is probably untrue; at least it is very suspicious because it is repeated about Tiberius's son, the famous agrarian reformer of the same name, and the daughter of Appius Claudius. But true or not, the stories are right in essence, for though the mothers may have been angry, they were powerless, and it is noteworthy that the more 'liberal' and enlightened wing of the senatorial aristocracy was involved. Presumably the wife of the fiercely traditional Cato the Censor would have kept her anger to herself in a similar situation; she would not have expected to be asked anyway. Surely the first of the Roman emperors, Augustus, consulted neither his wife nor any of the interested parties when he ordered members of his family and various close associates to marry and divorce and remarry whenever he thought (as he did frequently) that reasons of state or dynastic considerations would be furthered by a particular arrangement.

Augustus and his family personify most of the complexities, difficulties, and apparent contradictions inherent in the Roman relations between the sexes. He was first married at the age of twenty-three and divorced his wife two years later, after the birth of their daughter Julia, in order to marry Livia three days after she had given birth to a son. At the second ceremony Livia's ex-husband acted as *paterfamilias* and gave her to Augustus. Fifty-one years later, in A.D. 14, Augustus was said to have addressed his last words to Livia: "As long as you live, remember our marriage. Farewell." Livia had had two sons by her previous husband; gossip inevitably suggested that Augustus was actually the father of the second, and the first son, Tiberius, was in 12 B.C. compelled by Augustus to divorce his wife and marry the recently widowed Julia, daughter of Augustus by his first wife. Tiberius was eventually adopted by Augustus and succeeded him to the throne. Long before that, in 2 B.C., Julia was banished by the emperor for sexual depravity, and ten years later the same punishment was meted out to her daughter, also named Julia. That does not end the story, but it should be enough except for two further details: first, one reason for

2. GREECE AND ROME

Augustus's getting rid of his first wife was apparently her peculiar unwillingness to put up with one of his mistresses; second, Augustus was the author of a long series of laws designed to strengthen the family and to put a brake on licentiousness and general moral depravity in the upper classes.

Augustus was no Nero. There is no reason to think that he was not a reasonably moral man by contemporary standards (granted that his position as emperor created abnormal conditions). Ancient and modern moralists have a habit of decrying the decline in Roman moral standards from the old days. Talk of 'the good old days' is always suspect, but it may well be that while Rome was still an agricultural community on the Tiber with little power abroad, little luxury, and little urban development, life was simpler and standards stricter. However, the submissive and passive role of women was very ancient, and certainly by the time Rome emerged as a historic and powerful state, say after the defeat of Hannibal late in the third century B.C., all the elements were already there of the social and moral situation which Augustus both represented and tried in some ways to control. Nor is there any justification for speaking of hypocrisy. No one believed or even pretended to believe that monogamous marriage, which was strictly enforced, was incompatible with polygamous sexual activity by the male half of the population. Augustus was concerned with the social consequences of an apparent unwillingness on the part of the aristocracy to produce legitimate children in sufficient numbers, with the social consequences of extravagant and wasteful living, of *public* licentiousness, and in the upper classes, of *female* licentiousness (which may have been on the increase with the breakdown of political morality in the last century of the Roman Republic). It never entered his mind that moral regeneration might include the abolition of concubines, mistresses and brothels, the end of sleeping with one's female slaves, or a redefinition of adultery to extend it to extramarital intercourse by a married man.

There was no puritanism in the Roman concept of morality. Marriage was a central institution but it had nothing sacramental about it. It was central because the whole structure of property rested on it and because both the indispensable family cult and the institution of citizenship required the orderly, regular succession of legitimate children in one generation after another. There were neither spinsters nor confirmed bachelors in this world. It was assumed that if one reached the right age—and many of course did not, given the enormously high rate of infant mortality—one would marry. Society could not pursue its normal course otherwise. But the stress was always on the rightness of the marriage from a social and economic point of view, and on its legitimacy (and therefore also on the legitimacy of the offspring) from the political and legal point of view. If the relationship turned out also to be pleasant and affectionate, so much the better. It was taken for granted, however, that men would find comradeship and sexual satisfaction from others as well, and often only or chiefly from others. They were expected to behave with good taste in this respect, but no more.

Standards, whether of taste or of law, were profoundly influenced by class. Men like Sulla and Cicero openly enjoyed the company of actors and actresses, but by a law of Augustus and before that by custom, no member of the senatorial class could contract a legal marriage with any woman who was, or ever had been, an actress, whereas other Roman citizens were free to do so. Soldiers in the legions, unlike their officers, were not allowed to marry during their period of service, which was twenty years under Augustus and was raised to twenty-five later on. The reasons for this law were rather complicated, the consequences even more so (until the law was finally repealed in A.D. 197). Soldiers, of course, went on marrying and raising families all the time, and their tombstones are as full of references to loving wives and children as those of any other class. Nor, obviously, could they have acted in this way clandestinely. The law and its agents were not so stupid as not to know what was going on. They merely insisted on the formal unlawfulness of the relationship, and then proceeded to make and constantly to revise regulations for the inevitable confusion: confusion about inheritance, about the status of the children, about the rights of all the parties involved following honourable discharge.

Soldiers apart, we know very little about how these matters worked for the lower classes of Roman society. They were all subject to the same set of laws, but law codes are never automatic guides to the actual behaviour of a society, and neither poets nor historians nor philosophers often concerned themselves in a concrete and reliable way with the poorer peasantry or with the tens of thousands crowded together in the urban rabbit warrens which the Romans called *insulae*. Obviously among these people dowries, property settlements, family alliances for political purposes, and the like did not really enter the picture, either in the establishment of a marriage or in its dissolution. Neither could they so lightly dispense with a wife's labour service, whether on the farm or in a market stall, an inn, or a workshop. It was one thing to "work in wool", as did the Claudia whose epitaph I quoted earlier; it was something quite different to work in wool in earnest.

It would probably be a safe guess that women of the lower classes were therefore more 'emancipated', more equal *de facto* if not in strict law, more widely accepted as persons in their own right than their richer, more bourgeois, or more aristocratic sisters. This is a common enough phenomenon everywhere. No doubt they were freer in all senses—far less inhibited by legal definitions of marriage or legitimacy, less bound by the double standard of sexual morality. For one thing, the rapid development of large-scale slavery after the wars with Hannibal and the Carthaginians, combined with the frequent practice of manumitting slaves, meant that a large proportion of the free population, even of the citizen class, was increasingly drawn from ex-slaves and the children of slaves. This alone—and specifically their experience, as females, while they were slaves—would have been enough to give them, and their men, a somewhat different attitude towards the accepted, traditional, upper-class values. Add economic necessity, slum conditions, the fact that their work was serious and not a pastime, and the rest follows.

In all classes there was one inescapable condition, and that was the high probability of early death. On a rough calculation, of the population of the Roman Empire which succeeded in reaching the age of fifteen (that is, which survived the heavy mortality of infancy and childhood), more than half of the women were dead before forty, and in some classes and areas, even before thirty-five. Women were very much worse off than men in this respect, partly because of the perils of childbirth, partly, in the lower classes, because of the risk of sheer exhaustion. Thus, in one family tomb in regular use in the second and third centuries, sixty-eight wives were buried by their husbands and only forty-one husbands by their wives. A consequence, intensified by the ease of divorce, was the frequency of second and third marriages for both sexes, especially among men. This in turn complicated both personal and family relationships, economically as well as psychologically, and the prospect, even before the event, must have introduced a considerable element of tension in many women. Many, too, must have been sexually frustrated and unsatisfied.

None of this necessarily implies that women did not passively accept their position, at least on the surface. It would be a bad mistake to read our own notions and values into the picture, or even those of a century or two ago. The women of French provincial society portrayed by Balzac seem to have been more suppressed and beaten down than their Roman counterparts. The latter at least found their men much more open-handed with money and luxuries, and they shared in a fairly active dinner-party kind of social life and in the massive public entertainments. The evidence suggests that Balzac's women somehow made their peace with the world, even if often an unhappy and tragic peace, and presumably so did the women of Rome. We are told by Roman writers of the educated conversation of women in mixed company. Ovid in *The Art of Love* urged even his kind of woman not only to dress and primp properly, to sweeten her breath, to learn to walk gracefully and dance well, but also to cultivate the best Greek and Latin poetry. It is a pity we cannot eavesdrop on some of these conversations, but there is no Roman Balzac or Stendhal, no Jane Austen or Thackeray or Hardy, to give us the opportunity.

This brings us back to the silence of the women of Rome, which in one way speaks loudly, if curiously.

Where were the rebels among the women, real or fictitious—the George Sand or Harriet Beecher Stowe, the Hester Prynne or Tess of the D'Urbervilles? How, in other words, did 'respectable' women of breeding, education and leisure find outlets for their repressed energies and talents? The answers seem to lie within a very restricted range of activities. One was religion. It is a commonplace in our own civilization that, at least in Latin countries, women are much more occupied with their religion than are men. But it would be wrong to generalize too quickly: the same has not been true for most of Jewish history nor for most of antiquity. Much depends on the content and orientation of doctrine and ritual. Traditional Roman religion was centred on the household (the hearth and the ancestors) and on the state cults, and the male played the predominant part in both—as *paterfamilias* and as citizen, respectively—notwithstanding that the hearth was protected by a goddess, Vesta, and not by a god. To be sure, the public hearth, with its sacred fire which must never be allowed to go out, was in the charge of six women, the Vestal Virgins. Other rituals were reserved for women, too, such as the cult of *Bona Dea,* the 'good goddess', or such exceptional ones as the formal reception at the harbour, towards the end of the war with Hannibal, of the statue of *Mater Idaea* brought from Asia Minor in response to a Sibylline prophecy which guaranteed victory if that were done. However, the procession was led by a man, "the noblest in the state", as required by the same prophecy. And the Vestal Virgins were subject to the authority of a man, the Pontifex Maximus.

For most of Roman history, then, to the end of the Republic in fact, women were not very prominent even in religion. The change came under the Empire and with the great influx into the Roman world of various eastern mystery cults, carrying their new element of personal communion and salvation. Some of these cults—notably that of Mithras, the soldier's god *par excellence*—were closed to women. Others, however, offered them hope, ultimate release, and immediate status unlike anything they had experienced before—above all, the worship of the Hellenized Egyptian goddess Isis. She became (to men as well as women) Isis of the Myriad Names, Lady of All, Queen of the Inhabited World, Star of the Sea, identifiable with nearly every goddess of the known world. "You gave women equal power with men," says one of her hymns. In another she herself speaks: "I am she whom women call goddess. I ordained that women shall be loved by men; I brought wife and husband together, and invented the marriage-contract."

It was no wonder, therefore, that of all the pagan cults Isis-worship was the most tenacious in its resistance when Christianity ascended to a position first of dominance in the Roman world and then of near monopoly. Christianity itself was soon in some difficulty over the question of women. On the one hand, there was the unmistakably elevated, and for the time untypical, position of women in the life of Christ, and in many of the early Christian communities. Women of all classes were drawn to the new creed. There were women martyrs, too. But on the other hand, there was the view expressed in, for example, I Corinthians 14: "Let your women keep silence in the churches: for it is not permitted unto them to speak; but they are commanded to be under obedience as also saith the law." Women were not allowed to forget that Eve was created from Adam's rib, and not the other way round. Neither in this respect nor in any other did the early church seek or bring about a social revolution. Both the ritual of the church and its administration remained firmly in the hands of men, as did the care of souls, and this included the souls of the women.

Where Christianity differed most radically from many (though not all) of the other mystery religions of the time was in its extension of the central idea of purification and purity beyond chastity to celibacy. For many women this attitude offered release through sublimation. That the traditional pagan world failed to understand, or even to believe, this was possible is comprehensible enough. The Roman aristocracy had long been suspicious of the various new cults. A great wave of orgiastic Dionysiac religion had spread in Italy after the wars with Hannibal, soon to be suppressed by the Senate in 186 B.C. Even Isis-worship had a long struggle with the state before achieving official recognition. Anyone who reads the hymns or the detailed accounts of the cult in Apuleius or Plutarch may well find that hard to understand, but the fact is that Isis, though she attracted all classes, was particularly popular in the *demi-monde.*

Sublimation through religion was not the only outlet for pent-up female energies and female rebelliousness. There was another in quite the opposite direction. In the amphitheatres, among the spectators, the women achieved equality with their men: they relished the horrible brutality of the gladiatorial shows (and of the martyrdoms) with the same fierce joy. Gladiators became the pin-ups for Roman women, especially in the upper classes. And at the very top, the women became, metaphorically, gladiators themselves. The women of the Roman emperors were not all monsters, but enough of them throughout the first century of our era, and again from the latter part of the second century on, revealed a ferocity and sadism in the backstairs struggles for power that were not often surpassed— though they were perhaps matched in the contemporary court of the Idumaean dynasty founded by Herod the Great in Judaea. They were not struggling for the throne for themselves—that was unthinkable—but for their sons, brothers and lovers. Their energy and, in a curious sense, their ability are beyond argument. The outlets they found and the goals they sought are, equally, beyond all human dignity, decency, or compassion.

Obviously Roman women are not to be judged by their worst representatives. On the other hand, there must be something significant, even though twisted, in that small group of ferocious and licentious royal females. Under the prevailing value-system, women were expected to be content with vicarious satisfactions. It was their role to be happy in the happiness and success of their men, and of the state for which they bore and nurtured the next generation of men. "She loved her husband. . . .She bore two sons. . . . She kept the house and worked in wool." That was the highest praise, not only in Rome but in much of human history. What went on behind the accepted facade, what Claudia thought or said to herself, we can never know. But when the silence breaks, the sounds which come forth—in the royal family at least—are not very pretty. Most of the Claudias no doubt fully accepted and even defended the values fixed by their men; they knew no other world. The revealing point is that the occasional rebellion took the forms it did.

NERO, Unmaligned

Remembered for his excesses and little else, the eccentric emperor was a discriminating patron of the arts, a keen judge of men, and—while Rome burned—an energetic fire fighter

LIONEL CASSON

Gnaeus Domitius Ahenobarbus was a human beast. He once slaughtered a servant merely for refusing to drink as much as he was told. Driving on the Appian Way, he deliberately whipped up his horses to run over a child. When someone criticized him in the Forum, he gouged out the man's eyes on the spot. In A.D. 37 he was brought before the emperor Tiberius on charges of treason, adultery, and incest; only Tiberius's unexpected death saved him. About the one respectable thing he did was to marry a princess of the royal blood, Agrippina, a great-granddaughter of Augustus himself. He had one child by her, a boy whom they named Lucius Domitius; history knows him as the emperor Nero.

Nero's mother was a match for his father in cruelty, but in her it was disciplined by a calculating intelligence and cloaked by ostentatious deportment as a proper Roman matron. Her husband died in A.D. 40. Agrippina played her cards with such consummate skill that within nine years she had become the fourth wife of the emperor Claudius, despite his sworn resolve never to marry again (he had executed his third for publicly cuckolding him). A few months after the wedding Agrippina talked her new husband into adopting Nero, even though he had a son and two daughters of his own by previous marriages. In the ensuing years she manipulated the emperor into giving Nero all the outward

marks of preference, and in 53 she engineered the boy's marriage to Octavia, one of Claudius's daughters. Then, in 54, when her husband dropped dead—she had fed him a dish of poisonous mushrooms, so the rumors said—she got the troops of the palace guard to acclaim Nero as the successor.

And so a sixteen-year-old youth suddenly found himself heading an empire whose lands stretched from Gibraltar to the Syrian desert, from Britain to the Sahara, and whose subjects ran the gamut from primitive tribesmen to the highly civilized inhabitants of the ancient centers of Greece and the Near East. He was an absolute autocrat. His power rested, in the first place, on an army whose loyalty his predecessors had carefully secured, and, in the second, on the good will of Rome's multitudinous subjects to whom his predecessors had promised and furnished decent government. However, he was obliged to make it look as if he were but a partner in power, as if he shared the rule with the members of Rome's aristocracy who sat in the traditional governing body, the senate. This was a bit of theatre which, though it fooled nobody, for form's sake had to be maintained. Augustus, the founder of the Roman Empire, had devised the arrangement, and the elderly Tiberius and Claudius had kept it up, though with nowhere near his success, since they lacked his gift for public relations. In between was the brief reign of the young whippersnapper Caligula, who was clear-eyed enough to see that a Roman emperor was little short of a god on earth but not clear-headed enough to

realize he dare not act like one; he treated the senate with contempt—and was assassinated within four years.

However, Nero was no Caligula. What is more, he had some of the best brains in the nation at his side to guide him during his apprenticeship. Since the age of eleven he had been the pupil of Seneca, the philosopher and moralist; Seneca was now promoted from tutor to confidential assistant in the administration of the empire. One of Agrippina's adroit moves in paving the way for her son's elevation to the purple had been to get in her own man, Sextus Afranius Burrus, as head of the palace guard; he was made a high-level administrator and turned out to be a particularly able one. And then, at least in the beginning, there was Agrippina herself, the canniest politician in Rome, to keep the boy from any missteps.

The first five years or so of Nero's reign were, by all accounts, an unqualified success. His enemies—practically everything we hear about Nero comes in one way or another from his enemies—claimed that it was his advisers who were responsible for the operation of the government, and that the young emperor frittered away his time in frivolities and degeneracy. No doubt Seneca and Burrus did a great deal, but in many a key area Nero made his own contribution. He had a vast charm and an inborn sense of courtesy, gifts that helped him maintain harmonious relations with the stiff-necked senate, eternally resentful of their loss of power. He had a knack for selecting competent subordinates, and this resulted in the choice of a fine administrator for the city of Rome. His keen intelligence produced reforms in the law and the system of taxation (although a visionary proposal of his to abolish all indirect taxes and customs within the empire proved too heady for Rome's commercial interests).

Even in the quicksands of foreign policy he did well. He had inherited two troubling areas, Britain and the Near East, and he handled both with outstanding success, in good part because of the way he had of picking the right men for his jobs. Rome had invaded Britain in A.D. 43, during the reign of Claudius. A program of pacification followed, and this seemed to be going ahead without snags. Then, in 61, a revolt headed by a redoubtable native queen, Boudicca, exploded, the Roman forces that rushed to stop her were cut to pieces, her men massacred tens of thousands of Romans and other settlers, and the whole Roman position on the island hung by a thread. Nero's military appointee, however, kept his nerve and managed to save the day. At just the right moment Nero replaced him with a man whose talents lay in administration rather than leading troops, and Britain gave the emperors no further trouble for more than three centuries.

Beyond Rome's eastern border lay the only nation strong enough to be a political rival to Rome, Parthia. A century earlier Rome had tried war—and left the field licking her wounds. Augustus, astute and practical, settled for diplomacy, and that worked well enough for a time. However, when Nero ascended the throne, it had lost its effect; that year the Parthians invaded Armenia, which Rome up to then had carefully maintained as a buffer state. Nero's solution was to appoint as commander in chief of the forces in the area a certain Gnaeus Domitius Corbulo and leave it to him to rectify matters. Corbulo, a martinet of the old school, drilled and drilled his men into Rome's best fighting force, and by the year 60 he had the Parthians out and Armenia back in the hands of a local king.

No doubt about it, the young ruler was bright and able. Yet certain things about him gave people pause—his artis-

tic and cultural interests, for example. Nero was a passionate devotee of literature and music: he composed verse, acted parts from Greek tragedy, and assiduously listened to the lyre-playing of the greatest virtuoso of the day. These were not qualities one looked for in a Roman, least of all a Roman chief of state. Even worse, Nero was distressingly cavalier about doing what was expected of an emperor, such as maintaining a grave demeanor, taking an interest in army matters, and watching gladiators spill each other's blood.

And there were disturbing indications that he was, after all, the son of his father. With a gang of kindred spirits, he used to roam the streets at night incognito, having a wild time housebreaking, looting, raping, and mugging passersby. During one of these escapades his career was all but cut short when he barely missed being clobbered to death by a resolute husband who stood his ground to defend his wife.

It was Nero's relations with his mother that revealed once and for all the Mr. Hyde that this charming, youthful Jekyll had within him. Agrippina, having won a crown for her son, settled down to enjoy pulling the strings from behind the throne. Nero quickly discovered how strong-willed a partner in power his mother could be, and equally quickly decided that there was no reason he had to put up with her. He neatly cut her out of all official business and removed one of her most useful tools, the minister of finance (replacing him with a man so able that four subsequent emperors retained him in office—yet another instance of his gift for picking subordinates). And when Octavia, the dutiful princess to whom Agrippina had married Nero, turned out to be unable to handle the imperial sexual appetite, he took on as mistress one of his servants, a freed slave, thus thumbing his nose at his mother and court propriety. Agrippina flew into a rage and let it be known that she was thinking of taking up the cause of her stepson, whose claims to the succession were as good as Nero's, maybe better. This was a serious blunder. In 55 the emperor eliminated this rival—the story given out was that the

boy had died of an epileptic fit—stripped Agrippina of her bodyguard, and moved her out of the palace.

For three years she managed to steer clear of danger, until Nero met Poppaea, the *femme fatale* of the day. The new inamorata was no mere slave: she belonged to one of Rome's best and most wealthy families, and being Nero's mistress was not enough for her. But Nero was still married to Octavia, and Agrippina, though she willy-nilly had to stomach her son's liaisons, would under no circumstances swallow a divorce. In 59 Nero settled matters by committing his second bloody crime: he killed his mother. The murder, of course, had to look like an act of god, and the scheme he thought up reveals yet another facet of the man, his fascination with mechanical devices. He concerted with the admiral of the fleet to design a collapsible boat. While his mother was staying at her seaside villa on the Bay of Naples, he invited her to dinner at his own villa nearby and then sent her home in the death trap. The boat collapsed on schedule but, by a freak, Agrippina escaped and made it safely to shore. So Nero perforce sent assassins; the story goes that, as one raised his sword for the *coup de grâce*, she pointed to her womb and cried, "Strike here!"

Nero had consulted with Burrus and Seneca about the murder. If not before, certainly by this time they must have realized they had a tiger by the tail. Somehow they managed to hold their charge in check for another two years, largely by encouraging his artistic interests and his appetite for grandiose public works. His passion for taking the stage to declaim or sing was stronger than ever, and he indulged it by giving ever more elaborate private performances; a special "emperor's claque" of five thousand young men carefully drilled in the art of rhythmic handclapping guaranteed adequate applause. He instituted a festival, to be held every four years, that featured Greek events—contests in singing, dancing, and recitation, rather than gladiatorial fights, chariot races, and other typical Roman fare. He started the first of his great construction projects (and the only one he was ever to complete), a public gymnasium and bath in Rome not far from where the Pantheon stands. The building was vast and sumptuous, the forerunner of the celebrated edifices that Caracalla and Diocletian were to put up. "What was worse than Nero?" quipped the Roman wit Martial a half century later, "what better than his baths?"

Then, in 62, Burrus died, Seneca was allowed to resign his office and go into retirement, and Nero, just twenty-five, was on his own. In the first eight years of his reign he had committed but two murders, one a political execution and the other very likely inspired by tortured psychological drives. This year he added three more. Two of his victims were senators who had fallen under suspicion, the third was his unhappy wife. He had already divorced Octavia on the grounds of sterility and twelve days later had married Poppaea. Octavia was banished to a remote island, but somehow banishment was not enough for him, so the wretched woman was beheaded.

• • •

The year 64 was climactic. Nero's handling of its events graphically reveals the extraordinary mix of traits in his make-up—his sure hand in directing the affairs of his realm, his yearning to be recognized as a concert star, his feeling for art, his technological bent, and his brutal cruelty. The whole empire was at peace except for the old sore spot, Armenia. Two years earlier the country had slipped back into Parthian hands. Corbulo once again rescued it, and Nero then elected to try Augustus's method, diplomacy. He negotiated an agreement whereby the Parthians would put their man, Tiridates, on the Armenian throne but Nero would hand over the crown and scepter at Rome—in other words, give Parthia control of Armenia but make it look like Rome's free gift. When Tiridates arrived in Rome, Nero, with his flair for public relations and his taste for the theatrical, built up the ceremony into a stupendous spectacle. Backbiters griped at the fortune he spent on it; they had no way of knowing that the peace the money helped to buy was destined to last half a century.

While waiting for Tiridates to arrive,

Nero finally satisfied a wish dear to his stage-struck heart—he made his public debut as a concert performer. Too nervous to open in Rome, he went to Naples; after all, the population there, being largely of Greek origin, could be counted on to appreciate the finer things more than a Rome audience with its taste for gladiators and chariot racing. We may be sure he was a *succès fou*.

And then came the event that was to make the name of Nero a household word. On the night of July 18, fire broke out in part of the Circus Maximus. For six days it raged unabated until a firebreak, by heroic efforts, was finally opened and the conflagration checked. Then it flared up again, though less intensely, in other parts of the city for three days more. By the time it was all over, only four of Rome's fourteen districts were intact; three had been wiped out, and seven nearly so.

Nero had been at his seaside villa at Anzio, some thirty miles away, when the fire started. He raced back to town and swung into action: he welcomed the homeless into his own gardens and all public buildings still standing, ordered additional emergency housing to be hastily erected, rushed in food from the waterfront and neighboring towns, and drastically cut the price of grain. His enemies rewarded him by putting about the story that, inspired by the spectacle, he had gone into his private theatre and sung "The Burning of Troy." In fact, he had been directing the fire fighting in his palace, which was near where the flames had first broken out, so careless of his own security that he came within a hair of being assassinated.

Once the crisis was over, Nero planned the resurrection of the city in a way that only one with a talent for technology could have devised. The ravaged areas were to be rebuilt with regular rows of streets and wide avenues, in place of the old narrow, crooked alleys, and with houses of a uniform height. The houses were to have adjoining yards in the back and continuous arcades along the front; the yards guaranteed light and air and served as a firebreak, and the arcades would be a blessing in the summer heat and the winter rains.

He enacted ordinances requiring that a certain portion of every house be made of stone, with no wooden timbers or beams, that no house was to share a wall with its neighbor, and that the stone come from two specified quarries in the hills about Rome which furnished a particularly fire-resistant variety.

The populace, filled with helpless rage at the calamity, was ready to believe ugly rumors, assiduously spread by the many who had no love for Nero, that the emperor himself had started the blaze. Nero's defense was to supply a scapegoat. He picked out a small religious sect so un-Roman in its make-up and practices that the whole city, nobles as well as plebeians, viewed it with instinctive mistrust. Members of this sect were rounded up and given the full dose of Nero's cruelty: turning over his gardens for the spectacle, he had some torn to pieces by dogs, others made into human torches. It was Christianity's baptism of fire as a persecuted religion.

The devastation of Rome had included Nero's own palace. Its replacement, he decided, would be a totally new kind of imperial residence, a luxurious country home complete with farmland, woodland, flocks, game, and gardens, all in the very heart of the city. To accommodate all this he confiscated a vast piece of Rome's choicest real estate. The southern half of the Forum supplied one part of the grounds, the place where the Colosseum stands today was marked off for an ornamental pond, and the hill to the east of the Colosseum was cleared to take the main building, the Domus Aurea, or Golden House. After Nero's death, the emperor Trajan razed the structure and had a public bath put up on the site. Parts of the Golden House were incorporated in the foundations, and, by this quirk of fate, escaped total annihilation. These surviving remains lay hidden right till the end of the fifteenth century. Their sudden discovery brought a stream of artists and notables burrowing underground to visit them. Raphael sent a young assistant; he returned with sketches of the wall paintings he had seen, and Raphael was so impressed he included a number of motifs from them in his decorations for the Vatican loggias. The discoveries later inspired a school of painting.

Today art historians recognize that Nero's palace was strikingly avant-garde, that its murals represented a distinct new direction in painting and its architecture a veritable revolution. Its use of concrete rather than squared stone, its octagonal rooms and domed ceilings to provide novel interior spaces, and its other innovations made it a pioneer building, and prototype of such glories of Roman architecture as the Pantheon and Hadrian's vast villa at Tivoli. Quite possibly the radical departures were inspired by the art-minded emperor himself; at the very least he gets the credit for giving them his enthusiastic approval. There is no question that he had a hand in the ingenious mechanical gadgets the new palace boasted: overhead pipes in the dining rooms that sprayed perfume and overhead panels that opened to shower down flowers, a ceiling in the main banqueting hall that revolved in imitation of the heavens.

Rome's rank and file had nothing against Nero: his victims never came from their number, he was careful to see that their rations of bread and circuses were as regular as ever, and his cultural antics rather amused them. But the powerful aristocracy, the members of the senate, were not amused: on top of having to rubber-stamp whatever the young tyrant set his heart on, on top of having to pretend wild enthusiasm at his endless musicales, they now had to watch what they considered a pretentious and costly folly take over the very heart of their city. So, in the year 65, the eleventh year of Nero's reign, when the empire was still enjoying peace and a new Rome was rising from the ashes of the old, a powerful group formed a conspiracy to assassinate Nero. Its leader, a senator named Gaius Calpurnius Piso, was better known for degeneracy than political idealism, and most of the members were equally unsavory. The day before the murder was to take place, a freed slave got wind of the plot, and the affair was nipped in the bud.

The reaction was predictable: Nero became a killer for fair. Of the forty-odd people implicated in the attempt, sixteen who were undeniably guilty lost their lives (most were allowed to kill themselves), and a large number, including no doubt some who were innocent, were exiled and degraded. But it did not stop there: for the Roman aristocracy sudden accusation, conviction, and death became from that time on a routine part of daily life. Among the many who in these days received the order to do away with themselves was Petronius, Nero's "arbiter of taste" and the author of the unique and brilliant *Satyricon*; he went to his death in the elegant and unhurried style that had marked his life. Even old Seneca fell into disfavor and had to commit suicide.

With hate hanging heavy all about him, Nero serenely continued to pursue the passion of his life, his career as a concert artist. By now the Greek festival he had inaugurated was due again, and this time he did not hesitate to appear on the public stage in Rome. The senate, we are told, voted to award the prizes to him in advance, hoping to avoid the scandal of having the emperor appear in his own capital in a line-up of professional singers and actors, but Nero would have none of it. He insisted not only on being a contestant but on behaving exactly like the other competitors: he remained standing throughout, never let mucus from the nose or spittle from the mouth be visible, awaited the judges' decision on bended knee. We are further told that to ensure a full house spies informed on any who stayed away, and that spectators went home with their hands bruised from compulsory clapping.

All this acclaim still left Nero unsatisfied. He must needs reap laurels in the land of discriminating audiences—Greece. So, in September of 66, leaving the government in the hands of low-level subordinates, he set sail. The Greeks obligingly lumped together in 67 their four great festivals—the Olympian, Pythian, Isthmian, and Nemean games—which normally fall in different years, so he could attain what only the most renowned virtuosos had attained, victory in all four. He was applauded so wildly, carried off such a plethora of prizes, that, in an access of fellow feeling, he announced to the Greeks his decision to return to them their ancient freedom. It was a grand gesture which helped the Greek ego enormously, relieved them of the taxes they paid to Rome, and cost Nero very little, since the take from so poor a country was minimal. Also on behalf of his beloved Greeks, he launched the most ambitious public works project of his career, a canal through the Isthmus of Corinth, to spare ships the long and sometimes dangerous trip around the Peloponnese. At least three great rulers before him, including Julius Caesar, had gotten matters as far as the drawing board; Nero actually got the work under way, personally carrying off the first basketful of earth. Like his other brainstorms, it was dropped when he died, but the little that was completed shows his customary technological expertise: the French engineers who tackled the canal again in 1881 followed the course he had mapped out and even used some of the cuttings his men had made.

By now danger signals were flying all over the empire. In Palestine there had erupted the bitter revolt that was to end with the razing of Jerusalem and the destruction of Solomon's temple. Another uprising was brewing in Gaul. And from Rome came frantic reports of unrest and cabals. Finally Nero tore himself away and early in 68 returned to the capital.

By March the revolt in Gaul was in the open, and Galba, the governor of Spain, had joined the dissidents. Though the trouble in Gaul was soon snuffed out, leaving mainly Galba to worry about, it was clear that something had happened to Nero. His cause was far from lost; all he had to do was issue appropriate orders, as he had so successfully done for years. But instead of taking action he talked, and so wildly or so grandiosely or so irrelevantly that he seemed mad. One day, for example, when the situation in Gaul was at its most critical, he convened a meeting of his key advisers and spent most of the time demonstrating a new type of water organ he planned to install in theatres.

In June the commanders of the palace guard, a pair of opportunists who figured it was time to desert a sinking ship, talked their men into switching allegiance to Galba, and the curtain was rung down on Nero's career. The senate scrambled to declare Galba emperor and Nero a public enemy. Only his freed slaves showed any loyalty. He fled to the house of one of them and there committed suicide. It is reported that during his last hours he ordered a grave to be prepared and then kept crying out, "To die! An artist like me!"

. . .

Christians, the victims of Nero's most hideous act, have made his name anathema. Yet, in a sense, they only picked up where the Romans themselves had left off: the two Roman authors who are the only sources we have for the facts of Nero's life had already destroyed his reputation. The first, Tacitus, wrote about half a century after Nero died. A staunch member of the senatorial class, he purports to write history, but deliberately slants it to tell a tale of moral degradation: the decline that began with the subtle scheming of Augustus, was hastened by the hypocrisy of Tiberius, and reached its nadir with the mad and sinister antics of Nero. The second, Suetonius, who composed a short biography of Nero a few years later, gives us in effect a condensed version of Tacitus's account decked out with every lurid detail he could dig up. To judge Nero dispassionately is about as easy as judging Judas Iscariot.

As a leader of the state he deserves high marks, certainly for the first ten years of his fourteen on the throne. The bureaucracy of the empire functioned as efficiently and fairly as it ever had. The watchword of his reign was peace, and by and large he achieved it; his settlement of the Parthian problem, lasting as it did a full fifty years, was a masterstroke. He squandered money on spectacle and display, on public works that were often more showy than essential, but he avoided that most expensive luxury of all, wars of conquest. He was a murderer—but though he killed the innocent, he did not kill many; he was no Ivan the Terrible.

What made the opposition to Nero so intense was not his cruelty but his ever-burgeoning megalomania and the way it drove him to demean his high office.

When Nero died, this colossal statue of him was renamed Helios, in honor of the sun god. Now lost, the figure stood in Rome at least until the seventh century.

When he merely played at being a performing artist, he could be indulged, and, in any event, the spectacle was contained within the palace grounds. When he took himself seriously and paraded his talents publicly, he was not only being a fool but disgracing the office he held and by implication all who were associated with him in it, that is to say, the entire membership of the senate.

As for Nero's subjects in general, in their thinking the peace he maintained counted far more than the state of Rome's majesty. Indeed, among the masses of Greek-speaking peoples of the empire, his manifest partiality for all things Greek was a distinct asset. They mourned with true feeling when he died.

Many even refused to believe he was dead. During the next half century at least two imposters arose who claimed to be Nero, and both immediately gained a following.

Nero may have gone awry about his talents as a performer, but that was the only lapse of his critical sense. No other Roman emperor was a man of arts and letters in the way he was. He was a poet, and his verse, as we can tell from the few surviving samples, was not at all bad. His artistic taste is reflected in the coins struck during his reign; aesthetically they are the finest ever to come out of a Roman mint. Where art was concerned he had, too, the admirable quality of being receptive to new currents—witness the avant-garde architecture of the

2. GREECE AND ROME

Golden House and the novel paintings decorating its walls. He even managed to make a contribution in the world of music and song, though for the benefit of Rome's Tin Pan Alley rather than her concert halls: Suetonius reports that he used to act out "comic ditties about the leaders of the revolts [i.e., in Gaul and Spain], which . . . have become popular favorites."

And then there is that dimension that is uniquely his: no other Roman emperor, in fact no other Greek or Roman writer or thinker we know of, possessed his avid interest in matters scientific and technological. The fiendish contraption for killing his mother is of a piece with the gadgetry in his new palace, with the down-to-earth specifics in his plans for a fireproof Rome, with the new type of water organ he was puttering over while the world was collapsing about him. He tackled the greatest public works project of ancient times, the Corinth canal; he did not complete it, but for other than technological reasons. He was responsible for a scientific voyage of exploration to the reaches of the upper Nile (his men came back with an exact measurement for the distance between Aswan on the First Cataract and Meroë just north of Khartoum). In Greece he took time off from his artistic endeavors to try to sound the bottom of a lake that, tradi-tion had it, was bottomless. And what ruler or savant is there from any age who has earned renown in pharmacy? "A brimming tablespoon . . . of Nero's marvelous 'Quick Acting,' " states the author of a fourth-century treatise on medicines, "taken before meals . . . settles the stomach marvelously."

Nero deserves a better grade than history has assigned him. He was at times a monster, at times a fool, and he ended up a hopeless megalomaniac; but he was also a statesman, connoisseur, poet, songwriter and musician, mechanic, engineer, pharmacist—the closest equivalent to a "Renaissance man" to come out of the ancient world.

MURDEROUS GAMES

Gladiatorial shows in Ancient Rome turned war into a game, preserved an atmosphere of violence in time of peace, and functioned as a political theatre which allowed confrontation between rulers and ruled.

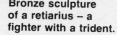

Bronze sculpture of a retiarius – a fighter with a trident.

Keith Hopkins

ROME WAS A WARRIOR STATE. AFTER the defeat of Carthage in 201 BC, Rome embarked on two centuries of almost continuous imperial expansion. By the end of this period, Rome controlled the whole of the Mediterranean basin and much of north-western Europe. The population of her empire, at between 50 and 60 million people, constituted perhaps one-fifth or one-sixth of the world's then population. Victorious conquest had been bought at a huge price, measured in human suffering, carnage, and money. The costs were borne by tens of thousands of conquered peoples, who paid taxes to the Roman state, by slaves captured in war and transported to Italy, and by Roman soldiers who served long years fighting overseas.

The discipline of the Roman army was notorious. Decimation is one index of its severity. If an army unit was judged disobedient or cowardly in battle, one soldier in ten was selected by lot and cudgelled to death by his former comrades. It should be stressed that decimation was not just a myth told to terrify fresh recruits; it actually happened in the period of imperial expansion, and frequently enough not to arouse particular comment. Roman soldiers killed each other for their common good.

When Romans were so unmerciful to each other, what mercy could prisoners of war expect? Small wonder then that they were sometimes forced to fight in gladiatorial contests, or were thrown to wild beasts for popular entertainment. Public executions helped inculcate valour and fear in the men, women and children left at home. Children learnt the lesson of what happened to soldiers who were defeated. Public executions were rituals which helped maintain an atmosphere of violence, even in times of peace. Bloodshed and slaughter joined military glory and conquest as central elements in Roman culture.

With the accession of the first emperor Augustus (31 BC – AD 14), the Roman state embarked on a period of long-term peace (*pax romana*). For more than two centuries, thanks to its effective defence by frontier armies, the inner core of the Roman empire was virtually insulated from the direct experience of war. Then in memory of their warrior traditions, the Romans set up artificial battlefields in cities and towns for public amusement. The custom spread from Italy to the provinces.

Nowadays, we admire the Colosseum in Rome and other great Roman amphitheatres such as those at Verona, Arles, Nîmes and El Djem as architectural monuments. We choose to forget, I suspect, that this was where Romans regularly organised fights to the death between hundreds of gladiators, the mass execution of unarmed criminals, and the indiscriminate slaughter of domestic and wild animals.

The enormous size of the amphitheatres indicates how popular

From *History Today*, June 1983, pp. 16-22. Reproduced by kind permission of History Today, Ltd., 83-84 Berwick Street, London W1V 3PJ England.

2. GREECE AND ROME

these exhibitions were. The Colosseum was dedicated in AD 80 with 100 days of games. One day 3,000 men fought; on another 9,000 animals were killed. It seated 50,000 people. It is still one of Rome's most impressive buildings, a magnificent feat of engineering and design. In ancient times, amphitheatres must have towered over cities, much as cathedrals towered over medieval towns. Public killings of men and animals were a Roman rite, with overtones of religious sacrifice, legitimated by the myth that gladiatorial shows inspired the populace with 'a glory in wounds and a contempt of death'.

Philosophers, and later Christians, disapproved strongly. To little effect; gladiatorial games persisted at least until the early fifth century AD, wild-beast killings until the sixth century. St Augustine in his *Confessions* tells the story of a Christian who was reluctantly forced along to the amphitheatre by a party of friends; at first, he kept his eyes shut, but when he heard the crowd roar, he opened them, and became converted by the sight of blood into an eager devotee of gladiatorial shows. Even the biting criticism quoted below reveals a certain excitement beneath its moral outrage.

Seneca, Roman senator and philosopher, tells of a visit he once paid to the arena. He arrived in the middle of the day, during the mass execution of criminals, staged as an entertainment in the interval between the wild-beast show in the morning and the gladiatorial show of the afternoon:

All the previous fighting had been merciful by comparison. Now finesse is set aside, and we have pure unadulterated murder. The combatants have no protective covering; their entire bodies are exposed to the blows. No blow falls in vain. This is what lots of people prefer to the regular contests, and even to those which are put on by popular request. And it is obvious why. There is no helmet, no shield to repel the blade. Why have armour? Why bother with skill? All that just delays death.

In the morning, men are thrown to lions and bears. At mid-day they are thrown to the spectators themselves. No sooner has a man killed, than they shout for him to kill another, or to be killed. The final victor is kept for some other slaughter. In the end, every fighter dies. And all this goes on while the arena is half empty.

You may object that the victims committed robbery or were murderers. So what? Even if they deserved to suffer, what's

your compulsion to watch their sufferings? 'Kill him', they shout, 'Beat him, burn him'. Why is he too timid to fight? Why is he so frightened to kill? Why so reluctant to die? They have to whip him to make him accept his wounds.

Much of our evidence suggests that gladiatorial contests were, by origin, closely connected with funerals. 'Once upon a time', wrote the Christian critic Tertullian at the end of the second century AD, 'men believed that the souls of the dead were propitiated by human blood, and so at funerals they sacrificed prisoners of war or slaves of poor quality bought for the purpose'. The first recorded gladiatorial show took place in 264 BC: it was presented by two nobles in honour of their dead father; only three pairs of gladiators took part. Over the next two centuries, the scale and frequency of gladiatorial shows increased steadily. In 65 BC, for example, Julius Cæsar gave elaborate funeral games for his father involving 640 gladiators and condemned criminals who were forced to fight with wild beasts. At his next games in 46 BC, in memory of his dead daughter and, let it be said, in celebration of his recent triumphs in Gaul and Egypt, Cæsar presented not only the customary fights between individual gladiators, but also fights between whole detachments of infantry and between squadrons of cavalry, some mounted on horses, others on elephants. Large-scale gladiatorial shows had arrived. Some of the contestants were professional gladiators, others prisoners of war, and others criminals condemned to death.

Up to this time, gladiatorial shows had always been put on by individual aristocrats at their own initiative and expense, in honour of dead relatives. The religious component in gladiatorial ceremonies continued to be important. For example, attendants in the arena were dressed up as gods. Slaves who tested whether fallen gladiators were really dead or just pretending, by applying a red-hot cauterising iron, were dressed as the god Mercury. Those who dragged away the dead bodies were dressed as Pluto, the god of the underworld. During the persecutions of Christians, the victims were sometimes led around the arena in a procession dressed up as priests and priestesses of pagan cults, before being stripped naked and thrown to the wild beasts. The welter of blood in gladiatorial and wild-beast shows, the

squeals and smell of the human victims and of slaughtered animals are completely alien to us and almost unimaginable. For some Romans they must have been reminiscent of battlefields, and, more immediately for everyone, associated with religious sacrifice. At one remove, Romans, even at the height of their civilisation, performed human sacrifice, purportedly in commemoration of their dead.

By the end of the last century BC, the religious and commemorative elements in gladiatorial shows were eclipsed by the political and the spectacular. Gladiatorial shows were public performances held mostly, before the amphitheatre was built, in the ritual and social centre of the city, the Forum. Public participation, attracted by the splendour of the show and by distributions of meat, and by betting, magnified the respect paid to the dead and the honour of the whole family. Aristocratic funerals in the Republic (before 31 BC) were political acts. And funeral games had political implications, because of their popularity with citizen electors. Indeed, the growth in the splendour of gladiatorial shows was largely fuelled by competition between ambitious aristocrats, who wished to please, excite and increase the number of their supporters.

In 42 BC, for the first time, gladiatorial fights were substituted for chariot-races in official games. After that in the city of Rome, regular gladiatorial shows, like theatrical shows and chariot-races, were given by officers of state, as part of their official careers, as an official obligation and as a tax on status. The Emperor Augustus, as part of a general policy of limiting aristocrats' opportunities to court favour with the Roman populace, severely restricted the number of regular gladiatorial shows to two each year. He also restricted their splendour and size. Each official was forbidden to spend more on them than his colleagues, and an upper limit was fixed at 120 gladiators a show.

These regulations were gradually evaded. The pressure for evasion was simply that, even under the emperors, aristocrats were still competing with each other, in prestige and political success. The splendour of a senator's public exhibition could make or break his social and political reputation. One aristocrat, Symmachus, wrote to a friend: 'I must now outdo the reputation earned by my own shows; our family's

The handle of a knife with the figure of a gladiator carved in ivory.

Graffiti of gladiators from the walls of Pompeii, showing their 'show-biz' appeal.

recent generosity during my consulship and the official games given for my son allow us to present nothing mediocre'. So he set about enlisting the help of various powerful friends in the provinces. In the end, he managed to procure antelopes, gazelles, leopards, lions, bears, bear-cubs, and even some crocodiles, which only just survived to the beginning of the games, because for the previous fifty days they had refused to eat. Moreover, twenty-nine Saxon

prisoners of war strangled each other in their cells on the night before their final scheduled appearance. Symmachus was heart-broken. Like every donor of the games, he knew that his political standing was at stake. Every presentation was in Goffman's strikingly apposite phrase 'a status bloodbath'.

The most spectacular gladiatorial shows were given by the emperors themselves at Rome. For example, the Emperor Trajan, to celebrate his conquest of Dacia (roughly modern Roumania), gave games in AD 108-9 lasting 123 days in which 9,138 gladiators fought and eleven thousand animals were slain. The Emperor Claudius in AD 52 presided in full military regalia over a battle on a lake near Rome between two naval squadrons, manned for the occasion by 19,000 forced combatants. The palace guard, stationed behind stout barricades, which also prevented the combatants from escaping, bombarded the ships with missiles from catapults. After a faltering start, because the men refused to fight, the battle according to Tacitus 'was fought with the spirit of free men, although between criminals. After much bloodshed, those who survived were spared extermination'.

The quality of Roman justice was often tempered by the need to satisfy the demand for the condemned. Christians, burnt to death as scapegoats after the great fire at Rome in AD 64, were not alone in being sacrificed for public entertainment. Slaves and bystanders, even the spectators themselves, ran the risk of becoming victims of emperors' truculent whims. The Emperor Claudius, for example, dissatisfied with how the stage machinery worked, ordered the stage mechanics responsible to fight in the arena. One day when there was a shortage of condemned criminals, the Emperor Caligula commanded that a whole section of the crowd be seized and thrown to the wild beasts instead. Isolated incidents, but enough to intensify the excitement of those who attended. Imperial legitimacy was reinforced by terror.

As for animals, their sheer variety symbolised the extent of Roman power and left vivid traces in Roman art. In 169 BC, sixty-three African lions and leopards, forty bears and several elephants were hunted down in a single show. New species were gradually introduced to Roman spectators (tigers, crocodiles, giraffes, lynxes, rhinoceros, ostriches, hippopotami) and killed for

their pleasure. Not for Romans the tame viewing of caged animals in a zoo. Wild beasts were set to tear criminals to pieces as public lesson in pain and death. Sometimes, elaborate sets and theatrical backdrops were prepared in which, as a climax, a criminal was devoured limb by limb. Such spectacular punishments, common enough in pre-industrial states, helped reconstitute sovereign power. The deviant criminal was punished; law and order were re-established.

The labour and organisation required to capture so many animals and to deliver them alive to Rome must have been enormous. Even if wild animals were more plentiful then than now, single shows with one hundred, four hundred or six hundred lions, plus other animals, seem amazing. By contrast, after Roman times, no hippopotamus was seen in Europe until one was brought to London by steamship in 1850. It took a whole regiment of Egyptian soldiers to capture it, and involved a five month journey to bring it from the White Nile to Cairo. And yet the Emperor Commodus, a dead-shot with spear and bow, himself killed five hippos, two elephants, a rhinoceros and a giraffe, in one show lasting two days. On another occasion he killed 100 lions and bears in a single morning show, from safe walkways specially constructed across the arena. It was, a contemporary remarked, 'a better demonstration of accuracy than of courage'. The slaughter of exotic animals in the emperor's presence, and exceptionally by the emperor himself or by his palace guards, was a spectacular dramatisation of the emperor's formidable power: immediate, bloody and symbolic.

Gladiatorial shows also provided an arena for popular participation in politics. Cicero explicitly recognised this towards the end of the Republic: 'the judgement and wishes of the Roman people about public affairs can be most clearly expressed in three places: public assemblies, elections, and at plays or gladiatorial shows'. He challenged a political opponent: 'Give yourself to the people. Entrust yourself to the Games. Are you terrified of not being applauded?' His comments underline the fact that the crowd had the important option of giving or of witholding applause, of hissing or of being silent.

Under the emperors, as citizens' rights to engage in politics diminished, gladiatorial shows and games provided

2. GREECE AND ROME

repeated opportunities for the dramatic confrontation of rulers and ruled. Rome was unique among large historical empires in allowing, indeed in expecting, these regular meetings between emperors and the massed populace of the capital, collected together in a single crowd. To be sure, emperors could mostly stage-manage their own appearance and reception. They gave extravagant shows. They threw gifts to the crowd – small marked wooden balls (called *missilia*) which could be exchanged for various luxuries. They occasionally planted their own claques in the crowd.

Mostly, emperors received standing ovations and ritual acclamations. The Games at Rome provided a stage for the emperor to display his majesty – luxurious ostentation in procession, accessibility to humble petitioners, generosity to the crowd, human involvement in the contests themselves, graciousness or arrogance towards the assembled aristocrats, clemency or cruelty to the vanquished. When a gladiator fell, the crowd would shout for mercy or dispatch. The emperor might be swayed by their shouts or gestures, but he alone, the final arbiter, decided who was to live or die. When the emperor entered the amphitheatre, or decided the fate of a fallen gladiator by the movement of his thumb, at that moment he had 50,000 courtiers. He knew that he was *Cæsar Imperator*, Foremost of Men.

Things did not always go the way the emperor wanted. Sometimes, the crowd objected, for example to the high price of wheat, or demanded the execution of an unpopular official or a reduction in taxes. Caligula once reacted angrily and sent soldiers into the crowd with orders to execute summarily anyone seen shouting. Understandably, the crowd grew silent, though sullen. But the emperor's increased unpopularity encouraged his assassins to act. Dio, senator and historian, was present at another popular demonstration in the Circus in AD 195. He was amazed that the huge crowd (the Circus held up to 200,000 people) strung out along the track, shouted for an end to civil war 'like a well-trained choir'.

Dio also recounted how with his own eyes he saw the Emperor Commodus cut off the head of an ostrich as a sacrifice in the arena then walk towards the congregated senators whom he hated, with the sacrificial knife in one hand and the severed head of the bird in the other,

(Above) Clay lamp showing gladiators' weapons. (Right) A clay pot depicting gladiators fighting.

clearly indicating, so Dio thought, that it was the senators' necks which he really wanted. Years later, Dio recalled how he had kept himself from laughing (out of anxiety, presumably) by chewing desperately on a laurel leaf which he plucked from the garland on his head.

Consider how the spectators in the amphitheatre sat: the emperor in his gilded box, surrounded by his family; senators and knights each had special seats and came properly dressed in their distinctive purple-bordered togas. Soldiers were separated from civilians. Even ordinary citizens had to wear the heavy white woollen toga, the formal dress of a Roman citizen, and sandals, if they wanted to sit in the bottom two main tiers of seats. Married men sat separately from bachelors, boys sat in a separate block, with their teachers in the next block. Women, and the very poorest men dressed in the drab grey cloth associated with mourning, could sit or stand only in the top tier of the amphitheatre. Priests and Vestal Virgins (honorary men) had reserved seats at the front. The correct dress and segregation of ranks underlined the formal ritual elements in the occasion, just as the steeply banked seats reflected the steep stratification of Roman society. It mattered where you sat, and where you were seen to be sitting.

Gladiatorial shows were political theatre. The dramatic performance took place, not only in the arena, but between different sections of the audience. Their interaction should be included in any thorough account of the Roman constitution. The amphitheatre was the

Roman crowd's parliament. Games are usually omitted from political histories, simply because in our own society, mass spectator sports count as leisure. But the Romans themselves realised that metropolitan control involved 'bread and circuses'. 'The Roman people', wrote Marcus Aurelius' tutor Fronto, 'is held together by two forces: wheat doles and public shows'.

Enthusiastic interest in gladiatorial shows occasionally spilled over into a desire to perform in the arena. Two emperors were not content to be spectators-in-chief. They wanted to be prize performers as well. Nero's histrionic ambitions and success as musician and actor were notorious. He also prided himself on his abilities as a charioteer. Commodus performed as a gladiator in the amphitheatre, though admittedly only in preliminary bouts with blunted weapons. He won all his fights and charged the imperial treasury a million sesterces for each appearance (enough to feed a thousand families for a year). Eventually, he was assassinated when he was planning to be inaugurated as consul (in AD 193), dressed as a gladiator.

Commodus' gladiatorial exploits were an idiosyncratic expression of a culture obsessed with fighting, bloodshed ostentation and competition. But at least seven other emperors practised as gladiators, and fought in gladiatorial contests. And so did Roman senators and knights. Attempts were made to stop them by law; but the laws were evaded.

Roman writers tried to explain away these senators' and knights' outrageous

Fresco showing riots between men of Pompeii and Nuceria in and around the amphitheatre in AD 59.

hope that the baby would imbibe a gladiator's strength and courage.

The victorious gladiator, or at least his image, was sexually attractive. Graffiti from the plastered walls of Pompeii carry the message:

Celadus [a stage name, meaning Crowd's Roar], thrice victor and thrice crowned, the young girls' heart-throb, and Crescens the Netter of young girls by night.

The ephemera of AD 79 have been preserved by volcanic ash. Even the defeated gladiator had something sexually portentous about him. It was customary, so it is reported, for a new Roman bride to have her hair parted with a spear, at best one which had been dipped in the body of a defeated and killed gladiator.

The Latin word for sword – *gladius* – was vulgarly used to mean penis. Several artefacts also suggest this association. A small bronze figurine from Pompeii depicts a cruel-looking gladiator fighting off with his sword a dog-like wild-beast which grows out of his erect and elongated penis. Five bells hang down from various parts of his body and a hook is attached to the gladiator's head, so that the whole ensemble could hang as a bell in a doorway. Interpretation must be speculative. But this evidence suggests that there was a close link, in some Roman minds, between gladiatorial fighting and sexuality. And it seems as though gladiatoral bravery for some Roman men represented an attractive yet dangerous, almost threatening, macho masculinity.

Gladiators attracted women, even though most of them were slaves. Even if they were free or noble by origin, they were in some sense contaminated by their close contact with death. Like suicides, gladiators were in some places excluded from normal burial grounds. Perhaps their dangerous ambiguity was part of their sexual attraction. They were, according to the Christian Tertullian, both loved and despised: 'men give them their souls, women their bodies too'. Gladiators were 'both glorified and degraded'.

In a vicious satire, the poet Juvenal ridiculed a senator's wife, Eppia, who had eloped to Egypt with her favourite swordsman:

behaviour by calling them morally degenerate, forced into the arena by wicked emperors or their own profligacy. This explanation is clearly inadequate, even though it is difficult to find one which is much better. A significant part of the Roman aristocracy, even under the emperors, was still dedicated to military prowess: all generals were senators; all senior officers were senators or knights. Combat in the arena gave aristocrats a chance to display their fighting skill and courage. In spite of the opprobrium and at the risk of death, it was their last chance to play soldiers in front of a large audience.

Gladiators were glamour figures, culture heroes. The probable life-span of each gladiator was short. Each successive victory brought further risk of defeat and death. But for the moment, we are more concerned with image than with reality. Modern pop-stars and athletes have only a short exposure to full-glare publicity. Most of them fade rapidly from being household names into obscurity, fossilised in the memory of each generation of adolescent enthusiasts. The transience of the fame of each does not diminish their collective importance.

So too with Roman gladiators. Their portraits were often painted. Whole walls in public porticos were sometimes covered with life-size portraits of all the gladiators in a particular show. The actual events were magnified beforehand by expectation and afterwards by memory. Street advertisements stimulated excitement and anticipation. Hundreds of Roman artefacts – sculptures, figurines, lamps, glasses – picture gladiatorial fights and wild-beast shows. In conversation and in daily life, chariot-races and gladiatorial fights were all the rage. 'When you enter the lecture halls', wrote Tacitus, 'what else do you hear the young men talking about?' Even a baby's nursing bottle, made of clay and found at Pompeii, was stamped with the figure of a gladiator. It symbolised the

Gladiator's dress helmet found at Herculaneum.

pared. One would have imagined that these were the pirates. The trumpets sounded their foreboding notes; stretchers for the dead were brought on, a funeral parade before death. Everywhere I could see wounds, groans, blood, danger . . .

He went on to describe his thoughts, his memories in the moments when he faced death, before he was dramatically and conveniently rescued by a friend. That was fiction. In real life gladiators died.

Why did Romans popularise fights to the death between armed gladiators? Why did they encourage the public slaughter of unarmed criminals? What was it which transformed men who were timid and peaceable enough in private, as Tertullian put it, and made them shout gleefully for the merciless destruction of their fellow men? Part of the answer may lie in the simple development of a tradition, which fed on itself and its own success. Men liked blood

Bronze tintinnabulum of a gladiator from Pompeii.

What was the youthful charm that so fired Eppia? What hooked her? What did she see in him to make her put up with being called 'The Gladiator's Moll'? Her poppet, her Sergius, was no chicken, with a dud arm that prompted hope of early retirement. Besides, his face looked a proper mess, helmet scarred, a great wart on his nose, an unpleasant discharge always trickling from one eye. But he was a Gladiator. That word makes the whole breed seem handsome, and made her prefer him to her children and country, her sister and husband. Steel is what they fall in love with.

Satire certainly, and exaggerated, but pointless unless it was also based to some extent in reality. Modern excavators, working in the armoury of the gladiatorial barracks in Pompeii found eighteen skeletons in two rooms, presumably of gladiators caught there in an ash storm; they included only one woman, who was wearing rich gold jewellery, and a necklace set with emeralds. Occasionally, women's attachment to gladiatorial combat went further. They fought in the arena themselves. In the storeroom of the British Museum, for example, there is a small stone relief, depicting two

female gladiators, one with breast bare, called Amazon and Achillia. Some of these female gladiators were free women of high status.

Behind the brave façade and the hope of glory, there lurked the fear of death. 'Those about to die salute you, Emperor'. Only one account survives of what it was like from the gladiator's point of view. It is from a rhetorical exercise. The story is told by a rich young man who had been captured by pirates and was then sold on as a slave to a gladiatorial trainer:

And so the day arrived. Already the populace had gathered for the spectacle of our punishment, and the bodies of those about to die had their own death-parade across the arena. The presenter of the shows, who hoped to gain favour with our blood, took his seat . . . Although no one knew my birth, my fortune, my family, one fact made some people pity me; I seemed unfairly matched. I was destined to be a certain victim in the sand . . . All around I could hear the instruments of death: a sword being sharpened, iron plates being heated in a fire [to stop fighters retreating and to prove that they were not faking death], birch-rods and whips were pre-

Terracotta relief of a gladiatorial circus.

and cried out for more. Part of the answer may also lie in the social psychology of the crowd, which relieved individuals of responsbility for their actions, and in the psychological mechanisms by which some spectators identified more easily with the victory of the aggressor than with the sufferings of the vanquished. Slavery and the steep stratification of society must also have contributed. Slaves were at the mercy of their owners. Those who were destroyed for public edification and entertainment were considered worthless, as non-persons; or, like Christian martyrs, they were considered social outcasts, and tortured as one Christian martyr put it 'as if we no longer existed'. The brutalisation of the spectators fed on the dehumanisation of the victims.

Rome was a cruel society. Brutality was built into its culture in private life, as well as in public shows. The tone was set by military discipline and by slavery. The state had no legal monopoly of capital punishment until the second century AD. Before then, a master could crucify his slaves publicly if he wished. Seneca recorded from his own observations the various ways in which crucifixions were carried out, in order to increase pain. At private dinner-parties, rich Romans regularly presented two or three pairs of gladiators: 'when they have finished dining and are filled with drink', wrote a critic in the time of Augustus, 'they call in the gladiators. As soon as one has his throat cut, the diners applaud with delight'. It is worth stressing that we are dealing here not with individual sadistic psycho-pathology, but with a deep cultural difference. Roman commitment to cruelty presents us with a cultural gap which it is difficult to cross.

Popular gladiatorial shows were a by-product of war, discipline and death. For centuries, Rome had been devoted to war and to the mass participation of citizens in battle. They won their huge empire by discipline and control. Public executions were a gruesome reminder to non-combatants, citizens, subjects and slaves, that vengeance would be exacted if they rebelled or betrayed their country. The arena provided a living enactment of the hell portrayed by Christian preachers. Public punishment ritually re-established the moral and political order. The power of the state was dramatically reconfirmed.

When long-term peace came to the heartlands of the empire, after 31 BC, militaristic traditions were preserved at Rome in the domesticated battlefield of the amphitheatre. War had been converted into a game, a drama repeatedly replayed, of cruelty, violence, blood and death. But order still needed to be preserved. The fear of death still had to be assuaged by ritual. In a city as large as Rome, with a population of close on a million by the end of the last century BC, without an adequate police force, disorder always threatened.

Gladiatorial shows and public executions reaffirmed the moral order, by the sacrifice of human victims – slaves, gladiators, condemned criminals or impious Christians. Enthusiastic participation, by spectators rich and poor, raised and then released collective tensions, in a society which traditionally idealised impassivity. Gladiatorial shows provided a psychic and political safety valve for the metropolitan population. Politically, emperors risked occasional conflict, but the populace could usually be diverted or fobbed off. The crowd lacked the coherence of a rebellious political ideology. By and large, it found its satisfaction in cheering its support of established order. At the psychological level, gladiatorial shows provided a stage for shared violence and tragedy. Each show reassured spectators that they had yet again survived disaster. Whatever happened in the arena, the spectators were on the winning side. 'They found comfort for death' wrote Tertullian with typical insight, 'in murder'.

FOR FURTHER READING:
An expanded version of this article with references appears in K. Hopkins, *Death and renewal, Sociological Studies in Roman History*, Volume 2 (Cambridge University Press, May 1983, £19.50). The most extensive review of the evidence on gladiatorial games is by L. Friedlaender, *Roman Life and Manners, Volume 2 with references in Volume 4 (London, 1913)*. A more accessible and readable account is given by M. Grant, *Gladiators*, (Weidenfeld and Nicolson, 1976). On the methods used here, see C. Geertz, *The Interpretation of Cultures* (Weidenfeld and Nicolson, 1973).

The Judeo-Christian Heritage

Western civilization took root in the Graeco-Roman world but, notwithstanding all we owe to the classical ideal, we are no less indebted to the Judeo-Christian tradition. If we derive humanism and materialism, philosophy and science, from the former, we derive our God and our forms of worship from the latter. Of course, it is difficult (and perhaps misguided) to separate these traditions, for the Judeo-Christian heritage comes to us through a Hellenistic filter.

On the political surface, the history of the Jews seems similar to that of other small kingdoms of the Near East, caught as they were between such powerful neighbors as the Babylonians, Assyrians, and Persians. Yet of all the peoples of that time and place, only the Jews have had a lasting influence. What appears to differentiate the Jews from all the rest, writes Crane Brinton, is "the will to persist, to be themselves, to be a people." The appearance of Israel on the map of the modern world two thousand years after the Romans destroyed the Jewish client-state is a testimonial to the spirit described by Brinton.

The legacy of the Jews is a great one. It includes the rich literary traditions found in their sacred texts; their unique view of history, which is at once linear and, based as it is on the Covenant idea, miraculous (God intervenes in history to punish his Chosen People); a messianic impulse that gave rise to Christianity and other cults; the elemental morality of the Ten Commandments and the higher morality of the prophets; and monotheism, the worship of their unique God, Yahweh.

A brief comparison of Yahweh and the Greek god Zeus illustrates the originality of the Jewish conception. Both gods began as warrior deities of tribal cultures. But as Zeus evolved he was concerned chiefly with Olympian rather than human affairs. Yahweh, on the other hand, was more purposeful and had few interests except his people. And unlike Zeus, who was in and of the universe, Yahweh was the creator of the universe. As Herbert Muller writes of Yahweh, "Once he had been endowed with benevolent purposes, and taught to concern himself with all mankind, he could become, as he did, the God of Judaism, Christianity, and Mohammedanism." The arti-

cle by Jenny Morris, "Jews and Judaism in the Ancient World," surveys relations among Jews, Greeks, and Romans.

Christianity bears the stamp of Judaism. Christ was a Jew. For his early followers, all of them Jews, he satisfied the powerful messianic impulse latent in Judaism. The New Testament recounts the growth and spread of Christianity from an obscure Jewish sect in Palestine to a new religion with wide appeal in the Roman world. Yet the central figure in this great drama remains shrouded in mystery, for there is a dearth of firsthand materials. The Gospels, our greatest and most reliable source, leave great gaps in their account of the life of Jesus. Nevertheless, they remain a profound record of early Christian faith, which is evident in "New Finds Cast Fresh Light on the Bible" and "Who Was Jesus?"

As it split away from Judaism, Christianity took on a new dimension: the promise of private salvation by sacramental means. In addition, according to "Who Was St. Peter?" St. Peter and St. Paul took the lead in spreading the faith to Gentiles. As it took hold in the Mediterranean, Christianity absorbed various Hellenistic elements. Among those trained in Greek learning, Stoicism and Platonism prepared the way for an amalgamation of classical philosophy and Christianity. Increasingly the personal God of the Jews and Christians became the abstract God of the Greek philosophers. Biblical texts were given symbolic meanings that might have confounded an earlier, simpler generation of Christians. Perhaps it was its combination of simple faith and abstract theology that explains the broad appeal of Christianity in the later Roman world.

Looking Ahead: Challenge Questions

How does the history of the Jews intersect with the main stages of Western civilization?

Describe the relationship between the Jews, Greeks, and Romans.

What evidence survives from biblical times, and how reliable is it?

On what evidence does the Church credit Peter with being the first Pope?

JEWS & JUDAISM IN THE ANCIENT WORLD

Jenny Morris

It was nearly a serious tumble – more serious than he anticipated. There were six in his party, all Hebrew gentlemen of position and intelligence, such as may be seen in these days filling a first-class carriage in the Cairo express on their way up to interview the government. In those days the Government was not at Cairo but at Rome, and the six gentlemen were on their way to interview the Emperor Caligula.

THESE ARE THE OPENING LINES of an essay by the novelist E. M. Forster, entitled 'Philo's Little Trip'. Forster's rather frivolous reconstruction of the Jewish deputation to Rome in 39 AD was based on Philo's own far more impassioned version of the mission which he led, *The Embassy to Gaius*. In another treatise, *Against Flaccus*, Philo describes the antecedents to the mission to Caligula to gain redress; Alexandrian Jews and the Graeco-Egyptian élite of the city had come into open conflict in the late 30s when the anti-semitic element in the Greek city gained the support – or at least the connivance – of the Roman prefect Flaccus. In the *Embassy* (the narrative of which is corroborated, in the main, by Josephus) Philo tells how Gaius demanded worship as a god, how the Jews (alone of his subjects) refused him such honours, and how the anti-semites of Alexandria exploited Caligula's annoyance with the Jewish people,

provoking further antagonism, and open violence, by introducing statues of the divine emperor into the synagogues. According to the Second Commandment, of course, and everything implied by Jewish monotheism and its an-iconic prescriptions, the Jews were to worship Yahweh and Yahweh alone. We can assume that Philo owed his position as leader of the deputation to Rome to his status as a member of a well-known and affluent family, and possibly also an official of some sort in the Jewish community of the city; his reputation to posterity rests on the vast corpus of treatises in which he endeavours to reconcile Greek culture with Jewish religious philosophy.

As a devout Jew, then, but a Jew with ample respect for Graeco-Roman culture, Philo was fitted to serve as a mediator between Jews, Greeks and Romans; his purpose was foiled by the intransigence and scorn of the mad emperor. Philo records, with patent bitterness and disillusionment, that the interview between the Jewish ambassadors and the Roman emperor was a charade. No audience was granted, but Caligula permitted the humiliated Jewish representatives to trail behind him while he toured some of his estate; they tried to put their case while the emperor discussed building projects with his staff, interjecting the occasional flippant remark to the Jews on the

nature of their faith and his grounds for offence. Dismissing them, Caligula left, as his Parthian shot, the remark 'they seem to me to be people unfortunate rather than wicked and to be foolish in refusing to believe that I have got the nature of a god'.

Setting the episode in the perspective of Jewish history, Forster concludes with a somewhat backhanded assertion of Jewish resilience:

> Yet did it signify – signify in the long run? The history of the Chosen People is full of such contretemps, but they survive and thrive. Six hundred years later, when Amr took the city [Alexandria], he found 40,000 Jews there. And look at them in the railway carriage now. Their faces are anxious and eloquent of past rebuffs. But they are travelling First.

Events after Forster wrote – the Holocaust, the foundation of the State of Israel, and the Middle Eastern War – have endowed the history of relations between Jews and gentiles with poignant relevance to the present. We are more inclined than Forster to attach significance to the nexus of conflict, incomprehension and intolerance which characterise Graeco-Roman relations with the Jews. The story of Philo's meeting with the mad Roman emperor captures the atmosphere of relations between Jews and pagans throughout much of antiquity. Anti-semitism, in the

From *History Today*, October 1981. Reproduced by kind permission of History Today, Ltd., 83-84 Berwick Street, London W1V 3PJ England.

general sense of prejudice against Jews as Jews, often erupting in outright persecution, appears to ante-date Christianity and the Christian grievance against the Jews by several centuries. But this label 'anti-semitism' can mislead; we should not diagnose the conflicts between Greeks or Romans and Jews in terms of more recent manifestations of hostility between Jews and gentiles. The responses of Greeks and Romans, in various social and political relationships with the Jews, can be instructive without being assimilated to the familiar categories of medieval or modern anti-semitism. Racial prejudice does not seem to have motivated the Greek and Roman failure to come to terms with Jewish subjects. Nor can we postulate economic grounds for resentment against Jews resident in Greek or Roman communities; papyri and literary evidence from Alexandria and Rome have now discredited the claim that the Jews held a monopoly over lucrative business deals: in fact the Jews would appear to have been among the poor residents in both cities. In scrutinising the sources of Greek and Roman attitudes to the Jews in the pre-Christian era, we are investigating behaviour patterns disturbingly similar to manifestations of anti-semitism nearer home; but the attitudes *underlying* this behaviour must not be conflated with the anti-semitic psychology which infected medieval Christendom or Hitler's Third Reich.

Considering the Graeco-Roman response to Judaism, in an attempt to derive lessons from the past, can, therefore, result in a distortion of the encounter between Jews and pagans. There is, however, an important reason for studying the encounter: the pivotal position in our cultural heritage occupied by the three civilisations concerned. The triple impact of Athens, Rome and Jerusalem shaped the legacy of the West. The achievements of the Greeks, in spiritual and material terms, were absorbed, assimilated and propagated by the Romans; they defeated the Greek mainland, and later the Hellenistic kingdoms, but (to paraphrase Horace) were themselves vanquished in the cultural field by their Greek captives. The Romans, of course, had their own gifts – notably administrative competence and legal expertise – and their culture had its own ethos. How did it come about that Christianity – a local Judaean *religio* in Roman eyes – assumed the status of orthodoxy in the West,

rather than, say, Mithraism, or the cult of Isis, or even traditional Roman paganism? Why, moreover, is European literature as rich in Biblical allusion (Jewish as well as Christian) as it is in Greek and Roman mythology?

The answer, at its simplest, is that during the fourth century AD, a Roman emperor was converted to Christianity. Constantine's adoption of Christianity was not, of course, the first occasion on which Graeco-Roman paganism and Judaism (of which Christianity was initially a sectarian offshoot) had been united. Nor did the entire Roman Empire automatically and irrevocably become Christian. But Christianity did ultimately prevail, and while the old Rome fell to the barbarian invaders soon afterwards (a sequence of events in which Gibbon detected a causal relation), Constantinople (Byzantium) remained as the new Rome until the fifteenth century: as the capital of the Christian Byzantine Empire it acted as the transmitter of both Classical learning and monotheistic faith.

By Constantine's time, the umbilical cord which linked Christianity to Judaism had long since been severed: Paul had opened the Christian community to gentiles, and the rabbis, for their part, has stressed Hebrew purism. (The emperor Julian even regarded Judaism as an ally with paganism, in his efforts to destroy the Church). But the Christians acknowledged that the historical and doctrinal dimensions of their faith were built upon the Old Testament – the Jewish Torah. In fact the Church Fathers had more difficulty in coming to terms with Greek and Roman literatures and its attractions. Tertullian cried out 'What has Athens to do with Jerusalem?', implying that pagan culture was incompatible with the education of a Christian. Others justified their continued study of Greek and Roman classics by asserting that the pagan authors had filched their ideas from Jewish thinkers. 'What is Plato', asked Numenius, 'but Moses speaking Greek?'

The notion that Graeco-Roman culture was derivative and parasitic upon Jewish wisdom was borrowed by the Church from Jewish apologists of the pre-Christian era. Josephus, for example, devoted much of his polemical treatise *Against Apion* to proving the priority of Jewish thought over Greek. His arguments are symptomatic of the tense relationship between Jews and

their Graeco-Roman contemporaries. Jewish writers like Philo and Josephus had discovered enough that they considered admirable in Hellenistic culture to wish to present their own culture in terms which would persuade disdainful gentiles that 'barbarians' could make contributions to civilisation. The encounter between Judaism and Hellenism had begun some three centuries before Josephus and Philo, when Alexander's conquest opened up the East to Greek influence. On the Jewish side, the encounter was marked by both resistance and assimilation; the Greeks, as we shall see, bothered very little with Judaism until the spread of Christianity.

It was common, in the last century, to talk of Judaism and Hellenism as two contrasting components in modern spiritual life. Matthew Arnold wrote an essay entitled 'Hebraism and Hellenism', in which he summarised the polarisation in the following terms: 'The uppermost idea with Hellenism is to see things as they really are; the uppermost idea with Hebraism is conduct and obedience.' He intended the dichotomy to be substantive, not merely terminological, for he continued: 'Hellenism is of Indo-European growth, Hebraism is of Semitic growth; and we English, a nation of Indo-European stock, seem to belong naturally to the movement of Hellenism.'

The Jewish historian Heinrich Graetz reached a different conclusion, but with a similar conviction in the existence of an ancient opposition between Jewish and Graeco-Roman world-views: 'Whereas the Latin race is more permeated with the spirit of Hellenism, the Anglo-Saxon race is penetrated with the Biblical/Judaic spirit, because its mind is more directed to truth than to beauty.'

The polarisation is unhistorical. Twentieth-century scholarship has revealed that the Judaism which gave rise to Christianity (and even, to a surprising degree, rabbinic Judaism, which persisted independently up to the present) was considerably modified by its contact with Hellenism. What is curious, and what prompts us to look more closely at circumstances in which Greeks and Romans encountered the Jews in antiquity, is that the process of acculturation appears to have been very much a one-way process; Jews imbibed Hellenistic culture, whilst the Greeks and Romans maintained, on the whole, a stolid distance from Jewish wisdom.

We can isolate two levels at which the

Graeco-Roman world came into confrontation with Jews and Judaism in the pre-Christian era. First, there were the violent clashes exemplified, at the level of civic strife, by the outbreak of Greek-Jewish hostility which occasioned Philo's fruitless journey to Rome. On an even more serious scale were the nationalistic rebellions of the Jews which culminated, in 66-70 and in 132-5 AD, in full-scale wars with Rome. As a consequence of the first Jewish War, the Temple was destroyed and Judaism outlawed to all intents and purposes. The rabbis' efforts to preserve and consolidate their faith in the face of oppression paradoxically provided the mainspring of that era of Jewish creativity and productivity which is now known as Classical Judaism. In 115-7 a revolt amongst Diaspora Jews in Cyrenaica, which rapidly spread to Egypt, was crushed with such force by Roman legions that the once-flourishing Egyptian Diaspora was virtually annihilated. The continuity of an affluent Jewish lifestyle, which Forster thought he saw in Egypt, was illusory.

It is fairly clear that on all these occasions the Roman authorities acted upon motives similar to those which led them to crush any imperial subjects provoking a nationalistic rebellion against Roman dominion. Conflict was often precipitated, on the Jewish side, by grievances against Roman insensibility to Jewish religious scruples, but there is little to substantiate the claim that Rome sent out the legions through a racial or ideological objection to Judaism as such. One violent confrontation between the Jews and their overlords which *may* have been instigated by pagan dislike of Judaism, is the persecution by Antiochus IV Epiphanes in BC 167. As Seleucid monarch of Syria, Antiochus attempted, for reasons which remain obscure, to replace the worship of Yahweh by the worship of Zeus at the Temple of Jerusalem. The revolt which this provoked – The Maccabean revolt – won independence for the Jews for the following century – until the intervention of Rome; its success is still celebrated by Jews at the festival of Hannukah. Some part of the violation of the Temple was played by a Hellenising element within Jewish society, the existence of which testifies to the infiltration of Greek culture among the Jews during the century and a half of Greek rule. The success of the Maccabean revolt did not put an end to this process of accultura-

tion, although it did arrest the erosion of Jewish culture.

Civil strife between Jews and pagans cannot be attributed to official Greek or Roman policy. It must be put down to unsanctioned antagonisms at the level of popular sentiment. It is here that we come to the second of the two levels of interaction between the Graeco-Roman world and the Jews. Most cases of civil strife date from the early Roman period. They involve the Greek intelligentsia of Alexandria, whose principal pretext for inciting the Jews appears to have been their objection to the Jews' claims to citizenship in Alexandria. Alexandrian Jews enjoyed a long halcyon period of civic equality with the Greeks under the Ptolemies, *de facto* if not *de iure*. When the Romans replaced the Ptolemies as governors of Egypt, Greek citizen status became a *sine qua non* for admission to Roman citizenship and all the rights and privileges which that entailed. What is more, the Romans imposed a system of taxation according to which Greeks, and Greeks alone, were entitled to exemption. The leaders of the Alexandrian *gymnasium*, which controlled admission to the citizen roll, became the ringleaders of the disturbances of the 30s AD. Philo will have been one of the last Jews to achieve admission to the *gymnasium* (where he received his Greek education). The Alexandrian troubles were by no means condoned by Rome. (Flaccus was acting on his own initiative in supporting the anti-semites, not on orders from Rome.) The Emperor Claudius, whose accession was timely for the Jews, sent a stern letter to the Alexandrians warning the Greeks of sanctions in the event of further harrassment of the Jews; but he also disposed summarily of the Jews' claims to citizenship, urging the Jews to behave graciously towards their hosts, in 'a city not their own'.

We cannot identify, as a prime motive for this sort of anti-semitism, resentment against the Jews for their favoured position vis-à-vis the ruling power. Jews were certainly enlisted by the Ptolemies to assist them in their struggle to maintain control over the Egyptians. But the leading opponents of the Jews in Egypt were Alexandrians, who were Greek, not Egyptian, in outlook if not by birth. The Jews were certainly accorded specific exemptions and concessions by Augustus (and some, though not all, of his successors); but these were offered in recognition of the Jews' religious distinctiveness, and were measures of prac-

tical import (such as permission t observe the Sabbath) not privilege Indeed if any subjects of Rome wer privileged, it was the Greeks themselve

For an explanation of the Alexandria troubles of the 30s AD we should loo beyond the Greeks' insistence on exclud ing Jews from citizenship, and thei protests against Jewish 'privileges', an consider the evidence for pre-existin sentiments of distrust and bad feeling Here we must turn to the literary evi dence for Greek and Roman sentimen towards the Jews. The earliest refer ences to the Jews, in Greek ethnographi cal literature of the early Hellenist period, are favourable, and present th Jews as a race of sages, rather like th Indian brahmins (to whom they wer sometimes thought to be related) Theophrastus, for example, called th Jews philosophers. Several writers ar respectful towards Jewish monotheism Monotheism was by no means unknow among Greek and Roman thinker Where the Jews differed from suc people, however, was in the Jewis insistence on the application o monotheistic principles to civic religio observance. The Jews were disposed t enforce their belief in one god in the daily religious conduct, because the possessed a religious mythology wit authenticising scriptures whic demanded monotheism. A Greek Roman philosopher could acknowledg monotheism according to philosophic speculation, but continue to act accor ing to the polytheistic framework of h traditional religious life.

Towards the end of the Hellenist period, through into the Roman er Greek and Roman references to Jev and Judaism become markedly mo hostile. A gamut of stock accusation and criticisms are found in the works many Greek and Latin authors, inclu ing Posidonius, Cicero, Juvenal, Tacit and Martial, as well as lesser-know antagonists, whose works Josephus s out to refute in his polemical treati *Against Apion*.

Caligula's jibes at Philo's deputati are fairly representative of the sort objections levelled against the Jews. T Jews, he shouted, were 'god-hater Although Caligula's main grievance w that the Jews refused to worship *him*, t charge of atheism is listed amongst t Jews' alleged crimes by several autho Apion, Josephus' main butt and t most dangerous of the Alexandri anti-semites, summed up the Graec

Roman response to Jewish religious exclusiveness when he asked 'If they are citizens, why don't the Jews worship the same gods as the citizens?' To demonstrate allegiance to the régime, in a Greek city, or under the Roman Empire, meant that one should show at least a token obeisance to the presiding deities, be they local gods or remote divine emperors. This the Jews would not do, and their offence was taken to be political as well as religious. They attempted to pacify Caligula, as they had pacified the Ptolemies, by sacrificing on his behalf – *for* him, rather than *to* him; but Caligula regarded this as evasion.

'Why do you refuse to eat pork?' taunted the emperor, and his question was greeted by peals of mirth from the attending Greeks. Jewish dietary scruples and various other features of the religious injunctions which pervaded the Jews' daily lives attracted attention and ridicule. Diet, Sabbath observance and so on made the Jew conspicuous; what was worse, they could make him appear stand-offish. Charges of separatism abound in Greek and Roman critiques of Judaism. Suspicion encouraged the propagation of legends purporting to account for various aspects of Jewish life. Apion gave the following facetious aetiology of the Jewish Sabbath:

> After six days' march, the Jews developed tumours in the groin, and that was why, after safely reaching the country now called Judaea, they rested on the seventh day, and called that day *sabbaton*, preserving the Egyptian terminology; for disease of the groin in Egypt is called sabbatosis.

Other Greek writers maintained that the Jews worshipped an ass in the Holy of Holies. Apion, again, is the source of the story that the Jews practised cannibalism:

> They would kidnap a foreigner, fatten him up for a year, and then convey him to a wood, where they slew him, sacrificed his body with their customary ritual, partook of his flesh, and, while immolating the Greek swore an oath of hostility to the Greeks.

Most of the aspersions cast against the Jews by Greek and Roman writers are founded upon ignorance of Jewish life and belief. Perhaps the most flagrant example of this ignorance of Jewish history, is the assertion, by an unknown Greek author, that the Jewish scriptures were composed by 'a Hebrew woman Mōsō'. Josephus is forced to give lengthy refutations of a series of anti-semitic travesties of the Exodus story, according to which the Hebrews were a band of leprous criminals, whose expulsion from Egypt was completely justified. Apart from familiarity with the basic story-pattern of the Exodus, none of the authors of these versions of the Exodus story show any knowledge of the Jewish Holy Books. Direct knowledge of the Torah, even in the Greek translation (the Septuagint) cannot be attributed with certainty to a single Greek or Roman pagan writer.

It is this ignorance – indifference even – of the true nature of Jewish culture, which characterises Greek and Roman attitudes towards the Jews on virtually all occasions. At least as far as appreciation of foreign literature is concerned, both Greeks and Romans were culpably insular. (One cannot understand Judaism without reading the Torah.) For one thing, the Greeks remained monolingual, and the Romans limited themselves to bilingualism in Latin and Greek. Barbarians eager for acceptance by their Hellenistic overlords translated their national epics or scriptures into Greek, but the Greeks showed little interest. The Septuagint was available from the Ptolemaic period, but it was only read by Hellenised Jews. Macaulay marvelled at the Greek and Roman indifference to the Jewish Holy Book:

> To the literature of other nations [the Greeks] do not seem to have paid the slightest attention. The sacred books of the Hebrews, for example, books which, considered merely as human compositions are invaluable to the critic, the antiquarian, and the philosopher, seem to have been unnoticed by them.

One can point to exceptions to this rule: Herodotus, in the fifth century BC, wrote his *Histories* with the express purpose of 'putting on record the astonishing achievements of both our own people and of the barbarians'. But his impartial presentation of the barbarian slant is unusual; Aeschylus, in his *Persians*, presented the Persian defeat with patent *Schadenfreude*. Among the Romans, Tacitus described the 'noble savage' Arminius as a model for corrupt Romans to imitate; but Tacitus is among the most unsympathetic and the most ignorant where the Jews are concerned. More representative is Plutarch's enterprise in writing his *Parallel Lives*: heroes from the Greek and Roman pasts are set side-by-side; there is no room for barbarian heroes.

In the Hellenistic period, when the Greeks began to move beyond the horizons of the city-state, they regarded their presence in barbarian lands as a *mission civilitrice*, and imposed, as far as they were able, a form of cultural imperialism, the ideology of which was maintained by the Romans. The civilisations of the Persians, Egyptians, Carthaginians and Etruscans are recoverable in part, thanks to archaeology; but Greek and Roman insularity silenced their cultural legacy effectively for thousands of years. The Jews resisted the onslaught of Hellenistic culture, and survived the misunderstanding and hostility which was a product of Greek and Roman disdain for the barbarian. The problem of pre-Christian anti-semitism resolves itself into a wider issue of Greek and Roman chauvinism towards foreign cultures. 'The Greeks', wrote Macaulay, 'admired only themselves, and the Romans admired only themselves and the Greeks.'

NOTES FOR FURTHER READING
Menahem Stern (editor) *Greek and Latin Authors on Jews and Judaism*, Israel Academy of Sciences and Humanities (Jerusalem, 1976 and 1980); Victor Tcherikover, *Hellenistic Civilization and the Jews*, Atheneum (New York, 1975); E. Mary Smallwood, *The Jews Under Roman Rule*, (Brill, Leiden, 1976); J. P. V. D. Balsdon, *Romans and Aliens*, Duckworth (London, 1979); J. N. Sevenster, *The Roots of Pagan Anti-Semitism in the Ancient World*, (Brill, Leiden, 1975).

New Finds Cast Fresh Light on the Bible

A wave of archaeological discoveries is altering old ideas about the roots of Christianity and Judaism—and affirming that the Bible is more historically accurate than many scholars thought.

Those are two of the main conclusions emerging from two decades of intensive probing of the ruins and artifacts of the Middle East and elsewhere. Among recent confirmed or suspected discoveries: King Solomon's mines, ruins of the cities of Sodom and Gomorrah, an Ark of the Covenant used by ancient Israelites and evidence of a catastrophe that may explain the Red Sea miracles in the Book of Exodus.

Other scholars say they are uncovering scientific support for the Bible by taking a fresh look at long-known artifacts. In Italy, a team of researchers is preparing for further tests to date the Shroud of Turin, believed by some to be the burial cloth of Jesus. Already investigators have ruled out contentions that the linen's image of a crucified man was a medieval fake.

Not all the new finds back up a literal reading of the Bible, and some assertions have been widely criticized. Fragments of wood hailed in a film as a likely remnant of Noah's Ark have since been dated by a carbon-14 test at only about A.D. 700—long after the great flood described in the Bible.

Also dismissed as farfetched is the hit movie "Raiders of the Lost Ark," describing a fictional discovery of the original 3,500-year-old chest containing the stone tablets of the Ten Commandments. The oldest ark ever found in ancient Palestine, revealed by three American scholars in early August, is a ceremonial imitation dating back only to about A.D. 300.

Even so, many scholars agree that the bulk of research reveals what University of Chicago archaeologist Lawrence Stager calls "a solid kernel of historical accuracy in the Bible."

Some of the most striking results were reported by American and European scientists using Space Age instruments to examine the so-called holy shroud in Turin, Italy.

X-rays, ultraviolet beams and computer-enhanced photographs were focused on the cloth's ghostly human image, said to have been imprinted by Christ's body. The image seems to be of a bearded man with bloodlike stains matching the wounds reportedly received by Jesus—lashes on the back, thorn pricks on the head and punctures in the side, wrists and feet.

The researchers say preliminary findings have all but disproved their most skeptical theory—that the picture was painted by forgers in the Middle Ages. That's when the shroud first surfaced in Europe, supposedly brought from the Middle East by knights returning from the Crusades.

Painting was ruled out because microscopes revealed that, except for the so-called bloodstains, the color is only on the very tips of the fibers, rather than penetrating as it would be if applied by hand or brush.

Some of the scientists have suggested that the shroud's image might have been produced by contact with burial ointments. Swiss criminologist Max Frei says he found traces of a Biblical-era ointment made from a plant found only on an island near South Yemen.

Other experts have prompted supernatural speculations by observing that cloths in Jesus' time were washed in a soapwort compound that turns precisely the color of the shroud's image when exposed to a burst of radiant energy. Religious scholars suggest that such a phenomenon might have accompanied the Resurrection.

Shroud investigators say their next step is to get permission from Roman Catholic authorities for a carbon-14 test that can determine whether the fabric dates from the time of Christ. No test, they stress, can ever prove that the shroud actually covered Jesus' body. Nevertheless, says the team's spokesman, New Orleans computer analyst Kenneth Stevenson, "all the evidence to date supports authenticity."

Digging deeper. Discoveries such as these have helped prompt even more expeditions and research. This summer, dozens of professors are leading squads of volunteers to the Holy Land, where at least 60 sites are under excavation. At dusty tells—mounds of buried debris left by ancient settlements—diggers are uncovering ruins and artifacts scientists say may have a profound impact on views about the Bible.

Until recently, most scholars dismissed the Biblical cities of Sodom and Gomorrah as legendary. Now two highly regarded American archaeologists, Walter E. Rast and R. Thomas Schaub, believe they may have found the remains of those cities, plus the three other settlements referred to in Genesis as the "cities of the plain."

The ruins lie where the Bible indicates they would be—within a few miles of the Dead Sea. Moreover, at least three of the cities appear to have been destroyed by fire, which the Bible says was rained down by God in vengeance. The cities are estimated to have been destroyed about the same time, 2300-2400 B.C.

Rast and Schaub remain cautious in evaluating their discovery. But the journal *Biblical Archeologist* reports, "One cannot avoid the impression that the sites surveyed by them are the long lost 'cities of the plain.'"

Thousands of tablets. Welcoming the find is an Italian professor, Giovanni Pettinato, who recently came under fire for asserting that Sodom and Gomorrah were real. His contention is based on a cache of 17,000 cuneiform tablets uncovered in Syria in 1976. The tablets, found in ruins of the 4,500-year-old city of Ebla, initially were hailed by at least one expert as "the most important find ever made" in relation to the Bible.

According to Pettinato's translation, now disputed by some colleagues, the tablets record commercial transactions involving at least two previously unproven Biblical places—Sodom and Gomorrah.

Another newly translated tablet found elsewhere may shed light on the Bible's seemingly miraculous account of the Hebrews' exodus from Egypt. The historical document reportedly gives the Egyptian side of the story, describing how the Pharaoh allowed rebellious "Asiatic ... immigrants" to depart and how their "footsteps" were "swallowed" by a flood.

One significant variation is the date ascribed to the event—1477 B.C., about 200 years earlier than previous datings of the exodus. The translator, a prominent Johns Hopkins University Egyptologist, Hans Goedicke, notes that a catastrophic volcanic explosion wrecked the Mediterranean island now called Santorin at that time. He says the blast could have produced the Biblical pillar of fire and a tidal wave that inundated Pharaoh's troops.

Scholars say these discoveries, if they prove true, tend to discredit the view that the first two books of the Bible, Genesis and Exodus, contain little historical truth because they were handed down for centuries by word of mouth. Instead, the Rev. Carlo Martini, rector of the Pontifical Biblical Institute in Rome, says new evidence shows "the memories of the Hebrews, later written in the Bible, were very old and very historical."

Additional evidence has come from the U.S. Geological Survey, which believes it may have located the site of King Solomon's 3,000-year-old mines. The agency's scientists tested an abandoned gold mine in Saudi Arabia, littered with old stone tools and lying on a major trade route to Israel. They found it was rich enough to produce the 1,086 talents—31 metric tons—of gold that the Bible says were hauled to Jerusalem.

But other discoveries are proving unsettling for some believers. One such find is a series of inscriptions and pictures at a shrine in the Sinai desert, possibly including God with a female goddess. Prof. Ze'ev Meshel, an Israeli expert who deciphered some of the ancient Hebrew writing, reported in *Biblical Archaeology Review:* "Two of the pictures may even be Yahweh (Jehovah) and his consort—a blasphemous concept never before suggested by an archaeological discovery."

Further controversy has been generated by scholars working to translate early religious writings called the pseudepigrapha—at least four dozen religious texts that some scholars say were unfairly excluded from the Bible.

Conflicting views. The manuscripts, scattered in libraries around the world, were composed by Jewish and Christian writers around the time of the 200-year gap between the Old Testament, believed to have been concluded about 100 B.C., and the start of the New Testament about A.D. 100.

Some experts say the texts were left out mostly because a few of their teachings, such as elaborate angel worship, conflicted with the views of religious councils that put versions of the Bible together between the second and 16th centuries A.D.

James H. Charlesworth, a Duke University professor coordinating the project, says his team is getting reaction from "fundamentalist groups who really don't want anyone studying the Bible critically," as well as groups "saying this or that book should probably be put in the Bible."

Another revelation from extra-Biblical texts is that many Christian teachings weren't as radically original as previously believed. More evidence along those lines came with recent publication of the last of the Dead Sea Scrolls, lost and later recovered after its discovery in caves near Qumran, on the Israeli-occupied West Bank, in 1947.

The text shows that the authors, a tiny sect of Jews, preached an end to Old Testament practices of polygamy and divorce several generations before Jesus did. One of the scroll's translators, Prof. Jacob Milgrom of the University of California, says John the Baptist, Jesus' cousin, could have picked up these and other beliefs when he lived near Qumran. "Moreover, the Gospels tell us that Jesus spent three years in the wilderness," says Milgrom. "Where else but among like-minded people in Qumran?"

Some dramatic evidence. Several major discoveries have been made by accident.

That's what happened when Greek Orthodox monks recently tore down a wall of their ancient monastery, St. Catherine's, at the foot of Mount Sinai. Inside the wall, they found thousands of parchment and papyrus fragments, some containing Bible passages from A.D. 300. The most dramatic discovery: Eight previously missing pages from the *Codex Sinaiticus,* a priceless fourth-century Greek version of the Old Testament uncovered at the same monastery 130 years ago.

Early texts such as these are important because they provide evidence on whether distortions have crept into the Bible through centuries of copying and translation. In general, says Suzanne Singer, associate editor of *Biblical Archaeology Review,* "there doesn't seem to have been much alteration because recently discovered texts coincide rather closely with those that were known before."

At present, discoveries and theories are cropping up faster than they can be evaluated. Scholars say that some of them are bound to be discarded. But when the dust clears, concludes Chicago's Professor Stager, "we're going to know a lot more than we ever have about what really happened during the period of the Bible."

By JAMES MANN

WHO WAS JESUS?

As Christians round the world gather to celebrate the birth of Jesus, once again they recite the story of a child born to a virgin. The details are familiar yet fabulous: harkening angels, adoring shepherds, a mysterious star. But is the story true? To the literal-minded, the infancy narratives of Matthew and Luke are the opening chapters in the official biography of Jesus. To scholars of the New Testament, however, they are not history at all but something infinitely more important: symbol-laden stories created to dramatize a deeper mystery—that the Jesus who was born 2,000 years ago was truly Christ, the Lord.

Since the nineteenth century, scholars have sought to isolate "the historical Jesus" from "the Christ of faith" proclaimed in the Gospels. But today, most Biblical scholars no longer make such a facile distinction. For one thing, there are no firsthand written accounts of Jesus' life from which a verbal or visual portrait (page 86) could be fashioned. For another, while there were eyewitnesses to his public ministry, it is highly unlikely that any of them can be identified with the authors of the four Gospels, which were written 40 to 60 years after his death. Thus scholars agree that the real Jesus can no more be separated from the theology of the Gospel writers than the real Socrates can be separated from the dialogues of Plato.

ORAL TRADITIONS: In their quest for the real Jesus, scholars today emphasize the creative role of the four evangelists. Each of the four Gospels, they say, presents a different portrait of Jesus fashioned to meet the needs of the community for which it was written and to rebut views of Jesus with which they disagreed. By using the modern tools of historical criticism, linguistics and literary analysis, Biblical scholars try to distinguish the layers of oral traditions embedded within each Gospel and to confront the essential mind-set—if not the actual words—of Jesus. "Primarily, the Gospels tell us how each evangelist conceived of and presented Jesus to a Christian community in the last third of the first century," says Father Raymond Brown, a leading expert on the Gospel of John and a professor at New York's Union Theological Seminary. "The Gospels offer only limited means for reconstructing the ministry and message of the historical Jesus."

Despite these limitations, New Testament scholars today know more about the Gospels themselves and the milieu in which they were formed than any previous generation of Biblical researchers. In the past decade alone, translations of several ancient texts from the period 200 B.C. to A.D. 200 have vastly enriched the Biblical trove. One is the Temple Scroll, longest of the Dead Sea Scrolls, which indicates that Jesus' strictures against divorce and other of his teachings were very similar to those held by the ascetic Essene sect at Qumran. Another is the recently translated Nag Hammadi codices, which contain gospels composed by second-century Gnostic rivals of orthodox Christians. And next year, Duke University professor James H. Charlesworth will publish the most complete edition of the Pseudepigrapha, a collection of some 53 texts by Jewish and early Christian scribes, many of which were regarded as sacred books by the Jews of Jesus' time.

MEANING OF TEXTS: In the effort to master all this new material, the burden of Biblical scholarship has shifted from Europe to the U.S. The 3,000 North American members of the Society of Biblical Literature now represent the largest group of Scripture scholars in the world, and their annual production of commentary and criticism outweighs that of all European countries combined. Moreover, modern Biblical research is thoroughly ecumenical; Roman Catholics teach the Bible at Protestant divinity schools, and Protestants publish books for use by Catholic schools and parish study groups. Equally important, first-rate Scriptural scholars now occupy chairs of religious studies at secular universities. This trend, together with a new wave of popular handbooks on Biblical criticism, has made access to the Gospels available to millions of Americans, including those who prefer to discover Jesus without joining a church.

Most New Testament scholarship purposely focuses on what the texts meant to first-century Christians, but some of its implications call into question the authority sometimes claimed by Christian churches today. Roman Catholic analysts, for example, agree that the papacy in its developed form cannot be read back into the New Testament and that the words of Matthew's Gospel, "Thou art Peter and upon this rock I will build my church," were not necessarily uttered by Jesus during his ministry. Protestants, on the other hand, can find little support for the claim that Scripture alone is the basis for Christian authority; on the contrary, modern scholarship demonstrates not only that the church existed before the Gospels were written but also that the church shaped the New Testament writings. "It is much more difficult now for Protestants to speak naïvely about Biblical faith or Biblical religion," says professor Donald Juel of Northwestern Lutheran Theological Seminary in St. Paul, Minn. "The diversity of Scripture is a fact and it is something to which Christian tradition must now speak."

The Christians most threatened by contemporary scholarship are those conservative evangelicals who insist that every statement in the Bible—whether historical, scientific or religious—is literally true. Scholars who accept any form of modern Biblical research are under attack in several Protestant denominations, including the nation's largest—the Southern Baptist Convention. The issue of Biblical inerrancy has already created a schism in the Lutheran Church-Missouri Synod and now, with the editorial blessing of Christianity Today magazine, influential fundamentalists are pressing a new battle for the Bible at the risk of splitting the already wobbly evangelical movement. In Rome, meanwhile, the Vatican began a formal inquiry last week against Dutch Catholic theologian Edward Schillebeeckx on the widely disputed ground that his recent book, "Jesus: An Experiment in Christology," uses modern Biblical criticism to deny the divinity of Christ.

Virtually all Biblical scholars would vigorously deny that their work undercuts the central message of the Christian faith: that God was incarnate in human form and that He died and rose again from the dead to redeem mankind from sin. To call into question some of the historical assertions in the four Gospels is not to dispute their spiritual truth. "The truth of the Gospels is not simply historical and anyone who tries to identify their truth with historicity is misunderstanding them completely," says Jesuit Joseph Fitzmyer, a top Scripture scholar at the Catholic University of America. The problem, Fitzmyer complains, is that "in Scripture matters, education today is so retrograde that one cannot even pose a critical question without shocking people."

FOUR SHADOWY FIGURES: What is known about the historical Jesus is that he was born in the last years of Herod the Great and died during the reign of Tiberius Caesar when Pontius Pilate was Procurator of Judea. He was an itinerant rabbi—his thinking was close to the liberal school of Pharisees—who ate with sinners and publicans, was regarded by some as a prophet and religious visionary, aroused the antagonism of influential Jewish leaders, violated at least some Sabbath laws, entered Jerusalem during the Passover celebration, was interrogated by the Sanhedrin, tried before a Roman court and crucified as a common criminal.

Aside from this bare outline, not much is certain. The four Gospels contain individual sayings and stories based on memories of Jesus' earthly ministry, which were transmitted—and inevitably stylized in the process—by the oral traditions of the various Christian communities. The four evangelists themselves are extremely mysterious figures. Although there have been many guesses about their identities, Matthew, Mark, Luke, and John are simply names attributed to shadowy figures who may even have been groups of people, not individual authors. Moreover, no one has yet pinpointed the Christian communities for which the Gospels were written, though several locations have been suggested.* What is known is that because of the Resurrection experience, followers of Jesus began to proclaim him as Christ, the Messiah, who would return shortly to judge the world.

PASSION: Most scholars now believe that the early Christians worked backward in developing their account of Jesus. At first, Christians focused on Jesus as the heavenly Messiah who would return soon in glory as the crucified redeemer who was raised from the dead. Only gradually did they incorporate into their preaching the earthly Jesus who had ministered to the people of Israel. The written Gospels, many scholars argue, also developed in reverse—from the Passion story to the earthly ministry (which is all there is in the earliest Gospel, Mark), to the infancy narratives (added by Matthew and Luke), to the pre-existence of Jesus as the eternal Word of God (unique to the last Gospel, John).

"Unfortunately, the majority of people carry around in their minds a composite picture of Jesus made up of whichever happens to be their favorite Gospel, plus some historical reminiscences about the first century and a whole lot of personal predilections which we all have," says Werner Kelber of Rice University, a specialist on Mark. "People do not take the trouble to read each Gospel separately or to recognize that each author gives us a different portrait of Jesus—and of all the other figures in the Gospel." Here, in brief, are the different slants of the four Gospels:

MARK: In this, the earliest and the shortest of the four, Jesus emerges as the long-awaited Messiah who redeems the world from Satan's grip by his own Passion and death. Mark signals his theological intent at

the outset when John the Baptist announces the coming Messiah and is shortly "delivered up" to his enemies. This presages what will happen to Jesus and what Mark himself believes all followers of Christ must expect. "Mark is putting all of the early traditions about Jesus under the interpretive control of the Passion story," says New Testament scholar Paul Achtemeier of Union Theological Seminary in Virginia.

When Jesus begins his ministry, Mark presents him as a stereotypical miracle worker, a stock figure of Hellenic culture familiar to his gentile readers. His miracles win him little faith: Mark's Gospel is the only one in which those who should best understand him—his family, the scribes and especially his own disciples—all fail to recognize him as the Messiah, or misunderstand his mission. In the same episode in which Peter acknowledges Jesus as Messiah, for example, his Master repudiates him—"Get behind me, Satan"—for failing to accept that "the Son of Man" has not come to rule the world through personal power, but to redeem it by his death. Mark's crucifixion scene is exceedingly lonely. None of the disciples is present. Jesus dies with a cry of ultimate abandonment: "My God, My God, why hast thou forsaken me?" And it is left to a Roman centurion—a pagan who has watched Jesus die—to profess what the disciples could not: "Truly this man was the Son of God." In Mark's original conclusion, the disciples are never informed of the resurrection and thus are never reconciled with Christ.

This conclusion has created a major controversy among New Testament scholars. Some point out that verses later added to Mark by another author or authors do indicate a reconciliation in Galilee between the disciples and the risen Christ. Others believe that Mark's negative assessment of the disciples was intended to shift the focus of Christianity away from the church in Jerusalem, which was identified with the disciples, after that city was destroyed by Roman forces in A.D. 70. But the most radical conclusion is that of Professor Kelber, who believes Mark's disciples were the chief opponents of Jesus, repudiated by him and so not saved. Mark's point, says Kelber, is that readers of his Gospel were to look to the cross for salvation—a Lutheran position—and not rely solely on Jesus' miracles and message. Jesuit scholar John Donahue of Vanderbilt University does not go that far, but he concedes Mark is suggesting that knowledge of the historical Jesus is inadequate for salvation without faith in the crucified Christ.

MATTHEW: Here, Jesus is presented as a royal Messiah, the last King of Israel and the Son of God, sent to teach his people as well as to die for them. He is also a remarkably humble king, as Matthew's story of the Nativity makes clear. Though descended

from the royal line of David, Jesus is born not in Jerusalem, but in Bethlehem, where foreign wise men come to worship him. This kingly image rivals that of Jesus as rabbi, which other scholars of Matthew emphasize. "In Matthew, Jesus' followers call him Lord and other royal titles," says New Testament specialist Jack Kingsbury of Union Theological Seminary in Virginia. "Only the Pharisees call him teacher and Judas alone calls him 'Rabbi'."

Matthew's Jesus is particularly antagonistic toward the Jewish establishment; he calls the scribes and Pharisees a "brood of vipers." In part, these passages seem to reflect Matthew's efforts to distinguish Christianity from rabbinical Judaism, which the Pharisees were developing in response to the catastrophic destruction of Jerusalem. Matthew's Jesus is presented as a new Moses when he delivers his Sermon on the Mount, one of five teaching discourses in the Gospel. But in Matthew's portrait, Jesus is not just an interpreter of the law; he is the lawgiver and personal fulfillment of Jewish prophecy. Christianity, Matthew wants to make clear, is a natural, long-expected development of Judaism. Time and again, the author follows an episode in Jesus' life with an Old Testament quotation introduced by a formula phrase such as, "This was done to fulfill what the Lord had spoken through the prophet."

Although Matthew incorporates a great deal of Mark's material, he bends it to his own theological purposes. Matthew's miracle stories, for example, are presented as demonstrations of Jesus' mercy and compassion, rather than as illustrations of his power. Where Mark's Jesus rebukes the disciples for failing to understand his power to walk on water, Matthew's Jesus helps the faltering Peter, whose hesitant faith nearly causes the disciple to drown.

LUKE: In this Gospel, Jesus is the innocent savior of the world, full of forgiveness and love, and the text follows the literary conventions of Hellenic culture. Written for a sophisticated gentile audience, Luke's portrait is the first effort to present a biography of Jesus. Gone is Mark's angst-ridden emphasis on the cross; in its place is a peaceful universality. Luke not only relates Jesus to events of Roman, Palestinian and church history, he goes on to trace his genealogy all the way back to Adam. In this way, the evangelist locates the words and deeds of Jesus within a scheme of "salvation history," which describes what God is doing—and will continue to do—for man.

Despite this universal framework, Luke's Jesus is very much concerned with teaching Christians how they should spend their lives from moment to moment. For example, Luke amends The Lord's Prayer so that it asks the Father to "give us each [Matthew says "this"] day our daily bread"; elsewhere, his Jesus reminds Christians that they must bear their burdens "daily." In part, this concern with time reflects the fact that by A.D. 85 or thereabouts, when Luke wrote his Gospel, the Christians were beginning to realize the Second Coming might not be imminent and therefore were more concerned with the here and now. Moreover, says Father Fitzmyer, an international expert on Luke's writings, "Luke is the only evangelist who stresses that Christians have to live ordinary lives, and he has played the Christian message to fit this fact."

But the dominant theme in Luke's verbal portrait is Jesus' ready forgiveness of sinners. They love him and he loves them and other social outcasts. When Jesus works a miracle, the typical response from the crowd in Luke's Gospel is joy, rather than Mark's wonder at his power or Matthew's show of faith. Luke's Jesus is perhaps best understood in his crucifixion scenes, where the innocent savior manages to pray for his executioners: "Father, forgive them, for they know not what they do."

JOHN: There is no need for a nativity scene in John; he simply asserts in his Gospel's famous prologue that Jesus is "the Word of God" made flesh. Thus John's Gospel begins where the others leave off, with the recognition of Jesus as the Son of God. In John, the disciples immediately know who Jesus is.

John's Gospel differs from the three Synoptic Gospels in other ways as well. His Jesus works only seven miracles—none of them exorcisms—preaches no ethical exhortations and issues no apocalyptic warnings about the end of the world. On the contrary, the kingdom of God has already arrived in the person of John's Jesus, who comes "from above" and therefore speaks with God's authority. The implications of this sometimes confuse his entourage. Nicodemus, a secret admirer, does not understand that disciples, too, must be "begotten from above"—a reference to Divine election that modern evangelists still sometimes interpret, instead, as requiring "born again" experiences.

Jesus' ultimate conflict with the Jews in the fourth Gospel reflects antipathies which were aroused when members of John's community were expelled from the synagogue for professing faith in Christ. "The key to current scholarly discussions about John is the extent to which conflicts in his own community are superimposed by the author on the struggles Jesus had in his ministry," observes Father Brown, author of the two-volume Anchor Bible commentary on John's Gospel. Both concerns are reflected in the controversy between John's Jesus and the Jews, who eventually con-

THE FACES OF JESUS

The Bible shows us Christ through a glass darkly; we see his figure, but not his face. None of the Gospels even hints at what Jesus might have looked like; there is no eyewitness account of his appearance. In painting him, therefore, artists have looked inward as often as heavenward. Picasso portrayed him as a bullfighter; Van Gogh, a redhead, gave him red hair. There have been black Jesuses and Oriental ones, and the American artist Richard West envisioned him as an Indian brave, praying on his knees in a tepee.

Historically, the most compelling vision of Christ has been that of the tortured martyr of the Cross, but this first appeared nearly a thousand years after his death. The vision that touched the earliest Christians was that of Christ as the Good Shepherd—a curly-haired, beardless youth rescuing his flock from the wolves, a familiar image in pagan art. From pagan sources also comes the "young philosopher" Christ, which decorated sarcophagi of the third and fourth centuries. He was a cleanshaven figure in the tunic and mantle of an itinerant Cynic, two fingers raised in blessing, a scroll or book under his left arm.

With the conversion of Constantine, there occurred what H.W. Janson of New York University calls an "exchange of amenities" between the Emperor and Christ. Jesus acquired the imperial nimbus, now recognized as the halo; he sits enthroned, judging mortal souls. In those early centuries, he is occasionally pictured on the Cross, but his eyes are open, his demeanor triumphant.

SECOND COMING: Only around the tenth century did artists begin to confront Christ's nature as both God and man who suffered and died. The reasons are obscure, but a new interest in death and resurrection took hold in philosophy about the same time, perhaps in anticipation of a Second Coming in the year 1000. Depictions of Christ suffering on the Cross appear first in Byzantine art and spread rapidly to the West, carrying with them the Eastern tradition that Christ was bearded. By the sixteenth century, artists had explored the macabre limits of the Passion: Grünewald's Isenheim altarpiece shows us a flayed and bloody Christ, his body studded with thorns, his livid lips drawn back in rictus. But that image was not universal. A latemedieval artist, flirting with the Gnostic belief that Christ was essentially a spiritual force, shows us an empty Cross with the centurion jabbing his spear into thin air—because the artist could not envision the Son of God made flesh.

The great artists of the Renaissance had no such mystical vision. The fifteenth century rediscovered God in the image of man. The Christ child changed from a solemn homunculus to Fra Angelico's plump-cheeked babe. Raphael's "Transfiguration" depicts an adult Christ of transcendent beauty—hair windblown, white robes trailing—but there are those who find the flame of his divinity obscured by the radiance of his physical perfection. The Christs of Rembrandt, drawn from models he found in Amsterdam's Jewish quarter, are masterpieces of portraiture, radiant yet unmistakably human.

By the nineteenth century, the decline of religion as a creative force was reflected in a devitalized Christian art. Those sentimental, effete images of Jesus—hands clasped in prayer, cow eyes turned deferentially heavenward—remain the mass-produced image of those who have seen Jesus only on calendars. In reaction to that saccharine vision, serious twentieth-century artists have given us "realistic" portraits, more or less. Diego Rivera has illustrated Christ's vaccination, an incident not recorded in the Bible. Max Ernst has shown us the Christ child on the Madonna's knee, receiving a spanking. For his Crucifixion painting, the American artist Rico Lebrun worked, in part, from concentration-camp photographs.

'FINAL VICTORY': Each generation adds its contribution to the understanding—or misunderstanding—of Jesus, each confronts in its own way the mystery of his nature. "You can't show an idealized Christ," says Father James Flanigan, chairman of the art department at Notre Dame. "But neither can you put too much emphasis on his death and suffering, or you miss the final victory." Flanigan points out that Michelangelo wrestled with the problem all his life. His early Pietà, the famous one in St. Peter's, tenderly evokes the death of a young man. But the Christ of his last Pietà, now in Milan, is stripped of human detail, little more than a trunk, barely emerging from the stone. The flesh, Michelangelo realized at the end of his long life, is incapable of holding the divinity.

JERRY ADLER

demn him for making himself equal to God.

Even in his passion and death, John's "Son of God" remains in full control. Unlike the other Gospels, John does not show Jesus suffering on his knees in Gethsemane. Instead, the Roman soldiers fall to their knees when they arrive to arrest him. And on the cross, Jesus is lucid enough to give John, his "beloved disciple," to Mary, a gesture symbolizing that he is leaving behind him a church. Then, satisfied that his work is done, he announces: "It is finished."

MIDDLE-CLASS ETHICS: At the very least, then, Biblical scholarship has shown that the Gospel writers all shaded the stories of Jesus' ministry according to their own interests and theological concerns. This is also true of the founders of modern Biblical criticism in the nineteenth century. In their various efforts to reconstruct a "naturalistic" life of Christ, they attempted to uncover the human Jesus before Christian doctrine had muddied the view. The result, with varying details, was a Jesus who looked very much like a nineteenth-century teacher of middle-class ethics. In his famous 1906 book, "The Quest of the Historical Jesus," Albert Schweitzer ended the life-of-Jesus movement by astutely observing that nineteenth-century scholars had looked into the well of the Bible and seen their own faces. In his patient dismantling of his predecessors' work, Schweitzer showed that Jesus was an apocalyptic Jew.

PARADOX The temptation to see Jesus through contemporary eyes will probably never cease. In our own century, German scholar Rudolph Bultmann sought to demythologize the Biblical Jesus and his message by translating the apocalyptic language into such modern, existential categories as angst and authenticity. Today, however, the search for Jesus is guided less by cultural or philosophical presuppositions than by the tentative assumption that scriptural analysis can yield more about him than old-fashioned rationalists ever imagined.

For example, after lengthy study of the miracle stories to determine whether they were purely literary inventions, Prof. Carl Holladay of the Yale Divinity School has concluded that Jesus was indeed a miracle worker and that the miracle stories are authentic. "Superimposing a post-Enlightenment view of such matters on the first century does injustice to what was truly going on," says Holladay. "But scholars must leave it up to believers to evaluate the claim that they were really the work of God."

What's more, most New Testament scholars believe that at least some sayings attributed to Jesus are authentically his, and a national conference is being planned in which scholars will try to reach a consensus on which passages qualify. Among the likeliest candidates are Luke's version of the Lord's Prayer, several proclamations that "the Kingdom of God is at hand," certain "aphorisms of reversal," such as Mark's "The first shall be last, the last first" and Jesus' familiar Aramaic word for God—"Abba," or Father—which many analysts believe captures the essence of Jesus' consciousness of his relationship to God.

Analysis of Jesus' parables has convinced other scholars that by understanding them as paradoxes readers can gain direct access to the mind of Jesus. This approach is based on the assumption that the deep structures of the human mind are universal, permitting twentieth-century readers to understand a first-century Jesus. For instance, they cite the famous parable of the good Samaritan, in which a Jewish traveler is robbed and left for dead. Both a priest and a Levite pass him by, but a Samaritan—a social and religious outcast—binds up his wounds and lodges him at the Samaritan's own expense. This story can be interpreted as a moral example of the neighborliness expected of Christians—as it often is in sermons—or as an allegory, as Saint Augustine did. But scholars see it as a paradox designed to transmit Jesus' special understanding of what God demands of everyone who would truly do his will.

WARY: "In this parable, Jesus is asking his Jewish audience to think the unthinkable by identifying goodness with the hated Samaritan," says theologian John Dominic Crossan, an expert in parable analysis at DePaul University in Chicago. In response, the listener either rejects the story or questions his deepest values and assumptions about life. When this happens consciousness changes, just as it does when a Buddhist solves a Zen koan. Mark takes this a step further. The crucified Jesus becomes Christ, the Messiah. And so the parable-teller becomes himself a parable told by the early church—the paradox of Christ crucified—which demands a conversion of consciousness.

Biblical scholars insist that better understanding of how the Gospels were written is a boon rather than an obstacle to faith. But defenders of traditional doctrine in all churches are wary of Biblical investigators. Catholic theologian Edward Schillebeeckx, for example, has tentatively argued from scriptural sources that Jesus' identity as Christ was evident even before the Cross—in the rejection he experienced during his life. Last week, during Schillebeeckx's secret hearing in Rome, Vatican inquisitors demanded to know instead whether he really believed that Jesus was divine. "Rome's inquisitorial behavior suggests they do not want Catholic understanding of the Bible enriched by contributions from the church's most gifted intellectuals," says one U.S. scholar.

Southern Baptists, meanwhile, are under increasing attack from Biblical fundamentalists who want to fire any teacher who does not agree that the Bible is literally true. At Baylor University, for instance, Prof. H. Jack Flanders has been criticized by fundamentalists for writing a book that questions the historicity of Adam and Eve and treats the story of Jonah in the whale as a parable. In Dallas, the administration of Dallas Baptist College has instructed all teachers to sign a statement of belief in Biblical inerrancy—a statement that Dr. Wallie Amos Criswell, the influential fundamentalist pastor of the nation's largest Southern Baptist church, wants the faculties of all Texas Baptist schools to affirm.

The fundamentalists' doctrine of inerrancy, says Professor Achtemeier, is rooted in the post-Reformation era, when Protestant scholastics countered the authority asserted by Rome with the authority of the Bible itself. The scholastics also came to regard the Bible as a sourcebook for systematic theology in which the verses were regarded as dogmatic propositions about scientific questions as well. When nineteenth-century scientists challenged the Christian world view, and historians discovered inconsistencies in the Bible, U.S. fundamentalists at Princeton University responded with a theory that fundamentalists still hold today: the Bible, they say, is inerrant in its original "autographs," or manuscripts, and even copies must be regarded as literally true.

TRUTH: To most Biblical scholars today, these demands for inerrancy are beside the point. The point is that the differences, even the contradictions, between the Gospel accounts do not detract at all from the spiritual truths that they contain. "God can reveal himself through inspired fiction, like the story of Jonah, just as well as through inspired history," says Father Brown.

Who was Jesus? Mark's Jesus dies alone, feeling forsaken but true to his Father's will. This Jesus will appeal to Christians who embrace life's tragedies with confidence. Matthew's Jesus dies only to return and promise his guidance to those who follow him. This Jesus will appeal to Christians who find assurance in the church. Luke's Jesus dies forgiving his enemies, knowing his Father awaits his spirit. This Jesus will attract Christians who have learned in life to trust God by imitating his mercy. John's Jesus dies in the confidence that he will return to the Father. This Jesus is for those Christians who have traveled the mystical way. All of these accounts express a truth; none of them is complete. All of these Jesuses are accessible only to those whose faith compels them on the search for "the way, the truth and the light."

KENNETH L. WOODWARD with **RACHEL MARK** and **JERRY BUCKLEY** in New York and bureau reports

Who Was St. Peter?

J. K. Elliott

NO READER OF THE NEW TESTAMENT can fail to be aware that one of the most important figures in the gospels and the *Acts of the Apostles* is Peter. Church tradition credits this disciple with being the founder of the church in Rome and consequently the first bishop of Rome and first Pope.

If we can accept that the gospels tell us the historical facts about the period of Jesus' ministry, then the importance of Peter in Jesus' movement revealed there would explain why he became the leader of the Jerusalem church after Jesus' death as recorded in *Acts* and in Paul's letters. Few scholars, however, would accept that the gospels can be read in this way: most would argue that the gospels, which for the most part were written at least thirty years after the events they speak of, were in fact influenced by the teaching, events and presuppositions of the early Christian communities which produced them. This means that the gospels are more likely to state Peter was the foremost of the disciples *because* he had been leader of the Jerusalem church, or founder of the church at the centre of the Empire.

It is unlikely therefore that Peter became head of the church after the first Easter merely because of his earlier prominence in Jesus' ministry. Similarly, it is unlikely he became leader because Jesus had appointed him to this position: passages in the New Testament gospels in which Jesus sets Peter up as the prime disciple are prophecies after the events.

Unfortunately there is a tantalising gap between Jesus' death at the end of the gospels and the emergence of the church in Jerusalem as recorded in *Acts* and as recognised by Paul. We therefore do not know the steps whereby the disciples reassembled with Peter as their head to inaugurate the spread of the church in the name of Jesus. The gospels are probably correct in recording that the disciples forsook Jesus at the time of his arrest. There is no reason to assume that this detail was an invention by the evangelists in pursuit of an anti-Jerusalem church bias because the later gospels are all at pains to justify and explain why Jesus did die forsaken by his erstwhile colleagues. What we do not know is how and when the disciples met up again in Jerusalem. Mark and Matthew assume that the disciples had returned to Galilee but the centre of the newly formed church began in Jerusalem according to *Acts* and Paul and it is in Jerusalem where *Luke* and *John* set their post-resurrection appearances.

Possibly one reason for Peter's assumption of leadership was that he was the first one among Jesus' former colleagues to come to the belief that Jesus was raised from the dead, and in the confidence of that belief he mustered the other disciples to continue Jesus' work. Belief in the resurrection involved the conviction that Jesus' movement and mission had not died with him. Peter therefore may well have been the first to encourage a reassembly of the disciples to continue to fight for the aims Jesus had died for. Certainly it is a strongly based tradition in the New Testament that the first of Jesus' post-resurrection appearances was to Peter.

Peter on this argument became the first leader of the Christian church not because of his prominence among the disciples during Jesus' lifetime or because Jesus nominated him for such a role but because it was believed – no doubt due to Peter's publicizing his own conviction – that Jesus appeared to him first after the crucifixion.

Peter's original name was Simon, or Symeon to use the Semitic form found on James' lips in *Acts*. According to *Matthew* he was Simon *baryona*. This might mean he was Simon son of Jonah, or, as interpreted in *John*, son of John, or that he was a zealot; some lexicographers connect the word *baryona* with the word for terrorist. If the latter is correct then Simon Peter would have been in good company with Simon the Zealot, Judas Iscariot (which may mean 'assassin") and the 'sons of thunder', James and John.

The reason why Simon was nicknamed Peter (meaning 'a rock') is given in *Matthew*, where it is stated that Simon is to be the foundation-rock of the church. Peter is the Greek for the Aramaic Kephas, a form of the name which is transliterated rather than translated in some parts of the New Testament, but neither Kephas nor Peter was a personal name until Simon the disciple was so named. Strictly speaking therefore we should speak of this apostle as Simon Rock if we are to preserve the shock and significance of the nickname. It is however very significant that Paul, almost exclusively in the New Testament, prefers to call Peter 'Kephas'. Of the ten references to this disciple by name in Paul's extant letters, only two call him 'Peter'. The rest name him as Kephas as if to emphasise that he belongs to the Semitic, pro-Jewish, branch of the church with which Paul was so regularly at loggerheads.

The animosity between Paul and the Jerusalem church leaders is particularly

From *History Today*, December 1981. Reproduced by kind permission of History Today, Ltd., 83-84 Berwick Street, London W1V 3PJ England.

apparent in *Galatians 2*. Peter here, and James and John, are referred to sarcastically as 'pillars of the church' and as 'people who are reputed to be of significance'. In fact, in reading this chapter the repeated 'reputed to be something' recalls Mark Anthony's repeated reference to Brutus as an 'honourable man'.

Paul's references to Peter and the Jerusalem church in other letters are no more cordial. What is important to note though is that whether Paul was writing to the church in Galatia, or in Corinth, he assumes his readers know Peter and what he stands for. *Acts* tells us little of Peter's missionary activity, and nothing of Peter in Corinth or Galatia, but *I Corinthians* suggests that Peter had been to Corinth, insofar as the Corinthians seem to be aware that Peter travels with his wife. What is probably of greater importance is that in *I Corinthians* Paul refers to the divisions in this nascent church between those who claim allegiance to Paul, and those who belong to Apollos or to Kephas. These factions are possibly rival parties among the Corinthians depending on which preacher's teaching they followed. Paul, characteristically, refuses to acknowledge that Kephas has any more importance, especially in Corinth (a church founded by Paul), than Paul himself. Paul argues against the schism and against the attempts made by others to win the Corinthian Christians over to their predominantly anti-Pauline cause. In *I Corinthians* Paul reminds his readers that he founded their church but warns that 'someone else is putting up the building' and that this workmanship will have to be tested in the last judgement. This contrasts with a passage in *Romans*, a letter sent to a church not founded by Paul, when Paul claims he does not wish to build on 'another man's' foundations. In both these verses it is not unreasonable to deduce that this mysterious 'other man' was in fact Peter.

The Acts of the Apostles which at face value appears to chronicle the events recorded in Paul's letters attempts to soften this rivalry. This is partly the result of the author's attempt to show how similar Peter was to Paul or rather Paul to Peter. Paul is consistently shown to be as good an apostle as Peter – and in many respects, the true successor to Peter as the main Christian evangeliser and missionary. In a recent article in *History Today* (August 1978) I tried to indicate the main theological tendencies at work in *Acts*. One of these is the attempt to

remove the differences between the two leading figures in the early church. Actions, speeches and attributes of one man are transferred to the other. The author, writing from a pro-Pauline angle, has attempted to rehabilitate Paul in the minds of readers whose church may well have been inclined to promote the memory of Peter, so that by robbing Peter to pay Paul the author has in effect diminished Peter's unique role in a far more subtle way than Paul himself did in his letters. Both Paul himself and the author of *Acts* have similar aims, even if both have a different style and approach, and these are to reduce the standing of Peter, as representing the Jerusalem church, and argue for the validity of the Gentile church.

We have already seen that Paul is strongly anti-Peter, whereas *Acts*, although giving us some interesting insights into the status of the earliest Christian community in Jerusalem, tries by and large to minimise the differences between Peter and Paul. With this knowledge, it is necessary now to examine how Peter is treated in the three synoptic gospels (*Matthew*, *Mark*, *Luke*) which, it is usually agreed, were written in the period between the letters of Paul and the composition of *Acts*. These gospels are likely to have been compiled in churches influenced, in some cases directly, by Paul's own teaching, and this probability may account for any Pauline traits in the way the gospels speak of Peter. But the gospels are intermediate between Paul and *Acts*, and as *Acts* is volume two of *Luke-Acts* it is important to recognise that the way *Acts* writes about Peter would be influenced by the way the gospels (or *Luke* in particular) portrayed him.

If we take *Mark* first as the gospel standing closest in time to Paul it is significant how the strongly anti-Petrine tone used by Paul has permeated this gospel. The attitude of the gentile church towards Peter in the ministry of the early church has influenced Mark's telling of Peter in the ministry of Jesus. This hostility is evidenced in those stories which emphasise Peter's failings, his impulsiveness, lack of understanding and ignorance. This anti-Petrine bias so characteristic of Mark's gospel reaches its climax in the stories of the denial. At a time when all the disciples are said to have fled, *Mark* brings Peter back into the scene of Jesus' questioning before the Sanhedrin in order to focus more specifically on what deserting Jesus

meant in the case of the main representative of the twelve disciples. The scene also provides a dramatic juxtaposition of stories: Jesus acts in a dignified courageous manner before the high-priest whereas Peter outside in the courtyard acts in a cowardly, undignified manner during his questionings by the high priest's servant. Peter's final appearance in *Mark* is when he curses Jesus (not in the parallels) and breaks down weeping after the threefold denial of association with Jesus.

Another example in this gospel which shows how the early pro-gentile branch of the church regarded Peter may be seen in the story of the confession at Caesarea Philippi. Here Peter acknowledges Jesus as 'Messiah', a title which Mark underplays as it could be an inadequate and limiting title liable to be understood to refer to a pro-Jewish or nationalist figure.

The early Christian writer Papias in a famous passage claims *Mark* to be Peter's interpreter. That tradition is true only in so far as *Mark* interprets the role of Peter in the judgement of the gentile church. A further derogatory reference to Peter interpreting him in this way occurs at another poignant moment in Jesus' career, namely the agony in Gethsemane. Here in *Mark* it is Peter who is addressed by Jesus as being unable to stay awake to share in Christ's vigil. Although this reference is retained by *Matthew*, *Luke* avoids mentioning Peter here. This scene in *Mark* anticipates the final desertion of Jesus by the twelve in general and by Peter in particular, and is typical of this gospel which denigrates all the disciples because they formed the nucleus of the Jerusalem church later.

The desertion by the disciples at the time of Jesus' arrest, and the treachery of Judas are unlikely to have been invented but these stories of failure were remembered and retold by Mark as symptomatic of the behaviour of the earliest close followers of Jesus. The later gospels try to find theological explanations why Peter, Judas, and the twelve in general behaved as they did. Such apologies are absent from Mark's stark account.

As far as *Matthew* is concerned although he preserves several of *Mark*'s derogatory references to Jesus' family, the disciples and Peter, it is in this gospel that some of the most honorific references to Peter occur. *Matthew* unlike *Luke* keeps faithfully to much of the material he found in his Markan source, but, like *Luke*, *Matthew* wrote after

70AD when the Jerusalem church had been destroyed along with the Jewish Temple. This event affected the later writers' judgement on the Jerusalem church. Whereas *Mark* and *Paul* were writing at a time when the Jerusalem church was still exercising its often restrictive influence, after 70 the gentile church was the dominant wing of Christianity. Hence those founder disciples tended to be viewed no longer as an immediate threat, but remembered as a cherished link with Jesus of Nazareth. This might explain why once Peter and the Jerusalem church ceased to exist and were no longer a bridle on the gentile mission, these early Christians were thought of not so much as church leaders but as erstwhile companions of Jesus.

Although *Matthew* keeps references such as Peter's vehement affirmation (taken from *Mark*) that he will not desert Jesus, he has sometimes added details about Peter to *Mark*'s account, and these are instructive. In one passage it is Peter who asks Jesus for the meaning of a parable and is rebuked for being as dull as the rest of the disciples. In this *Matthew* is close to *Mark* and it is significant to note that when Peter as spokesman makes a similar request for the interpretation of a parable in a different context in *Luke* Jesus there answers Peter without any rebuke. But *Matthew* nevertheless can be seen to be moving away from *Mark* towards the stand taken by *Luke* regarding the twelve. A more favourable reference to Peter occurs in *Matthew*, when Peter as spokesman asks Jesus for an authoritative statement on the nature of Christian forgiveness. There is no hostility to Peter here.

Generally, it is the peculiar references to Peter in *Matthew*, rather than in his additions to Markan material, that give an enhanced view of Peter and show us Matthew's distinctive contribution to the rehabilitation of this disciple. These unique stories occur in *Matthew* in that section of the gospel dealing with the church. *Matthew* tells of Peter's attempt to walk on the water. This is the only place in the gospels where Jesus performs a miracle just for Peter. This story can be seen as an intermediate stage between *Mark*'s stark portrayal of Peter the failure and the later idealised picture of him in *Luke-Acts*. Here Peter is rebuked by Jesus as a man of little faith but nevertheless it is Peter's action which gives the other disciples their faith and they confess Jesus as Son of God. There is thus an ambiguity in the scene and it seems as if *Matthew* working on material similar to that found in *Mark*'s sources tried to find a favourable interpretation in a scene originally anti-Petrine.

A story in which there is no trace of an anti-Petrine tradition is *Matthew*'s radical adaptation of the confession at Caesarea Philippi, in which Peter is made to confess not that Jesus is Messiah but that he is a Messiah reinterpreted as 'Son of the living God' (*Matthew* 16). In this Peter repeats the confession recorded earlier where the disciples address Jesus in this way. What is more important for *Matthew* in this account of the confession by Peter is that it results in Jesus' proclamation of Peter's superiority. This represents the early Jerusalem church's belief that because Peter was their first leader then Jesus himself must have ordained it. Peter is given here his highest acclaim to be the foundation rock of Jesus' church. Although all the gospels agree that Jesus named Simon 'Peter' it is only here that the explanation of this nickname is preserved. It is in this passage also that Peter is blessed – the only disciple to be blessed in the whole of the New Testament. Peter is then told he will be given the 'keys to the kingdom of heaven' and that he will have power to 'bind and loose'. These difficult sayings have inevitably been subjected to much investigation. The theological importance and significance of the sayings is best discussed elsewhere, but there is no denying the high estimate of Peter and the exalted role for the disciples in these verses. It is of course on these verses that the unique position of Peter as first Pope is usually justified. What is significant is that the language and style of this passage is very Semitic in tone, which suggests that the sayings, even if not authentic to Jesus, certainly seem to reflect the language of the Jerusalem-based church. It is interesting that Matthew twenty years later than Mark felt able to incorporate in his gospel this old tradition.

It is unlikely that the sayings in *Matthew* 16 actually came from Jesus himself in so far as it is improbable that Jesus anticipated the founding of a church. This question is naturally much debated but on the basis of the New Testament his intentions are ambiguous. If Jesus did in fact intend the establishment of a church it is likely he saw it as a New Israel in which the twelve disciples would rule the twelve tribes (*Matthew* 19:28) As far as the remembrance of the sayings in *Matthew* 16 is concerned it seems as if Peter's eminence and importance apparent in this early tradition went through a period of reaction, initiated by Paul and reflected in his letters and in *Mark*, but by the time Matthew wrote there was an attempt to reappraise his real significance both in the life of Jesus and in the life of the church. *Matthew* in other words seems to reflect the early need to reestablish the apostolic links with the Jerusalem-based church after 70. A similar motive may be seen below when we consider *John* 21.

Another story concerning Peter peculiar to Matthew's gospel is the episode of the Temple tax (17:24-7). The position of the Christians *vis à vis* the Roman state as exemplified in the individual's need to pay tax to Rome is evidenced not only in *Romans* 13 where civic obligations are enjoined on Christians, and in the dominical saying 'Render unto Caesar . . .' in the gospels, but also in stories telling of Jesus' consorting with taxgatherers thus making them acceptable and 'respectable'. These, together with this story in *Matthew* 17, were doubtless of apologetic importance in the early Christians' dealings with the Roman authorities on whose goodwill their existence depended. As with the other two Petrine stories unique to *Matthew* in the synoptic tradition noted above, this story of the half-shekel has its parallel in *John* 21 (the chapter in the Fourth Gospel most favourably disposed to Peter) in so far as the story here could be a Matthaean adaptation of the account which reached *John* (and possibly *Luke* also) as the miraculous draft of fishes. As with Peter's walking on the water, the miracle as told in *Matthew* is performed for the benefit of the miracle worker. It seems as if for Matthew's church it was relevant for Peter to be able to provide a Christian answer to questions about tax.

Having examined the treatment of Peter in *Acts* it is not surprising to find a similar portrayal of Peter in *Luke*'s gospel. *Luke* has refined the Markan description of Peter even more than *Matthew*, and it is in this gospel that Peter is idealised. *Luke* avoids most of the derogatory designations of Peter. For example he deletes Jesus' rebuke of Peter after the confession. He also softens the references to Peter in the Passion story. Similarly in the story of the woman with a haemorrhage *Luke* has Peter gently point out the crowds thronging Jesus and this is in contrast to the more petulant comment of the disciples in the Markan parallel. In the predictions of the denials *Luke* adds the prophecy that Jesus is praying for Peter in his ordeal and that afterwards Peter will 'turn again and strengthen his brothers'. This is comparable to the rehabilitation of Peter in *John* 21 to be discussed below. Another link with *John* 21 already referred to is at *Luke* 5:1–11 which is a story unique to *Luke* in the synoptic tradition. Here Peter alone is given a personal call by Jesus and told he will be a fisher of men (even though two others are present in the story) unlike *Matthew* and *Mark* who have all the disciples described as fishers of men.

In another incident unique to *Luke* (24:34) Jesus' appearance to Peter is recorded. It is the recording of the resurrection appearance to Peter that makes Peter the last named discile in the gospel just as it is Peter who is the first disciple to be named in the second volume, *Acts*. In all the three episodes peculiar to *Luke* it is significant that Peter is referred to by his original Jewish name Simon suggesting that these stories all came to *Luke* from a Palestinian source. (The name Peter, present in some MSS at 5:8, is unlikely to be original to the story.) These were used by *Luke* as being consonant with the image of Peter which he wished to preserve.

Despite the fact that the majority of scholars date the Fourth Gospel about 90 thus making it the last of the four gospels to be written, its treatment of Peter in chapters 1–20 is closer to *Mark* than *Luke*. The softening of Mark's anti-Petrine motif which we have traced through *Matthew* to *Luke-Acts* is not carried forward to the Fourth Gospel. The extent to which this gospel is independent of the synoptics is a crux of Biblical scholarship but if the author of the Fourth Gospel really was unaware of the material as written in the synoptic gospels (especially outside the Passion narrative) then he seems to have been aware of the traditions concerning Peter which find their place in *Mark*'s gospel. However, unlike Mark, the Fourth Gospel has a typically idiosyncratic way of dealing with the perfidy and inadequacies of Peter.

The Fourth Gospel tells six stories concerning Peter which do not include his mysterious extra character, 'the beloved disciple'. Four of these – the call of Peter, the confession, Peter's inability

to understand the significance of Jesus' words and the prediction of Peter's denials, and the denials – have synoptic parallels. In addition the Fourth Gospel has two further stories concerning Peter without the beloved disciple which do not have synoptic parallels: both of these follow the Markan pattern and show Peter to be impulsive. Neither shows Peter in a favourable light. In one of these stories the Fourth Gospel adds the detail that the previously unnamed person who cut off the servant's ear during the fracas in the garden of Gethsemane was in fact Peter. The story which tells of the footwashing is an episode that replaces the institution of the eucharist in this gospel and in many ways may be an allegory of the need for humility expressed more directly in the saying found in *Luke* that no one disciple is to be deemed superior to another. In the footwashing episode it is Peter who is cast as the man most in need of humility.

Among the stories *John* has in common with the synoptics, it is significant to note that in his telling of the call John tries to demote Peter from the assumption of priority. It is not Peter who is the first to recognise Jesus, but, according to the most likely text here, Andrew. Nor is Peter the first disciple called. The other three stories repeat derogatory episodes known to the synoptics.

The remaining stories in the Fourth Gospel involving Peter also include the enigmatic beloved disciple. It has already been pointed out that elsewhere in the New Testament Peter is compared to and contrasted with Paul, and in other places is in apparent conflict with James. In the Fourth Gospel there is a further rivalry, this time between Peter and the beloved disciple. In the first of these stories (at the Last Supper) it is the beloved disciple who is accorded pride of place at Jesus' breast and it is only through this mysterious disciple that Peter is able to find out from Jesus which of the twelve is to be the betrayer. The superior influence of this disciple is also seen in the story of the trials, when unlike Peter who has to wait outside the high-priest's courtyard, 'another disciple', presumably the beloved disciple, has the authority to follow Jesus inside. It is only through this man's influence that Peter eventually gains access to the courtyard.

The superiority that this disciple is able to wield over Peter is also evidenced in the uniquely Johannine story at the cross when the dying Jesus entrusts his mother to the beloved disciple. This

man is the only disciple not to have denied or deserted Jesus and is therefore unlike Peter who is absent when Jesus is, in the language of the Fourth Gospel, 'lifted up' in glory onto the cross.

By means of this regular comparison with the beloved disciple Peter's role is diminished and his relationship to Jesus distanced as it is evident that Peter is not the beloved disciple of Jesus – only among the most important of the *named* disciples, and even in this Peter does not predominate. Other disciples such as Thomas or Philip or Judas act as spokesmen.

Another episode in which Peter and this disciple are contrasted to Peter's disadvantage is in the Easter story. Here in *John* the beloved disciple and Peter race to Jesus' tomb. The beloved disciple outruns Peter, and when he subsequently follows Peter into the tomb 'he sees and believes' in the significance of the empty tomb, unlike Peter who merely looks. Other references to the beloved disciple occur in *John* 21, which needs to be treated as separated from chapters 1–20.

This Appendix to the Fourth Gospel has a different style and the theology is in some ways different from the bulk of the gospel to which it is attached. It is in this section that Peter is rehabilitated by having to confess his love for Jesus three times. This episode therefore provides an antidote to the earlier denials. As a result of the words of Peter pastoral authority is laid on him by Jesus. Whereas *John* 1–20 betrays an attitude to Peter similar to *Mark*'s or Paul's, chapter 21 seems to have been influenced by the growing veneration of Peter seen in *Matthew* and particularly in *Luke-Acts*. The Appendix may have been composed in the first instance in order to correct the image of Peter expressed in the first draft of the gospel (*John* 1–20).

It might be thought that the two letters of Peter in the New Testament canon would give a particularly intimate insight into the character of their author. Each probably does – but is unlikely to help us in our search for the historical St Peter. Most scholars doubt if the two letters bearing Peter's name were by the same author because the style, language and theology of both are so different. The consensus of academic opinion is that neither was written by Simon Peter. Several New Testament epistles were written in the name of a famous apostle. This was done not from a desire to deceive but in order to pay honour to the memory of a man whose views – supposed or actual – were being promulgated by his admirers and followers. In the case of the Petrine epistles it is obvious that some later Christians were prepared to honour Peter by composing letters in his name.

As far as *I Peter* is concerned it is interesting to note that this circular letter is addressed to churches with which Paul had also been associated. This suggests that Paul's presence in these communities had not succeeded in eliminating the outlook and influence of Peter. In the case of *II Peter* one of the purposes of the letter was to comment on the views of Paul and warn against unprincipled men who were apparently using Paul's words in a way the author disapproved of. This letter is probably a fairly late composition and likely to be the latest in the canon to have been written: it assumes the existence of a Pauline corpus which in the eyes of the author was creating misinterpretation. The authority for the viewpoint in *II Peter* seems to have been St Peter's eyewitness and apostleship.

These letters therefore do not tell us anything about the historical Peter, but they are powerful witnesses to a continuing dichotomy between Pauline and Petrine forces at work in the first century church even at a time later than the composition of *Luke-Acts* with its intended palliative effect.

This survey of the Biblical evidence about Peter shows his evident importance in the life of Jesus and the primitive church but also reveals the varying opinions and attitudes to him as his role was interpreted and remembered by later writers. The two most important traditions about Peter are his martyrdom and his being the first bishop of Rome. Yet these traditions cannot be read directly from the Biblical evidence.

Acts tells us nothing about the founding of the church in Rome. All we know is that there was a Christian community there when Paul arrived. When *Acts* tells us Peter went off *elsewhere* the author could have been suppressing knowledge that the 'elsewhere' was in fact Rome, but this can only be guessed at. However it may be a deduction that can be substantiated.

The epistle to the *Romans* was sent by Paul early in his missionary career to a well-established church not founded by him. If Peter had founded that church, this may explain why Paul is so concerned in this letter above all to express his beliefs about God's purposes for gentiles and Jews and to clarify his own distinctive theological position to a church which in Paul's eyes had been based on a perverted view of the gospel. A similar need to correct Peter's teaching may have lain behind the composition of Mark's gospel which is of Roman provenence and written about the time Paul was in Rome.

A further claim that could help sustain the traditional linking of Peter with Rome is found in *I Peter*. Even if this letter was pseudonymous the letter eminated from a section of the church which venerated Peter. The letter claims to be sent from Babylon thought by many – probably correctly – to be an euphemism for Rome.

It is therefore possible to elicit some Biblical support for the tradition that Peter was the founder of the church in Rome, but what of his alleged martyrdom? With the wisdom of hindsight Peter's death by crucifixion is possibly predicted in *John* 21:18. Another New Testament indication that Peter was venerated as a martyr figure may be seen in *I Peter*, which is a letter written to give comfort and encouragement to Christians about to experience persecution. Such Christians could well have found a letter in Peter's name exemplary.

However, the tradition of Peter's martyrdom in Rome is not firmly stated in extant documentary evidence until the second half of the second century although there are one or two allusions in the earlier *I Clement* and Ignatius of Antioch's letters to Rome. Prior to the second century early Christian writers are silent about Peter's death. The archaeological evidence that seeks to identify some bones buried under St Peter's Basilica in the Vatican as those of Simon Peter is inconclusive, and the real 'proof' for Peter's martyrdom in Rome must still be sought from literary evidence.

Peter as first Pope may be difficult to prove because the connexion with Rome is dubious. He was obviously the first leader of the Jerusalem church but because of his special history his authority was greater than that of just a local church leader. He certainly seems to have had an influence over churches founded by other Christians, although *I Peter* 5:1 remembers him as only one elder among others. Peter as leader and spokesman of the twelve in the gospels; Peter as Jesus' choice to be the foundation stone of his church; the pastoral commission bestowed on Peter by the risen Jesus in *John 21* are all pointed to by defenders of the church's tradition. But if it is accepted that these sayings are creations of the early Jerusalem church in the light of Peter's assumption of leadership there, then the sayings cannot be used as divine commands regarding Peter's prominence.

The church tradition nevertheless may be historically accurate in stating that Peter was the leader of the church in Rome before his martyrdom but the Biblical basis for this tradition is inconclusive. The later career and ultimate fate of Peter are not recorded in the New Testament. This may be because even those parts of the New Testament most favourably disposed to Peter are working from sources contaminated at an early date by the pervading influence of Paul and his anti-Petrine reaching. An attempt was begun in New Testament times to review Peter's career and rehabilitate him but the process was never completed in the first century. Vital early evidence once suppressed was doomed never to resurface. Apologists in later centuries may have tried to tap memories but for the most part the deeds of the historical Peter had been forgotten. Only the Biblical evidence gets us close to the real man but even this is woefully inadequate and needs to be carefully sifted if any factual evidence is to be found in it.

NOTES FOR FURTHER READING
Oscar Cullmann: *Peter: Disciple, Apostle, Martyr* SCM, 2nd edition, 1962. Raymond E. Brown, Karl P. Donfried, John Reumann (editors): *Peter in the New Testament*, Geoffrey Chapman, 1973. J. K. Elliott: 'Κηφᾶς: Σίμων Πέτρος: ὁ Πέτρος: An Examination of New Testament Usage', *Novum Testamentum*, XIX (1972), pp 241–56.

The Contest for Men's Souls

A rich and scholarly show traces Christianity's competition
with early spiritual rivals, and its eventual triumph

LIONEL CASSON

Lionel Casson is chairman of the classics department at New York University.

The titles museum curators and scholars give to the exhibitions they mount are sometimes enough to discourage all but the most crusading art lover from sampling the objects on display. Age of Spirituality: Late Antique and Early Christian Art, Third to Seventh Century *is the dry and perhaps intimidating label for a remarkable show now at the Metropolitan Museum in New York. Though there are no long lines waiting to get in, and no Mona Lisas are to be seen there, the exhibition is an art history event with a reward for any visitor.*

According to the Metropolitan staff, which took five years to organize Age of Spirituality, *it is the "most important exhibition ever assembled of the art of the period." More than 450 objects—sculptures, paintings, ivories, ceramics, mosaics, glassware, silverplate, jewelry, textiles, manuscripts—have been assembled from some 100 collections in this country, Europe, and other parts of the world. Thanks to the simplicity and clarity of the arrangement in five galleries,* Age of Spirituality *is a visual essay on the slow and subtle establishment of Christianity in the pagan world and a high and complicated culture little known to us today. The 71 carved ivories—many of them more than 1,500 years old, yet speaking in crisp and vivid figures—would make a fabulous show in themselves.*

Here, Lionel Casson, a distinguished professor and an expert in the period, describes how well those fascinating times are defined through the beautiful images of a rare art.

In the second century of the Christian Era, the empire of Rome comprehended the fairest part of the earth, and the most civilized portion of mankind.... Peaceful inhabitants enjoyed and abused the advantage of wealth and luxury." So wrote Edward Gibbon to open his monumental study of the later Roman Empire.

The decline and fall began the very next century. The "fairest part of the earth" became a bloody battlefield in the third century A.D., as one army leader after another struggled to capture the throne. When the soldiers were not engaged in civil war, they were at the frontiers trying to check the Gauls, Goths, and other barbarians on the move. On top of all this, toward the end of the century an astronomical inflation hit: in 30 years the price of wheat, the staff of life for most of the population, went from 1,300 drachmas a bushel to 84,000. It is no surprise that all over Rome's realm men gave up on the grim and unpredictable world about them and pinned their hopes on an unchanging, eternally serene world beyond.

But which path to salvation was one to choose? There were any number of religions that guaranteed it, and all of them boasted flocks of adherents. Was one to follow Orpheus, the god from Thrace, whose power was such that he could soothe the savage breasts of wild beasts? Or Isis, the goddess from Egypt, whose selfless love for her young son made her especially appealing to women, above all mothers? Or Cybele, the goddess from Asia Minor, whose frenetic ritual brought worshipers to a pitch of ecstasy? Or Mithras, the god from Persia, who slaved tirelessly to save men from evil and better their lot? Or Christ, the savior from Palestine, who was, uniquely, god and man?

The contest to capture men's souls was in full swing by the third century, and it was not finally resolved until the seventh, when Christianity put the finishing touches to its total victory. The rivals used a variety of weapons: words, music, dance, ritual, spectacle, art. The music, dance, ritual, and spectacle have been almost wholly lost. The words can still be read, but the fire breathed into them when they were written has long since burned out. Only the art is intact—or, rather, a portion of it has survived. These precious relics of a critical period in western history are what make up the current exhibition at the Metropolitan Museum. This is not great art in the style of a Rembrandt painting or a Michelangelo sculpture. But many pieces are rare and beautiful, and fascinating for what they portray. And all are of supreme importance in reflecting men's ideas and feelings during the centuries that saw the rise and triumph of Christianity.

• • •

The pagan religions were not all-out competitors: joining one of them did not preclude joining others; the prudent pagan hedged his religious bets. But for Christianity it was

3. THE JUDEO-CHRISTIAN HERITAGE

winner take all: those who entered the ranks had to renounce forever all other forms of worship. Eventually the church was able to carry this stand to its logical conclusion and stamp out the other religions.

Inevitably, the victor's art drove out of existence the art of the defeated rivals. Christian art consequently plays the lead role in the Metropolitan's show. There is a sampling of the losers' art: a relief showing Mithras slaying the bull whose blood will flow upon the earth and thereby inseminate it so that men may reap crops; an ivory box decorated with a carving of Isis at a solemn banquet; a silver dish with a picture of Cybele in a chariot drawn by lions and surrounded by followers whirling in a frenzied sword dance. But the greater part of the exhibition is given over, and properly, to Christianity. The first room introduces, through a selection of portrait-sculptures, emperors such as Constantine the Great and Justinian, who were instrumental in giving the new religion its start and promoting its advance. The last room contains a stunning assemblage of varied objects from the sixth and seventh centuries, by which time art was devoted almost exclusively to the greater glory of the Christian god.

• • •

The term *Christian art* is, in a way, a misnomer. Victors in art, as in war, gain the right to exploit the losers, and the art that was turned out for Christianity was simply the art of the times adapted for new patrons and customers. It was essentially the art the Greeks had created long before, as far back as the fourth century B.C. when Alexander the Great wrought such tremendous changes in the Mediterranean world. Greek

CINCINNATI ART MUSEUM

Memorial marble bust of an upper-class matron from the fifth or sixth century

METROPOLITAN MUSEUM OF ART, THE CLOISTERS COLLECTION

Jonah saved from the whale, in a third-century marble, symbolizes the Resurrection.

gods and heroes and the events of Greek mythology were favored as subject matter. To this repertoire was added, in response to the needs of the time, portraits of the great: the kings who after Alexander's death ruled the lands he had conquered, and also the notable poets, dramatists, philosophers. Whether gods or men, they were rendered naturalistically, in the round, in some casual pose. The Romans had taken over this art, and since they welded the Mediterranean into a single political unit, gave it the chance to spread from one end to the other. Well established, international in appeal, such an art was an ideal instrument for Christian leaders.

They did not try to change it; on the contrary, artists merely adapted it to the needs of Christianity. Shops took on the new clientele without abandoning the old, simultaneously turning out illuminated manuscripts of Virgil and of the Bible, objects decorated with scenes from the life of Achilles and objects with scenes from the Old Testament (which derived, as we are shown in a special portion of the exhibition, from Jewish art). Sculptors and painters rendered the new rulers and notables, sacred and secular, in the same way they had the old. This gave the impression—art creates artful propaganda—that the new had taken over the mantle of the old and were possessed of their majesty, authority, powers, and virtues.

Thus Christ is represented seated on a gorgeous throne like a Roman emperor; an Evangelist is posed as a Greek phiiosopher; Saint George killing the dragon looks like Bellerophon killing the Chimera; and David slaying a lion that attacked his flock is very like Hercules slaying the mythological lion of Nemea. Some curious combinations resulted from this melding of pagan and Christian. In one wall painting we see a musician charming wild beasts; he is neither the Orpheus of Greek mythology nor the Orpheus of the Orphic religious sect, but David, the skilled musician of the Bible. A statuette portrays a shepherd carrying a lamb on his shoulders, a motif that goes back to very early Greek art; here, however, the figure is no longer an anonymous Greek lad but Christ, the Good Shepherd. A fine silver plate is decorated with the encounter between David and Goliath, but they look like gladiators in the arena—a swordsman, armed head to foot, is pitted against an opponent clad in a light tunic. A casket made for a Christian couple bears a picture of Aphrodite, the seductive Greek goddess of love. An ivory plaque depicting the emperor Justinian includes, above him, a bust of Christ offering a blessing, and, alongside him, a Roman winged victory offering a crown or wreath.

• • •

The spirituality mentioned in the title of the exhibition is most apparent in the way faces are rendered: they show, rather than a miscellany of emotions or interests, only a solemn thoughtfulness. The eyes are especially revealing: they are made to gaze, wide open, past the spectator, as if looking upon another world. This was by no means something introduced under the influence of Christianity; it had entered in pagan times when men began turning to religion en masse, and like so much else, had been taken over by Christianity. Pagan and Christian figures share it indiscriminately. A portrait of Constantine the Great, the emperor whose Edict of Toleration set Christianity on its triumphal march, has this spiritual gaze—but so does a portrait of Maxentius, the emperor who was Constantine's bitter opponent. The artists of both were seeking to concentrate attention on their subject's inner life.

Another way the artists brought out the spiritual side was by dematerializing the bodies of their subjects, by abandoning the naturalistic way of rendering them in favor of a more abstract and two-dimensional depiction. This is why they preferred shallow relief, painting, and mosaic to sculpture in the round: the latter smacked too much of the material world. We know what Augustus, Claudius, Trajan, and other noted emperors of pagan times looked like from the fine portrait statues of them that have survived. The best portrait we have of Justinian, the great emperor of the sixth century who did so much for the cause of the church, is a life-sized figure in a mosaic at Ravenna (a copy is included in the exhibition) in which he is almost an abstract figure, his body devoid of corporeality, his face stylized, and his eyes, of course, staring into space.

What may start out as a genuine way to express certain feelings or thoughts can end up as mere stylistic convention. So it was with these ways of indicating spirituality. A finely carved ivory plaque shows Justinian on horseback; not only the emperor but also his horse gaze abstractedly into the distance. Another plaque of roughly the same age pictures the mythological heroine Ariadne, whose undoing was caused by her flaming sexual passion, flanked by a satyr, the Greek symbol of lechery. But there is nothing erotic about either of them here; both have the spiritual look.

The rendering of figures in abstract fashion is so much the style of the age that the pieces done in the earlier style stand out, sometimes dramatically. A case in point is a series of statuettes illustrating scenes from the life of Jonah (his story was a particularly popular subject since the whale's swallowing him up and then disgorging him safe and sound upon land offered a nice parallel to the death and Resurrection of Christ). Most Jonah versions were done in the new style, but these sculptures, dating back to the third century, are fully rounded, naturally modeled, and in vigorous movement. The illuminations in manuscripts—the art of illumination flourished mightily in these centuries, and some strikingly beautiful examples are among the best things in the show—even in later centuries tended to be done naturalistically. This was especially true of those in scientific works, treatises on animals and plants, and the like, where man's inner feelings were beside the point.

• • •

There are any number of objects on display that make one wonder just how genuinely spiritual this age of spirituality was. Its people are consistently portrayed with their eyes fixed upon a world beyond, yet they certainly enjoyed to the full the good things of this world. We see specimens of the gorgeous gold and gem-encrusted jewelry they wore, the magnificently decorated silverplate they displayed, the fine furnishings they surrounded themselves with. In their pictures they are garbed in what obviously was expensive and elaborate clothing. And all classes, poor as well as rich, never lost their enthusiasm, at times fanatical, for such unspiritual activities as horse racing or gladiatorial games and other bloody spectacles. One beautifully carved ivory, dating to the first part of the fifth century, vividly pictures hunters slaughtering wild elk in the arena.

How deeply spiritual the age was is of minor importance, however. It was the age during which Christianity forged ahead to become the dominant religion first of Europe and then of most of the globe, the age in which a venerable old world died and a new one was born. The *Age of Spirituality* at the Metropolitan Museum is one of the finest collections of art objects of these crucial centuries ever put together.

Moslems and Byzantines

With the fall of Rome three emergent orders came to dominate the Mediterranean world. In Europe various Germanic kingdoms filled the vacuum left by Rome. In the Balkan peninsula and Asia Minor the eastern remnants of Rome evolved into the Byzantine Empire. The Middle East and North Africa fell to an expanding Arab empire, according to "The World of Islam." Each area developed a unique civilization, based in each instance upon a distinctive form of religion—Roman Catholicism in Western Europe, Orthodox Christianity in the Byzantine sphere of influence, and Islam in the Arab world. Each placed its unique stamp upon the classical tradition to which all three fell heir. The articles in this unit, however, concentrate on the Byzantine and Moslem civilizations. The medieval culture of Europe is treated in the next chapter.

Western perceptions of Islam and Arabic civilizations have been clouded by ignorance and bias. To European observers during the medieval period, Islam seemed a misguided version of Christianity. In the wake of Arab conquests, Islam increasingly came to represent terror and devastation, a dangerous force loosed upon Christendom. Reacting out of fear and hostility, Christian authors were reluctant to acknowledge the learning and high culture of Arabic civilization.

Moslem commentators could be equally intolerant. Describing Europeans, one of them wrote: "They are more like beasts than like men. . . . Their temperaments are frigid, their humors raw, their bellies gross . . . they lack keenness of understanding . . . and are overcome by ignorance and apathy."

The stereotypes formed in early encounters between Christians and Moslems survived for generations. Centuries of hostility have tended to obscure the degree of cultural exchange between the Arab world and the West. Indeed, as William H. McNeill has observed, Moslems have been written out of European history.

However, the domain of Islam encroached upon Europe at too many points for the two cultures to remain mutually exclusive. In western Europe, Islam swept over Spain, crossed the Pyrenees, and penetrated France. In the central Mediterranean, it leapt from Tunis, to Sicily, and then into Italy. In eastern Europe, Islam finally broke through Asia Minor and into the Balkans and Caucasus. It is useful to recall, too, that early Islam was exposed to Jewish, Christian, and classical influences. History and geography determined that there would be much cross-fertilization between Islam and the West, a theme taken up by Harvey Cox in "Understanding Islam."

Yet there is no denying the originality and brilliance of much of Islamic civilization. For a start, there is Islam itself, unquestionably one of the great religions of mankind. Additional evidence of Arabic creativity can be found in the visual arts, particularly in the design and decoration of the great mosques.

The medieval West borrowed extensively from the Arabs. The magnificent centers of Islamic culture—Baghdad, Cairo, Cordoba, and Damascus—outshone the cities of Christendom. Islamic scholars surpassed their Christian counterparts in astronomy, mathematics, and medicine—perhaps because the Arab world was more familiar than medieval Europe with the achievements of classical Greece. (European scholars regained access to the Greek heritage at least partially through translations from the Arabic!)

As for the Byzantine Empire, it was for nearly a thousand years a Christian bulwark against Persians, Arabs, and Turks. Its missionaries and statesmen spread Orthodox Christianity, with its unique tradition of Caesaropapism, to Russia. Its scholars and lawmakers preserved much of the classical heritage, though Byzantine Greeks rejected some facets of Hellenism as Arnold Toynbee reports in "The Byzantine Greeks' Heritage from the Hellenic Greeks." Even hostile Islam was subject to a "constant flow of ideas" from the Byzantines.

Looking Ahead: Challenge Questions

Do medieval hostilities between the Arabs and the West color relations between the two in the modern world?

Do the articles in this unit betray any bias toward Islam and the Arabs?

Why did Byzantine Greeks reject some elements of Hellenism?

THE BYZANTINE GREEKS' HERITAGE FROM THE HELLENIC GREEKS

Arnold Toynbee

THE HELLENIC GREEKS' LEGACY to the Byzantine Greeks was potent and massive. In the course of the three centuries (AD 284-602) of cultural overlap, during which the Hellenic civilization was not yet extinct, while the Byzantine civilization was already in being, the Byzantines rejected a number of key elements in Hellenism. City-states had already become incapable of serving even as non-sovereign municipal organs of local self-government. The Byzantine Greeks rejected the city-states' pre-Christian religion, the outward-facing rectilinear architecture of the Hellenic temples in which the rites of this religion had been performed, the naturalistic representation of the human form in monumental sculpture (bas-reliefs, as well as statues), and Hellenic philosophy. These rejected elements of Hellenism were of its very essence, and it might have been thought that so radical a cultural revolution would have enabled the Byzantine Greeks to jump clear of their Hellenic past. However, the Byzantines' repudiation of their Hellenic heritage, though sweeping, was not complete. The Byzantines failed to make a break with some of the naturalistic post-Alexandrine Hellenic minor arts, and they were haunted by two major bequests from Hellenism, the Hellenic

paideia* and the Roman Empire (a political dispensation which was the antithesis of city-states and was the nemesis of the Hellenic city-states' failure to give the Hellenic World peace, unity, and order). The paideia and the Imperial regime dominated Byzantine Greek life, and their dominance was one of the causes of the Byzantine Greek civilization's breakdown and disintegration.

In the Byzantine Greek World, there were still some city-states to be found, and some of these – for instance, Khersón (the Hellenic Khersónesos) in the Crimea and Neapolis (Naples) in southern Italy – were survivals from the Hellenic age of Greek history. Others, however – for instance, Amalfi on the Sorrento Peninsula, Ragusa, originally just off, and later just on, the coast of Dalmatia, and Venice in her lagoon – were settlements of refugees who had fled from their former homes during the age of anarchy and Völker-

wanderung (circa AD 378-678). The constitutions of these Byzantine city-states differed, de facto, from those of the former municipal city-states of the Roman Empire, and still more from those of the previous sovereign Hellenic Greek city-states. The local bishop now usually played an important part in the civil administration, and in the Byzantine city-states in Italy and Dalmatia the principal lay officers had originally been imperial officials and retained this status in theory long after they had become, in practice, representatives of the local population. Moreover, there were only fourteen Byzantine city-states in all, including the nine on and off the Dalmatian coast, and all of them were on the fringes of a Byzantine Greek World whose heart-land was Asia Minor with a European ferry-terminal at Constantinople. This heart-land was held by a resuscitated Roman Imperial Government, with Constantinople – 'the New Rome' – as its capital. Compared with the territories under the East Roman Imperial Government's direct administration, the autonomous outlying city-states were insignificant so long as the East Roman Empire flourished. The Empire's slow decline and long-delayed fall opened the way for Venice – and for Ragusa, too, on a smaller scale – to become sovereign

---

*Editor's note. In an earlier chapter of his book Toynbee gives the following definition of paideia: 'Together with atheletics, the study of "literae humaniores" provided the materials for paideia— the Greek word corresponds to the German Bildung (the formation of a cultivated mind) rather than to the more technical Erziehung (the German counter-part of the English word "education").'

     From *History Today*, November 1981. History Today, 83-84 Berwick Street, London W1V 3PJ. Reprinted by permission.

city-states, and for Naples to become eventually the capital of the Kingdom of the two Sicilies.

The Byzantine Greeks' repudiation of the Hellenic city-states' religion was an even greater formal break with the Hellenic past than the liquidation of the city-states themselves. This religious revolution was symbolised in a change in the connotation of a famous name. For Greeks of the Hellenic Age, the name 'Hellenes' signified 'civilized men' in contrast to 'barbarians'; for Greeks of the Byzantine Age, the name signified 'pagans' in contrast to 'Christians'. In other words the name 'Hellenes' meant, for the Byzantine Greeks, no longer 'insiders' but 'outsiders'; and these deplorable Greek-speaking recalcitrants, whose survival had been a reproach to Christian Greek civilization, had become extinct when their last representatives, the Maniots, had been converted to Christianity in the reign of the Emperor Basil I (867-86).

This reversal of the connotation of the name 'Hellenes' was dramatic, but the actual break in the continuity of the Greeks' religious life was not so great as this terminological revolution suggests. The break was on the surface; it did not extend to the subsoil. The popular religion remained what it had been since the Neolithic Age. A *genius loci* who had been honoured in the Hellenic Age as a hero or as a tutelary goddess was now honoured as a saint or as 'the All Holy Mother of God' ('The Panayía', 'the Theotókos'). The religious revolution at the official level passed over the peasants' heads, and most Greeks were still peasants till within living memory.

The reversal of the fortunes of Hellenism and Christianity was abrupt, because it could be, and was, brought about by acts of autocratic Roman Emperors. Constantine I and Licinius lifted the ban on Christianity in AD 313; Theodosius I imposed a ban on all non-Christian religions, except Judaism and the kindred religion of the Samaritans, in AD 380-92. The corresponding revolution in the architectural form of the Greek World's places of public worship was, by its nature, a change that could not be produced instantaneously by Imperial decrees; inevitably it was a gradual process.

This architectural revolution had two aspects: in being transformed into a Christian church, the Hellenic temple, like the word 'Hellenic' itself, was turned inside-out, and its rectilinear lines were dissolved into curves. Visually, the second of these two revolutionary changes is the more striking; psychologically, the first is the more significant.

The transfer of attention from the building's exterior to its interior was not only first in importance; it also came first chronologically. The Hellenic temple had been designed to please, not the god or goddess to whom it was dedicated, but the human public. The divinity's statue was housed – or immured – in lonely darkness within walls whose inner faces were not relieved either by windows or by decorations. The decorations were placed on the temple's outer faces, in the sunlight, for the delectation of the public. In the ensuing architectural revolution the contrast between the building's two faces was maintained, but their treatment was now reversed. This happened when the temple's lay-out was taken over for designing secular buildings in which the interior was to be used, not for housing the statue of a divinity, but by human beings.

Human users needed the comforts, namely sunlight and decorations, which had been unnecessary for a statue – however holy, and however great a work of art, this inanimate representation of the divinity might have been. Therefore, when the temple's layout was adapted for designing a basilica,[1] in which ceremonial, judicial, administrative, and other public business was to be transacted indoors, the basilica, unlike the temple, had to have windows. These might either be pierced in the walls or be provided by a clerestorey. The second alternative would require the replacement of the temple's traditional unitary gable roof by a roof in three sections, with the middle section elevated, in the clerestorey, to a higher level than the other two. For supporting the clerestorey and its roof, it was convenient to

transfer to the interior the rows of columns that had previously been set along the long sides of the temple's outer face. Besides being useful for the architect, this transfer was agreeable for the human users of the basilica, since the columns were major elements in the decoration of the building.

For the same reason, all the other decorations were now transferred from the exterior to the interior. They would be visible and enjoyable there, now that the interior was lighted by windows. The exterior could be stripped of its decorations, in order to embellish the interior with these, without any aesthetic loss for the human users. These, unlike statues, had sensibilities that required consideration. So long as the building had been a temple into which there was no admittance except, periodically, for a few priests, the public ordained its aesthetic satisfaction from the building by standing, or strolling round, outside it and enjoying its decorated exterior. Now that the interior of the building had become a place for the transaction of human business, no one would any longer wish to linger, gazing, outside; everyone would wish to enter promptly in order to get his business, inside the building, done. The exterior would not now receive more than a passing glance, so the architect could afford to leave it unadorned.

The rectilinearity of a basilica might be broken by apses, since an internal recess would be a convenient location for a public officer who was giving audience or was passing judgement in public. The public could then fill the main body of the hall. An apse would have to be roofed by a semi-dome, and this would break the rectilinearity of the roof as well. The way was now open for the development of the secular pre-Christian basilica into the Byzantine Christian church, in which the secular officer, transacting business with the public, would be replaced by a priest, officiating in partnership with a congregation.

In the architecture of the church, a square replaced the basilica's oblong ground-plan. This square was roofed by a circular dome, and the walls bulged out into apses roofed by semidomes. These led the eye up, by stages, to the crown of the central dome. The Hellenic rectilinear gable-roofed oblong temple had thus been

---

[1] The word means 'a royal building', and this suggests that the first basilicas must have been built in one or other of the Persian Empire's monarchical Greek successor-states. However, the earliest surviving basilica is the Aemilia at Rome, and this was preceded there by the Porcia. Both these basilicas at Rome were built at the beginning of the second century BC.

4. MOSLEMS AND BYZANTINES

4. MOSLEMS AND BYZANTINES

transformed into a non-rectilinear hollow pyramid. The roofing of a Byzantine church is pyramidal in its general effect; but, instead of mounting from its base to its apex in smooth surfaces meeting each other at sharp angles, the Byzantine church's roofing mounts in a crescendo of billowing curves. The optical effect is wave-like, and, to a modern observer, it feels like a piece of symphonic 'classical' Western music translated into visual form.

The Byzantine architects never carried their transformation of the Hellenic temple to its logical conclusion. This would have been a dome-roofed round building on the plan that, in the Pantheon at Rome, had been executed in concrete at an early date in the second century of the Christian Era.[2] The Byzantines did not take up the Roman invention of concrete, and therefore, with a single famous exception, they did not build on the gigantic scale of the Baths of Caracalla and of Diocletian at Rome. The exception is, of course, the Church of the Ayía Sophía at Constantinople (532-7). The architects achieved their *tour de force* of building on this scale without using concrete by countering the outward thrust of the huge non-monolithic dome with massive buttresses, and by making the dome, at the first essay, of such light materials that it had to be replaced (558-62).

The sixth-century Church of Saints Sergius and Bacchus at Constantinople ('the Little Ayía Sophía') is a variation on the plan of the Great Ayía Sophía, executed on a miniature scale, but the normal scale of later Byzantine churches is still smaller. The eleventh-century churches of the Kapnikaréa and the Saints Theodore at Athens are more characteristic, in both their scale and their style. The still tinier Old Metropolitan Church at Athens, whatever its date, conveys the quintessence of the Byzantine ecclesiastical architects' spirit.

The abandonment of monumental sculpture was, no doubt, partly a consequence of impoverishment. Statues of Emperors and even of popular racing charioteers continued to be made until the Empire's economic collapse in the East in and after AD 602. But,

though statues of human beings were still tolerated till then, statuary was too intimately associated with Hellenism, and Hellenism with paganism, to be looked upon with favour by the Christian ecclesiastical authorities. Moreover, when Hellenic temples were replaced by Christian churches, there was no longer a place for the statue of the divinity to whom a temple was dedicated. The statue had been the focal point of a temple's interior; the focal point of a church's interior was the place at which the rite of the Eucharist was performed. There was no room in a church for a rival centre of attraction in the form of a dominating statue. Nor could the Christian Trinity-in-Unity or the duality-in-unity of the person of Christ have been represented acceptably in the round. Christians fell out with each other in trying to convey these theological paradoxes even in the supple medium of the vocabulary of Hellenic Greek philosophy. In the use of art in the service of Christianity, the Byzantines eschewed sculpture in the round, and bas-relief too. They compensated for this renunciation by decorating the inner walls of their churches two-dimensionally with mosaics and paintings.

Even the flat representation of human forms is a breach of a Jewish tabu which the Christian Church has never avowedly repudiated; and when it has failed, as it has at most times and places, to observe the second of the Mosaic Ten Commandments, the Church has had periodic misgivings about its laxity on this important point. These misgivings have produced occasional outbursts of iconoclasm. There has been the Protestant outburst in Western Christendom in and after the sixteenth century; and this was anticipated by an outburst in the eighth century which was let loose by an East Roman Emperor, Leo III (717-41).

The conflict in the East Roman Empire over *eikóns* went on from 726 to 843. During these 117 years, except for the twenty-six years 787-813, the iconoclasts were in power in the Empire, and they enforced their veto on images in that part of Eastern Orthodox Christendom (and it was the greater part) over which the East Roman Imperial Government's authority was effective in the eighth and ninth centuries. In 843 the conflict

was ended by a compromise in which the champions of images got the best of the bargain. Two-dimensional images were reinstated, and it was agreed that the devotion paid to them was not to be condemned as idolatrous. The images, so their champions[3] claimed, were not being worshipped in themselves; they were being venerated as visual symbols of the divine or saintly persons whom they depicted.

This decision, which has never been called in question, demonstrated that the East Roman Imperial government's autocratic power was not so potent as public feeling. A majority of the Eastern Orthodox Christian public was deeply attached to the cult of images, and its devotion to them had not been weakened by two bouts of repression which, between them, ran to ninety-one years. In the end the iconoclastic-minded minority was compelled to recognize that, in spite of having had the Imperial Government on its side, it must acquiesce in a compromise that was a thinly disguised defeat. The settlement of AD 843 ensured that the two-dimensional representation of human form should be countenanced in Eastern Orthodox Christendom. The veneration of *eikóns*, both publicly in church and privately in the home, had been vindicated.

To judge by such evidence as we have for the style of the Hellenic art of painting, the Byzantine and the Hellenic treatments of the human figure were worlds apart. Their difference in style reflected a difference of spirit and aim. Hellenic pictures, like Hellenic bas-reliefs and statues and busts, were attempts to give a naturalistic portrayal of the human body, on the assumption that this was the best, and indeed the only possible, way of revealing human nature. On the other hand, Byzantine *eikóns* were attempts to adumbrate in visual form the invisible soul, on the assumption that the soul is Man's essence; and Byzantine painters and mosaicists did not hesitate to abandon naturalism if, by misrepresenting bodily appearances, they could succeed in conveying spiritual realities that a naturalistic treatment of the body would have failed to express.

I have elsewhere suggested that the Early Hellenic decorators of Pro-

---

[2] The Pantheon's Hellenic-style rectilinear portico is a perfunctory excrescence on the circular plan of the rest of the building.

[3] eg Saint John of Damascus (d AD 749).

their own non-naturalistic style. the Hellenic style was used by the Byzantines mainly for the trivial decoration of secular buildings; but they also used it, on occasion, for treating solemn religious themes. Moreover, their missionaries carried this Hellenic style, as well as the Byzantine style, to the regions beyond the East Roman Empire's frontiers that they converted. Examples of works in this Hellenic style survive in Russia and Serbia.

Thus, in the field of painting and mosaic-making, the Byzantines' attitude towards their heritage from Hellenism was equivocal; and so was their attitude towards Hellenic philosophy. Christian theology had been elaborated in terms of Hellenic philosophy. The Greek texts — and these are the original texts — of the Christian Church's creeds are composed in the Hellenic philosophy's vocabulary, and the value of Hellenic philosophy's service to Christianity was always recognized even by the strictest guardians of Eastern Christian Orthodoxy. Moreover, Christian Greeks preserved, by the laborious copying of manuscripts, the writings of those Hellenic philosophers who happened to have written in a form of Attic Greek that had passed the censorship of the Atticizing purists of the Augustan Age. They also preserved

Hellenic pictures and statues were attempts to portray the natural human body, for, as they believed, this was the best and only possible way of revealing human nature. This realism is exemplified in this drawing of a statue depicting Hebe and Cupid feeding Venus' doves.

togeometric vases broke with the Minoan style of Mycenaean naturalism deliberately, and that their successors in the age of mature Geometric art were also acting deliberately when they 'geometricized' the figures of human beings and horses that they admitted into their subtly worked out abstract patterns. These are only guesses. But, in the apparently parallel case of the non-naturalistic style of the Byzantine *eikóns*, we have positive evidence that their departure from naturalism was not the involuntary consequence of a loss of mastery of the technique of painting or mosaic-making in the naturalistic Hellenic style. There are surviving specimens of the Byzantines' continuing use of this Hellenic style, side by side with

Byzantine painters and mosaicists did not hesitate to abandon naturalism if, by misrepresenting objective figures, they could succeed in conveying spirituality. This design from a Byzantian woven silk fabric typifies this art form.

even Aristotle's unpolished lecture-notes. Yet, in the Byzantine Age, to study Plato's works for their content, and not just for their style, was usually a dangerous adventure. The institutes of philosophy at Athens[4] were closed by the Emperor Justinian I in AD 529. Seven philosophers who were unwilling to become apostates from Hellenism to Christianity had to find asylum in the Persian Empire; and they were able to return home, without having to choose between conversion and penalization, only because the Persian Emperor exacted from Justinian a special amnesty for them.[5] These were the last Greek students of Hellenic philosophy who were able to follow their bent with impunity.

[4] The separate institutes of the four major schools (Plato's Academy, Aristotle's Lyceum, Zeno's Stoa, Epicurus' Garden) had still been going concerns in the second century of the Christian Era. We do not know whether they retained their separate identities till 529. We know only that the teaching of Hellenic philosophy continued to be carried on at Athens until that date.

[5] In the Perso-Roman peace treaty of 523-3 (see Agathias: *Historiae*, Book II, chapters 30-1).

Phótios in the ninth century, Michael Psellós and John Italós in the eleventh century, and Yemistós Pléthon in the fifteenth century, each in turn got into trouble on this account. Italós and Pléthon asked for trouble; Phótios and Psellós did not; they tried to be discreet, but this did not save them. They were suspected of having secretly relapsed into the pre-Christian paganism that Pléthon afterwards professed openly and aggressively.

The two important elements in the legacy of Hellenism that the Byzantines failed to shake off were the Hellenic *paideia* and the Roman Imperial regime. In the latter part of the sixth century, the monks succeeded in putting the *paideia* out of action temporarily, but it was resuscitated in the ninth century. In the Eastern Orthodox Church's eyes the Hellenic *paideia* was innocuous, because all that it inculcated was an adulation of literary form. It had deliberately divorced form from content, and it did not take the content seriously; it did not regard this as having an intrinsic value of its own. As for the Roman Imperial regime, the Hellenes had begun by resenting and resisting its imposition but had ended by recognizing retrospectively that it had given the Hellenic civilization an unexpected and perhaps undeserved new lease of life. After that, the Hellenes had identified themselves with the Roman Empire and had appropriated it. The Greeks' captivation of their Roman conquerors was completed when they took to calling themselves Romans (Rhomaíoi) instead of Hellenes. Now that the word 'Hellenes' had come to signify 'pre-Christian Greeks', the Christian Greeks needed a new appellation for themselves, and in 'Rhomaíoi' they found the word that they were seeking. In Byzantine Greek parlance, 'Rhomaíoi' came to mean, not Latin-speaking Romans, but 'Greeks who were Eastern Orthodox Christians', in contrast to outsiders, extinct and extant. The extinct outsiders were the Hellenes; the extant outsiders were the inextinguishable barbarians beyond the East Roman Empire's frontiers, and, in Byzantine Greek eyes, these now included Old Rome's barbarized and non-Greek-speaking inhabitants.

The World of Islam

The Messenger of Allah

In a cave at the foot of Mount Hira near Mecca, where he had spent six months in solitary meditation, the vision came to Muhammad. The Angel Gabriel roused him from his bed with the stern command: "Proclaim!" Rubbing his eyes, the startled Muhammad gasped, "But what shall I proclaim?" Suddenly his throat tightened as though the angel were choking him. Again came the command: "Proclaim!" And again the terrified Muhammad felt the choking grip. "Proclaim!" ordered the angel for a third time. "Proclaim in the name of the Lord, the Creator who created man from a clot of blood! Proclaim! Your Lord is most gracious. It is he who has taught man by the pen that which he does not know."

Thus it was, according to Islamic tradition, that an unremarkable Arab trader from Mecca was inspired to preach God's word in the year A.D. 610. Compared with Jesus or the Buddha, information about the life of the man who became known as the Messenger of Allah is relatively abundant, although the facts have been embellished with pious folklore. Some have claimed that at Muhammad's birth the palace of the Persian emperor trembled, or that a mysterious light ignited at his mother's breast, shining all the way to Syria, 800 miles away. It was said that his body cast no shadow and that when his hair fell into a fire it would not burn. Muhammad himself disdained any miraculous claims, insisting that he was merely the all-too-human conduit through which God had revealed himself.

It is known that the Prophet was born about A.D. 570 to a member of the respected Meccan clan of Hashim. His father died shortly before Muhammad was born, and his mother when the boy was only six. Two years later, his doting grandfather Abd al-Muttalib died, leaving the orphan in the care of a poor uncle, Abu Talib. As a youth, Muhammad was set to work tending his uncle's herds; he later recalled that task as a mark of divine favor. "God sent no prophet who was not a herdsman," he told his disciples. "Moses was a herdsman. David was a herdsman. I, too, was commissioned for prophethood while I grazed my family's cattle.

As a young man, Muhammad was exposed to the currents of religious debate then swirling through the Middle East. He would listen avidly as Jews and Christians argued over their faiths. Those discussions may have fed his dissatisfaction with the traditional polytheistic religion of the Arabs, who believed in a panoply of tribal gods and jinn, headed by a deity known as Allah. Says Muhammad's French biographer, Maxime Rodinson: "Both Jews and Christians despised the Arabs, regarding them as savages who did not even possess an organized church."

At 25, Muhammad accepted a marriage proposal from Khadijah, a rich Meccan widow 15 years his senior, for whom he had led a successful caravan. With his financial security assured by Khadijah's wealth and business, he began to venture into the desert, to contemplate and pray, as had other Arab holy men before him.

According to legend, Muhammad had earned a reputation as a wise and saintly man even before his first revelation from the angel on Mount Hira. Looking out from the balcony of his Mecca home one day, he saw the members of four clans arguing over which of them should be allowed to carry the Black Stone, a huge meteorite that the Arabs regarded as sacred, to its new resting place in a rebuilt shrine called the Ka'ba. Unknown to Muhammad, they had resolved to let the first man who walked into the sanctuary decide the matter. Entering the holy place, Muhammad proposed a satisfactory compromise: placing the Black Stone on a blanket, he instructed each tribe to lift one corner. Then he personally laid the meteorite in its new niche.

At 40, Muhammad began to preach the new faith of Islam, which was gradually being revealed to him on his sojourns in the desert. Some of this religion was familiar to Arabs who knew about the monotheistic teachings of Jews and Christians. His countrymen, for example, could readily accept Muhammad's assertion that Allah, long regarded as the highest of the desert gods, was the same God worshiped by Jews and Christians. But Meccan traders felt threatened by Muhammad's growing power. Both Jews and Christians questioned his claim that he was revealing the true word of God to the Arabs, in effect joining them as "People of the Book." In 622, after being harassed by his opponents, Muhammad and his followers escaped to Medina in a migration known as the hegira.

To a growing body of converts, Muhammad began to elaborate on his new religion. Revelations came to him in trances; his descriptions of those encounters, memorized and recorded by his adherents, were later collected as the Koran. As his followers grew in strength and numbers, Muhammad began a series of raids on Meccan caravans, which led to several indecisive battles with their avenging war parties. In 628 the Meccans agreed to let Muhammad's followers make their pilgrimage to the Ka'ba, which the new faith continued to regard as a sacred shrine. Muslims believe it is the spot where Abraham prepared to sacrifice his son Ishmael at God's command. Two years later the prophet led an army of 10,000 into his former city, taking control in a bloodless victory.

For all the pious legends that grew up even in his lifetime, Muhammad remained a humble and, in some ways, unfulfilled man. He occasionally incurred the wrath of his wives and concubines. All of his sons died in childhood, leaving him with no male heir. In 632 he led a pilgrimage to Mecca, where he declared, "I have perfected your religion and completed my favors for you." Three months later he fell ill in Medina and died. To his zealous followers went the task of spreading the word of Allah, not only throughout Arabia but far beyond it as well.

A Faith of Law And Submission

God's grandeur, and a path to follow

Eight words in Arabic sum up the central belief of the world's 750 million Muslims: "There is no god but God, and Muhammad is the Messenger of God." Five times a day, from Djakarta to Samarkand to Lagos, this *shahada* (confession of faith) is recited by the devout as meuzzins (callers to prayer) summon them to worship God.

In the prescribed daily prayers, a pious Muslim does not beseech God for favors, either material or spiritual, so much as for guidance and mercy. The word Islam means submission, and the true Muslim submits his life to the divine will of a deity who is the Compassionate, the All Knowing, the Strong, the Protector, the All Powerful—to cite only a few of the traditional 99 "most Beautiful Names" of God.

Muslims believe that God decrees everything that happens in the cosmos. Some critical Western scholars contend that this doctrine leads to a kind of passive fatalism, but Islamic theologians strongly deny that *qadar* (divine will) negates a person's freedom to act. It merely means, says Muhammad Abdul Rauf, director of the Islamic Center in Washington, that "when some misfortune befalls us, we resign ourselves to it as something coming from God, instead of dispairing."

Islam stresses the uniqueness of the Creator, and strictly forbids *shirk*—that is, the association of anyone or anything with God's divinity. Along with Moses and Abraham, Jesus is revered by Muslims as one of the 25 scriptural prophets of God, and Islam accepts both his virgin birth and his miracles. But Muslims believe that Christian faith in the divinity of Jesus is polytheism. They resent being called "Muhammadans," which suggests that Muhammad's role in Islam is similar to that of Jesus in Christianity. The Prophet is revered as God's final Messenger to mankind, but is not worshiped as a divine being.

Because they accept the Bible, Jews and Christians have a special status in Islam as "People of the Book." Muslims also believe that the Bible in its present form is corrupt and that the true faith was revealed only to Muhammad. Those revelations are contained in the Koran, the Arabic word for recitation. Slightly shorter than the New Testament, the Koran has little narrative. There are evocations of divine grandeur in rhymed prose, florid descriptions of the harsh fate that awaits those who knowingly ignore God's will, and detailed instructions on specific ways that man must submit to his maker.

The basic spiritual duties of Islam are summed up in the so-called five pillars of faith. They are: 1) accepting the *shahada;* 2) the daily prayers to God while facing Mecca; 3) charitable giving; 4) fasting during the daylight hours of Ramadan, a 29- or 30-day month in Islam's lunar calendar* and 5) making the hajj, or pilgrimage, to Mecca at least once in an individual's lifetime—if he or she is financially and physically able. Some Muslims argue that there is a sixth pillar of the faith, namely jihad. The word is frequently translated as "holy war", in fact, it can refer to many forms of striving for the faith, such as an inner struggle for purification or spreading Islamic observance and justice by whatever means.

During the hajj, pilgrims throng Mecca, the men clad in two seamless white garments and sandals, the women in white head-to-toe covering. The pilgrims walk seven times around the Ka'ba, a cubical stone building covered by a gold-embroidered black canopy, in the exterior wall of which is set the Black Stone. The interior, now empty, once housed pagan idols, which Muhammad destroyed. The pilgrims also visit other holy sites, act out the search for water by Hagar, the mother of the Arab nation, perform a vigil on Mount 'Arafat (site of the Prophet's last sermon) and conduct a ritual sacrifice of goats, sheep and camels.

The devout Muslim is also expected to observe the Shari'a, which means "the path to follow." Based on the Koran, the deeds and sayings of Muhammad and the consensus of Islamic scholars, the Shari'a is not just a compilation of criminal and civil law, but a complex, all embracing code of ethics, morality and religious duties. It is a sophisticated system of jurisprudence that summarizes 1,400 years of experience and constantly adapts, in subtle ways, to new circumstances.

In Western eyes, however, the Shari'a all too often is denigrated as a relic of the Dark Ages. Some of its provisions do seem awesomely harsh:

habitual thieves are punished by having a hand cut off; adulterers are either scourged or stoned to death; falsely accusing a woman of adultery calls for 80 lashes—the same penalty imposed on a Muslim caught drinking alcohol. The equivalence of the two punishments exemplifies the time-honored logic of the Shari'a. The Koran forbade the drinking of wine, but did not specify a punishment; 80 lashes, however, was decreed for those who bore false witness. Making the analogy that drink leads to hallucination and to telling untruths, Islamic sages decided that the punishment for the two sins should be the same.

Muslim jurists contend that stoning is no more typical of Islamic justice than extra-tough state laws against the possession of drugs are representative of the American legal tradition. Beyond that, the threat of the Shari'a is usually more severe than the reality. As in Western common law, defendants are presumed innocent until proved guilty. To convict adulterers, four witnesses must be found to testify that they saw the illicit act performed. Moreover, there are loopholes in the law and liberal as well as strict interpretations of it. For example, a thief can lose his hand only if he steals "in a just society"; the provision has been used by Islamic courts to spare men who steal because they are poor and have no other means to feed their families.

In Iran particularly, the reintroduction of the Shari'a under an Islamic republic is seen as a threat to rights that women won under the monarchy. Feminists do have reason to complain. Islamic law tolerates polygamy, so long as a husband treats his wives equally, and he can end a marriage simply by saying "I divorce thee" three times in front of witnesses. A woman may request a divorce under certain circumstances—for example, if she is mistreated or her husband is impotent. Women must dress modestly, and their inheritance is limited to a fraction of that of men. In defense of these sexist inequities, scholars of the Shari'a note that Islamic law was advanced for its time. Before Muhammad, women in Arabia were mere chattel. The Koran emphatically asserts a husband's duty to support his wife (or wives), who are allowed to keep their dowries and to own property—rights that did not emerge until much later in Western countries.

All Muslims accept the Koran as God's eternal word, but Islam to some extent is a house divided, although its divisions are not as extensive as those in Christianity. About 90% of all Muslims are Sunnis (from *sunna,* "the tradition of the Prophet"), who consider themselves Islam's orthodoxy. In Iran and Iraq, the majority of Muslims are Shi'ites ("partisans" of 'Ali), who differ from

*By the Islamic calendar, this is the year 1399, dated from Muhammad's Hegira to Medina.

the Sunnis in some of their interpretations of the Shari'a and in their understanding of Muhammad's succession. The Prophet left no generally recognized instructions on how the leadership of Islam would be settled after his death. The Sunnis believe that its leader should be nominated by representatives of the community and confirmed by a general oath of allegiance. Shi'ites contend that Muhammad's spiritual authority was passed on to his cousin and son-in-law, 'Ali, and certain of his direct descendants who were known as Imams. Most Iranian Shi'ites believe that 'Ali's twelfth successor, who disappeared mysteriously in 878, is still alive and will return some day as the Mahdi (the Divinely Appointed Guide), a Messiah-like leader who will establish God's kingdom on earth. Meanwhile, Shi'ite religious leaders, such as Iran's Ayatullah Khomeini, have wide powers to advise the faithful on the presumed will of the "Hidden Imam." Sunni religious scholars, the ulama, have less authority, though both branches of Islam consider their leaders to be teachers and sages rather than ordained clergymen in the Western sense.

Both Sunni and Shi'ite Islam include Sufism, a mystical movement whose adherents seek to serve God not simply through obedience to the law but by striving for union with him through meditation and ritual. Sufism is considered suspect by fundamentalist Muslims like the puritanical Wahhabis of Saudi Arabia, because it allows for the veneration of *awliya*—roughly the equivalent of Christianity's saints. Islam also has spawned a number of heretical offshoots. One is the Alawi sect, a Shi'ite minority group to which most of Syria's leaders belong. The Alawis believe in the transmigration of souls and a kind of trinity in which 'Ali is Allah incarnate. Another is the secretive Druze sect of Israel, Lebanon and Syria, which split away from Islam in the 11th century. America's so-called Black Muslims were once generally regarded by Sunni Muslims as followers of a new heresy. By adopting orthodox beliefs and discarding a rule that limited membership to black Americans, the World Community of Islam in the West, as the movement is now known, has been accepted as being part of the true faith.

Islam is not a collection of individual souls but a spiritual community; its sectarian divisions, as well as the man-made barriers of race and class that Islam opposes, dissolve dramatically at the hajj. Once a pilgrimage made mostly by Muslims of the Middle East and North Africa, the hajj has become a universal and unifying ritual. For those who have taken part in it, the hajj acts as a constant testament to Islam's vision of a divine power that transcends all human frailties.

Some sayings from a Holy Book

The grandeur of the Koran is difficult to convey in English translation. Although Islam's Holy Book is considered God's precise word only in Arabic, a generally recognized English text is that of Abdullah Yusuf 'Ali.

THE OPENING PRAYER. In the name of God, Most Gracious, Most Merciful. Praise be to God, the Cherisher and Sustainer of the Worlds; Most Gracious, Most Merciful; Master of the Day of Judgment. Thee do we worship, and Thine aid we seek. Show us the straight way, the way of those on whom Thou hast bestowed Thy Grace, those whose (portion) is not wrath, and who go not astray.

THE NATURE OF GOD. God! There is no god but He—the Living, the Self-subsisting, Eternal. No slumber can seize Him, nor sleep. His are all things in the heavens and on earth. Who is there can intercede in His presence except as He permitteth? He knoweth what (appeareth to His creatures as) Before or After or Behind them. Nor shall they compass aught of His knowledge except as He willeth. His Throne doth extend over the heavens and the earth, and He feeleth no fatigue in guarding and preserving them.

DRINKING AND GAMBLING. They ask thee concerning wine and gambling. Say: "In them is great sin, and some profit, for men: but the sin is greater than the profit."

THEFT. Male or female, cut off his or her hands: a punishment by way of example, from God, for their crime: and God is Exalted in Power. But if the thief repent after his crime, and amend his conduct, God turneth to him in forgiveness; for God is Oft-forgiving, Most Merciful.

POLYGAMY. If ye fear that ye shall not be able to deal justly with the orphans, marry women of your choice, two, or three, or four; but if ye fear that ye shall not be able to deal justly (with them) then only one, or (a captive) that your right hands possess.

CHRISTIANS. They do blaspheme who say: "God is Christ the son of Mary." But said Christ: "O Children of Israel! Worship God, my Lord and your Lord." Whoever joins other gods with God— God will forbid him the Garden, and the Fire will be his abode.

THE DAY OF JUDGMENT. When the sun is folded up; when the stars fall, losing their lustre; when the mountains vanish; when the she-camels, ten months with young, are left untended; when the wild beasts are herded together; when the oceans boil over with a swell; . . . when the World on High is unveiled; when the Blazing Fire is kindled to fierce heat; and when the Garden is brought near;—(Then) shall each soul know what it has put forward.

PARADISE. (Here is) a Parable of the Garden which the righteous are promised: In it are rivers of water incorruptible; rivers of milk of which the taste never changes; rivers of wine, a joy to those who drink; and rivers of honey pure and clear. In it there are for them all kinds of fruit, and Grace from their Lord. (Can those in such bliss) be compared to such as shall dwell forever in the Fire, and be given, to drink, boiling water, so that it cuts up their bowels?

Islam, Orientalism And the West

An attack on learned ignorance

In an angry, provocative new book called Orientalism *(Pantheon; $15), Edward Said, 43, Parr Professor of English and Comparative Literature at Columbia University, argues that the West has tended to define Islam in terms of the alien categories imposed on it by Orientalist scholars. Professor Said is a member of the Palestine National Council, a broadly based, informal parliament of the Palestine Liberation Organization. He summarized the thesis of* Orientalism *in this article*

One of the strangest, least examined and most persistent of human habits is the absolute division made between East and West, Orient and Occident. Almost entirely "Western" in origin, this imaginative geography that splits the world into two unequal, fundamentally opposite spheres has brought forth more myths, more detailed ignorance and more ambitions than any other perception of difference. For centuries Europeans and Americans have spellbound themselves with Oriental mysticism, Oriental passivity, Oriental mentalities. Translated into policy, displayed as knowledge, presented as entertainment in travelers' reports, novels, paintings, music or films, this "Orientalism" has existed virtually unchanged as a kind of daydream that could often justify Western colonial adventures or military conquest. On the "Marvels of the East" (as the Orient was known in the Middle Ages) a fantastic edifice was constructed, invested heavily with Western fear, desire, dreams of power and, of course, a very partial knowledge. And placed in this structure has been "Islam," a great religion and a culture certainly, but also an Occidental myth, part of what Disraeli once called "the great Asiatic mystery."

As represented for Europe by Muhammad and his followers, Islam appeared out of Arabia in the 7th century and rapidly spread in all directions. For almost a millennium Christian Europe felt itself challenged (as indeed it was) by this last monotheistic religion, which claimed to complete its two predecessors. Perplexingly grand and "Oriental," incorporating elements of Judeo-Christianity, Islam never fully submitted to the West's power. Its various states and empires always provided the West with formidable political and cultural contestants—and with opportunities to affirm a "superior" Occidental identity. Thus, for the West, to understand Islam has meant trying to convert its variety into a monolithic undeveloping essence, its originality into a debased copy of Christian culture, its people into fearsome caricatures.

Early Christian polemicists against Islam used the Prophet's human person as their butt, accusing him of whoring, sedition, charlatanry. As writing about Islam and the Orient burgeoned—60,000 books between 1800 and 1950—European powers occupied large swatches of "Islamic" territory, arguing that since Orientals knew nothing about democracy and were essentially passive, it was the "civilizing mission" of the Occident, expressed in the strict programs of despotic modernization, to finally transform the Orient into a nice replica of the West. Even Marx seems to have believed this.

There were, however, great Orientalist scholars; there were genuine attempts, like that of Richard Burton (British explorer who translated the *Arabian Nights*), at coming to terms with Islam. Still, gross ignorance persisted, as it will whenever fear of the different gets translated into attempts at domination. The U.S. inherited the Orientalist legacy, and uncritically employed it in its universities, mass media, popular culture, imperial policy. In films and cartoons, Muslim Arabs, for example, are represented either as bloodthirsty mobs, or as hook-nosed, lecherous sadists. Academic experts decreed that in Islam everything is Islamic, which amounted to the edifying notions that there was such a thing as an "Islamic mind," that to understand the politics of Algeria one had best consult the Koran, that "they" (the Muslims) had no understanding of democracy, only of repression and medieval obscurantism. Conversely, it was argued that so long as repression was in the U.S. interest, it was not Islamic but a form of modernization.

The worst misjudgments followed. As recently as 1967 the head of the Middle East Studies Association wrote a report for the Department of Health, Education and Welfare asserting that the region including the Middle East and North Africa was not a center of cultural achievement, nor was it likely to become one in the near future. The study of the region or its languages, therefore, did not constitute its own reward so far as modern culture is concerned. High school textbooks routinely produced descriptions of Islam like the following: "It was started by a wealthy businessman of Arabia called Muhammad. He claimed that he was a prophet. He found followers among other Arabs. He told them that they were picked to rule the world." Whether Palestinian Arabs lost their land and political rights to Zionism, or Iranian poets were tortured by the SAVAK, little time was spent in the West wondering if Muslims suffered pain, would resist oppression or experienced love and joy: to Westerners, "they" were different from "us" since Orientals did not feel about life as "we" did.

No one saw that Islam varied from place to place, subject to both history and geography. Islam was unhesitatingly considered to be an abstraction, never an experience. No one bothered to judge Muslims in political, social, anthropological terms that were vital and nuanced, rather than crude and provocative. Suddenly it appeared that "Islam" was back when Ayatullah Khomeini, who derives from a long tradition of opposition to an outrageous monarchy, stood on his national, religious and political legitimacy as an Islamic righteous man. Menachem Begin took himself to be speaking for the West when he said he feared this return to the Middle Ages, even as he covered Israeli occupation of Arab land with Old Testament authorizations. Western leaders worried about their oil, so little appreciated by the Islamic hordes who thronged the streets to topple the Light of the Aryans.

Were Orientalists at last beginning to wonder about their "Islam," which they said had taught the faithful never to resist unlawful tyranny, never to prize any values over sex and money, never to disturb fate? Did anyone stop to doubt that F-15 planes were the answer to all our worries about "Islam"? Was Islamic punishment, which tantalized the press, more irreducibly vicious than, say, napalming Asian peasants?

We need understanding to note that repression is not principally Islamic or Oriental but a reprehensible aspect of the human phenomenon. "Islam" cannot explain everything in Africa and Asia, just as "Christianity" cannot explain Chile or South Africa. If Iranian workers, Egyptian students, Palestinian farmers resent the West or the U.S., it is a concrete response to a specific policy injuring them as human beings. Certainly a European or American would be entitled to feel that the Islamic multitudes are underdeveloped; but he would also have to concede that underdevelopment is a relative cultural and economic judgment and not mainly "Islamic" in nature.

Under the vast idea called Islam, which the faithful look to for spiritual nourishment in their numerous ways, an equally vast, rich life passes, as detailed and as complex as any. For comprehension of that life Westerners need what Orientalist Scholar Louis Massignon called a science of compassion, knowledge without domination, common sense not mythology. In Iran and elsewhere Islam has not simply "returned"; it has always been there, not as an abstraction or a war cry but as part of a way people believe, give thanks, have courage and so on. Will it not ease our fear to accept the fact that people do the same things inside as well as outside Islam, that Muslims live in history and in our common world, not simply in the Islamic context?

UNDERSTANDING ISLAM
No More Holy Wars

Harvey Cox

Harvey Cox teaches at Harvard Divinity School and writes widely on the varieties of religious experience.

> *No cask without an end stave or a head*
> *E'er gaped so wide as one shade I beheld,*
> *Cloven from chin to where the wind is voided.*
> *Between his legs his entrails hung in coils;*
> *The vitals were exposed to view, and too*
> *That sorry paunch which changes food to filth.*
> *While I stood all absorbed in watching him*
> *He looked at me and stretched his breast apart,*
> *Saying: "Behold, how I split myself!*
> *Behold, how mutilated is Mahomet!*
> *In front of me the weeping Ali goes,*
> *His face cleft through from forelock to chin;*
> *And all the others that you see about*
> *Fomenters were of discord and of schism:*
> *And that is why they are so gashed asunder."*
>
> Dante, *Inferno*, Canto 28

Odious Western images of Muhammad and of Islam have a long and embarrassingly honorable lineage. Dante places the prophet in that circle of hell reserved for those stained by the sin he calls *seminator di scandalo e di scisma.* As a schismatic, Muhammad's fitting punishment is to be eternally chopped in half from his chin to his anus, spilling entrails and excrement at the door of Satan's stronghold. His loyal disciple Ali, whose sins of division were presumably on a lesser scale, is sliced only "from forelock to chin." There is scandal, too. A few lines later, Dante has Muhammad send a warning to a contemporary priest whose sect was said to advocate the community of goods and who was also suspected of having a mistress. The admonition cautions the errant padre that the same fate awaits him if he does not quickly mend his ways. Already in Dante's classic portrait, we find the image of the Moslem linked with revolting violence, distorted doctrine, a dangerous economic idea, and the tantalizing hint of illicit sensuality.

Nothing much has changed in the 600 years since. Even the current wave of interest in Eastern spirituality among many American Christians has not done much to improve the popular estimate of Islam. It is fashionable now in the West to find something of value in Buddhism or Hinduism, to peruse the *Sutras* or the *Bhagavad Gita,* to attend a lecture by Swami Muktananda or the Dalai Lama, even to try a little yoga or meditation. But Americans in general and Christians in particular seem unable to find much to admire in Islam. As G. H. Hansen observes, with only a modicum of hyperbole, in his book *Militant Islam*, the mental picture most Westerners hold of this faith of 750 million people is one of ". . . strange bearded men with burning eyes, hieratic figures in robes and turbans, blood dripping from the amputated hands and from the striped backs of malefactors, and piles of stones barely concealing the battered bodies of adulterous couples." Lecherous, truculent, irrational, cruel, conniving, excitable, dreaming about lascivious heavens while hypocritically enforcing oppressive legal codes: the stereotype of the Moslem is only partially softened by a Kahlil Gibran who puts it into sentimental doggerel or a Rudolph Valentino who does it with zest and good humor.

There is, of course, one important exception to the West's rejection of the religious value of Islam. This exception's most visible representatives have been Muhammad Ali and the late Malcolm X. Most Americans who seem genuinely drawn to the call of the minaret are blacks. But given the racial myopia that continues to affect almost all American cultural perceptions, this exception has probably deepened the distrust most white Christians feel toward Islam. The dominant image was summed up brilliantly in a Boston newspaper's cartoon showing a Moslem seated in prayer. Over his head the balloon contained one word: "Hate!"

This captious caricaturing of Moslems and Arabs is not confined to the popular mentality. In his *Orientalism,* Edward Said describes a study published in 1975 of Arabs in American textbooks that demonstrates how prejudices continue to be spread through respectable sources. One textbook, for example, sums up Islam in the following manner:

> The Moslem religion, called Islam, began in the seventh century. It was started by a wealthy businessman of Arabia, called Muhammad. He claimed that he was a prophet. He found followers among the other Arabs. He told them they were picked to rule the world.

This passage is, unfortunately, not atypical. Although phrased with some degree of restraint, it coheres all too well with the popular medieval picture of Muhammad as a sly trickster or the current comic-book depictions of the sated, power-mad Arab. Moreover, Dante's unflattering portrait of the prophet was rooted in traditions that existed long before his time. These primal shadowgraphs have notoriously long half-lives, and they continue to darken our capacity to understand Islam to this day.

Allah works in mysterious ways. Through the stubborn geopolitics of oil, Westerners are being forced, like it or not, to learn more about Islam than they ever thought they would. Inevitably this reappraisal has begun to include a rethinking of the relationship between Islam and Christianity. In the fall of 1979, the World Council of Churches sponsored a conference on the subject in Kenya, and Christian scholars with direct experience of Islam were invited from all over the world. The results were mixed since, ironically, theologians from countries where Islam is a small minority seemed much more eager to enter into dialogue with their Moslem counterparts than did those from countries where Christians form a small minority in an Islamic world. Still, the recent upsurge of Islamic visibility will surely increase enrollments in courses on Islam wherever they are offered, and sales of books on the subject are up.

All such activities are welcome. But what about the shadowgraphs? Conferences and courses will help only if their participants become aware of the deeplying, nearly archetypal images that subvert the whole enterprise from the outset. Along with study and analysis, a kind of cultural archaeology or even a collective psychoanalysis may be necessary if we are to leave Dante's Inferno behind and live in peace with our Moslem neighbors on the planet Earth. The question is, How can Westerners, and Christians in particular,

begin to cut through the maze of distorting mirrors and prepare the ground for some genuine encounter with Moslems?

The first thing we probably need to recognize is that the principal source of the acrimony underlying the Christian–Moslem relationship is a historical equivalent of sibling rivalry. Christians somehow hate to admit that in many ways their faith stands closer to Islam than to any other world religion. Indeed, that may be the reason Muhammad was viewed for centuries in the West as a charlatan and an imposter. The truth is, theologically speaking at least, both faiths are the offspring of an earlier revelation through the Law and the Prophets to the people of Israel. Both honor the Virgin Mary and Jesus of Nazareth. Both received an enormous early impetus from an apostle—Paul for Christianity and Muhammad for Islam—who translated a particularistic vision into a universal faith. The word "Allah" (used in the core formula of Islam: "There is no God but Allah and Muhammad is his prophet") is not an exclusively Moslem term at all. It is merely the Arabic word for God, and is used by Arabic Christians when they refer to the God of Christian faith.

There is nothing terribly surprising about these similarities since Muhammad, whose preaching mission did not begin until he reached forty, was subjected to considerable influence from Christianity during his formative years and may have come close—according to some scholars—to becoming an Abyssinian Christian. As Arend van Leeuwen points out in his thoughtful treatment of Islam in *Christianity in World History,* "The truth is that when Islam was still in the initial stages of its development, there was nothing likely to prevent the new movement from being accepted as a peculiar version of Arabian Christianity." Maybe the traditional Christian uneasiness with Islam is that it seems just a little *too* similar. We sense the same aversion we might feel toward a twin brother who looks more like us than we want him to and whose habits remind us of some of the things we like least in ourselves.

The metaphor of a brother, or perhaps a cousin, is entirely germane. Muhammad considered himself to be in a direct line with the great biblical prophets and with Jesus. The title he preferred for himself was *al-nabi al-ummi,* the "prophet of the nations" (or of the "gentiles"). He believed he was living proof that the God who had called and used previous prophets such as Abraham and Job, neither of whom was Jewish, could do the same thing again. Later on, Moslem theologians liked to trace the genealogy of Muhammad back to Hagar, the bondwoman spouse of Abraham. The Old Testament story says that Hagar's giving birth to Ishmael stirred up such jealousy between her and Sarah, Abraham's first wife and the mother of Isaac, that Sarah persuaded Abraham to banish the bondwoman and her child into the desert. There Hagar gave up hope and left the child under a shrub to die. But God heard the child's weeping, created a well of water in the desert to save them both, and promised Hagar that from her son also, as from Isaac, He would "create a great nation." According to the symbolism of this old saga, the Jews and the Arabs (and by extension all Moslems) are the common offspring of Abraham (called "Ibrahim" in Arabic). This makes Christians and Moslems cousins, at least by legendary lineage.

The similarity between Christians and Moslems does not stop with religious genealogy. The actual elements of the Koran's message—faith, fasting, alms, prayer, and pilgrimage—all have Christian analogues. Despite its firm refusal to recognize any divine being except God (which is the basis for its rejection of Christ's divinity), Islam appears sometimes to be a pastiche of elements from disparate forms of Christianity molded into a potent unity. Take the Calvinist emphasis on faith in an omnipotent deity, the pietistic cultivation of daily personal prayer, the medieval teaching on charity, the folk-Catholic fascination with pilgrimage, and the monastic practice of fasting, and you have all the essential ingredients of Islam. All, that is, except the confluence of forces which, through the personality of Muhammad and the movement he set off, joined these elements in the white heat of history and fused them into a coherent faith of compelling attractiveness.

Like Paul, who said his apostleship was to both Jews and gentiles, Muhammad believed his mission was twofold. He felt called by God to bring the law and the Gospel to the heretofore neglected peoples of Arabia. But he also felt he had a mission *to* those very peoples—Christians and Jews (whom he called "peoples of the book")—*from* whom the original message of salvation had come. In one important respect, therefore, Muhammad's mission was different from St. Paul's. Since Muhammad carried on his preaching in the early decades of the seventh century, he not only had to deal with a Judaism he considered corrupted (as Paul had too); he also had to face an even more corrupted form of Christianity. Fortunately for St. Paul, since the Christian movement was only a decade or so old when he lived, he had to cope only with a few legalizers and gnostics. The infant Church had not yet tasted the corruption that comes, perhaps inevitably, from power and longevity. From a certain Christian perspective, Muhammad was as much a reformer as an apostle. A prophet of the gentiles, he also saw himself as a purifier of the faith of all the "peoples of the book," Christians and Jews, calling them away from the ornate and decadent versions of the faith they had fallen into and back to its simple essence, at least as he understood it. There is always something of this urge to simplify, to return *ad fontes*, in any reformer. And Muhammad was no exception.

No one should minimize the fact that in any genuine conversation between Christians and Moslems certain real differences in theology and practice will have to be faced, what scholars often call "rival truth claims." But such conflicting assertions can be properly understood only against the flesh-and-blood history that has somehow made them rivals. Religious teachings do not inhabit a realm apart. They mean what they do to people because of the coloration given to them by long historical experience. Therefore a previous question has to be asked. It is this: If Christianity and Islam share such common roots and, despite real differences, some striking similarities, why have they grown so bitter toward each other over the centuries? Why did the average white American feel less sympathetic to Islam than to any other world religion even *before* our current flap with the ayatollahs?

The explanation for this hostility is not a pretty story. Its major lineaments can be indicated with the names of three figures who symbolize its most critical stages. The first is Alexander the Great, whose career corresponds to what might be called the prehistory of Christianity. The second is Constantine the Great, who exemplifies its early period. The third is Pope Urban II, who expresses its classical phase, one of the most formative in the Christian–Moslem interaction.

Christopher Dawson, the late Roman Catholic cultural historian, once remarked that "Muhammad is the Orient's answer to Alexander the Great." At first this sounds like one of those wonderfully sweeping but highly improbable aphorisms. Muhammad, after all, lived and preached a full thousand years after Alexander. The prodigious Macedonian disciple of Aristotle conquered everything between Greece and northern India before he was thirty-three and spread the culture and values of Hellenism wherever his soldiers trod. But a thousand years is not a long time when one is dealing with cultural domination and the backlash it ultimately elicits. This is what Dawson had in mind.

Alexander did more than conquer everything before him. Unlike previous conquerors, who sought mainly booty and tribute, he wanted to convert his colonized peoples into Hellenists. Alexander's conquest mixed military, political, and religious power. It was obviously going to require a comparable fusion of elements to throw off his conquest. After a thousand years that response finally came. It was Islam.

As Albert Memmi writes in his classic book *The Colonizer and the Colonized*, ". . . the colonized can wait a long time to live. But, regardless of how soon or how violently the colonized rejects his situation, he will one day begin to overthrow his unlivable existence with the whole force of his oppressed personality. . . . He attempts to . . . reconquer all the dimensions which the colonization tore away from him." When the Islamic response to Roman–Hellenistic domination exploded in the early seventh century, the entire world was stunned by its vitality. In retrospect, however, we can understand its religious ideology in large measure as a reverse mirror image of what it was overthrowing. Take its rejection of the divinity of Christ, for example. Alexander had allowed himself to be viewed as a divine being, a god-emperor, and this ideology persisted through centuries of European culture in one form or another. The Koran's strenuous insistence that there was only one God, and its rejection of all semidivine beings, must be seen at least in part as a rejection of the political use of Christology to sacralize various forms of human rule.

The Moslem rejection of the divinity of Christ is not just simpleminded monotheistic stubbornness. It began as "political theology." For the Arabians, living on what were then the outskirts of the Eastern Empire, it marked a rejection not only of the non-Semitic categories in which the doctrine of Christ's divinity were elaborated in the Church councils (the "being of one substance with the Father") but also of the political hierarchy the doctrine helped to sanctify, especially in the Byzantine environment. When the Pantocrator Christ began to sacralize an empire in which the Arabians were the underdogs, their refusal of the doctrine made perfect sense. Alexander the Great had created the cultural imperium for which Christianity eventually supplied the sacred ideology. The Islamic revolt against this system was a revolt not against the Gospel as they understood it but against what Christianity had come to be. Islam's implacable insistence on one God not only freed thousands of people from their fear of the evil jinns and united the feuding tribes of Arabia (and later a vast part of the known world); it also served as a counterideology to the political function that Christian trinitarianism was beginning to serve. No "rival truth claim" debate between Christians and Moslems can begin until this history is recognized.

Islam began as a liberation theology, but, like Christianity, which had a comparable beginning, it could not resist the wiles of worldly power. As in the case of most successful liberation movements, Islam incorporated many of the cultural and political characteristics of its enemies. Though Muhammad was hounded out of Mecca by its local power elites, one hundred years after his death a glittering capital for the new Islamic empire was founded at Baghdad, the "Constantinople of Islam." Moslems became imperialists themselves, although in most instances they allowed Christians and Jews to practice their faiths. Forced conversions were rare. Above all, Moslems became the supreme masters and cultivators of the very Greek wisdom that had been imposed on them by Alexander. They became devout disciples of the same Aristotle whose zealous pupil had set out to spread his master's learning in their lands a millennium before. It was the Arabs, after all, who brought Aristotle back to the West and eventually to the cluttered desk of Thomas Aquinas. At its height, Islamic culture vastly outshone that of the Christian West, which most Moslems more or less accurately regarded as a barren outpost. But at the same time, the original liberating impulse of Islam had begun to run out. Today, paradoxically, this very spoiling by success may provide a needed bridge between Christians and Moslems, since Christians have experienced the same sad, familiar story in their own history.

Muhammad's judgment on the Christianity of his day is one of the great ironies of history. This Christianity, which began in the life of a Palestinian Jew who was executed because he was viewed as a threat to the Roman Empire and to the Hellenistically inclined rulers of his colonized nation, was seen a few centuries later by Muhammad, the prophet of another downtrodden nation, as the religious sanction for his own people's domination. What is remarkable about Muhammad is not that he rejected current theories about the divinity of Christ but that he did *not* reject Jesus himself. Rather he tried, from his own vantage point, to bypass the caricature of the Gospel which imperial Christianity had elaborated and to reclaim the faith of a people much like his own who had once looked to Allah for justice and mercy.

Jesus, then, is another vital link between the two faiths. To this day, Jesus holds a central place in Islamic teaching and is sometimes even depicted as a kind of supreme exemplar of what is meant by "submission to God" (the meaning of the word "Islam"). In popular Islamic belief, Jesus often occupies an even more important position. Thus many Moslems believe that when the long awaited "Twelfth Iman," whose name is *al-Mahdi*, finally appears to usher in the reign of justice on earth (*not* in the sky, incidentally), he will either be accompanied by Jesus or will turn out to be the same one whose "coming in Glory" the Christian creeds confess. Obviously there is much to discuss here between these two "Jesus traditions," if the ground can be cleared of spiteful stereotypes and the sibling rivalry can be held at bay.

Both Christianity and Islam began as visions of captive peoples who yearned for deliverance and caught a glimpse of hope in the promise of God. The two can understand each other only when both begin to acknowledge these common roots, step out of the long shadow of Alexander the Great, and try to learn from each other what has gone so terribly wrong over the years of their common history.

Constantine the Great, Roman emperor from 313 to 337 A.D. represents the historical turning point that eventually created the second great obstacle between Christians and Moslems. The Christian movement began not only as a message of hope to a colonized nation but also as the faith of the poor and the brokenhearted. But three centuries later, when Emperor Constantine beheld the cross shining across the sun and later claimed to have won the imperial throne with the help of Jesus Christ, all that changed. Although St. Paul could write to one of his fledgling congregations that there were "not many wise, not many powerful" in their midst, and the common name for Jesus' followers in those earliest days was simply "the poor," Constantine's well-timed and canny conversion totally altered all that for good. It is impossible to understand Muhammad's view of Christianity unless one remembers that he was basing it not on the Gospel accounts but on his observation of how the Church was actually functioning in his world. By their fruits ye shall know them.

Muhammad claimed to be one of the poor, at least when he started, and he never tired of reminding his followers that he was only an illiterate camel driver. He saw his humble origins not as a disgrace but as a wondrous proof that God could raise up from the very stones children unto Abraham. The *al-ummi* with whom Muhammad identified himself has a double sense. The word means not only the "gentiles," or "people without the Law," but also the unlettered, something close to the *am-ha-aretz*, the poor "people of the land" with whom Jesus sided against the learned scribes and Pharisees. The historian H. G. Reisman says that Muhammad was "a leader of the masses against the privileged minorities of wealth and sophistication." This may also explain in part the popular Islamic belief, baffling to many Christians, that every child is a "born Moslem." With growing up and education comes sophistication and corruption. In the Koran, similar to an idea St. Paul defends in the first chapter of his Epistle to the Romans, every person has an inborn, natural awareness of God. We all start out pious but are misled by a fallen civilization and perfidious religions. It is the task of preaching to call us back to what we were, or were intended to be, in the first place.

The Koranic vision of a simple faith by which the poor and the unlettered can withstand manipulation at the hands of the powerful and the better educated makes Christians uncomfortable today, and understandably. It is painfully reminiscent of the "Blessed are the poor" with which Jesus began the Sermon on the Mount and the subsequent "Woe to you rich" with which he made sure he was not misunderstood. The Church has never completely lost its recognition of this aspect of its history. It surfaces repeatedly in such places as Simone Weil's life-shaking discovery that Christianity is essentially a faith of the poor, or in the Latin American bishops' declaring that the Church's special responsibility is to stand with the jobless and landless. Nor has Islam, despite prodigiously rich oil sheiks, ever completely lost this central core of its

tradition either. Each faith will find it easier to appreciate the other when this special role of the *al-ummi* becomes the major rather than the minor theme of its message. In this respect, Christianity probably has more recovering to do than Islam has.

Pope Urban II, who occupied the throne of Peter from 1088 to 1099, is the third great actor in the tragedy of Christianity's cumulative falling-out with Islam. He was an energetic reformer who became Pope during a period of divisiveness in the Church; his main challenge was to bring it into some semblance of unity. Like many other rulers before him, religious and secular, Urban hit upon a surefire unifying idea. Realizing that nothing unites like an external foe, and inspired by requests from the beleaguered Christians of the East, he preached a holy war against the infidels who were even then holding the Holy Sepulchre and promised the fullest spiritual benefit to those who would take up the cross. Christians and other Americans who criticize the concept of the jihad, or holy war, and decry the taking of hostages and conversion at sword's point are right, of course. But it does not require much reading in this not-so-glorious chapter in Western Christian history to see that Moslems were neither the first nor the only guilty parties in this department. In fact, there is at least one prominent school of historical scholarship that sees the first Moslem expansion not as a jihad but as a large-scale migration similar to the one that had brought the Germanic tribes into the Roman Empire from the other direction. The concept of holy war can be found in more than one Old Testament verse. It did not originate with Islam. To many Arabs it must have seemed the only sensible response to the not entirely pacifist manner in which the Christian empire dealt with its recalcitrant provinces and with those forms of Christianity, such as Nestorianism, that the bishops deemed unacceptable.

Like all wars, holy or unholy, the Crusades produced their quota of atrocity stories on both sides. They also produced countless incidents of generosity and unexpected interfaith respect. The mutual admiration that developed between Richard I of England and the theologically articulate Saladin, celebrated in legend, seems to have had a factual basis. Still, it was the Crusaders and not the Saracens who boasted that when they first took Jerusalem the blood of the infidels, including wives and children, flowed through the streets as deep as the horses' stirrups. Such memories do not die easily, and it is important to recall that although Westerners would sometimes like to reduce the "wars of the cross" to tales of chivalry and late-night movie fare, for many Moslems the Crusades—Christian jihads—remain the most graphic expression of what the cross means. All the more amazing, then, that even the Ayatollah Khomeini, talking to a group of visiting American clergy on Christmas Day, 1979, could ask why, as those who worship the wounded Jesus, Americans were so incapable of understanding a wounded people such as his own. Apparently some feeling for the real meaning of the cross has survived in Islam, despite the Crusades.

If it took Muhammad a thousand years to respond to Alexander the Great, perhaps it should come as no surprise that it has taken the Islamic peoples another 900 years to respond to Pope Urban II, Peter the Hermit, and the hordes of idealists, adventurers, and thugs who in successive waves burned and pillaged their way across Europe toward the Holy Land for nearly 400 years. True, some historians hold that the Crusades might never have occurred had it not been for the previous threat of militant Islam to the West. Still, once the Crusades began, they acquired a lethal momentum of their own. Christian armies started by burning the nearest ghetto, and when their attempts to seize the Holy Sepulchre did not fully succeed, turned their cross-bedecked banners toward the pagan Baltic peoples and the Albigenses of southern France. It is an ugly history. But until the sorry story of Crusade versus jihad is faced frankly and then replaced by a more generous and conciliatory attitude, the hatred and suspicion between Christians and their Moslem cousins can only escalate.

No discussion of the relations of Moslems and Christians can proceed very far without raising the parallel question of the equally long and similarly vexed interaction of Moslems and Jews. The Jewish historian S. D. Goitein is the leading scholar in the study of what he calls the "symbiosis" between Jews and Arabs. Now at the Institute for Advanced Study in Princeton, after having taught at the Hebrew University of Jerusalem, Goitein has spent a lifetime probing Moslem religious literature, the medieval Geniza (documents written in Hebrew characters but in the Arabic language), and the fascinating histories of the so-called Oriental Jewish communities—those of the Arab and Moslem worlds. His *From the Land of Sheba* is an anthology of Yemenite literature. It would be hard to find a more reliable guide to this intricate area.

Goitein believes that Islam is actually far closer to Judaism than to Christianity in its core ideas. In taking this position, he joins a debate that has been going on for years (the other side contending that the similarity with Christianity is more important). Goitein bases his case on the obvious fact that both Islam and Judaism are religions of the Holy Law, and that Moslem law is in many respects similar to the Jewish Halakah, which he calls its "older sister." Both therefore differ, at least in this respect, from Christianity, which, with its emphasis on grace, has always harbored a certain suspicion of religious law (even though Christian theologians have managed to spin out yards of it over the years).

Goitein's "sister" image of the bond between Islam and Judaism should not be surprising when one bears in mind the saying, attributed to Muhammad, "You will follow the traditions of those who preceded you span by span and cubit by cubit—so closely that you will go after them even if they creep into the hole of a lizard." This colorful advice takes on even more significance in light of the fact that there were large Jewish settlements in the city of al-Medina, the birthplace of the first Moslem community, and that the biographers of the prophet almost all agree that these communities, far from being an obstacle to the spread of Islam, were in fact wondrous evidence of Allah's merciful and providential preparation of the people for a monotheistic faith. As with Christianity, the early years of Islam seem in retrospect to have promised mostly fraternal—or in this case sororial—congeniality with Judaism. But again, the roiling history of Jewish and Islamic peoples has often turned familial ties into tribal vendettas. Must it always be so?

In his informative book *Jews and Arabs: Their Contacts Through the Ages,* Goitein does what only a seasoned scholar ever dares to do. He compresses eons of history into one volume, risks a few well-grounded generalizations, and even hazards some guesses about the future. He divides the millennia-long give-and-take between these two peoples into four periods. The first, corresponding perhaps to the Alexandrian age of the Christian–Islam story, begins before historical memory and reaches up to the sixth century A.D. and the appearance of Islam. During this early period, a critically formative one for the Jews since it saw the compilation of both the Bible and the Talmud, Goitein believes Jews and Arabs had quite similar social patterns and religious practices. He firmly rejects any notion of a common Semitic race, however, as a modern idea concocted from the misapplication of a term invented by a German scholar in 1781 to denote a group of related languages, not "races," or even peoples. The distinction is an important one. There are several examples of peoples who for a variety of historical reasons now speak a language spoken by other peoples with whom they have no ethnic consanguinity at all. Black Americans are a case in point. Likewise, Jews and Moslem Arabs are related, according to Goitein, but by history and tradition, not by race.

The period from, roughly, 500 A.D. to 1300 A.D. is Goitein's second one. He describes it as one of "creative symbiosis," in which early Islam developed in a largely Jewish environment. Although he agrees that Christian influences, coming especially from monastic groups, played some role in this primal period, he believes that Judaism was even more important, so much so that he is willing to say—with some reservations—that Islam appears to be "an Arab recast of Israel's religion." But the influence was not one-way, and the impact of Islam and the Arabic language on Jewish thought and the Hebrew language was, he adds, at least as considerable. Goitein also reminds his readers that although Jews experienced some legal disqualifications under Moslem rule, they almost always fared better than they did under Christian dominance.

Goitein's third period begins in about 1300, when the previously high-riding Arabs began to "fade out" of world history at the same time that the Oriental Jews began to fade out of Jewish history. During this phase, which lasted until about 1900, the Arab nations fell to various conquerors until the entire Arab world had become a colony of the modern West. Meanwhile Jewish religious and intellectual life flourished in Europe, while Jews living in the beleaguered Moslem world, though they nurtured a rich internal culture, shared the suffering and obscurity of their Moslem neighbors.

The present period in Goitein's scheme begins in about 1900 with the coincidental revival of Jewish and Arab cultural and national identities, both influenced by the growing nationalism of nineteenth-century Europe. Since Zionism was an almost exclusively European (and American) movement, however, it was perceived by Arabs and other Moslems more as a new Western intrusion into the East, a pattern going back at least to the Crusades, than as something essentially Jewish, at least at the beginning. But shortly after the founding of the State of Israel, Israelis had to cope with a kind of mirror image of this "intrusion" as Jewish immigrants from Arab countries, the "forgotten Jews" of the previous period, streamed into Israel, making it less "European" with every passing day. The paradox of this apparent double intrusion was illustrated recently when an Oriental Jewish scholar living in Israel complained to a visitor about all the remarks he heard from his European colleagues lamenting the "Levantizing" of Israel. "How," he asked, " can you 'Levantize' something that is already the Levant?" His comment underscores Goitein's thoughtful prophecy that since the future of Jewish–Moslem relations has everything to do with the relations between Israel and its Arab neighbors, Israel's internal policy toward its Oriental Jews and its Arab citizens will be of decisive importance. Whether or not this turns out to be true, remembering the roller-coaster history of Jewish–Moslem relations helps one not to become too depressed about the steep decline these relations have taken in recent decades. There have been downs before, and ups, and it is not impossible that the tiny minority of Arab-Israeli citizens who are also Christians might eventually be able to play a conciliatory role. Likewise, though it seems far-fetched today, the global Jewish community, with centuries of experience in the Christian and the Moslem worlds, might someday provide an essential bridge between these two faith traditions, both in some ways its offspring. In any case, whatever happens to facilitate the conversation that must go on among Christians, Jews, and Moslems is bound to benefit all three.

Jews may help, but in the final analysis, given the role our religions play in both our cultures, no real rapport between the Arabs and the West seems possible unless Christians and Moslems make a more serious effort to understand each other. Curiously, after being warned for years that our greatest enemies in the world were godless and atheistic, Americans are now faced with a challenge that emanates from profoundly religious sources. Although Islam has never accepted the dichotomy between religion and the civil polity that has arisen in the West, there can be little doubt that the present Islamic renaissance is not a deviation but an authentic expression of the elements that were there at its origin. So we are now told that, instead of atheists, we are dealing with "fanatics," or "Moslem fundamentalists." This language is not very helpful either.

Sometime soon a real conversation must begin. Perhaps the moment has come to set aside Dante, Urban II, and the rest; to remember instead the two children of Father Abraham, from both of whom God promised to make great nations; to recall that Jesus also cast his lot with the wounded and wronged of his time; to stop caricaturing the faith of Arabia's apostle; and to try to help both Christians and Moslems to recover what is common to them in a world that is just too small for any more wars, especially holy ones.

The Medieval Period

In the aftermath of barbarian incursions, Western civilization faced several massive challenges: to integrate Roman and Germanic peoples and cultures, to reconcile Christian and pagan viewpoints, and to create new social, political, and economic forms to fill the vacuum left by the disintegration of the Roman order. In sum, it was necessary for Western civilization to shape a new unity out of the chaos and diversity of the post-Roman world. The next millenium (c.500-c.1500) saw the rise and demise of a distinctive phase of the Western experience—medieval civilization.

Medieval man developed a uniquely coherent view of life and the world, summarized here by literary scholar C.S. Lewis:

> "Characteristically, medieval man was not a dreamer nor a spiritual adventurer; he was an organizer, a codifier, a man of system. . . . Three things are typical of him. First, that small minority of his cathedrals in which the design of the architect was actually achieved (usually, of course, it was overtaken in the next wave of architectural fashion long before it was finished). . . . Secondly, the *Summa* of Thomas Aquinas. And thirdly, the *Divine Comedy* of Dante. In all these alike we see the tranquil, indefatigable, exultant energy of a passionately logical mind ordering a huge mass of heterogeneous details into unity. They desire unity and proportion, all the classical virtues, just as keenly as the Greeks did. They have a more varied collection of things to fit in. And they delight to do it."

This outlook also expressed itself in a distinctly medieval social ideal. In theory medieval society provided a well-ordered and satisfying life. The Church looked after men's souls, the nobility maintained civil order, and a devoted peasantry performed the ordinary work of the world. Ideally, as Crane Brinton explains, "a beautifully ordered nexus of rights and duties bound each man to each, from swineherd to emperor and pope."

Of course, medieval society often fell short of this ideal. Feudal barons warred among themselves. Often the clergy was ignorant and corrupt. Peasants were not always content and passive. Medieval civilization also had other shortcomings. During much of the Middle Ages there was little interest in nature and how it worked. While experimentation and observation were not unknown, science (or "natural philosophy") was secondary to theology, which generally attracted the best minds of the day. An economy based on agriculture and a society based on

hereditary status had little use for innovation. Aspects of medieval society are treated in "The Natural History of Medieval Women," and "Murder and Justice, Medieval Style."

All this is not to suggest that the medieval period was static and sterile. Crusaders, pilgrims, and merchants enlarged Europe's view of the world. And there were some noteworthy mechanical innovations: the horse collar, which enabled beasts of burden to pull heavier loads; the stirrup, which altered mounted combat; mechanical clocks, which made possible more exact measurement of time; the compass, a giant step toward the age of exploration; and the paper-making process, which made feasible the print revolution, and which in turn played key roles in the Reformation and the scientific revolution. Medieval ideas and technical innovations are surveyed in "The Viking Saga," "Student Power in the Middle Ages," and "Medieval Roots of the Industrial Revolution."

The medieval order broke down in the fourteenth and fifteenth centuries. Plague, wars, and famines produced a demographic catastrophe that severely strained the economic and political systems. Social discontent took the form of peasant uprisings and urban revolts. Dynastic and fiscal problems destabilized France and England. The Great Schism and new heresies divided the Church. Emergent capitalism gradually undermined an economy based on landed property. Yet these crises generated the creative forces that would give birth to the Renaissance and the modern era. The nation-state, the urban way of life, the class structure, and other aspects of modern life existed in embryonic form in the Middle Ages. As William McNeill has written, it was in medieval Europe that the West prepared itself for its later role as "chief disturber and principal upsetter of other people's ways."

Looking Ahead: Challenge Questions

Does the collapse of a civilization constitute an opportunity as well as a calamity?

How and why did women's lives change during the medieval period?

Were the Vikings destroyers or agents of progress?

Why did students have so much power in medieval universities?

What motivated medieval pilgrims and crusaders?

Is is possible to bridge the gap between modern and medieval outlooks?

The Natural History of Medieval Women

They began to live longer, but they lost economic and social ground

David Herlihy

Versed in reconstructing all dimensions of past human experience, many modern social historians have become especially interested in women. Partly inspired by the contemporary feminist movement (whose advocates have correctly pointed out that the history of roughly half of humanity has been systematically slighted), these historians also recognize that in the natural and social history of any society, women have unique and critical functions. They carry the new generation to term, sustain children in early life, and usually introduce the young to the society and culture of which they will be a part. Women begin the processes through which human cultures strive to achieve what their individual members cannot—indefinite life, immortality.

Few historians are willing to accept the claims of sociobiologists, who find culture already programmed in genes and who subordinate cultural history to natural history. But most would agree that human societies and civilizations cannot be properly evaluated or appreciated without considering the basic biological experiences of their members. These crucial events—including the duration of life itself under various social and historical conditions, as well as the timing of nursing and weaning, sexual maturity, marriage and mating, reproduction, menopause, and aging—are often by no means parallel experiences for both men and women and can have radically different consequences for each sex.

The biological experiences of women throughout the Middle Ages are interesting because of the length of this particular period: we can observe a thousand years of women's careers and the contours of their lives. Data concerning the Middle Ages are notoriously intractable —difficult to find, difficult to interpret. But medieval scholars advanced some general comments on the biology of women, and a few of these ideas have come down to us; even some precious statistical information that illuminates how women fared in the real world. Finally, some biographies, chiefly of saints and queens, support our rudimentary knowledge of women's situations. All these sources have manifest gaps, but taken together, they present coherent pictures of medieval women. Although medievalists are often obliged to be jugglers and prestidigitators, they are not without pins or beans with which to play.

In the Middle Ages, life expectancies apparently varied sharply, in accordance with epidemiological conditions. For unclear reasons, western Europe was practically free of epidemics from the sixth to the fourteenth century, when the infamous Black Death of 1348–1349 introduced an epoch of recurrent and devastating plagues. From the thirteenth century on, we know the birth and death dates of many medieval nobles and townspeople, predominantly male, and can venture some estimates. In the plague-free years of the thirteenth century, people could expect to live between 35 and 40 years. In the stricken generations including and immediately following the Black Death, life expectancies fell to only 17 or 18 years. It thereafter slowly lengthened and averaged about 30 years during the fifteenth century.

Life expectancies for women shifted up or down in phase with this general movement. But simultaneously, a small, significant change was taking place. Women were beginning to survive better than men; they were acquiring an advantage in longevity that, in the Western world, they have not since relinquished.

Medieval natural philosophers concluded that women's chances for life were improving. The biologists of the ancient world—of whom the foremost was Aristotle—had affirmed that, saving unusual circumstances, males of all species live longer than females (hard work or excessive sexual indulgence might frustrate nature's intent and artificially shorten the male life span). Males represented the perfection of the human species; females were an imperfection of nature, albeit a happy one, in view of their essential contribution to propagation. The defective females passed through all stages of life quicker than the male. They reached sexual maturity sooner, aged earlier, and were the first to die. The ancient biologists thought that specific humors determined a person's temperament and believed that women's temperaments, dominated by cold and dry humors, hurried them toward the cold and dry state of death.

In the twelfth century, when a renaissance of learning began in western Europe, scholars reexamined the biological writings of Aristotle and other classics. Initially, medieval natural scientists repeated without elaboration the ancients' opinion that men, as perfect representations of the species, live longer than women. Then, in the thirteenth century, the foremost biologist of the age, Saint Albertus Magnus (Albert the Great), who died in 1280, treated the question of the relative longevity of the sexes in a novel fashion. In Albertus's view, the Philosopher, Aristotle, was indeed correct. Men live longer than women *naturaliter*, "according to the natural order." But women live longer than men *per accidens*, "by accident," by which Albertus apparently meant under the distinctive conditions of his period. He gives three reasons for women's longer life expectancy: sexual intercourse is less demanding on women than on men; menstruation flushes impurities from women's bodies; and women "work less, and for that reason are not so much consumed." We can question what Albertus meant by the judgment that the demands of sexual intercourse or the purgative functions of menstruation were accidental, but his observation that the burdens of labor lowered men's natural life expectancies is worth remembering.

Subsequently, other medieval authors also concluded that women live longer than men. Some even occasionally pointed out that women must be the superior sex because they live longer and thus fulfill nature's intent better than males. Learned opinion shifted and the ancient belief in the greater life expectancy of males was slowly abandoned.

This change in scholarly attitudes corresponded with an actual improvement in life expectancies for women. From the opening centuries of the Christian Era, we have tens of thousands of funeral inscriptions, from visible standing monuments and from tombstones uncovered by archeologists' excavations. These epigraphs give age at death and allow a rough calculation of the duration of life according to sex. The evidence seems to confirm Aristotle's opinion that at their death, men in these populations of the late ancient era were four to seven years older than women. However, there may be a bias in the data; presumably, the young wife who died prematurely was more likely to earn a memorial than the aged and forgotten widow. But we are certain that women were in short supply in ancient society, either through systematic infanticide of girls or through shorter life expectancies. The biological experience of the women—or baby girls—of classical antiquity was not especially happy.

Unfortunately, we have no comparable epigraphic evidence from medieval populations. The earliest surviving relevant data are sporadic surveys made by the great European monasteries, which wanted clear records of the rents they could expect from their lands. We have between fifteen and twenty of these studies, dating from the ninth century on and enumerating populations settled on particular estates or manors. The largest census was taken by the monastery of Saint Germain-des-Prés in Paris and covers lands that are now mainly Parisian suburbs. Monasterial surveys of the early medieval world characteristically show more men than women, with ratios as high as 130 men per 100 women. Women continued to be in short supply.

Of course, the monasteries may have counted males more carefully. Still, much indirect evidence suggests that women were both few and highly valued in early medieval society. The barbarian legal codes, passed down orally and finally redacted between the fifth and ninth centuries as Christianity spread and introduced literacy, characteristically imposed a fine, usually called a *Wergeld*, on anyone who caused a person's injury or death. The fines protecting women were usually as high as, and sometimes higher than, those

protecting men, and women of childbearing age sometimes enjoyed special value. Moreover, in marriage arrangements, the groom brought the dowry to the bride. The male or his family assumed the principal costs of setting up the new household. This reverse dowry suggests that grooms had to compete for relatively few brides.

About 965, an Arab geographer, Ibrahim ibn-Iakub, described Slavic marriage customs, which, in many respects, were typical of all barbarian Europe. Ibrahim reported that the "marital price" required of grooms was so high that "if a man has two or three daughters, they are as riches to him; if, however, boys are born to him, this becomes for him a cause of poverty." Nearly the same complaint would be widely heard again in Europe during the late Middle Ages (1350–1500), but the sexual references would be exactly reversed.

From the eleventh or twelfth century, the relative number of women in medieval society, and presumably their life expectancies, rose. A rough estimate of life expectancies for the urban and rural population of Pistoia in Italy in 1427 is 29.8 years for women; 28.4 years for men. The shift is most apparent among the high nobility and in the towns. In Bologna in 1395, there were only 95.6 men for every 100 women; in fifteenth-century Nuremberg, there were 83.8 men per 100 women. Even in cities where the sex ratio favored men—as in Florence in 1427—women grew more numerous in the progression up the scale of ages and held an absolute majority among the elderly. Although many older women may have migrated to the city, women probably also survived better under conditions of urban life.

There are several reasons for women's improving chances of survival during the central Middle Ages (1000–1350). The establishment of strong governments and a stable political order lowered the level and reduced the incidence of violence. New ideals of chivalry restricted—although they by no means completely ended—women's active participation in warfare as fighters or as victims. Women fare better under peaceful conditions, when they do not run the constant risk of attack, rape, or abduction. But the most decisive changes were economic. Primitive agricultural economies, with their low production levels, used predominantly the labor of women, children, and the aged. In a famous description written in A.D. 98, the Roman historian Tacitus observed that among the barbarian Germans, women and children maintained the household economy, while adult males gave themselves over to war and indolence. This pattern probably was preserved well into the Middle Ages. But intensive cultivation requires heavy field work, which women cannot readily perform; peasant women in the late Middle Ages worked hard on their farms, but they were no longer alone.

Finally, the new urban economy offered little employment for women. They spun at home, prayed in convents, and labored as household servants, but they did not constitute a significant part of the urban labor force. Families considered their daughters burdens, unable to earn their keep. Girls were also burdens to prospective husbands, and so the terms of marriage

Month of February, from the Breviario Grimani, *a manuscript in the Biblioteca Marciana, Venice.*

turned against women. The reverse dowry all but disappeared, and the girl or her family had to meet the principal costs of marriage. Throughout the late Middle Ages, the social position of women visibly deteriorated, but so also did the social demands and pressures laid upon them. For women, less participation in economic life and diminishing social importance meant better chances of biological survival.

The other principal biological events in women's lives, menarche and menopause, are difficult to examine historically. Medieval medical writers, who abounded from the eleventh century on, commonly placed menarche at between twelve and fifteen years of age and menopause at fifty. But we have no way of knowing whether they were recording their own observations or merely echoing the ancient authorities. Both Roman law and canon law of the medieval Church set the age of puberty and of binding marriage at twelve years for girls and fourteen years for boys. Saint Augustine, who lived from 354 to 430, contracted to marry a girl "two years below the marriageable age"; presumably, she was ten. "I liked her," he reports in his *Confessions*, "and was prepared to wait." He was then thirty years old. Had his conversion to celibacy not intervened, the girl would have been married at age twelve or soon after, to a groom twenty years older. The pattern seems typical of Roman marriages within the privileged orders.

The medieval canonical requirement that girls be at least twelve years old at the consummation of their marriage was a lower bound. There are many indications that girls at menarche were closer to age fifteen than to age twelve. In the law of the seventh-century Visigoths, a girl was not considered capable of bearing children until age fifteen. In a manorial survey of the early ninth century, from the church of Saint Victor of Marseilles, girls are called "marriageable" only from age fifteen. The customs of Anjou in 1246 similarly give age fifteen as the date of presumed maturity for women.

Still, the traditional estimate of age twelve for menarche was not entirely unrealistic. To judge from marriage patterns, which we can discern from the fourteenth and fifteenth centuries on, rich urban girls tended to be very young at first marriage—younger than those of lower social station and younger even than peasant women. Chaucer's wife of Bath, a middle-class, urban woman, was first married at age twelve, and many urban women were already mothers by age fifteen. Social factors were important here: the rich were apparently eager to settle the future of their daughters as early as possible. But the evidence also hints that menarche came sooner among rich women, and amenorrhea (abnormal absence or suppression of the menses) was presumably less common among them. In consequence, rich women in marriage tended to be consistently more prolific than the poor.

Some dietitians argue that girls must achieve a certain critical amount of body fat to trigger menarche and also to sustain menstruation. The better diet and ease of living that rich Roman girls and their medieval counterparts enjoyed gave them low ages of menarche, close to the thirteenth year anticipated in Roman and canon law. Girls in the countryside and among the poor classes were probably at menarche closer to age fifteen—the year most commonly encountered in the barbarian codes, manorial surveys, and customary laws. Perhaps these same groups also experienced relatively early menopause. The laws of the Visigoths assume that a woman would no longer be fertile after age forty. Apart from what we have gleaned from legal sources, we can say little with certainty about these principal events in the female life cycle.

To add flesh and features to our portrait of women, we can rapidly review the lives of three real people—a peasant, a queen, and a bourgeoise. Our peasant is a woman named Alpaix. She was eventually canonized in the late nineteenth century, and even during the Middle Ages, her sanctity was so well recognized that, unlike most peasant women, she attracted a biographer.

Alpaix was born about 1155 in a village near Sens in northern France. Her biographer says that her father, a poor man, "earned his bread by the sweat of his face," by laboriously tilling the soil. Alpaix was the eldest child with several younger brothers. From an early age, she had to assist her father in the heavy work of cultivating the fields. As he drove his two oxen at the head of the plow, she marched alongside, goading the animals to more strenuous effort. When so ordered, she carried manure and sheep dung on her slight shoulders to the fields and gardens. Her young frame could not easily bear the weight, and her father, who seems to have felt no particular sympathy for her, lashed the burdens to her back. Besides her other chores, she had to lead the cattle and sheep to pasture and guard them as they grazed.

All this she did willingly, even on Sundays and festivals, when other peasant girls gave themselves over to dancing and "frivolous things." But then, at the age of twelve, she could no longer sustain the charges laid upon her. According to her biographer, "the tender maiden could no longer bear such heavy labors. Rather, her entire insides were broken and torn from the magnitude of unrelieved work. Drawing deep sighs from the depths of her heart, with the color of her lovely face all marred, she finally gave external, visible signs of her internal suffering. What more can be said? Gripped by unyielding weakness, she remained for an entire year recumbent on her hard and bitter bed, made of straw, without mattress and sheets. . . ." Ugly lesions appeared on her skin, and her body exuded such a repulsive odor that her family isolated her in a hut. For her sustenance, they delivered black bread daily to her door. But because she could no longer contribute to the household, her brothers demanded that no food be wasted upon her. Their heartless proposal implies that the favorable social position of the peasant woman was indeed linked to her labors.

After a year of excruciating pain, Alpaix was visited in a vision by the Virgin Mary, who cured her of her sores and smell. But Alpaix never recovered the use of her limbs and remained bedridden the rest of her life. She took no food apart from Communion, and died in 1211. Before the eyes of this ignorant, invalid peasant girl, spectacular visions paraded; she was allowed to contemplate the splendid court of heaven and terrifying scenes of hell. Her powerful visions gave her a reputation for sanctity, and pilgrims began to find their way to her bedside. Eventually a biographer arrived and preserved for modern historians an account of a girl's hard childhood in the medieval countryside.

Our medieval queen was also acquainted with holiness; she is Blanche of Castile, mother of Louis IX, or Saint Louis, king of France. She was born on March 4, 1188, in Palencia, Spain, the third daughter of King Alphonso VII and the granddaughter, through her mother, of Eleanor of Aquitaine, who had been, in succession, queen of France and of England. Blanche was taken to France, where on May 23, 1200, not long after her twelfth birthday, she married the French heir apparent, who would later reign as Louis VIII (1223–1226). The marriage was not consummated until 1205, when Blanche was sixteen years old. The delay probably indicates, not her own retarded menarche, but the youth of her husband, only a few months older than she.

According to differing sources, Blanche's marriage, which ended when Louis died in 1226, gave her either eleven or twelve children. Blanche's deliveries included one set of twins, born dead in 1215. The spacing of her children suggests that Blanche initially tried to nurse her babies, although the king's disposition and his absences on royal business may also have affected the

rhythms of her births. Thus, three and a half years elapsed between the birth of her second baby, Philip (born September 9, 1209), and her next delivery on January 26, 1213, when the dead twins were born. No period of nursing followed here, and her next child, the future Louis IX, was born only fifteen months later. Another lengthy interval of two and a half years followed until the next child, presumably because Louis was being nursed by his mother. Thereafter, births in rapid succession (five or six of them in the eight years from 1219 to 1227) suggest that Blanche—now maturing and occupied with children, household, and the affairs of state—no longer suckled her babies but instead relied on wet nurses. Several tracts on nursing have survived from the thirteenth century, and the assumption in all of them is that the nurse was not likely to be the child's mother.

Blanche's career illustrates the powerful position that women could still attain among Europe's high nobility in the thirteenth century. Of course, given the shortage of males, many noble girls did not marry. Most of those who remained single were forced into the religious life and all but excluded from lay society. A woman lucky enough to marry, often did so very young, produced babies in rapid succession, did not nurse her own children, and was likely to be relieved of the risks and burdens of childbearing by her husband's early death. Women frequently figured prominently as administrators and regents for their often absent, or short-lived, husbands and sons. At this elevated social level, a widow with children was not likely to remarry; rather, she would dedicate herself to defending and advancing her children's interest.

Blanche herself was effectively regent of France during the minority of her son Louis (1226–1234), and regent again during his absence on the ill-fated Egyptian crusade (1252). She dominated her son and tyrannized her daughter-in-law; she even tried to prevent the royal couple from chatting together before retiring for the night. Surviving her husband by twenty-eight years, Blanche died at the age of sixty-four in November 1254.

The woman who for us perhaps best represents the medieval bourgeoise is Alessandra, daughter of Bardo dei Bardi. She was born in Florence in 1414. We know a good deal about her because a Florentine book dealer named Vespasiano da Bisticci wrote the story of her life. His work, probably the oldest surviving biography of a European woman who was neither a princess nor a saint, tells us, for example, that Alessandra grew to be the tallest young woman in Florence, delighted ambassadors by her grace in promenading and in dancing, learned to read, and could do excellent needlework. She was engaged to be married at age fourteen, but for unknown reasons, the marriage was delayed until 1432, when she was eighteen years old. She was close to the average age of first marriage (17.8 years) for Florentine women in 1427. We can make refined estimates because in that year, a large census was taken of the city. Alessandra's husband, Lorenzo, was the son of Palla di Nofri dei Strozzi, who in 1427 was Florence's richest citizen. Then twenty-seven years old, Lorenzo was young by Florentine standards. The average age of first marriage for males in 1427 was 29.9 years. As Lorenzo was the first-born son in Palla's family, he was probably permitted to marry somewhat earlier. His new wife quickly produced three children in four years—an indication that she was not nursing her own babies.

Disasters then struck Alessandra's family. In 1434, her father, an opponent of the Medici family, was exiled. He was sixty-six years old at the time; Alessandra was twenty. This long generational distance of forty-six years between father and child seems typical of Florentine households. Alessandra's unmarried sisters, left without dowries, were desperate. "What will become of us?" they protested to their departing father. "In whose care will you leave us?" Amid the continuing tumult of Florentine politics, Alessandra's husband, Lorenzo, was similarly exiled in 1438, freeing her, at the age of twenty-four, of the risk of further pregnancies. In 1427, the average age of mothers at the birth of their middle children was twenty-six, the fathers' average age was forty.

Lorenzo eked out a living as a tutor in the town of Gubbio, but in 1451 he was assassinated by a disgruntled student. He was forty-six at the time. Alessandra, now widowed, had to raise her children alone. Her biographer presents her as a model of dedication and sober deportment for young widows, of whom there were many in Florentine society. He mentions one other, Caterina degli Alberti, who was married at fifteen, bore two children over the next twenty-three months, lost her husband, and remained a widow for the following sixty years. Alessandra herself remained a widow for seventeen years, and died in 1468, at the age of fifty-four.

The bourgeois woman, like the lady of the landed nobility, was very young at first marriage, and her groom was even older than among the nobles. She, too, bore her babies in rapid succession, did not herself nurse them, and through the death of her older husband, was more likely than the noblewoman to be free of the dangers of continual pregnancies. As a child bride married to a mature man, she probably had little influence on her husband and his generation. But as a young mother destined to have intimate and usually extended contact with her children, she could be a respected and influential figure for the young. Married women occupied a strategic position. As intermediaries between the distant generations of fathers and their children, they could readily shape the tastes and values of the young and thus profoundly influence the culture of the city. And widowhood seems to have suited women well. In Florence in 1427, more than half the adult population of women were widows.

Both the biological and social experiences of women changed substantially during the long medieval centuries. In the overwhelmingly rural world of the early Middle Ages, women enjoyed a high social value and entered marriage under favorable terms. But the bases of their preferment seem to have been the taxing physical labor they performed and the substantial contribution they made to the peasant household. With the growth and transformation of the medieval economy—and in particular the rise of towns from the twelfth century on—women's participation in the domestic economy grew restricted. Daughters no longer made a father rich and the terms under which they entered marriage turned against them. But this partial exemption of women from hard labor conferred some benefits: "they work less," observed Albertus Magnus, "and for that reason are not so much consumed." Women in modern Western history still enjoy some of the advantages and bear some of the penalties bequeathed to them by medieval society. We have yet to see what will happen to these advantages and penalties, in our own, rapidly changing times.

The Viking saga

Magnus Magnusson

MAGNUS MAGNUSSON, *Icelandic-born author and journalist, is well-known in the UK as a TV and radio broadcaster specializing in archaeology and history. He wrote and presented in 1980 a major TV series on the Vikings which has been shown in many countries and has appeared in book form as* Vikings! *(BBC Publications with Bodley Head). Among his many other published works are the award-winning* Introducing Archaeology *(1972),* Viking Expansion Westwards *(1973), and* Iceland *(1979).*

THE term "Viking" has come to mean anyone who happened to be a Scandinavian in the Middle Ages, whether he was a seaman, a farmer, a merchant, a poet, an explorer, a warrior, a craftsman, a settler—or a pirate. And the term "Viking Age" has been applied by historians—somewhat indiscriminately, it must be said—to cover three centuries of dynamic Scandinavian expansion that took place from around 800 AD onwards.

It has become popularly associated with an age of terror and unbridled piracy, when Norse freebooters came swarming out of their northern homelands in their lean and predatory longships, to burn and rape and pillage their way across civilized Europe. They have always been portrayed as merciless barbarians, heedless of their own lives or of the lives of others, intent only on destruction. They were anti-Christ personified; their emblems were Thor's terrible Hammer and Odin's sinister Ravens, symbolizing the violence and black-hearted evil of their pagan gods.

This deep-rooted popular prejudice about the Vikings can be traced back directly to the lurid sensationalism of ecclesiastical writers who were the occasional victims of smash-and-grab Viking raids. In a turbulent age, when piracy and casual raiding were a commonplace of everyday life all over Europe the Vikings happened to be more successful at it than most other people; and they paid the price for it by getting an extremely bad reputation.

But, curiously enough, no one knows for certain what the word "Viking" actually means! It may be related to the Old Norse word *vík,* meaning "bay" or "creek", suggesting that a Viking was someone who lurked with his ship in a hidden bay. Some think it may come from the Old Norse verb *víkja,* meaning "to turn aside", so that a Viking was someone who made detours on his voyage—presumably to go raiding. A third school of scholarly opinion looks for a derivation in the Anglo-Saxon word *wic,* itself borrowed from the Latin *vicus,* meaning a fortified camp or trading-post, so that "Viking" might mean a raider or a trader, or both!

But not every Scandinavian was a professional warrior or Viking; and not every Viking was a pirate. Modern scholarship is now beginning to highlight the constructive, rather than the destructive, impact of the Viking Age. Spectacular archaeological excavations like Coppergate in York, which unearthed a whole street from the Viking Age, are revealing the ordinary Viking man-in-the-street as a diligent and skilled artisan—the Viking as man, not the Viking as myth.

If the origin of the word "Viking" is obscure, so too are the motive causes of the so-called Viking Age itself. There is no

Photos © L. A. East.
The British Museum, London

Coins struck by the Vikings attest to their receptiveness to the cultures with which they came into contact. Above, 10th-century silver pennies from the Viking kingdom of York. Left, coin inscribed "Anlaf Cununc" (King Olaf) is decorated with a raven, traditionally associated with Odin. Right, penny with the name of St. Peter shows a sword and also Thor's hammer, a symbol as potent to a Viking as a cross to a Christian.

Reproduced from the *Unesco Courier,* December 1983, pp. 10-13.

123

5. THE MEDIEVAL PERIOD

Carved out of elkbone, this helmeted head of a warrior (c. 10th century) was found at Sigtuna, Sweden.

Photo Soren Hallgren © ATA, Stockholm

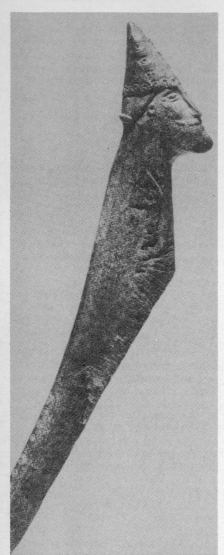

Viking expansion was made possible by the development in 8th-century Scandinavia of strong, swift sailing ships whose construction and shallow draught enabled them to land on sloping beaches and manœuvre in waters unsuitable to most European vessels of that time. Well-preserved Viking longship, right, was found in a burial mound at Gokstad on Oslo Fjord in 1880 and is now in the Viking Ship Museum, Oslo. It is 23 metres long and 5.25 metres wide amidships, but even when fully laden would only have drawn 1 metre of water. Its keel consists of a single timber 17 metres long. A replica of the Gokstad Ship crossed the Atlantic in 1893.

Photo Toni Schneiders © Rapho, Paris

To relieve the tedium of the long nor-thern winters, the Vikings played various board games, including dice games and a game similar to chess. Pieces were made of bone, amber or glass. Left, 10th-century wooden Viking gaming board from Ireland.

Photo © National Museum of Ireland, Dublin

single, simple reason why the Scandinavians should suddenly have burst upon the European scene late in the eighth century (in the history books, at least—it probably wasn't as sudden as it has been made to appear). All major historical shifts have complex roots. We know that in the seventh century, the Scandinavians began developing new sources of iron, which had several consequences: improved iron production made for bet-ter weapons, and better farm implements; better farm im-plements led to agricultural improvements, which led in turn to better nutrition and a correspondingly lower mortality rate amongst infants. There is evidence about this time that land that had formerly been thought unsuitable for farming was be-ing vigorously cleared of forest and scrub to make new farms for new generations of vigorous, well-nourished younger sons who wanted a place in the sun for themselves.

So an acute shortage of land was probably a major factor, which led to considerable settlement overseas; there is evidence of peaceful co-habitation between the Picts of nor-thern Scotland and Norwegian emigrant farmers long before the outbreak of the Viking Age.

But there were other consequences, too. With its surplus iron production, Scandinavia had a new and much-prized product to sell to its neighbours; and the traders had sharp, well-tempered weapons with which to defend themselves from pirates that swarmed in the Baltic and along the shores of northern con-tinental Europe. But in order to trade effectively, the Scandina-vians needed good ships. They came in all shapes and sizes, from small six-oared boats for coastal waters to the enormous ''dragon-ships'' of royalty. In between came a versatile variety of cutters, ferries, pinnaces, plump-bellied cargo-boats, ocean-going ships and galleys.

But the pride of the fleet, the ship that has become the univer-sal symbol of the Viking Age, was the lordly longship, un-disputed master of the northern seas. These ships were the out-come of centuries of technological innovation and evolution which have been charted by chance archaeological discoveries, from flat-bottomed punts to the splendour and sophistication of the single-masted, square-sailed longships. Without the ships, the Viking Age would never have happened at all.

The Viking Age was not a concerted effort at empire-building. The Vikings were never a single, homogeneous people imbued with the same aims and ambitions. The three countries of the Scandinavian peninsula, as they are now defined by political geography, were not really nations at all in the modern sense of the term. Norway, for instance, was a scatter of in-habited areas under independent tribal chieftains along the western seaboard; even the name Norway *(Norvegur)* simply meant ''North Way''—not so much a nation as a trade-route. And the three countries had distinct if sometimes overlapping ''spheres of influence''—the Swedes in the Baltic and Russia, the Danes on the Continent and in England, and the Norwegians in Scotland and Ireland and the North Atlantic islands.

The first recorded Viking raid took place in the year 793, with a seaborne assault by prowling Norwegian marauders on the Holy Island of Lindisfarne, just off the north-eastern shoulder of England. But long before that, the Swedes had been busy in the Baltic, growing rich on trade. At the outset of the Viking Age, Swedish entrepreneurs started to penetrate the hinterland of Russia (they called it ''Greater Sweden'') in pursuit of the rich fur trade and the exotic markets of Arabia and the Far East. Swedish pioneers made their way through Russia by way of the major rivers like the Volga and the Dnieper, dragging their ships in exhausting overland portages on the way to the Caspian Sea and the Black Sea.

By the ninth century they had reached the capital of the greatest power in the western world, the successor to Rome— the Byzantine Empire centred on Constantinople. There, Viking mercenaries formed the elite bodyguard of the Byzantine emperors, the feared and famous Varangian Guard, a kind of Scandinavian Foreign Legion. But the Swedes never conquered Russia, as such; they contented themselves with taking control of existing trading posts and creating new ones to protect the trade-routes, but within two or three generations they had become totally assimilated and Slavicized.

5. THE MEDIEVAL PERIOD

While the Swedes looked east, the Danes looked south-west along the northern coasts of Europe and towards England. Danish warriors were soon hammering at the cities of the crumbling Carolingian empire after the death of Charlemagne in 814 AD: Hamburg, Dorestad, Rouen, Paris, Nantes, Bordeaux —all river-cities, notice. The Viking longships, with their exceptionally shallow draught, could go much further up-river than had been thought possible before, and the effect was rather like that of dropping paratroops behind the enemy lines.

To start with, the Danish Vikings acted as pirates with official or unofficial royal backing. Later on, Danish designs on Europe, and especially England, became openly territorial; the flag followed the trade, just as trade had followed the piracy. But here, too, the Danes, just like the Swedes, became assimilated whenever they settled. In the year 911, one marauding army accepted by treaty huge tracts of land in Northern France in what is now called Normandy—"Northmandy", the land of the Northmen; 150 years later, the descendants of these Norse-Frenchmen would conquer all England under William the Conqueror. Before then, but only briefly, under King Knut (Canute) in the eleventh century, there was a united Scandinavian empire of the North Sea, comprising England, Denmark and Norway; but it quickly fell apart.

Norwegian adventurers joined Danish Vikings in subjugating the whole of northern England (the Danelaw, as it was called) before settling there as farmers and traders, where they developed great mercantile cities like York. They also took over much of mainland Scotland, the Hebrides, and the Northern Isles of Shetland and the Orkneys. In Ireland they played a lusty part in the endless internecine squabbles of rival Irish clans, and founded Ireland's first trading posts: Waterford, Wexford, Wicklow, Limerick and, most especially, Dublin. They were insatiable explorers in search of new trade opportunities to exploit, new lands to settle, new horizons to cross. They discovered Spitzbergen and Jan Mayen Island; they discovered and colonized the Faroes, far out in the heaving Atlantic; they discovered and colonized Iceland, where they established Europe's first Parliamentary republic—a new nation that is still regarded as the oldest democracy in Europe, and which has left us the most enduring cultural monument of the Viking Age, the Icelandic Sagas.

From Iceland, they discovered and settled Greenland. And it was from Greenland, round about the millennial year of 1000, that the Vikings launched their last and most ambitious expeditions of all, the discovery and attempted settlement of the eastern seaboard of North America: "Vinland", the land of wild grapes, as it was called in the two Icelandic Sagas that record the first undisputed European discovery of the New World.

The discovery of North America, and the abortive attempts at colonization which were thwarted by the indigenous Red Indians, used to be considered mere legend; but now archaeology has unearthed authenticated evidence of a Viking settlement at L'Anse aux Meadows, in northern Newfoundland. All other alleged Viking "finds", like the runic Kensington Stone, have long since been exposed as forgeries or hoaxes, or merely wishful thinking.

The impact of the Vikings was ultimately less lasting than might have been expected. Why was that? They had all the necessary energy, they had their own administrative systems of justice and royal authority, they had become converted to Christianity, they had their own coinage, they seemed to have everything. They had criss-crossed half the world in their open boats and vastly extended its known horizons. They had gone everywhere there was to go, and beyond. They had dared

Photo © ATA, Stockholm

In the Viking age silver jewellery such as this delicately worked pair of ear-rings found in Sweden was imported into Scandinavia from the territory of the western Slavs, south of the Baltic.

Photo Toni Schneiders © Rapho, Paris

Left, timber richly carved with interlaced fighting animals is a structural detail from the 12th-century Stave Church at Urnes in western Norway. It was incorporated into the Church from an even earlier building. A remarkable example of the art and architecture of northern Europe at the end of the Viking period, Urnes Church is today inscribed on Unesco's World Heritage List of cultural and natural properties of outstanding universal value.

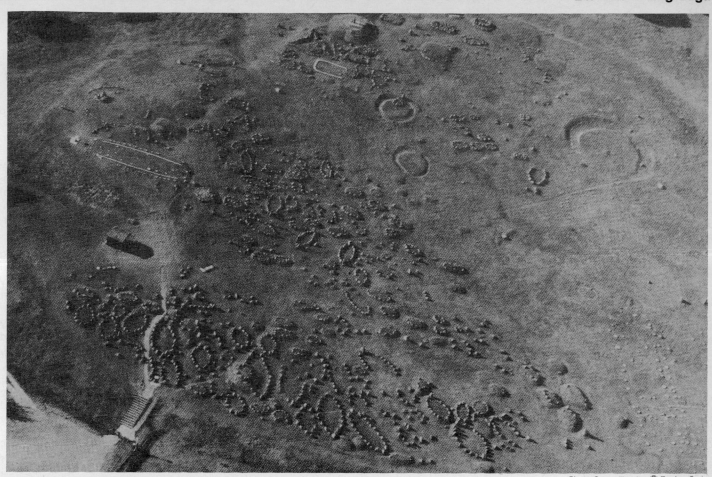

Air view of the Viking cemetery at Lindholm Hoje, northern Jutland. Low boat-shaped mounds and stone settings in different forms mark the graves.

everything there was to dare. They had given Europe a new trading vigour, vigorous new art-forms, vigorous new settlers.

But they had neither the manpower nor the staying-power, neither the reserves of wealth nor the political experience, neither the cohesion at home nor the confidence abroad, to master effectively the older, richer, more stable States they tried to overrun. Instead, being rootless men of the sea, they put their roots down where they landed, and then blended into the landscape. Somehow or other, the dynamic simply petered out.

But they left in the annals of history, a heritage of heroic endeavour and courage, a legacy of robust audacity, that has won the grudging admiration even of those who would otherwise deplore their incidental depredations.

STUDENT POWER
IN THE MIDDLE AGES

Alan B. Cobban

Far from being a recent development, student control was a factor in the early growth of the university as an institution

Student power is virtually coeval with the emergence of the medieval universities. In southern Europe it became endemic, in one form or another, for about 200 years. The motives that gave rise to medieval student rebellion find a distant echo in the student scene of the 1960s and 1970s. But there are important dissimilarities and it would be unhistorical to press analogies too far. Medieval students had, for the most part, a highly utilitarian view of the university as an institution of direct community relevance that might well be regarded as too narrowly conceived by a large proportion of present-day students and staff. The priority of educational utility conditioned students into accepting innately conservative attitudes vis-à-vis the Establishment. Revolutionary student activity in the medieval situation was rarely directed against the prevailing order of things: it seems to have been either a defence mechanism or was channelled towards the winning of greater student participation in university structures.

For the majority of medieval undergraduates education was a severely practical business: there was simply not the surplus wealth available to support non-vocational courses on any scale. As the

student was bereft of a state system of financial aid and as the rate of graduate production was often in excess of the rate of graduate absorption, the pressure on the average student was to seek, as rapidly as possible, a lucrative employment within the established order. As vehicles for community needs, the medieval universities were largely vocational schools training students in the mastery of areas of knowledge and analytical skills which could be utilised in the service of the State or Church, in teaching or in the secular professions of law and medicine. The movements of student protest in the Middle Ages were not the explosive outgrowth of pent-up anti-establishment feelings. Nowhere does it appear that direct student action within the universities was orientated towards the ultimate reformation of the wider community. To imagine that medieval students thought of the university as a microcosm of society would be anachronistic. Medieval student power did not embody this degree of self-conscious awareness.

Nor were student protest movements concerned with the content of university courses if by this is meant the selection of the ingredients of the syllabus or curriculum. The medieval undergraduate

was not faced with the bewildering range of options that confront the modern student. There was an agreed core of studies in the medieval universities derived from a series of time-honoured texts and supplemented by the commentaries of contemporary academics. It would appear that medieval students acquiesced in current educational assumptions and none of their rebellions had, as its aim, the widening or modernisation of the syllabus.

The earliest European universities were not specifically founded but were spontaneous creations which evolved in the course of the twelfth century. They first emerged at Bologna and Paris and these were the archetypes which determined the twofold pattern of university organisation in the Middle Ages: the latter, Paris, gave rise to that of the masters' university; the former, Bologna, to that of the concept of the student-controlled university.

The first student power movement in European history had crystallised at the University of Bologna by the early thirteenth century. The idea of guilds of students directing the affairs of a university and keeping the teaching staff in a state of subservience has been alien to

First published in HISTORY TODAY, 30 (February, 1980).

European thinking for about 600 years. But one of the two original universities was, shortly after it came into being, a student-dominated society and the prototype for a large family of universities either partially or mainly controlled by students.

The rise of the student university at Bologna has to be seen in relation to the prevailing concept of Italian citizenship, a possession of the utmost importance in a country fragmented by the spread of communes. The students who had converged on Bologna to study law from many parts of Europe were, in Bologna, non-citizens and, as such, aliens who were vulnerable in the face of city law. The teaching doctors should have been the natural protectors of their students: this is what had happened at Paris. But at Bologna the commune succeeded in drawing the doctors within its orbit and driving a wedge between the teachers and their students. Without their natural protectors the students had to take the initiative in the matter of organisational defence. By the beginning of the thirteenth century the pristine contractual arrangements that had operated between individual students and doctors had been superseded by a student guild powerful enough to exact the obedience of the doctors to its members.

It is important to stress that at first the student guild at Bologna was a mutual benefit society designed to give its members protection under city law and to provide a measure of defence against hostile parties. The student movement did not, from the start, set out to gain control over the university and its teaching staff. There was no blueprint plan as to how a university ought to be organised. Possibly the students never thought about this. But in order to survive they had to adopt a trade union attitude and carve out for themselves a position of strength within the university. Once this had been attained, the momentum of their power could not be stemmed. In the course of the thirteenth century the students moved from the defensive to the offensive and this resulted in their winning the initiative in university affairs: this was the first student take-over bid in European history.

Although the teaching doctors had to accept the reality of student power they never conceded its legality: that is to say, they contested the alleged right of the students to organise themselves into guilds with elected officers, statutes, and legal independence. It was argued that the students by themselves did not constitute a profession: students were merely the pupils of the doctors, the academic equivalents of trade apprentices and, as such, were devoid of professional status. But the reluctance to give a legal recognition to the student guild could not check student militancy and the teaching doctors were forced to acquiesce in a university situation wherein they were very obviously employed as the functionaries of the students.

It needs to be stated that a fair number of the Bologna law students were older than the majority of students in northern Europe. It has been reckoned that their average age lay between eighteen and twenty-five, and some were on the borders of thirty upon entry to the university. And it is established that a sizeable proportion held ecclesiastical benefices or offices upon their enrolment as law students, and that a significant number of them were laymen from easy social backgrounds. It is clear, then, that many of the Bologna law students were young men of substance with experience of the world and accustomed to administering responsible offices in society, all of which makes the fact of students controlling power in a university more intelligible.

Under the student governmental system at Bologna the teaching doctors were excluded from voting in the university assemblies, although they may have been allowed, as a concession, to attend as observers. Yet all lecturers had to obey the statutory wisdom emanating from these student congregations. The students seem to have elected their prospective teachers several months in advance of the beginning of the academic session in October. Upon election the successful doctors took an oath to submit to the student rector in all matters affecting the life of the university. Student controls over the lecturing system were impressive. The lecturer's life proceeded in an anxious atmosphere of impending fines. A lecturer was fined if he started his lecture a minute late or if he continued after the prescribed time: indeed, if the latter occurred the students were required to leave the room without delay. At the opening of the academic session the students and the teaching doctors elected by the students reached agreement on how the material of the lecture course was to be distributed over the year. The harassed lecturer had to reach stipulated points in the set texts by certain dates in the session. Failure to do so resulted in a heavy fine. It would hardly be an exaggeration to say that lecturing performance in thirteenth-century Bologna was continuously assessed by the students on both a qualitative and quantitative basis. A doctor who glossed over a difficulty or who failed to assign an equal emphasis to all parts of the syllabus would incur financial penalties. As a surety for his lecturing performance the lecturer, at the beginning of the session, had to deposit a specified sum with a city banker, acting for the students. From this deposit, a student review court would authorise the deduction of fines incurred by the lecturer for infringements of the statutes. If the fines were of such an order of magnitude that the first deposit was used up, the lecturer was required to make a second deposit. Refusal to comply was pointless: no lecturer with fines outstanding was permitted to collect student fees for his teaching and thus his source of university income would be cut off. In any event, a recalcitrant doctor could be rendered less obstinate by means of the student boycotting machinery which was fundamental to the workings of the student-university. Even in normal circumstances a lecturer had to have an audience of at least five students at every ordinary lecture: if he failed to attract that number he himself was deemed to be absent and incurred the stipulated fine. This whole gamut of student controls was underpinned by a system of denunciations by secretly elected students who spied on the doctors. Controls extended even into private areas: for example, if a lecturer got married the students allowed him only one day and one night for his honeymoon.

Why were university teachers prepared to submit to this kind of student dominion? They rejected the legitimacy of the student university and yet they consented to serve as its acolytes. The main reason for the submission of the teaching doctors stems from the circumstance that in southern Europe student controls derived ultimately from the economic stranglehold the students had over their lecturers. Before the salaried lectureship became the established norm the majority of teachers depended for their university livelihood on teaching fees collected from the students. The threat of the boycotting of lectures hung like the sword of Damocles over the university teachers as a permanent reminder of where their main economic interests lay. Against the disadvantages of student controls, however, one has to balance the consideration that a successful lecturer in a populous university such as Bologna could expect to earn a good remuneration from student fees. Also, as a group, university teachers did not easily put down roots: many of them stayed in one university for only a year or two before migrating to another or beginning a spell of non-academic employment. The ease with which lecturers alternated between the academic and non-academic life may go some way towards explaining why teaching staff were prepared to endure the irritation of student controls for a limited period.

In Bologna and in the student-universities of the Bolognese type the exercise of power tended to be concentrated in the hands of a few long-tenured student officers. Even during the high-noon of student power at Bologna the theoretically democratic form of government was offset by the consideration that the executive student committees functioned as the hub of administrative government. The student population would be assembled to vote on issues of major importance, but the cumbersome nature of this procedure made the summoning of the sovereign body less frequent than might be expected. For the average Bolognese law student the mass meeting was a means by which he was kept informed on the governmental and educational life of the university: but while he could make his voice heard in these assemblies and record his secret vote in response to a limited agenda, most of the policy-making remained with the executive committees. The sovereign body must often have appeared a rather impotent one, a passive reflector of the decisions of executive government.

The Bologna students, at the dawn of the university movement, acted from the dictates of necessity and not according to an ideological view of the student role in university affairs. This came later, as a rationalisation of an achieved position of power. The student-university emerged as an attempt to solve empirical problems: it was not advanced as a visionary thesis of European university organisation. But at Padua student power in the early fourteenth century bore the stamp of a conscious imitation which embodied the assumptions on which the Bolognese system was based. The Paduan model expressed the belief that the form of university which had evolved at Bologna should serve as a prototype for university organisation in southern Europe. The planned adoption of the Bolognese structure helped to promote the idea that the core and essence of a university was the student guild. Teaching doctors were necessary adjuncts who were to be selected, continuously assessed, supervised and disciplined by the students. Respect was to be paid to their scholarship but within the university organisation they were to be in the nature of academic consultants who have a specialised commodity to sell and who were to be denied the exercise of power: this was the epitome of the student republic embodying the fundamental principle of direct accountability of teaching staff to the student mass.

In the event, the model of the student-university which evolved at Bologna and was refined at Padua proved too extreme for general adoption. Almost everywhere in Italy it was accepted that students might participate to some appropriate degree in university government: to that extent student aspirations were widely met. But the fully-fledged concept of the student-university was quickly overtaken by compromise and replaced by mixed constitutions whereby power was to be shared between staff and students and external bodies. From Italy the student-power movement spread to the universities of provincial France where, in the fourteenth and fifteenth centuries, it assumed varying degrees of student participation in university affairs. And here, in France, at universities such as Orléans, Angers and Montpellier, the students seem to have played a prominent role in the winning of university autonomy from diverse forms of ecclesiastical control. To a limited extent student power found an expression in some of the Spanish universities of the medieval period from whence it was exported to South America: and South America has kept alive into the twentieth century varieties of student participation which ultimately derive from the medieval University of Bologna.

The establishment of the salaried lectureship as the normal method of academic payment sounded the death knell of student power. In the course of the fourteenth and fifteenth centuries the bristling array of student controls was reduced to a set of hollow forms. The restoration of the authority of the teaching masters in European universities is associated with the mounting disquiet felt about the efficacy of student government. Apart from the belief that student power was an actual or potential menace to both academic and urban peace, there was the general complaint that the students had a bad to indifferent record in university administration. There were repeated allegations that student officers were men without capacity or integrity who were not above rigging their own re-elections or ruling in arbitrary fashion with cliques of drinking companions. But it cannot be supposed that irresponsibility was confined to the student body. There was a great deal of it among university teachers. We hear complaints of academic simony in the sense that university chairs were being disposed of to the highest bidder: there were even attempts, at one time, to make chairs hereditary at Bologna. And everywhere the students complained of the negligence or absence of their lecturers who discharged their functions by means of ill-qualified substitutes. In particular, there was much student resentment at the absence of teachers who involved themselves in business, civic or wider political affairs.

The extent of academic irresponsibility and corruption and how it was apportioned between the students and their lecturers in the Middle Ages cannot be assessed by any quantitative means. Nevertheless, west European establishments came to the conclusion that university government was to be the preserve of university teachers, with or without the aid of external bodies, and that the students were to be reduced to the ranks of the listeners and the learners. Student power had been tested for a respectable length of time by the fifteenth century and it had been found wanting. After about 200 years it had come to be regarded as a more or less permanently disruptive force in university and urban society. Rightly or wrongly, the collective European experience had judged that professional maturity was a more hopeful directing force of stable university development than the erratic uncertainties of youth.

Medieval student power was chiefly a phenomenon of southern Europe having its roots in Italy, parts of provincial France and, to some extent, in Spain. It was shaped and directed mainly by the relatively mature law students. In the northern universities of England, Scotland, Germany, Bohemia, the Low Countries and Scandinavia student power did not materialise as a serious challenge to the dominion of the teaching masters. In these universities of the medieval period the arts faculties loomed larger than in those of southern Europe, where they were often mere adjuncts to legal and medical studies. Consequently, a great deal of the university's effort in the north went into the training of young men, for the majority of whom the BA degree would be the academic ceiling. In terms of maturity and worldly expertise these adolescents were ill-equipped to organise and spearhead movements of student protest. The average northern student was less politically and legally sophisticated than his southern fellow. The product of a fairly humble background, he was likely to regard university as one of the few or even the sole means of social advancement. These considerations would make him predisposed to accept the hierarchical assumptions upon which the university was built and to acquiesce, albeit with the reluctance of youth, in the disciplinary code imposed by the masters' guilds. Moreover, in the northern universities the protectionist functions of the masters' guilds were extended to embrace the associated students. And this, along with the fact that the masters often took an effective lead in the struggle against hostile external parties, sheltered the students from many of the hazards to which their counterparts were exposed in southern Europe, thereby lessening the motivation for student power enterprise.

Medieval student power ultimately failed. The universities, overwhelmingly orientated towards the professional needs of society, became increasingly reflective of the establishments which they served. The unsettling nature of student power, with its weapons of the boycott and the migration, posed too great a threat to the more ordered, sedentary character that the universities were acquiring in the fourteenth and fifteenth centuries. Society expected an adequate return for the investments sunk in the universities, investments in the form of endowed lecturerships, colleges, permanent university buildings and so forth. That return was deemed to be put in jeopardy by the machinations of student politics. The indifferent student record in university administration provided the secular and ecclesiastical authorities with a more immediate reason for the phasing out of student participation as a vital force in west European universities. But looking back over the kaleidoscopic richness of all the diverse forms of student power in the medieval universities, it is clear that the modern phenomenon of student power is, by comparison, in its infancy. And an appreciation of the historical perspective of student power provides a

necessary defence against those who would contrast present hierarchical university regimes with the supposedly open student democracies of the Middle Ages. Where student powers were most extensive the oligarchical rule of students by students often led to a brand of intolerance and a narrowing of democratic channels that ill accords with romantic or propagandist notions. While student power could be a creative movement in the struggle for university autonomy, as in the French provincial situation, it could also be a self-defeating and divisive force. After about two centuries the medieval universities reverted to the belief that the teaching masters were better conductors of their craft than their student apprentices.

NOTES ON FURTHER READING

A. B. Cobban, *The Medieval Universities: their development and organization*, Methuen (London, 1975); 'Medieval Student Power', *Past and Present*, LIII, 1971, pp. 29–66; H. Rashdall, ed. F. M. Powicke and A. B. Emden, *The Universities of Europe in the Middle Ages*, 3 vols, Oxford University Press (Oxford, 1936), especially vols I and II; P. Kibre, *The Nations in the Medieval Universities*, Medieval Academy of America Publication 49 (Cambridge, Mass., 1948); *Scholarly Privileges in the Middle Ages*, Medieval Academy of America (London, 1961).

WANDERING FOR THE LOVE OF GOD

Dianna L. Dodson

Stepping outside the gates of his native town for the first time, a fledgling traveller in the Middle Ages had reason to question the wisdom of his impending journey. Behind him lay a lifetime of predictable routine, where his neighbours, both friend and foe, were known to him by name as well as by face. Before him stretched a world of unknowns. The residents of the next shire, or even the next town, were sure to view him as an "incomer" or "foreigner". His only defence against a possible charge of vagrancy lay with the warrant which he carried in his *Scrip* or purse: written by the hand of an educated clerk and sealed with the ensign of his local bishop, it declared him to be "a good and suitable person", fulfilling a religious vocation. He had taken upon himself the obligation of a pilgrimage.

Much to his surprise, he soon discovered that the highways of his native Britain and of mediaeval Europe as a whole were well travelled by men and women who sought "to live as pilgrims on earth that they might be welcomed by the saints when they were called away from their earthly sojourn". Their peregrinations spanned not only the miles but the centuries, and his fellow countrymen figured so frequently in their throng that it was thought "the habit of traveling is part of their nature". Many of these victims of wanderlust ventured not once but several times upon the same pilgrimage route!

The pilgrim shrines of Britain were so numerous that one 12th Century visitor from Norway found it necessary to cast lots as to which he should visit. Each shire had its own tutelary saints from whom the devout could expect aid for a variety of life's problems. The county of Norfolk alone boasted 38 such memorials to "the glorious confessors there resting". The popularity of these saints and sites was largely determined by changing fashion; the major shrines, however, retained their fame throughout the Middle Ages. Among these ranked St. Andrew's in Scotland, St. David's in Wales, St. Swithin at Winchester, Our Lady of Walsingham, and the martyr, Thomas Becket of Canterbury. The numbers offering tribute at these holy places were considerable: 200,000 worshippers annually knelt upon the site of Becket's murder in Christ Cathedral as compared to the 500,000 wayfarers "for the love of God" who yearly traversed Europe as a whole.

The obligation of a pilgrimage was assumed by members of all classes under all circumstances, to achieve a variety of goals, both "bodelie and ghostlie". The man or woman burdened by illness would pray before the altar of St. John of Beverley or some other well-known patron of healing. When his illness prevented his making the journey in person, a concerned relative or friend often assumed the responsibility. A visit to the shrine of a saint or martyr was often recommended to the sinner by his confessor as the quickest way to cleanse his soul of the sins threatening his salvation. If the sinner himself was unable, or unwilling, to spend his time and energy upon the road, a professional pilgrim or *Palmer* was found to journey as his spiritual deputy. Rescue from danger, the reaping of a bountiful harvest and the birth of an heir were all considered reasons for a pilgrimage of thanksgiving. And when rescue or harvest or heir was desired, a vow to perform a pilgrimage was often forthcoming.

Not all those who took to the pilgrim roads were moved by need or religious zeal. Often the *Palmer* was an inveterate traveller who had no desire to send down roots in either a place or a profession. The man who found himself overburdened with a growing family and equally prolific debts used the pilgrimage as an opportunity for escape as well as for acquiring respectability in the eyes of the religious. Farm labourers and town apprentices, dissatisfied with the regimen of their employment, could find a new situation under pretext of a pious journey. The occasional woman sought freedom from the "moral safety" of home or convent by assuming the pilgrim's vocation. For these, as for the genuinely religious, the hardships of the road were worth enduring in order to enjoy fresh experiences while securing their admission to Paradise.

In spite of the benefits and honour associated with a pilgrimage, the news that a man had decided to set out for some shrine as often as not caused his friends and family to break "into sobs instead of into song". The state of mediaeval roads, and of travelling conditions in general, was not such as to inspire them with confidence in his safe return home. Most "pilgrim streets" winding their way through Britain's growing urban centres were "full feebly paved, and full perilous and jepardous" for horseman and foot-traveller alike. The causeways and bridges of the countryside were scarcely less in need of repair, and often a pilgrim found himself faced with a flooded river and a washed out bridge. Were he lucky, some enterprising local would have established a ferry service across the water for which he would pay dearly from his journey money. It is little wonder that the upkeep of roads and bridges was considered a "true charity", as praiseworthy as feeding the hungry or clothing the naked.

Where the pilgrim's path took him into the "remote and craggy hills", he ran the risk of losing his way. The boundaries of counties and kingdoms, the localities of cities and the courses of rivers were vaguely marked upon the map which he might have acquired before his departure. If he could not afford the services of a cartographer or if he could not read, he depended upon directions given to him by those who lived in the regions through which he passed. Even should he avoid unexpected detours, he travelled in constant "feere of robbyng". The highways of Britain were notorious for their population of "wolves heads" and "pyrates", who were considered "the most desparatest people of the earth". He was not a prudent traveller who did not prepare for the possibility of robbery and assault by arming himself or joining with a group of fellow pilgrims. Yet even in the choice of his companions he risked much; as one well-seasoned wanderer of the 15th Century warned: "If a man has a comrade with whom he cannot agree, woe betide them both during their pilgrimage." Least noticeable, but not least annoying, of the traveller's burdens were lice and fleas for "unless a man spends several hours in the [the hunting and catching of vermin] when he is on pilgrimage, he will have but unquiet slumbers".

The financial benefits extended to those on pilgrimage may have influenced many a would-be traveller to ignore the dangers of the road. Since the status accorded to a pilgrim amounted to that of a religious vocation, he was above all law except that of St. Peter. If he were a priest the Church allowed him to draw his full stipend during his journey, provided he did not remain away longer than three years. The lay pilgrim was excused from the payment of all taxes; his property was declared secure from confiscation and injury and his wife was threatened with excommunication should she think to remarry during his absence.

To guarantee these benefits for himself, the aspirant pilgrim procured a *Testimonium* or warrant from his spiritual lord, the bishop of his diocese, verifying his status. Were he a serf or indentured workman, the permission of his temporal lord or master was likewise required. Such a warrant served at once as a licence to travel, a safeguard against indictment before a civil court and his recommendation to the pious and charitable along his way.

Once he had received his patent from his bishop or lord, the pilgrim set out to arrange his finances, both for his family during his absence and for himself on the road. In this he received assistance from the professional or religious guild of which he was a member. The Resurrection Guild of Lincoln required that each member give the pilgrim brother "a half-penny at least" as long as he took care to forewarn the guild of his departure. In addition, each guild released its pilgrim member from payment of his dues for the period of his journey and promised to meet him at the gates of his city upon his return, provided that the day of his homecoming was not a working day.

From the time he declared himself intent upon a pilgrimage, the pilgrim was expected to let his beard grow "from a face which is serious and pale". He procured for himself a simple *Gown* of grey or russet wool, cowled similarly to that worn by members of the monastic orders. Around his waist or over his shoulder he fastened a belt, from which he hung his *Bol* or drinking flask, his begging bowl which he would use to receive alms-meals during his journey, and his *Scrip* in which he stored his traveller's warrant and whatever coin of the realm he would use to purchase what charity did not supply. In his *Scrip*, too, he carried the crosses, "paternosters" (rosaries) and trinkets which his family and friends entrusted to him to have blessed once he reached his sanctifying destination. To protect him from the assault of wind, rain and sun, he wore a heavy woollen travelling cloak and a wide-brimmed hat of black or grey felt. It was only at the time of Chaucer, when pious pilgrimage was suffering from decline, that a *Canterbury Tales* could be written in which each pilgrim wore clothing individual to his class and personality.

The pilgrim's *Bourdon* or staff was perhaps most emblematic of his vocation in the eyes of his contemporaries. Measuring from six to seven feet in length, the staff was topped with a heavy iron knob, upon which was inscribed the prayer, HAEC IN TUTE DIRIGATITER ("May this guide thee safely on the way"). Useful for pole-vaulting over ruts and chuckholes in the road, the staff also proved an effective weapon when held spearlike against the attacks of bad-tempered village dogs or as a cudgel against highwaymen. Attempts were made by churchmen to induce wanderers to carry crosses and banners instead of staves, but these proved less satisfactory weapons of defense and were politely but firmly declined.

Dressed in his travelling garb, his mind at ease concerning the state of his property during his absence, the pilgrim visited a church dedicated to one of Christendom's patron saints of travel where he made supplication to Saints Raphael, Michael, Christopher or Martin for a safe journey, "good and honourable" lodgings, "or at all events. . . . patience to bear the shortcomings of our inns during our long journey". His last visit was to his own parish church. There he declared before his neighbours what he intended to accomplish on his pilgrimage. Prostrating himself before the altar, he lay with his arms extended in cruciform while a dedicatory Mass was said over him. He then rose to his feet and presented the accoutrements of his costume to be blessed by the officiating priest: his *Scrip*, "the badge and habit of thy pilgrimage", and his *Bourdon*, "thy strength and stay in . . . . toil and travail", were consecrated with holy water and returned to him. Finally, blessed and dressed, he was escorted to the edge of his parish, a processional cross carried before him and his neighbours and family laughing and weeping behind him.

The pilgrim carried out his journey on foot unless he were a wealthy merchant or a court grandee. Only those of considerable financial means could afford the dubious luxury of a carriage which, for all its gilded frame and embroidered canopy, tended to lumber and jolt along even the best of mediaeval roads. Walking was considered the most efficient, as well as efficacious, means of completing a pilgrimage. Should the pilgrim prefer to spare himself a pair of aching feet, he could exercise his option to travel on horseback. The large majority of wayfarers in the Middle Ages preferred to ride from one place to another, and did so on everything from plow horses to asses. If the footsore traveller did not own a horse, he could rent one at a local inn. Also available for hire were boats and barges along Britain's many navigable waterways. But regardless of what means of transportation was chosen, the pace was always a relaxed one. It is from the leisurely gait of the Canterbury pilgrim's horse that we gain our term to "canter"; our ambling "saunter" was used to describe the progress of pilgrims to the "Sainte Terre" or Holy Land; and our modern "roaming" refers to those who made their visit to the city of St. Peter a pleasurable outing rather than a hurried tour.

Walking alone from town to town, the pilgrim often found himself humming a familiar melody or improvising verses to add to a song. Were he to fall in with a group of pilgrims, his singing was joined by the bagpipes or recorder of a fellow traveler. Their ditties were not always of a religious nature: "wanton" songs of hunting and love-making were often interspersed, or even joined, with biblical themes and the legends of the saints. The progression of pilgrims was often so exuberant "with the noise of singing and the sound of their piping . . . . and with the barking out of dogs after them, that they make more noise than if the King came that waye with all his clarions and minstrells". To those who criticised their display it was countered that the tribulations involved in travel were justification enough for a veneer of gaiety.

The pilgrim sought refreshment and lodging for the night by begging for alms. It was considered an act of charity, "like unto Saint Martin" to "clothe the pylgrym's nakedness" and provide him with food and shelter. By offering him a bowl of milk or a mat by the fire, the almsgiver shared in his merits, and even the wife of the poorest cottar felt that she had participated in, if not completed, a pilgrimage. With this same purpose in mind, the various guilds established *Domus Dei* or hospitals to minister to the needs of "poor travelers who cross the country going on pylgrymage, or from any other pious motive". Where there were no hospices or Christians willing to share their provender, the pilgrim sought shelter at one of Britain's many monasteries. He was welcomed into the chapter's *Hospitum*, or guest house, with the kiss of peace from the prior or his delegate. There he dined and dozed with the monastery's other guests in a common hall. Nobles and wealthy merchants might be invited to take their meal with the brothers in their own refectory, but they were expected to pay for their privileged hospitality. Only in the centuries immediately preceding the Reformation did many monastic houses limit their welcome to a luxury clientele.

Many pilgrim travellers, however, preferred the informality and worldly atmosphere of a public inn for their evening's repast and rest. Of these there were many across Britain, particularly in the vicinity of major religious shrines. Entering the inn, the pilgrim was faced with "as great a confusion of tongues and persons as there was at the building of the tower of Babel". The innkeeper extended his services of food and drink not only to travellers from a distance but also to local customers. "Marriners, waggoners, husbandmen, children, women, sick and sound" all gathered together there to finish their day with a companionable drink. Whatever wandering *jougeleurs* and acrobats had passed by the door of the monastery would likewise gather at the inn, entertaining the guests in return for a few coins and a free meal. Once the patrons came to be "warm with wine", the noise within the room was great: one pilgrim states tersely that "it deafens a man".

The sleeping situation in most inns was communal: the traveller shared not only his room, but also his bed with as many as three other guests, usually strangers. The disadvantages associated with this arrangement were great, for, in addition to the lack of privacy and the possibility of acquiring a bedpartner who snored, the lone traveller was often a victim of theft while he slept.

All the pains of the road and the dangers of the inn were forgotten when first the pilgrim sighted the object of his pilgrimage. The point from which the shrine or its town first came into view was designated the *Mons Gaudii* or *Montjoie* ("mountain of delight"). Had he reached that point on horseback, the traveller dismounted and joined his footsore brethren in walking barefoot over the last mile or so to their goal. His pilgrimage was fulfilled when he knelt before the shrine. To accomplish this, however, was not always an easy task. The worshippers who crowded their way toward the shrine were often unruly, and many a pilgrim's staff was turned on those who pressed around him. Angry words were often exchanged: the liturgy of the Mass which was celebrated for the new arrivals was punctuated by such oaths as: "For the sake of the Holy Virgin, keep your sharp elbows out o' my ribs" and "Hell pursue you, you old sinner, can't you keep the spike of your crutch off my foot?"

The focal point of the shrine was the reliquary of some saint or group of saints. Ranging from a simple casket to an elaborate tabernacle; it was made from metal, wood or stone, and decorated lavishly. A *Feretrum* (coffer) was used to hold all or part of the body of a saint. If the relic was no more than a severed limb or splinter of bone, the *Feretrum* was crafted in the shape of the original or whole. When not being carried in solemn procession, the *Feretrum* rested on a *Throne,* a fixed stone base. The *Throne* also was used to house the complete bodies of saints; trefoiled or quatrefoiled peepholes were carved through its sides so that the devotee might share in the spiritual virtue of the relics by reaching his hand through the aperture. One slim and pliable pilgrim to Canterbury managed to slip his entire body through a porthole in the *Throne* enshrining Thomas Becket so that he could lie full-length on the coffin. Most visitors, however, settled for touching the tomb with their fingers, though they were warned against chipping at the stones for souvenirs and noblemen were asked to refrain from carving their coats-of-arms on the walls and pillars of the church.

A list of relics available to the pilgrim demonstrates, if nothing else, the creative scope of the mediaeval mind. Items like slivers from the True Cross and the limbs of various saints and martyrs seem pale when compared to such treasures as a phial containing the breath of Christ or the tip of Lucifer's tail. The Mark of Cain and the pealing of the bells of Solomon's Temple were no doubt more difficult to preserve than a few droplets of the blood from Christ's circumcision. They were no less susceptible to theft, however. The value set upon relics explains much of the fraud, forgery of records and intermonastic feuds which run through much of mediaeval ecclesiastic history. Monks and priests were not so awed by the saints that they were above clipping a piece of their relics to carry to their own chapel or monastery. The larger shrines served not only to enhance the glory of the saint but also to preserve it from unauthorized division or disappearance.

A considerable business was likewise done in faked relics, added to which were innumerable copies of holy objects presented to pilgrims which, in a generation or so, became accepted as originals by the residents of the pilgrims' home towns. The more progressive theologians of the time commented that the number of splinters of the True Cross which were reputed to exist across Europe constituted enough wood to build a good sized ship; they were told that, if one accepted Christ's miracle of feeding a multitude with seven loaves and a few fishes, it was certainly not stretching credibility to believe that the Holy Rood likewise was imbued with the power of miraculous multiplication. This uncounterable argument allowed a host of parish churches, conventual chapels, cathedrals and almshouses to reap the benefits of owning one of many duplicate relics.

The rewards of a pilgrimage were many. The earning of indulgences, either for the pilgrim or his sponsor, was a common objective: the altars at many shrines bore the inscription: "Every Mass celebrated at this altar frees a soul from Purgatory." For those who were confident in their salvation, material gain was to be had. Visitors to the shrine at Walsingham were encouraged to kneel beside the Virgin's wishing well, drinking as much of the water as they could hold in their cupped palm while whispering to the Virgin the desires of their hearts. The most lauded achievement of the saints, however, was that of healing. Touching the shrine was considered enough to cure some ailments, while the dust from around its base, dissolved in water, was seen as a potent cure for most diseases "both of men and cattle". Not all reputed healings were accepted unquestioned by contemporaries, however. One 15th Century witness to the supposed healing of a man blind from birth was Humphrey, Duke of Gloucester. Intrigued, he quizzed the man by asking him to identify certain colours. When the newly-sighted man answered correctly, he was ordered committed to the stocks as a fraud.

The granting of pilgrims' petitions resulted in a wealth of offerings for the saint's shrine. A candle of expensive beeswax or a model of the body part healed, sculptured in wax or precious metals, was left by the man who had experienced a faith cure. Miniature ships, trimmed with jewels, were left by travellers offering thanks for a safe journey overseas. Gifts of personal clothing and jewellery, oil, timber and "ymages of silver and gilt" in the form of the giver were all offered for the enrichment of the shrine. As these accumulated over the centuries of the saint's popularity, the shrine developed into a museum of immense value where rich and poor alike could gaze upon the treasures of their kingdom's history.

Rich bequests were looked upon with more favour than were simple gifts, such as the staves and crutches abandoned by the poor or the parchment of Greek verse left at Walsingham by the 16th Century scholar Erasmus. Unless a church was well endowed by a patron, the gifts of its pilgrims were its primary source of income. For many shrines, this was considerable: in one year alone, the canons of Hereford Cathedral received enough offerings to allow them to rebuild the church's central tower. Offerings not spent on upkeep of the shrine or its housing church were preserved from sale and theft by being incorporated into it. To protect these enriched reliquaries, wooden boxes were used to cover the *Throne* and *Feretrum;* raised and lowered by a system of pulleys, the *Canopy* could be locked at night or when the shrine was closed to the public. Custodians were appointed at the most visited shrines to keep an eye out for light-fingered paupers as well as relic-collecting clergy. In addition, fierce "ban-dogs", or watchdogs, were used to patrol the shrine, particularly during the winter months when human curators preferred to be sitting beside a warm fire rather than in a draughty sanctuary.

Before he departed from the shrine, the pilgrim took care to purchase a souvenir as a testimonial to his "holy travels". Available to him were many "sygnys or brochis", religious medals emblematic of the places he had visited. Crafted in lead or pewter, the medal displayed a figure of the saint performing some characteristic action. The medals sold to travellers to Walsingham portrayed the Annunciation to the Virgin Mary, while pilgrims to the shrine of St. Cuthbert at Durham wore home *Ampullae,* flasks filled with holy water. Sewn to his cloak, such tokens served to verify that the pilgrim had accomplished his originally declared purpose. The display of "a hundred of ampulles on his hat set . . . and many a crutch on his cloak" was not always a reliable witness, however, for some travellers made themselves appear more worthy by purchasing imitations or tokens which they had not earned.

The returning pilgrim was greeted at the edge of his parish with general rejoicing on the part of his family and friends. Pewter medals jangling on his dusty clothes, he was led into his home church where he dedicated his staff and some of his tokens on the altar. The great journey of his life had come to an end, unless he had been so infected with the desire to travel that he chose to relinquish the comforts of hearth and home for a life on the road. He returned to his work as a blacksmith or ploughman but he often found himself asked to repeat the story of his pilgrimage. The temptation to elaborate upon his adventure was great, and the more conservative members of society complained that "if these men and women be a month out. . . many of them shall be, a half-year after, great janglers, tale-tellers, and liars". But whether or not he became a spinner of fables, the pilgrim had benefited spiritually from his travels and, more importantly, he had learned about the peoples and lands which lay beyond the horizon of his day-to-day existence. He had proven the truth of the mediaeval proverb: "The further ye go, the more ye shall see and know."

FURTHER READING
Pilgrim life in the Middle Ages, by Sidney Heath (London, 1911)
English Wayfaring Life in the Middle Ages (XIVth Century), by J.J.Jusserand (London, 1920)
The Pilgrim Shrines of England, by B.C. Boulter (New York, 1928)
Travellers and Travelling in the Middle Ages, by E.L. Guildford (London, 1924)
English Mediaeval Pilgrimage, by D.J.Hall (London, 1965)
Memoirs of a Medieval Woman, by Louise Collis (New York, 1964)

MURDER AND JUSTICE, MEDIEVAL STYLE

The Pashley Case, 1327-8

The murder of young Edmund de Pashley uncovered a family feud that illuminates the realities of late-medieval crime

Pashley Manor, Sussex, as it is today.

Nigel Saul

ON MARCH 13TH, 1328, THIRTEEN-YEAR old Edmund de Pashley and his valet were murdered at Coulsdon in Surrey, some forty miles from their home in Sussex. A callous crime certainly, even by the standards of the fourteenth century, but seen in isolation it is no more than that. Seen in the context of the family feud that followed, however, it can shed light on the causes of upper-class crime in the late middle ages. What makes the double-murder at Coulsdon interest-

ing for the historian is that the body of documentation to which it gave rise enables us to say something about the motive of the assailants and to examine the consequences of their actions.

The sources for the history of crime in the middle ages are plentiful, not to say voluminous. There are the court rolls themselves, of which those of King's Bench are the most informative. There are also files of indictments, and literally thousands of peti-

tions. Small wonder, then, that some writers have been led by the sheer bulk of these records to conclude that public order was breaking down by the time of the three Edwards. As K.B. McFarlane once pointed out, it is the very richness of the sources for the late middle ages that have given them their bad name. And, as if to complete the gloomy picture that they paint of disorder in the countryside, there are the lamentations of the chroniclers and the constant demands of the

From *History Today*, August 1984, pp. 30-35. Reproduced by kind permission of History Today, Ltd., 83-84 Berwick Street, London W1V 3PJ England.

5. THE MEDIEVAL PERIOD

Commons in Parliament for the better enforcement of the King's Peace. Plentiful though they may be, these sources present a number of problems of interpretation. Does, for example, the fact that the court rolls become bulkier mean that crime was getting worse, or the rate of detection better? What proportion of the total volume of crime came to the attention of the authorities? Until these and other questions can be answered, there is little point in approaching late medieval crime in terms of modern statistical analysis. It is far better to attempt a qualitative approach by seeking to look at the kind of cases which came before the courts and the manner in which they were dealt with. The Pashley murders represent as good a starting point as any.

Young Edmund, the victim of the assault at Coulsdon, was the son of Sir Edmund de Pashley, a lawyer and Sussex landowner who had himself died in mysterious circumstances a year before. Evidently a man of some ability, Edmund senior had combined the life of a country gentleman with a successful career in the courts. He became a king's serjeant in 1309 and a baron of the Exchequer in 1323; and the higher he rose in his profession, the richer he grew on retaining fees from local landowners who valued his services. As his income swelled, so he added to the Pashley estates in Kent and Sussex.

That his son was done to death at Coulsdon on March 13th, 1328, no one seems to have denied. Why and by whom were the questions that had to be answered. A year after the event King Edward III ordered the sheriff and coroners of Surrey and Sussex to hold an inquest, and the jury returned that the assailants were Adam Saule and Edward le Peleter, acting on instruction from Margaret de Basing, who also gave them shelter afterwards. The King forwarded these findings to Sir Geoffrey le Scrope, the Chief Justice of King's Bench, who ordered that the three of them should be brought before the court in Michaelmas. When the time came, the sheriff reported that neither Saule nor Peleter could be found – hardly a great surprise to anyone acquainted with the workings of the medieval courts – but it was then testified that Saule had been detained and was in the Sheriff of London's gaol at Newgate. His case

was set to be heard later that term, and meanwhile the sheriff was instructed once more to seek Peleter and if necesary to initiate outlawry proceedings.

Meanwhile, the record continues, the sheriff had been given to understand that Margaret was living at her manor of Pashley, which is near Ticehurst in Sussex. So three men were sent to arrest her, Thomas de Ledred, the under-sheriff, Nicholas de Ledred, probably his brother, and John de Northton, bailiff of the Rape of Lewes, and accompanying them was Robert de Pulesdon, a clerk assigned to supervise the operation. On August 27th, 1329, they made their way to Ticehurst, and tried to serve the writ, but as soon as they did so they were attacked by a gang led by Margaret's sons and forced to flee in fear of their lives. Whether because he came off the worst or because he was employed at Westminster near the courts, Robert de Pulesdon subsequently decided to prosecute his assailants, and to do this he used the method known as 'appeal' which entailed giving a detailed account of the circumstances of the attack and offering to support the veracity of the charge in court. Thanks to this we are

afforded a wealth of picturesque if somewhat spurious detail illuminating what happened that day outside Margaret's house. The engagement took place at noon. According to Robert, Reginald de Basing struck him across the right hand with his sword, roughly between the thumb and the fingers, making a wound five inches long and cutting open the veins and the nerves. Reginald then fled, leaving his hapless victim to raise the hue and cry.

Before tracing the story of Robert's appeal any further, it is necessary to investigate further the circumstances of the double-murder which had taken place at Coulsdon a year-and-a-half before, because the record in King's Bench is not the only source. There is also a petition written in or after 1331 by a woman called Joan who claimed to be the widow of young Edmund's father, Sir Edmund de Pashley, the Exchequer judge. Now Sir Edmund had made his will on February 23rd, 1327. Just over month later, on March 27th, a writ wa issued for the holding of an inquisi tion *post mortem*, indicating that b then he had died. As his widow, Joar should have been entitled to a third o his lands in dower. But she had rur

138

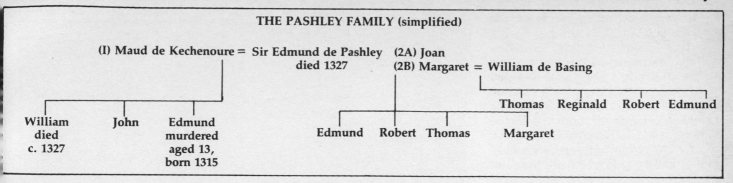

THE PASHLEY FAMILY (simplified)

(I) Maud de Kechenoure = Sir Edmund de Pashley   (2A) Joan

died 1327   (2B) Margaret = William de Basing

William died c. 1327   John   Edmund murdered aged 13, born 1315

Edmund   Robert   Thomas   Margaret

Thomas   Reginald   Robert   Edmund

into difficulties – hence her petition, the contents of which are worth summarising. She could not, she alleged, obtain the dower lands to which she was entitled because they were occupied by Margaret, the widow of William de Basing, with whom Sir Edmund had been living for some time, though instructed by his confessors to return to his lawful wife. Margaret saw that Edmund would never marry her, but she wanted her sons by him to inherit the Pashley estates. So first she had him poisoned, and then his eldest son William. Yet she could not murder his youngest son, Edmund, 'without shedding Christian blood', so she had him and his page killed at Coulsdon. These crimes, Joan concluded, were common knowledge in the counties around Sussex. Therefore she pleaded redress.

This petition raises a number of problems. It seems that there were two women claiming to be the rightful wife of Sir Edmund de Pashley – Joan and Margaret. Which of them was telling the truth? Sir Edmund's first marriage had been to one Maud de Kechenoure, who had died by 1318. Young Edmund was presumably her son, because he was said to have been aged thirteen at the time of his murder in 1328 – that would place his date of birth at 1315. We know also that Sir Edmund had two other sons who grew to maturity – William, who had died by 1327, and John, of whom more will be heard later. After Maud's death the person who appears in the records as his second wife is Margaret, widow of William de Basing. In November 1318 Edmund and Margaret, described as his wife, obtained the grant of a market at their manor of Empingham (Rutland). And in the hearings of King's Bench in the 1330s Margaret calls herself widow and executrix of Edmund de Pashley.

Equally though, her adversaries call her 'Margaret, who was the wife of William de Basing'.

How is this evidence from the records to be reconciled with Joan's claim in her petition? The petition certainly cannot be dismissed out of hand. It makes statements which can be supported from other sources. The young boy and his valet *were* murdered at Coulsdon; Sir Edmund, his father, had died less than a year before, and his eldest son William disappeared from the scene at about the same time. It is possible, then, that Margaret did, as Joan alleged, have them poisoned. There is one other piece of evidence which has some bearing on the problem. Joan backed her claim by suing in Common Pleas for recovery of the dower lands which she said Margaret was detaining. According to the entry on the court roll, Joan maintained that Edmund had dowered her at the church-door of St Mary Magdalene next 'Oldfysshestreete', London, when he had espoused her. The Bishop of London testified to the truth of this, and Joan was adjudged to have proved her case.

Two possible interpretations can be considered. Either, Sir Edmund had been betrothed to Joan and no more, leaving him free to marry Margaret. Or, if Joan's petition is taken at face value, Edmund had indeed married Joan, but later left her to live with Margaret. This at least can be said for the latter interpretation, that if it is accepted then everything else falls into place. Whatever the legal status of his relationship with Margaret, there can be no doubt that Edmund spent the rest of his life with her. She bore him four more children – Edmund, Robert, Thomas and Margaret. And who can doubt the truth of the allegation Joan makes in her petition that this ambitous woman

wanted her own offspring to succeed to the Pashley estates? The only trouble was that the three sons by Edmund's first marriage stood in the way. So she planned to dispose of them one by one. William disappeared in about 1327, and Edmund we know was murdered. That left John. He must have been beyond Margaret's reach, for there is no suggestion in the petition that she was able to get rid of him. Quite the contrary. It was John who was to carry on the fight against Margaret and her designs for the next ten years.

Edward III who, in 1329, ordered an inquest following the death of Edmund de Pashley.

5. THE MEDIEVAL PERIOD

He started launching attacks on the property of Margaret and her Basing relatives on March 9th, 1327 – perhaps as soon as he heard the news of his father's death, and realised that unless he acted promptly he would stand no chance of succeeding to the estates. A couple of months later he was reported to have taken livestock worth £100 from Margaret's custody at Frant and goods worth £20 from her at Parrock-in-Hartfield. Predictably retaliation followed. On August 10th, 1327, a commission was issued to look into attacks that the Basings had made on property of John's at Peasmarsh and elsewhere in Sussex. He replied in turn by renewing the attacks on their property and making off with the harvest.

There matters seem to have rested until the murder of young Edmund and his servant at Coulsdon in the following year, 1328. As we have seen, it was said in court that Margaret had masterminded the attack and had offered shelter to the assailants afterwards. The Sheriff sent three officials to arrest her, but these had had to give up the attempt when they were overwhelmed by a crowd of her men. Robert de Pulesdon, the clerk, subsequently appealed Reginald de Basing of mayhem. Before tracing the later stages of that 'appeal', however, we must see what came of the charges against the murderers and those who had sheltered them. Adam Saule, who had been named as one of those who had perpetrated the deed, had been arrested and detained in Newgate. He appeared in King's Bench in Michaelmas 1329 and was acquitted. The case against Margaret and her Basing sons of procuring the murder and of harbouring those responsible for it was adjourned from term to term in the absence of the defendants. Writs were issued for their attachment, and Margaret finally made an appearance in Michaelmas 1330, when she gave mainprise and was told to appear in Hilary 1331. This she did and was acquitted. So few defendants ever troubled to turn up in court in the middle ages that when one did it is tempting to suppose that pressure had been brought to bear beforehand to ensure that a verdict of 'not guilty' would be returned by the jury.

There still remained of course Robert's appeal, which was entered

The Court of the King's Bench, the court that dealt with most of the criminal cases in medieval England.

on the rolls term after term. In the summer of 1331 the Sheriff of Sussex initiated outlawry proceedings against some of the Basings' hangers-on – John Aleyn and John de Beggebury being the most prominent of them. He issued five summonses in the county court between April and July, and on the fifth, when the outlawries were due to be pronounced, John de Beggebury surrendered himself. He was taken into the sheriff's custody pending his appearance in King's Bench, but when the time came for the hearing he could not be produced, and the hapless sheriff was fined 20 shillings. His prisoner had presumably escaped.

Reginald de Basing and the others, meanwhile, had decided to offer a defence against Robert's appeal. In Michaelmas 1331 they gave mainprise and were told to appear the following term. This they did, and Margaret, who came too, said on their behalf that she had with her a quitclaim from Robert dated February 12th, 1332, in which he dropped all charges against them. What lies behind this sudden *volte face* on Robert's part is hard to say for certain – the arid record on the court roll gives not the slightest hint of what went on behind the scenes – but it must be supposed that Margaret and her sons did everything they could to make him abandon his appeal against them. As for the accessories whose attendance the Sheriff had been trying in vain to secure the previous summer, they presumably were left in peace. Only John Aleyn troubled to obtain a pardon from the King. This was in July 1332: and thereafter no more is heard of Robert de Pulesdon's appeal.

However, that was not the end of the affair. There were still the actions which John de Pashley, the one surviving son by Sir Edmund's first marriage, was bringing against Margaret and her Basing sons in both Common Pleas and King's Bench and the actions which they were bringing against him. In Easter 1337 a verdict was finally given in the plea of trespass which Margaret had brought against John, Richard de Ashby and John de Preston for the attack on Peasmarsh ten years before. John was convicted, his accomplices acquitted. Several other actions against them, however, were still pending, and as they showed no inclination to attend court the Sheriff initiated outlawry proceedings at Chichester. At the third summons on September 24th, 1338, they came, and the Sheriff placed them in custody. Yet when he had to deliver them to King's Bench they had gone. A familiar tale, and one that was to be heard again in 1340. On that occasion it was John de Pashley who was to slip through the Sheriff's fingers when the time came for his appearance in court.

For a few more terms the adjournments dragged on until they finally disappear from the records in the

Sir Edmund de Pashley had been an Exchequer judge from 1323 until his death. Brass of Sir John Cassy, a judge of the Exchequer Court; from Deerhurst Church, Gloucestershire.

early 1340s, probably as a result of Margaret's death on October 15th, 1341. It should not be forgotten, however, that the object of her design in the first place had been to secure the Pashley estates for her own son Robert. John seems to have realised this because within weeks of his father's death he was not only harrassing Margaret and the Basings at Ticehurst but also occupying the properties at Wadhurst, Brightling and Eastbourne which she aimed to secure for her son. To regain these lands Robert (or, as he was probably still a minor, his mother acting on his behalf) brought an assize of novel disseisin which was heard before the justices at Horsham on October 5th, 1327. The jury found in Robert's favour and awarded him damages of 300 marks which he was still trying to recover thirteen years later. John was not one to give in without a fight. Evidently realising that he was losing the battle in the courts, he resorted to direct action again. In 1335 Robert complained that his half-brother and ten others had broken into his property at Merstham in Surrey and made off with goods and chattels.

The long dispute drew to a close in the following decade. In 1345 an out-of-court settlement was reached whereby John released to his half-brother his claim to all the lands the latter held in Surrey. Maybe a similar settlement was made of their respective claims in Sussex. When John died in 1366, he held no lands in chief, and the main Pashley estates can be shown to have descended through one or other of Margaret's sons. To that extent it seems she accomplished her design.

The story of the Pashley murder case is of more than purely local or antiquarian interest because it lends further support to the view that many of the violent feuds which were apt to erupt within or between gentry families in the late middle ages grew out of disputes over the descent of land which the courts were unable to resolve. Sir Edmund de Pashley, lawyer though he was, left a more than usually tangled legacy for his relatives and friends to contend with. He had left two women simultaneously claiming to be his widow, one of whom was prepared to go as far as murdering her stepsons one by one to ensure that her own offspring would succeed to the Pashley estates. The

141

Stone effigy of a fourteenth-century Lady of the Manor from Lowick Church, Northamptonshire.

The inadequacies of the courts are too self-evident to merit further comment: delays, adjournments and procedural pitfalls dogged the path of every suitor. The law must be slow in order to be fair, said Maitland. But the delays which meant safety for some meant frustration for others, frustration which was apt to spill over into violence. Yet if the courts were indeed as inadequate as they seem, why were people still so eager to use them? For eager they were. Ever since Henry II (1154-1189) had opened the royal courts to all his free subjects by making available writs to initiate the possessory assizes, the justices had been overwhelmed by a volume of business that showed few signs of abating. G.L. Harriss has recently highlighted this paradox by describing late medieval England as a 'law-seeking and law-keeping' society. 'Law-keeping' it may not quite have been, but 'law-seeking' it certainly was. An enormous appetite for litigation existed in fourteenth-century England. Evidently, then, the courts did serve a function in society, even if it was different from the one they serve today. It is that function which needs to be identified.

Whatever assumptions may have guided the king's justices in their actions, they were certainly not ones based on a theory of deterrence. The insignificant penalties imposed for most offences show that. Conviction for a felony, it is true, automatically carried sentence of death. But conviction for a trespass would have incurred no more than a light fine – a few pounds at the most. Very likely the limited range of punishment available, particularly for felonies, was a major reason for the notorious reluctance of juries to convict. Very likely, too, it limited the practicability of making the punishment fit the crime. Deterrence, in other words, could play little part in medieval sentencing. Instead, the emphasis was placed on reconciliation and on restoration of the social framework. Since much of the business that came before the courts involved family quarrels and disputes over property, that preference made sense. But it follows that so long as reconciliation was achieved, it mattered little whether was achieved inside the court or outside. This is why out-of-court settlements were so common in the four

law, it seems, could do little to stop her. Ignorance of her intentions can hardly be an explanation. Joan's petition might perhaps be dismissed as an *ex parte* statement; but the coroner's inquest had confirmed that Margaret had procured the double murder. All the same, she herself was acquitted, and her Basing relatives were to browbeat the Privy Seal clerk into submission and to defy the law for years on end.

Court Rolls	The records kept by the clerks of the proceedings in the courts.
Common Pleas	One of the two main courts into which the king's court had divided by the thirteenth century.
King's Bench	The second of the two main courts into which the king's court had divided, hearing the bulk of the criminal business.
Mainprise	The medieval equivalent of bail.
Assize of Novel Disseisin	The process for recovering possession of a tenement of which you had been dispossessed.

teenth century. This is also why the appointment of arbitrators became so common in the fifteenth.

One consequence of this outlook was that litigants, which in this context means principally landowners both great and small, viewed resort to the law as merely one of several means by which the defence of property rights could be achieved. They regarded the law less as an objective set of rules than as a set of procedures by which self-interest could be served. It was the king's law certainly. But they had long seen how it could be turned to their advantage. The evolution of the law of villeinage in the thirteenth century is an early and illuminating example of how they did this. The inflationary pressures of the day were compelling landowners to cut costs by reimposing labour services on their tenants, but the resistance that this understandably provoked resulted in disputed cases being brought before the courts. The result was usually a victory for the lord; and the terms of villein tenure were defined in such a way as to give him complete authority to exact performance of the labour services in question.

In the fourteenth century landowners needed to use the law not so much to overcome the opposition of their tenants as to defend their estates against the machinations of neighbours and relatives. Not that this was anything new, of course. Land had always been the principal source of wealth and thus of status in medieval society. What aggravated the problem in the late middle ages was the growing complexity of the law, in its turn probably a consequence of the diffusion of property rights among a wider community of proprietors. If these rights had to be secured, as Margaret thought they had for the benefit of her children by Sir Edmund, then it mattered little whether they were secured by using, bending or simply by breaking the law. The distinction was, it seems, one that hardly bothered contemporaries. When we remember these attitudes, it does not seem so strange that the men who enforced the law could often be the men who broke it.

If it illuminates the causes of crime and the spirit in which plaintiff and defendant regarded the law, the Pashley case sheds far less light on the vexed question of whether lawlessness was on the increase in the late middle ages. Appearances suggest that it was. But the historian has to distinguish appearance from reality. The story told by his sources may not be as straightforward as it seems. The court rolls grow bigger certainly. The justices seem busier than ever. And if there is a reason for this, it appears to be that disputes over the descent of land were becoming commoner. But whether these threads of evidence are enough to support the general theory of a late medieval breakdown in order is open to question. Gentry feuding, though better documented in the fourteenth century, was surely nothing new. If all had been well in the twelfth century, Henry II would never have needed to introduce his possessory assizes. That these were intended principally to afford better protection for the rights of property suggests that even then conflicting claims to land were seen as a major temptation to lawlessness. The historian knows more about such cases in the fourteenth century than in the twelfth. But that is not to say that they had necessarily become more common. Thus it is preferable to approach the study of medieval crime by looking at particular episodes, like the Pashley murders, than by attempting to measure it statistically.

FOR FURTHER READING:
For late medieval crime in general see J. Bellamy, *Crime and Public Order in England in the Later Middle Ages* (Routledge & Kegan Paul 1973) and for gentry crime in particular, N.E. Saul, *Knights and Esquires: the Gloucestershire Gentry in the Fourteenth Century* (Oxford University Press, 1981). On the courts A. Harding, *The Law Courts of Medieval England* (Allen & Unwin, 1973) is useful.

ROBIN HOOD REVISED

The legend of the merry outlaw began more than 700 years ago. His history is vague but, says a British historian, one thing is clear: Robin never robbed the rich to give to the poor.

James C. Holt

Robin Hood is regarded by many, including some historians, as an archetypal hero who successfully defied unjust authority—personified by the wicked sheriff of Nottingham—and righted the ills of society by robbing the rich and giving to the poor. His legend has survived for more than seven centuries, with some changes and adjustments certainly, but with the essentials preserved: so far no film maker has armed Robin with a space-gun or dared to change the sheriff into a good cop.

But where did the legend come from, and how much of it is true? The story has been told and retold so often, acquiring layer after layer of accretions catering to the tastes of each new generation. What do we really know about Robin Hood?

The first known reference to Robin Hood occurs in a version of William Langland's *Piers Ploughman*, composed in 1377, in which Sloth is made to say:

I do not well know my Paternoster as the priest sings it.

But I know rhymes of Robin Hood and Randolph Earl of Chester.
So far so good, but the question of origins remains, for plainly Langland's "rhymes" were already current. How old was the legend when he alluded to it and how was it transmitted?

The first tales to survive in manuscript come from about 1450. *Robin Hood and*

the Monk, found in a manuscript collection that includes a prayer against thieves and robbers, is a thriller, a story of treachery and revenge. Robin is betrayed to the sheriff by a knavish monk and is then rescued from Nottingham Castle by Little John and the rest of the gang. *Robin Hood and the Potter*, part of a manuscript collection of romances and moralistic pieces probably written shortly after 1503, is by contrast almost a burlesque. Robin, after challenging and fighting a traveling potter, takes the potter's dress and wares to inveigle his way into Nottingham Castle and lure the sheriff to the outlaw lair in Sherwood.

The *Gest of Robin Hood*, most probably written in the 15th century, is a collection of the current tales of Robin Hood. It attracted the attention of early printers, and between the last years of the 15th century and the middle of the 16th century there appeared no less than five editions of this lengthy poem describing the deeds (gest) of Robin Hood. The *Gest*, a minstrel's serial to be recited at intervals, includes what is perhaps the earliest story of all, the tale of the impoverished knight. In this story, Robin assists a knight who has mortgaged his lands to the Abbot of St. Mary's York, by robbing the monks themselves to repay the loan. The *Gest* also includes the encounter of the King and Robin in Sherwood Forest and a summary tale of Robin's death at Kirklees.

These early versions contain nothing of the legend that is taken for granted by 20th-century readers. There is nothing of King Richard the Lionheart or of his ill-famed brother, Count John; the only king given a name is Edward "our comely king," which leaves a wide choice—by 1327 there were three Edwards.

There is no Maid Marian; she only came into the story about 1500, when it was already centuries old. Robin is not of noble birth; that was a social gloss first applied in the 16th century and given color by fictitious pedigrees of the 18th century which made him Earl of Huntingdon. In origin, Robin Hood is a simple yeoman.

He did not lead the English resistance to the Normans; that element came into the legend in 1819, with Scott's *Ivanhoe*. He does not resist royal taxes; the only tax mentioned in the earliest tales is pavage, a tax imposed for the paving of market-places and the like. And Robin, far from resisting the tax, is trying to levy it.

The earliest tales contain next to nothing of Robin's robbing the rich to give to the poor. That he was a "good outlaw" who "did poor men much good" was tacked on to one tale almost as an afterthought.

"Robin Hood and Maid Marian in Their Bower," from **Bold Robin Hood and His Outlaw Band,** *"penned and pictured by Louis Rhead" (Harper & Bros., c. 1912).*

5. THE MEDIEVAL PERIOD

The question of Robin Hood's origins remains, and there are several routes to an answer. One, of course, is to identify the "real" Robin Hood. The earliest candidate for the role is one Robert Hod, who was recorded as a fugitive before the King's justices at York in July 1225. The account recurred in the following year when the name appeared in the more colloquial form, Hobbehod. Unfortunately, the plea roll which might have contained details of the charges against him has not survived. Only one thing is certain: Robert Hod had fled the jurisdiction of the court. He was an outlaw. He is the only possible original of Robin Hood, so far discovered, who is known to have been an outlaw. Without more evidence, however, the matter is inconclusive.

Another path is the study of literary analogues. This approach links the legend with some of the knightly romances of the 13th century, particularly the tales of Fulk fitz Warin, a baron of the Welsh Marches who was an outlawed rebel against King John (1200–3), and of Eustace the Monk. This monk took to the woods in 1203 against his lord, the Count of Boulogne, and ended his days as a soldier of fortune when he was defeated at the battle of Sandwich in 1217. Fulk and Eustace live their lives as outlaws in the forest, just as Robin Hood does. All show a remarkable prowess with arms. There is no one to resist them; they may be undermined by treachery or overpowered by numbers but, if so, they gain release through skillful ruse and the base stupidity of their captors. Some of the analogous material must have been transmitted from one tale to another.

Approaching the legend through its geographic background links it with the great baronial estates of Pontefract, which encompassed parts of both Lancashire and Yorkshire and through which the major roads north from London led. Barnsdale and Clitheroe were both Yorkshire properties of the de Lacy family, lands which came to the earls of Lancaster through the marriage of Alice de Lacy to Thomas of Lancaster in 1292. The yeomen who served, and the minstrels who often stayed

When "Robin Hood meeteth the tall Stranger on the Bridge," Little John dunks the outlaw. From **The Merry Adventures of Robin Hood of Great Renown,** *illustrated by Howard Pyle.*

at, such households helped disseminate the legend throughout the Pontefract holdings—and beyond.

Finally, there is the study of names: not place-names, for they mark the subsequent dissemination of the legend, but surnames in the form of "Robinhood" or some equivalent. The earliest example has long been thought to be Gilbert Robinhood, who appears in Fletching, Sussex, in 1296. Other examples occur in London in the early 14th century. (There is no difficulty in understanding how the fame of the legendary outlaw might have been carried from Barnsdale in south Yorkshire down the Great North Road to the London taverns. In contrast, Fletching, to the south of London in Sussex, seems a far cry from Barnsdale: but not in terms of feudal property, for the lord of Fletching in 1296 was

none other than Thomas of Lancaster, husband of Alice de Lacy of Pontefract.)

Such evidence is admittedly wondrous thin and the logic finespun. After all, the name Hood was not uncommon; men called Robert Hood appear frequently enough in the existing records to preclude the snap identification of any one of them with the legendary outlaw. But the combination Robinhood is extremely rare. Even so, all such surnames could simply be dismissed as straightforward patronymics. In the same vein, children of a Robert Hood could also be known as fitz Robert, or Robertson, or Robinson, or Hudson, or Hodson, or even just plain Hood. And, more commonly, they were. In fact, Robinhood was a very rare form of surname, and so the hunch, the historian's sixth sense remains: The tales were sufficiently well known by the end of the 13th century to account for the adoption of a rather strange surname.

The weight of the accumulated evidence indicates that the legend's central locus is Barnsdale. (Most probably, Nottingham was later emphasized simply because it was a larger, better-known town.) The first tales, like that of the knight in debt to the abbot, had a knightly flavor that seems suited to a 13th-century audience. And it is likely that the tales have at their base a real outlaw.

An exciting new lead has recently been found by Dr. David Crook of the Public Record Office, London. Dr. Crook has now found yet another Robinhood surname (which is the subject of a note by him shortly to appear in *English Historical Review*). The name occurs in the Memoranda Roll of the King's Remembrancer of 1262, where the Prior of Sandleford, Berkshire, was pardoned a penalty imposed on him for seizing the chattels of one William "Robehod," fugitive.

That mention advances the earliest of such names by a matter of 34 years. And it has proved to be of much greater significance. For, by the luckiest chance of survival, the entry on the Memoranda Roll can be matched with an entry on the roll of the Justices in Eyre in Berkshire in 1261. The Eyre entry is an indictment of a criminal gang, both men and women, suspected of robberies and the receiving of robbers, who had fled the jurisdiction of the court and were outlawed. They included William, son of Robert le Fevere (Fevre=Smith), and there is no doubt, considering the precise details available, that this man and the William Robehod of the Memoranda Roll are one and the same.

Quite simply, somewhere along the administrative chain between the Justices in Eyre and the Remembrancer in the Exchequer, one of the clerks—perhaps even the Remembrancer's clerk—changed the name. And what led the clerk to do so was the fact that William son of Robert was a member of an outlaw gang indicted for robbery. The outlaw became William Robehod.

The clear inference is that the man who changed the name knew of the legend. And thus the earliest reference to Robin Hood as a legendary figure must now be taken to be not 1377 (*Piers Ploughman*), but 1261–2. In all senses, that is an enormous advance.

This discovery by Dr. Crook demonstrates beyond serious doubt that Robin Hood surnames did indeed derive from the legend, rather than the reverse. But its importance stretches far beyond that. First, the new discovery imposes strict limits on the search for a historical Robin: All candidates later than 1261–2 can now be firmly eliminated. Much Robin Hood scholarship concerned with establishing him in south Yorkshire in the 1320s must now be jettisoned. Robert Hod, fugitive of the York justices in 1225, now has a clearer field; indeed, the nickname that he was given on the rolls in 1226, "Hobbehod," may well reflect the emergence of the legend.

Old, well-known evidence, which has been played down in recent years, suddenly looks refreshed. The Scottish historian John Major, writing in 1521, believed that Robin Hood and Little John were active in 1193–4. A tomb with epitaph that survived at Kirklees in the late 17th century recorded that Robin died in 1247. The persistence with which these and other sources associated Robin with the late 12th and early 13th centuries is now explicable. John Major was probably right, and many modern scholars are proved wrong.

A second consequence of Dr. Crook's discovery will be more difficult to assess. Until now literary scholars, relying on 1377 as a rough point of origin for the legend, have assumed very reasonably that the analogues that the tales of Robin share with the knightly romances of the 13th century arose in the earlier knightly romances of Fulk fitz Warin and Eustace the Monk and spread to the later yeoman ballads of Robin Hood. It now appears that romances and ballads all took shape at one and the same time; it is easier to understand how they came to share material, but it can no longer be so certain which was the source and which the recipient. The earlier the Robin Hood legend is pressed, the more original it is likely to be.

A third consequence is even more important. If any real Robin Hood existed, it was thought, he had to exist before 1377, the *Piers Ploughman* reference. Early manuscript tales of Robin appearing around 1450 then made sense, because it seemed reasonable that a story should take 50-odd years to move from fireside tale into written form. But an interval stretching back from c.1450 to before 1261–2 is a much more serious gap. The inference is that the stories known in 1261–2 by the clerk who called the outlaw William son

Perhaps the earliest tale of all: "Merry Robin Stops a Sorrowful Knight." The Howard Pyle illustration appears in the 1925 edition published by Scribner's.

of Robert "Robehod" were probably very different from the diversified tales which appear in written verse from the middle of the 15th century.

What went on in the intervening years? There are only a few indications of what the Robin Hood stories contained at any particular point. In 1432, for instance, the clerk of the sheriff of Wiltshire concocted an acrostic in his parliamentary return for the county that associates "Reynold" with Robin's gang: From that clue, it seems certain that the clerk knew the tale in which Little John assumed the alias of Reynold Greenleaf—or that he knew some similar yarn. The tale of the King's visit to Sherwood is plainly based on the progress of Edward II through the northern counties in 1323; therefore it cannot have been embodied in the legend before that date. Besides those two reasonably fixed points, it is possible to say that some elements in the legend—such as the tale of the Knight and the Abbot of St. Mary's, with its connections to Barnsdale, where the tales are thought to have begun—are likely to have been earlier, others later. And that at present is all we can say.

Within this long period of gestation there are continuous, consistent themes. In 1261–2 the legend was known to a clerk at work most probably in the Exchequer—in our parlance, the clerk was a civil servant. So the legend was circulating at that social level. What triggered the clerk's consciousness was not a tale of some heroic medieval prototype of Che Guevara but the record of a gang of outlawed criminals: robbers and receivers of robbers. The same statements can be made about the references to Robin in the late 14th and 15th century. Such references come mostly from a middling social level and they are largely derogatory. (The sheriff's clerk in Wiltshire in 1432 is apparently the first to describe Robin as a good man. He included in his acrostic the phrase, "Good man was hee.")

The story's origins are intermingled with the aristocratic and gentle household; the geographic detail both in the tales' content and in the distribution of personal names suggests that one great household, that of Lacy/Lancaster, played a role that is still reflected in the evidence. The legend's heroes are yeomen—middling household

5. THE MEDIEVAL PERIOD

officers, youths at the beginning of their careers. The tales are remarkable for the absence of sex, family, and family property. They were retailed by minstrels who passed through, or who were permanently employed by, the household.

And that is how the legend spread and changed. Such households were itinerant. Yeomen in particular ranged afar as archer-bodyguards, messengers, sometimes as foresters and huntsmen. Minstrels, above all, traveled, performing not only before noblemen and gentry but also before bishops, in monasteries, and especially in the marketplace; anywhere, indeed, with a sufficient audience to suggest the possibility of reward. The legend's resulting diversification was already apparent in the first surviving tales. There are scenes in *Robin Hood and the Potter,* for example, that would have made the most sense, and perhaps had the most immediate appeal, to the folk of Nottingham.

By the middle of the 14th century, Robin seems to have been invading popular iconography. The sculptures in the north aisle of Beverly Minster (c. 1340), which celebrate the Beverly Guild of Minstrels, include a spandrel carving of a remarkably convincing longbowman. Furthermore, one of the misericords (c. 1430) in St. Mary's Beverly, which was the Guild's church, has been taken by some to represent Robin Hood and the King.

The most important development of all was that the legend overflowed the bounds of minstrelsy and invaded both folk festival and theater. Much new light was shed on this development by David Wiles's *The Early Plays of Robin Hood* (Boydell and Brewer, 1981). Indeed, Wiles is disposed to argue that in the developing tradition, the plays were primary and the ballads secondary. This is unlikely to be accepted. Still, Wiles rightly draws attention to the fact that the first recorded performance of a Robin Hood play took place before the Mayor of Exeter as early as 1427.

Certainly within 50 years or so of that date came a theatrical development that involved Robin Hood in the May Festival, first as a participant in the May Games and ultimately as King of May. It was in this last development, in my view, that Robin at last—near the start of the 16th century—

"Robin Shooteth his Last Shaft," by Pyle. ". . . and sett . . . mine arrowes at my feete," says Robin in the Gest.

acquired the reputation of robbing the rich to give to the poor.

The celebration of the Spring Festival is, of course, very ancient. In medieval England it began with youths and maidens returning from the woods at dawn on the first May morning, adorned with sprigs, branches, and flowers. As they processed, they decorated houses and sought payment for their display. This collection, "gathering," or *quete* was an almost inevitable concomitant of such processions.

Now, what could be more natural than that the most famous human denizen of the greenwood should accompany the youth on their return? And what more suitable role was there for the most successful of all robbers than that he should be put to the charitable purpose of conducting the *quete?* For that is plainly what Robin did.

Robin Hood's gatherings, which begin to appear in local records before the end of the 15th century, are not riotous assemblies of men but charitable collections of money. In some southern townships, especially at Reading and Kingston upon Thames, these celebrations were controlled by the church wardens and are recorded in their accounts. At Kingston, the wardens provided for the expense of the

display: Kendal (green) cloth for Robin, Little John, and Maid Marian, white cloth for the Friar, and other items. The wardens received sums from the gathering.

And, perhaps most significant of all, the wardens accounted for expenditures on items that indicate how the gathering was done and how many contributions were expected: in 1506, 4s. 2d. to John Painter, who supplied 1,000 "liveries" or badges, 3s. 8d. to William Plott, who supplied 1,200 "liveries and 40 great," and 10d. to the same for 2,500 pins. Robin had become the central figure in a flag-day.

A flag-day is an occasion, now almost peculiar to Britain, in which ladies of charitable instincts conduct well-organized collections by selling lapel flags or badges—in aid of wounded veterans before Remembrance Sunday (when the badge is a Flanders poppy), or for the national Life-Boat Service, or for national societies for the protection of children or the support of orphans.

Robin collected from those who had money to give and accounted for his collection to those who administered the charitable funds of the parish. Thus he took from the rich to give to the poor.

This could have happened by a kind of easy elision of associations. Or it could equally have been the brainstorm of some long-forgotten church warden who envisaged exploiting Robin's reputation for charity. At all events, it left an enduring mark on Robin's reputation.

Something else also endured. At Kingston in 1506 the contributor bought a pin or livery great or small. The livery was a sign that he had joined Robin's *mesne,* band, or company. Those who buy their flags on similar charitable occasions today rarely reflect that they identify themselves with a mark that originated as a feudal livery—or with an outlaw hero.

James C. Holt is the author of Robin Hood *(Thames and Hudson, 1982). Professor of medieval history at the University of Cambridge, where he is also master of Fitzwilliam College, Holt is president of the Royal Historical Society. He first became interested in Robin Hood when he taught at the University of Nottingham.*

The Social Influence of the Motte-and-Bailey Castle

The motte was a medieval mound fort; the bailey was an associated enclosure. Their appearance in the second half of the 10th century diminished central authority in Europe and gave rise to chivalry

Michel Bur

The first project of military engineering ordered by William the Conqueror after his landing in England was the hasty construction of a motte, a fortification of a kind unknown in the British Isles. Designed to provide the Normans at Hastings with a strongpoint, the motte was primarily a mound of earth surrounded by a ditch. Embedded in the mound were heavy timbers that supported a tower put together out of prefabricated members. In the years that followed the Norman victory the occupiers built similar mottes throughout England, thus securing a firm hold over the vanquished.

The Normans brought their knowledge of mottes with them from France, where the building of such simple fortifications had enabled nobles, great and small, to defy the central authority of Charlemagne's successors and to establish their own domains. It is not too much to say that this novel defensive weapon revolutionized medieval Europe. Politically it was the instrument of the feudalism that replaced rule from a single center. Socially its effects were perhaps even more important: the motte served as a kind of schoolroom where the medieval seigneurs and their retinue learned what was needed to create the form of civilized behavior known as chivalry.

Until a few years ago little was known about the mottes of France. The only archaeology concerned with the Middle Ages was the study of major medieval buildings, a subdiscipline of history concerned with describing and analyzing the technical aspects of masonry construction. The examination of other remains of medieval life was left to geog-raphers; archaeologists did not bother to probe them. Recently, however, scholars at universities and other institutions have begun investigating the medieval countryside, and their work has begun to transform long-established patterns of historical thought.

Among the areas where progress in such research is being made is the study of fortified rural habitations. The motte has proved to be the most significant of these primitive seigneurial strongholds of the late 10th century through the 12th. Thanks to archaeological studies outside France, particularly those in Britain, where the details of the Norman Conquest continue to be investigated, French defensive earthworks of the period are well known.

A typical motte, appearing in profile either as a truncated cone or as part of a sphere, could be up to 100 meters in diameter at its base and as much as 20 meters high. Adjacent to most mottes was a large earth-walled enclosure, known as a bailey, surrounded by a ditch and topped with a wood palisade. Hence this type of dual defensive earthwork is called a motte-and-bailey castle. Another type of earthwork consists of a miniature bailey without a motte: a circular or oval bank 30 to 100 meters in diameter, surrounded by a ditch and topped with a palisade. Some of these enclosures served only as pens for livestock. Others, particularly those flanked by separate stock pens, were actually earthen castles of a lesser type.

Since 1961 a systematic inventory of these primitive seigneurial habitations has been under way in France, beginning in the Auvergne. Normandy was added to the survey in 1968 and Champagne in 1972. Since then the work has been extended both eastward and westward to include French Flan-ders, Dauphiné, Gascony and Saintonge. Its objective is to find, describe, measure and map (on a scale of 1 : 1,000) every vestige of these medieval earthworks that remains before modern agricultural machinery has erased them. The field work is being co-ordinated with archival research aimed at determining the date of construction and of abandonment or razing, the name given to each motte (such as "stronghold" or "castle") and the role in society of its inhabitants, such as "count" (*comes*), "knight" (*miles*) or "seigneur" (*dominus*). The standardization of such inquiry should result in a uniformity of collected data and so provide, if need be with the help of computer programs, a solid quantitative base for historical speculation.

A mere sampling of sites would not be acccptable. The survey must, like oil poured on water, spread outward from one community to the next until the census is complete. In brief, the study, both methodical and exhaustive, is simultaneously examining in depth the medieval archives and what remains of the medieval landscape.

The motte-and-bailey castle was known as a *château*, a word that like "castle" is from the Latin *castellum*. It was an establishment that served as a permanent abode for a seigneur and his men-at-arms. The *château* differed in size and function from similar but much larger defensive enclosures that had in the past served as places of refuge for the general population. The distinction is of particular importance because the motte, from the military point of view, was the most significant technological innovation of the latter part of the 10th century.

Mottes appeared first in low-lying marshy areas in the region between the Loire and the Rhine and next on the steep hills of the same region. From this "homeland" they spread across Europe from the Atlantic to the Vistula and from Scandinavia to the Mediterranean. With their wood tower—in some instances simply a watchtower, in others a larger residential structure—these earth mounds were, with one significant difference, equivalent to the nearly contemporaneous great stone donjon keeps of the Loire and Normandy. The difference was that in western Europe the medieval mottes were much more numerous than the stone castles were then or at any time later.

The time when the mottes quickly spread across Europe was an eventful one. Even before A.D. 1000 parts of western Europe (at first France and Ita-

ly and later Germany) had undergone a profound political and social transformation. The structure of Charlemagne's empire was in ruins and smaller political entities were forming everywhere. In place of the Carolingian system of state control from the center, men grouped themselves around feudal lords. The locally powerful who were sought out as protectors by lesser men now intended to exercise for their own benefit the authority they had previously drawn from the king. It was a revolution of the landed aristocracy, the very group from whose ranks the sovereign had traditionally recruited his administrators and officers. In France the landed aristocracy eventually dethroned the descendants of Charlemagne and in A.D. 987 gave the

crown to one of their own, Hugh Capet. In the years that followed the interests of the landed aristocracy stifled those principles of peace and common weal that had formerly had the support of the central authority.

Such an upheaval could not take place without fierce strife: the great nobles against the monarch, the same nobles among themselves and so on down to second- and third-tier seigneurs against one another. The 10th century was a time of particularly violent competition for land and power. If a seigneur was to dominate, he needed abundant resources: the means to maintain troops and reward the fidelity of the rank and file. In the long run, however, even the most determined adventurer was always at

LARGE MOTTE in the Ardennes of northeastern France is seen to the left of the church in this aerial photograph of Cornay, a village near the canal town of Vouziers. Although eroded for more than seven centuries, this earthwork is still 18 meters high, 60 meters in diameter at the base and 35 meters in diameter at the top. The summit, which covers an area of 110 square meters, now serves as a cemetery.

risk of chance defeat, perhaps only a temporary setback, perhaps death in a skirmish. No territorial takeover could have been lasting without the motte, a weapon that enabled those who controlled it to defy their adversaries and to transform that defiance into irreversible victory.

Just as the waterwheel mill and the draft-animal harness revolutionized the economics of agriculture, so was the motte an instrument of political and social revolution. An unskilled peasant labor force could easily erect the earthworks in a short time. Moreover, except for its wood superstructure the motte was virtually indestructible. When in the 11th century provincial authority (itself a product of the breakdown of central authority) was challenged in such strongholds as Normandy and Champagne, what followed? Mottes sprang up all over the two provinces; without that weapon those up in arms against the provincial authorities could neither have initially held their ground nor have eventually sunk their roots.

Motte tactics were not unlike those of a huge but simplified game of chess. The primary objective was to advance one's own pieces without having them captured. One pushed forward and built a motte, strongly barricading one's forces within it to resist the siege that one's rival, hoping to regain lost lands, was sure to begin immediately. In general such sieges were failures, and after the seigneur and his garrison had survived a few such efforts the motte, by now upgraded to the status of a *château*, was guaranteed to endure at least until treason opened the gates or the seigneur himself was captured.

Contemporaneous accounts show that the early seigneurs lived in constant fear of treason, never being entirely sure of their followers' fidelity. They had to avoid capture at all costs, a consideration that explains why, when things went adversely in formal open battles, the seigneur in command of the losing side was the first to leave the field. The reason was that once the loser was in the hands of the winner he was exposed to intolerable pressure, as were his kin and others left behind to guard his domain. Many a captive seigneur was brought to the door of his *château*, to be hanged there if his wife did not open the gates. Many a noble who held as hostages the children of a traitorous seigneur threatened to hang them or blind them if their father did not give himself up. Less dramatic than such episodes but fully as effective in putting pressure on a captive was one involving the comte de Blois in 1044. After his capture by the comte d'Anjou

a mere three days of imprisonment convinced him to yield the city of Tours and its surrounding countryside in exchange for his freedom.

Two schools of medieval historians disagree on how the mottes came to proliferate so rapidly. One school takes the view that most such *châteaux* were legally built by those endowed with authority. The other, echoing a phrase coined by Norman chroniclers, sees almost every motte as a *château adultérin*, that is, an unlawful construction. In effect anyone who declares some action to be a revolution necessarily defines as unlawful the means by which the revolution triumphs. Actually whether most of the *châteaux* were built by properly authorized persons or more informally by adventurous landed proprietors matters little since what counts is not so much the source of the power as the purpose to which the power was put. This argument leads to a complementary one. If the act of revolution renders unlawful all other actions against the challenged authority (in this instance a violation of the monopoly on fortifications held by the crown or by lesser nobility), the revolt, if it is successful, soon creates its own legality. One is reminded of a 16th-century epigram of John Harington: "Treason doth never prosper: what's the reason? / For if it prosper, none dare call it treason."

In a military aristocracy social relations were based on the vassal's homage and oath of allegiance to his superior. In other words, the weak became dependent on the strong in return for a reward in the form of land: the fief. This principle, occupying the middle ground between strength and weakness, gradually became the criterion of a new kind of legality that applied equally to kings and to great nobles: to be accepted as a legal occupant the master of a *château* had to hold the fortification in fief from a sovereign or a nobleman. In the give-and-take that naturally put the holders of existing fortifications in opposition to those who sought to build new ones, an equilibrium began to develop. This situation owed nothing to a policy of direct confrontation, an always violent and often sterile course of action. It came about because of recourse to the legal formula of feudalism. For the more politically skilled nobles the building of a stable establishment called not for destroying (or trying to destroy) the *châteaux adultérins* but for bringing them into vassalage. Thus the mottes on the fringe of any particular jurisdiction were progressively transformed into "feudal" mottes, with their existence no longer contested.

The network of the first French mottes had no connection with existing population centers; the formidable mass of the palisaded fortress was raised in total disregard of the local population. Keeping close watch on their rivals, each seigneur's forces camped in the flat countryside like an army of occupation, their ties with the countryfolk limited to levies and labor drafts. Above all, the *château* sought isolation. After that other strategic factors could be weighed. The chosen site might be at a point controlling travel by road, at a central location on a private domain, on property stolen from the Church or even in a town or close to the wall of a fortified city. Beyond any such long-term considerations, however, the seigneur selected a setting that would enable him and his forces both to survive siege and to go over to the offensive effectively.

Under these circumstances it is not surprising that a good many of the earliest *châteaux*, erected in unsatisfactory locations, were later abandoned by their builders. A number of anonymous vestiges still bear witness to the precariousness and instability of the first seigneurial habitations. The process of site selection, however, soon came to favor locations that were easy to defend, had a good view of the countryside and commanded terrain over which it was possible to venture in all directions.

What was *château* life like? Here is a 12th-century description of the dwelling tower of Ardres in French Flanders. The tower of this sizable *château* had three levels. At the ground level were kept the stores of grain and wine. On the next level was the seigneurial chamber, adjoined by smaller rooms occupied by the master's younger children, his table attendants (bearers of wine and bread) and some other servants. On the top level, which was also the level of the guard walk, were communal sleeping quarters for the master's older children, one for the sons and another for the daughters. Adjoining the dwelling tower was another three-story structure. There at the ground level meat was stored; on the next level were the kitchens and quarters for the cooks, and on the top level was the chapel, facing east. Actually few if any of the early *châteaux* were as spacious and comfortable as Ardres; a sensible fear of fire must have made most *château* builders place the kitchens farther away from the dwelling tower.

Nevertheless, at least at Ardres, the seigneur, his family, their table attendants and other servants all lived in the dwelling tower. Their cooks lived in the adjacent building and perhaps so did

FORTRESS BOURG OF DAMPIERRE-LE-CHÂTEAU in the department of the Marne, depicted in this drawing after a 15th-century engraving, had grown from a motte-and-bailey castle between the 12th century and the time when the engraving was made. Only one structure remained on the summit of the motte. The associated bailey was surrounded both by a rampart and by a moat. Some of the bailey outbuildings, seen in the foreground, are on low ground. Others stand on higher ground with a guard tower at the right. Beyond the rampart and moat at the left are commercial, residential and religious structures, their occupants attracted by the stability of the bourg.

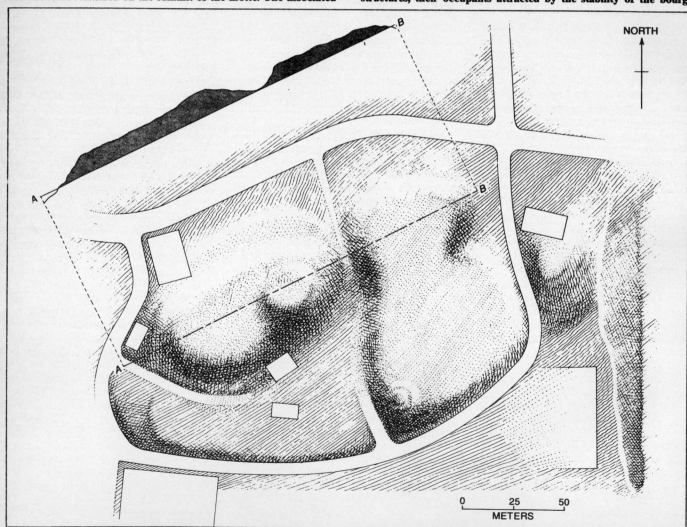

PLAN VIEW OF MOTTE AND BAILEY in the illustration at the top of the page shows its substantial dimensions: 120 by 60 meters at the base and 75 by 35 meters at the top. The motte earthwork itself was 15 meters high. The relation between the motte and the bailey is shown in a section along the line A–B that appears at the top left. It shows why that part of the bailey was known as the upper town.

the chaplain and the sentries of the watch. The rest of the establishment—the knights of the garrison, the administrators of the seigneurial domain, artisans such as the blacksmith and others needed for the upkeep of arms and equipment, and lesser personnel such as stable boys—occupied buildings within the adjacent palisaded bailey. There stables, barns, ovens, workshops and similar outbuildings formed a small, self-contained community that existed only for the seigneur's service and under his protection. The small population of the typical early *château* scarcely interacted at all with the much more numerous peasants who inhabited the villages of the countryside.

This aloofness did not continue for long. By about A.D. 1050 clusters of outsiders began to establish themselves near the *châteaux*. The root causes of this shift appear to have been population growth and a resulting social instability. Carolingian Europe had been covered with deep forest, and in the 11th and 12th centuries forests were actively cleared to allow agricultural expansion. In such newly cleared areas the interests of two quite different groups converged. The first group consisted of surplus labor hungry for land. The second was entrepreneurial: the younger sons of noble families, eager to set up their own domain. The convergence of interests led to the construction of a new kind of fortified site, where the seigneur's *château* and his followers' village all stood inside a single defensive earth wall. Examples are found in southern Aquitaine and Champagne.

Next, beginning in about A.D. 1070, local towns arose, particularly in the west of France. Churches and marketplaces were built in the immediate vicinity of one *château* or another. The population attracted to such amenities swelled the numbers in the growing settlement and soon the seigneur of the *château* found himself master of the adjacent bourg, or borough, economically and administratively the center of a sizable district.

Such bourgs were variants of other settlements, both in the open country and close to the few cities, that were multiplying everywhere at this time. They benefited from the same social dynamics and often enjoyed the same legal privileges. In any event villages without *châteaux* remained more numerous than villages with them. This suggests that a seigneur's effort to recruit a cadre of peasants in order to profit from the economic growth of the newly established village did not always conclude with a company of happy householders settled in the shadow of his tower.

When the fortuitous union of *château* and village gave birth to a bourg, the presence of the seigneur, his entourage and the other clientele of the same social class was certainly crucial to making the enterprise flourish. Yet for the bourg to become firmly rooted other factors favorable to growth had to exist. One such factor was the fertility of the local soil. Another was a location on a main road. Without such advantages there could be little probability of success. Negative factors also played a part; many a bourg withered away when its adjacent *château* was destroyed by chance or by malice.

These observations, concerned with the period of seigneurial consolidation from the middle of the 11th century into the 12th, have taken us a long way from the initial feudal period, a time of struggle when ordinary methods of defending habitations were shaky and when the new weapon, the motte, first came into service as a means of territorial domination. Let us now return to that earlier period in order to see the role the motte played in the evolution of a new kind of man and the molding of his behavior. In effect one cannot separate the feudal warrior from his environment.

To begin with, consider the contradictions of the times: on the one hand freedom and on the other a subjugated and exploited peasantry; on the one hand war and on the other a clergy preaching peace as the ideal. A seigneur inhabited a world of isolation and danger where—in order to protect himself and his family, to sleep in safety, to raise children to be knowledgeable about that harsh and hazardous life—he needed to hide behind an earth rampart and barricade himself on a motte. The only way to soften those harsh conditions was to depend on the links of kinship or, better, on the parent-surrogate links of vassalage and an oath of fealty.

Even with those assurances constant vigilance was necessary. At home the seigneur lived in fear of treason. In battle the knowledge that the stakes were high sharpened cunning and incited treachery. Even a task as simple as finding a wife became enmeshed in haggling or led to matchmaking that left little room for personal choice.

Then, little by little, the violence and insecurity of these early feudal times gave rise, as it were, to their own antibodies. The fear of treason served in the end to reinforce the fidelity of the vassal and to exalt the loyalty of the warrior. The art of war, learned through continuous training from an early age, was not sidetracked into becoming the art of ambush. Instead it evolved into straightforward prowess, so that a victor faced by a valiant but unlucky adversary—virtu-

ally a mirror of himself—was careful to exercise fair play. By the same token the young warrior's lust, stimulated by the presence of both unmarried and married women within the *château*, was transformed into civility.

This kind of courtesy was not limited to the men's attitude toward women. It defined the deportment of the men in the seigneur's retinue. Within the confines of the *château* the choice was to live either in fellowship or in antagonism. Clearly the best course was to adhere to certain rules that made life as pleasant as possible or, at the least, to refrain from violence. Thus it was that in the confined world behind the palisade there slowly developed the moral standards that, when feudal society entered its second age at the end of the 11th century, inspired the troubadours. They sang of chivalry and love, but what the songs actually celebrated was the dual achievement of stabilization and colonization. Those foremost figures of chivalry, the seigneur's retinue of knights, began as simple warriors who had attained a higher estate through the practice of cavalry warfare. At the same time their garrison duties imposed on them specific values of courtesy and honor: the rules of the game.

One can conclude that the motte of the 10th and 11th centuries has a historical significance that has not attracted enough notice. As an instrument of domination par excellence it should be evaluated in terms of technological efficiency. The waterwheel mill and the draft-animal harness played a comparable technological role in the economic revolution of the Middle Ages. Consider, however, another factor. The authority of Louis XIV, who ruled France for more than half of the 17th century and on into the 18th, is regarded as having been nothing less than absolute. The fact remains that the Sun King in all his glory was not as well obeyed as any minister in the French republic of today. His orders reached the farthest boundary of his realm, but they got there slowly, and the functionaries on the spot were left a certain margin for interpretation. It is not so today. For example, it is enough for the Minister of the Interior to book a conference call, to lift his telephone and have some 100 departmental prefects standing at attention at the other end of the line. Moreover, any ambiguity in his orders can be eliminated as he goes along. As a means of exercising authority in government the telephone not only is faster than the written order but also can carry more weight.

Viewed in proportion and at a somewhat different level the motte played a role similar to the telephone's but in reverse. It diminished the king's prerogatives, affording the seigneurs a means of weakening central authority and giving birth to as many seigneuries as there were *châteaux*. Unable to exercise sovereignty, the king could only act the part of a feudal overlord, hoping for obedience no longer from subjects but

FORTRESS BOURG OF RETHEL in the Ardennes, depicted in another drawing after a 15th-century engraving, had also grown from a motte-and-bailey castle. By then both the motte and the bailey had been faced with blocks of chalk and surrounded with a stone wall that had towers placed at regular intervals. The same wall had been extended to protect the community that grew up around the priory of Notre Dame, at the center. As at Dampierre-le-Château, the security offered by the original motte had transformed it into a major town.

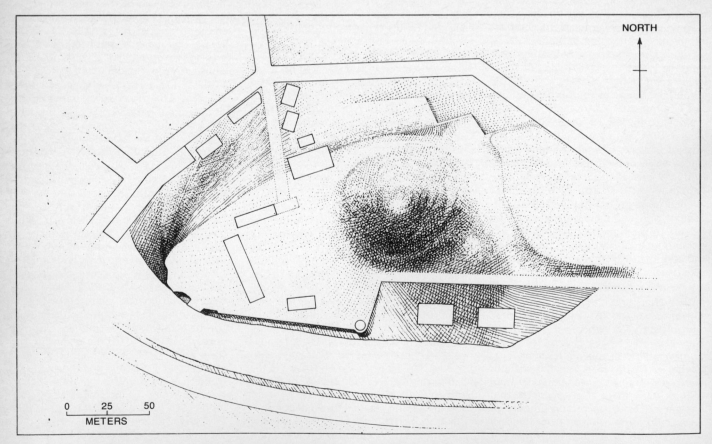

PLAN VIEW OF MOTTE shows how it took advantage of irregular terrain. The motte itself was on a rocky spur that extended eastward with an almost vertical drop on its south side and an only slightly shallower slope to the east and the north. The motte was 70 meters in diameter at the base and 10 meters in diameter at the summit. Probably built before A.D. 1026, it rose 21 meters above its base.

rather from vassals. The conclusion is self-evident: however powerful the ruler and however determined the unruly, the outcome for both remained moot as long as neither had an effective technological advantage.

A second conclusion is that the motte certainly affected the mass of the rural population. From having been more or less self-sufficient they found themselves tied to the *châteaux* and their seigneurs and forced to pay taxes to these new overlords. The effect on the behavior of the overlords, however, was even more profound. Accustomed to a life in large open dwellings in a country-side populated with peasant freemen, the seigneurs in a matter of decades found themselves huddling behind ramparts, armed to the teeth in order first to grasp power and then to keep it. Clinging to this technological instrument of terror, the motte, the seigneurs and their retinues began to evolve a culture both primitive and original. On the one hand the culture was two-faced and dedicated to naked power; on the other it was a culture of courage and faithfulness to the given word. Certain of the popular medieval ballads, the chansons de geste, captured this evolving culture as if in a living mirror.

Little by little, as the generations passed, a certain equilibrium arose. A set of new values acknowledged seigneurial mutuality and made it possible to live less at sword's point. The *châteaux* became open to friends and neighbors; tournaments took the place of warfare; shields, once anonymous, carried symbols indicating the identity of the bearer. Where there had reigned ruse and brutality there now flourished virtues such as prowess, generosity, courtesy and honor. Such is the legacy the period bequeathed us from its second stage of development, a legacy, bred in the environment of the motte, that deserves to be called the civilization of the *châteaux*.

Medieval Roots
of the Industrial Revolution

*The revolution is generally dated to the arrival of steam power
in the 18th and 19th centuries. It is now clear that long before
then a significant role was played by water-powered machines*

Terry S. Reynolds

The origins of modern industry are often dated only to the late 18th and early 19th centuries, when manual labor was displaced by steam-powered machines, first in the cotton-textile industry and later in other industries. This period is commonly called the Industrial Revolution, a term strongly suggesting that there had been a sharp break from developments in the preceding centuries.

The history of water power in medieval and early modern Europe presents a different picture. Powered machinery had begun to displace manual labor long before the 18th century, and in some areas of Europe it had done so on a substantial scale and in many industries. In other words, the rise of European industry should more properly be regarded as an evolutionary process going back at least to the eighth or ninth century, when European engineers began to aggressively apply water power to industrial processes.

Although water power can be harnessed by a variety of devices, the commonest device is of course a wheel fitted with blades or buckets. Such a wheel can be mounted either horizontally or vertically. Until the introduction of the water turbine in the 1830's horizontally mounted water wheels were the simpler of the two types. In the early horizontal water mill the lower end of a vertical shaft carried a small horizontal wheel consisting only of blades. The upper end of the axle was linked directly, without gearing, to a rotating millstone. This kind of mill was cheap to build but usually delivered no more power than a donkey or a horse (less than one horse-power). Even that power it generated wastefully, operating at an efficiency of only 5 to 15 percent. The horizontal mill was also not as easily adapted as the vertical one to tasks other than milling grain. Hence it did not play an important role in the early evolution of water-powered industry in Europe.

Vertical water wheels, on the other hand, did. There were two main sub-types of vertical wheel: undershot and overshot. The undershot was the simpler. It had flat radial blades attached to its circumference, and it was energized by the impact of water flowing under the wheel and pushing against the blades. The undershot could work in almost any stream as long as there was enough water flowing at a modest speed, but it worked most effectively in a confined channel. Its typical output was three to five times as great as that of a horizontal wheel (namely about two to three horsepower) and its efficiency was 20 to 30 percent.

With the overshot wheel water was fed over the wheel into "buckets" built into the wheel's circumference. There the weight of the water, rather than its impact, turned the wheel, with each bucket discharging its water at the bottom of the wheel and returning empty to the top to begin the cycle anew. Overshot wheels were usually more expensive to build than undershot or horizontal wheels, since they called for a dam and an elevated water channel, and they could not handle large volumes of water. With a small volume and a head of water ranging from three to 12 meters, however, they were capable of operating at an efficiency of from 50 to 70 percent and delivering anywhere from two to 40 horsepower. (The average was from five to seven horsepower.)

Although ancient engineers devised both undershot and overshot wheels, neither were widely built. For example, in the first century B.C. the Roman engineer Vitruvius described the undershot wheel in a section of his *De architectura* dealing with machines rarely employed. Indeed, there are fewer than a dozen known literary references to the use of water power in all antiquity.

In medieval Europe social and economic conditions increased the need for such power and initiated the trend toward replacing manual labor with powered machines. One of the most critical elements in the changing technological climate of western Europe was the monastic system, based on the rules laid down early in the sixth century by St. Benedict. These rules had two features that encouraged the introduction of water power. First, monks were to devote certain rigidly regulated periods to manual labor, to reading and study and to spiritual duties such as meditation and prayer. Second, the monastery was to be self-sufficient and to isolate itself from worldly influences.

These rules provided an incentive for the development of water power because only by harnessing power for time-consuming manual tasks such as grinding grain could the monastery ever become self-sufficient or give the monks time for study and prayer. The monastic order that was perhaps the most aggressive in developing water power was the Cistercian. By 1300 there were more

MULTIPURPOSE ORE MILL powered by a single water wheel at the upper left was illustrated in Georgius Agricola's *De re metallica,* published in 1556. Gold ore was processed in the following steps. First the ore was crushed by a cam-lifted stamp (*c*), just visible to the left of the water wheel. Next the crushed ore was ground to a powder in a pair of millstones to the right of the wheel. Two spare dome-shaped upper millstones (*d, e*) are on the ground on each side of a spare lower millstone; one of the upper millstones is turned upside down to show the hole that admitted the crushed ore. The outlet for the powdered ore (*h*) in the lower millstone deposited the powder into the first of three settling tubs (*o*). The slurry of powdered ore in the tubs was agitated by paddles driven by cogs (*x*) attached to the axle of the wheel. The agitation separated the heavier gold from the lighter dross, which eventually spilled from the last of the settling tubs.

5. THE MEDIEVAL PERIOD

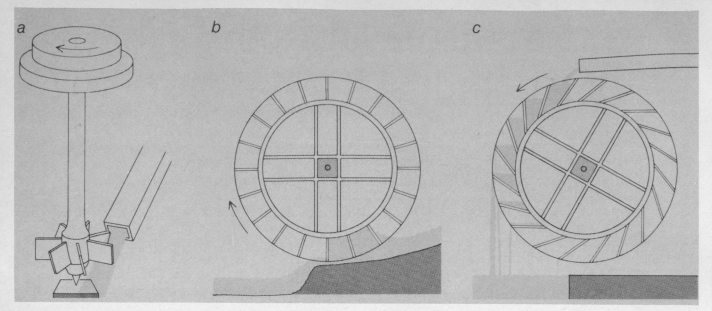

MEDIEVAL WATER WHEELS rotated either horizontally on a vertical axle (*a*) or vertically on a horizontal axle (*b*, *c*). The horizontal wheel, an ancestor of the turbine, was called a Norse mill; it was inefficient and was not widely used for anything but flour milling. The earliest vertical wheel (*b*) is known as an undershot wheel because the water passes under it; its chief virtue is its low cost and simplicity of installation. The overshot wheel (*c*) usually requires either a substantial fall of water (three meters or more) or a dam to provide such a fall.

than 500 Cistercian monasteries. Virtually all of them had a water mill, and many had five or more mills.

One other social class contributed to the diffusion of water power in the medieval West. It was the feudal nobility. The nobles saw in the introduction of water power an additional means of getting revenue from the peasantry. In a number of areas of Europe lords imposed on their serfs the obligation to bring their grain for grinding only to the lord's mill. That milling monopoly, at first limited to grain mills, was sometimes extended to other water-powered processes, for example fulling: the finishing of wool cloth. Thus in western Europe two major groups—the clergy and the landed nobility—developed an interest in expanding water power. They were later joined by a third group: the merchant class, which saw in milling a way to make a profit.

Other economic pressures in medieval Europe contributed to the extension of water power. By the seventh century the labor surplus that had plagued the Roman Empire at its height and may have discouraged the adoption of water power had completely disappeared. The ensuing labor shortage encouraged the adoption of laborsaving devices such as the water wheel. Europe's geography may also have contributed to the development. The heart of medieval European civilization lay in the drainage basins of rivers that flowed into the Bay of Biscay, the English Channel and the North Sea. In this region were hundreds of small to middle-size streams with a fair-

ly regular flow, which was convenient for the development of water power. The heart of Classical civilization, on the other hand, was in the Mediterranean basin, where because of the dry climate stream flow tended to be erratic and seasonal.

As a result of these social, economic and geographic factors the use of water power in Europe steadily grew, particularly from the ninth century on. By 1500 water wheels were in operation throughout Europe. At some sites the concentration of powered machines was quite comparable to that in the factories of the 18th- and 19th-century Industrial Revolution. Let us look at three elements of medieval water-wheel technology: growth in numbers, growth in applications and concentrations of power.

The best source of data for the number of water mills in any part of medieval Europe is William the Conqueror's late-11th-century census of his newly acquired English domain. The areas of England under Norman rule in the late 11th century had 5,624 water mills at more than 3,000 locations. This amounted to one mill for approximately every 50 households. Moreover, in some areas the mills were close together: as many as 30 mills might be found along 16 kilometers of the same stream. Whether these mills had horizontal, undershot or overshot wheels and what work they did was not recorded. Most of them probably ground grain, a tedious task that if done by hand would have

consumed from two to three hours of each housewife's day.

Even figures as incomplete as these do not exist for other European countries of the same period. Presumably some of those areas were technologically ahead of England. Later evidence, however, indicates the substitution of water power for manual labor must have been growing at a rate at least comparable to that in England. For example, in 1694 the Marquis de Vauban, a French military engineer, estimated that France had 80,000 flour mills, 15,000 industrial mills and 500 iron mills and metallurgical works. This is a total of more than 95,000 mills, although some of them, particularly the flour mills, were powered not by water but by wind.

Even in industrially backward regions of Europe, such as Russia and Poland, water wheels were common before the introduction of steam power. A 1666 survey of the northern tributaries of the Dnieper River in Russia, from the Sula River to the Vorskla River, lists 50 dams and 300 water wheels. One of these tributaries alone, the Udai River, had 72 water mills. By late in the 18th century the part of Poland under Austrian occupation had more than 5,000 water mills.

The steady numerical growth of water wheels was accompanied by a steady geographic diffusion. By the 13th century water wheels were turning throughout Europe: from the Black Sea to the Baltic, from Britain to the Balkans, from Spain to Sweden.

Ancient engineers had applied the rotary motion of the water wheel in only two ways: in the flour mill and in what was called a noria, a wheel to raise water. In the noria the motion was harnessed directly; it was not transformed by any kind of gearing. In the flour mill, however, right-angle gearing at one end of the wheel's axle changed the speed of rotation and transformed the wheel's motion in the vertical plane into motion in the horizontal plane in order to turn a millstone. Beyond this ancient engineers evidently did not go, although one poem of the fourth century Roman poet Ausonius suggests the possibility of wheel-driven saws.

Beginning in the ninth century millwrights started to extend the developments of antiquity. For example, medieval European millwrights applied the vertical water wheel to several processes that, like water-raising with the noria, called for rotary motion in the same plane as the wheel itself. One was the grinding and polishing of metals in cutlery mills. These mills are first mentioned in documents dating from early in the 13th century. In such mills gears were installed not to alter the plane of rotation but to step up the rotational speed of the water-wheel axle and in some instances to shift the direction of the plane of rotation to grindstones mounted on shafts set at right angles to the water-wheel axle.

Other examples of new applications of water power that harnessed the rotary motion of vertical water wheels in the same plane were lathes (the earliest evidence of the use of water power for this purpose was in the 14th century), pipe borers (in the 15th century), rollers for producing metal sheets and rotary cutters for cutting the sheets (also in the 15th century), fans for mine ventilation, mine hoists and ball-and-chain mine pumps (all in the 16th century).

In a similar way medieval engineers extended the combination of the water wheel and vertical-to-horizontal plane gearing. As early as the ninth century in France traditional water-powered flour mills were modified to turn millstones not for grinding wheat into flour (the only Roman use of the combination of gearing and the water wheel) but for grinding malt for beer mash. Later vertical-to-horizontal plane gearing was applied in order to replace manual labor in such activities as grinding metal ores into powder.

By the 11th century vertical-to-horizontal gearing arrangements had been further developed to turn millstones set on edge, which crushed rather than ground. Water mills with such edge-rolling stones may have served to crush oil out of olives as early as the 11th century

and were definitely serving this purpose and others by the 12th century. Early in the latter century the mills were adopted by the tanning industry: they reduced oak bark to powder preparatory to the leaching process that extracted the tannin. Water-powered edge rollers may also have been used to crush sugarcane

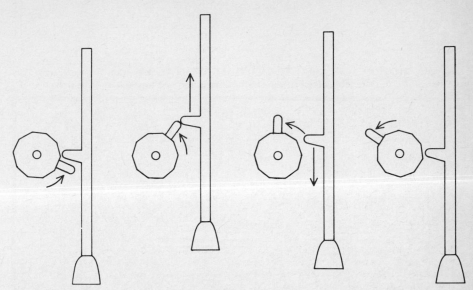

TRANSFORMATION OF ROTARY MOTION into linear motion can be achieved by having a cam on the axle of the wheel. The rotating cam engages a matching cam on a stamp shaft; as the shaft turns, the stamp is first raised and then dropped to deliver a powerful impact.

CAM PRINCIPLE WAS APPLIED in a rock-crushing mill illustrated in *De re metallica*. Cams on the axle engage and then release a tappet (*g*) attached to each of the iron-shod stamps.

5. THE MEDIEVAL PERIOD

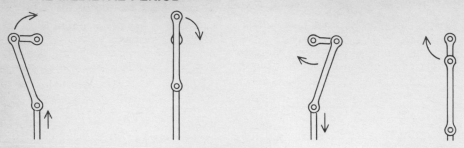

ROTARY MOTION WAS ALSO TRANSFORMED into linear motion by the crank. This one requires a flexible joint between the shaft being raised and lowered and the driven shaft.

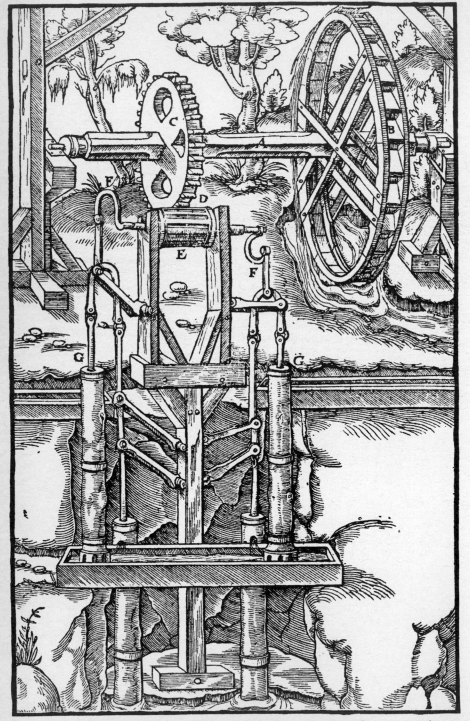

PAIR OF CRANKS driven by an overshot wheel rotating a two-gear train are converting rotary motion into linear motion in this illustration from *De re metallica*. The linear motion is being conveyed to pistons of two pairs of mine pumps. The lower pump of each pair lifts water from the mine shaft to a trough in the foreground for further raising by the upper pumps.

in Sicily as early as the 12th century. Later such mills served to crush mustard seed (the earliest evidence of the application of water power for this purpose is in the 13th century), poppy seed (also in the 13th century) and dyeing substances (in the 14th century).

Although the rotary motion of water wheels—speeded up, slowed down or translated into another plane of rotation—could be applied to many tasks, other tasks called not for rotary motion but for linear motion. For example, many industries employed pummeling or hammering actions. They included washing wool cloth, crushing ore for a smelter, forging iron and separating the fiber from flax plants. Medieval technicians between the 10th and the 15th centuries devised two solutions to the problem of transforming rotary motion into the linear motion needed to actuate hammers: the cam and the crank.

The cam was the earlier of the two devices and was long the more widely applied. It was a simple device, basically a small projection fixed on an axle. Not a medieval invention, it had appeared in small-scale mechanisms in antiquity but had never been applied to large-scale production devices. It came of age in medieval Europe, and in conjunction with water wheels it served mostly to actuate hammers. By 1500 European engineers had developed two forms of water-actuated hammer: the vertical stamp and the recumbent stamp. In the vertical stamp a cam on a horizontal shaft rotated against a similar projection on a vertical rod with a hammerhead at its lower end. As the cam rotated it lifted the rod until contact was lost; the rod then dropped, delivering the hammer blow. With the recumbent stamp the cam was rotated against the hammer end of a horizontal rod pivoted at the other end, first lifting the hammer and then, as the rotation continued, dropping it.

Water-actuated trip hammers could have been used instead of modified millstones in the beer mills of the ninth century, but the first industries to definitely take up hydraulic hammers were the fulling and hemp industries of the 10th and 11th centuries. After wool has been woven into cloth it must be pounded or pummeled in a cleansing solution. This action serves three purposes. First, it washes the cloth and removes much of the remaining sheep's grease from it. Second, it shrinks the wool so that it can be safely sewn to size afterward. Third, it felts the wool fibers, strengthening the weave.

In antiquity and on into early medieval times fulling had been done by hand. The water wheel and the cam—

actuated trip hammer mechanized the process beginning in the 11th century. By the 13th century mechanized fulling was done over much of western Europe. In England, for example, the earliest water-powered fulling mill recorded dates from 1185. By 1327 there were 130 such mills, and before the end of the century the English woolens industry had shifted almost entirely to sites where water power was available.

The hemp industry was also among the first industries to adopt the mechanized trip hammer. Traditionally hemp fibers, which are formed into rope and cord, had been separated from the woody plant tissue by being pounded and picked by hand. Water-powered hammers were substituted for this manual labor in Alpine France late in the 10th century and early in the 11th. By the 12th century there were water-pow-ered hemp mills throughout France.

As time passed many other tasks were taken over by water-powered hammers. Ever since paper had been invented in Asia the pulp for making it had been produced by manually pounding rags in water. Western Europeans learned how to make paper only at the beginning of the 12th century. By the late 13th century European papermakers had taken a step that Chinese and Arabic ones never

SIXTEENTH-CENTURY SMITHY had bellows driven by an undershot wheel to achieve high furnace temperature. Again a crank converted rotation of the shaft into reciprocating motion. The plate is in Agostino Ramelli's *Le diverse et artificiose machine*, dated 1588.

5. THE MEDIEVAL PERIOD

had: they substituted the water-powered trip hammer for the manual hammering. By the early 17th century England alone had 38 water-powered paper mills. By 1710 the number was 200 and by 1763 it was 350.

One of the most important European industries to be partially mechanized by the combination of the vertical water wheel and the cam was the iron industry. Early in the Middle Ages, European ironmasters smelted ore in a small furnace with air supplied to the burning mixture of charcoal and ore by a hand- or foot-powered bellows. The process did not yield temperatures high enough to liquefy iron. Thus almost daily the ironmaster had to shut his furnace down and take it apart to remove the sponge-like mass known as bloom, consisting of a porous mixture of metallic iron and slag. In order to get a usable form of iron the ironworkers had to heat and hammer the bloom repeatedly, with each cycle further consolidating the iron and eliminating the slag. The bloom, like the ore, was heated in a furnace with a draft that was supplied by a manually operated bellows.

The introduction of water power significantly affected both processes. Water-powered hammers in iron forges may have appeared as early as the 11th century; they were certainly in service by the 13th century, and they were commonplace in the 14th. Cam-actuated bellows, powered by water wheels, were operating in forges by early in the 13th century and were common in the 14th.

By late in the 14th century the combination of a vertical water wheel and a cam-actuated bellows had moved from the forge to the smelting furnace and iron production underwent an even more radical change. Larger and more powerful bellows, made possible by water power, enabled ironmasters to get higher temperatures in their smelters, so that the iron was liquefied. The bottom of the smelting furnace could be tapped, and the liquid metal would run out to solidify in "pigs." Shutting down and taking apart the furnace to get the bloom came to an end, and iron production was transformed from a batch process into at least a semicontinuous one, with significant reductions in labor requirements. This new application of water power spread rapidly. For example, in the Siegen area of Germany all 38 pig-iron works and steelmaking forges were relying on water power by 1492.

Still other industries were transformed by the combination of the water wheel and the cam. In water-powered sawmills the cam served to pull down a ripsaw; the saw was pulled back up by a spring pole. Mills of this kind are first mentioned in documents of the early 13th century. Apparently the practice spread rapidly. In 1304 deforestation in the area of Vizille in southeastern France was being blamed in part on the proliferation of water-powered sawmills. Two centuries later the water wheel and the cam were being employed to lift hammers for the crushing of ore and to operate piston pumps for mine drainage.

The alternative to the cam for converting rotary motion into linear motion was the crank (or crankshaft). Known in China by the second century A.D., the crank appeared in Europe somewhat later. Cranks may have been used to rotate millstones by hand late in Classical times; they appear in mature form in Europe only in the ninth century, when the Utrecht Psalter depicts a crank attached to a hand-powered grindstone. Late in the medieval period the crank was combined with the water wheel and began to replace the cam for certain tasks. The double action provided by the crank was more advantageous than the single action of the cam in water-powered pumps, sawmills and bellows. The crank was also combined with manually operated grippers and drawplates in wire-drawing mills, which emerged in the 14th or 15th century.

By the 16th century at least 40 different industrial processes in Europe had come to depend on water power. The trend continued in the ensuing centuries. As one example, water power was first applied to spinning silk some-

PAPER MILL relied on an undershot wheel with cams (c) to lift and drop hammers (d, e) that reduced rags to pulp. Thereafter the process was manual: the pulp was transferred to a vat (g), dipped out with a seive and formed into a sheet in a press (f). The sheets were hung on racks to dry. The plate is from Georg Andreas Böckler's *Theatrum machinarum novum* of 1662.

time between 1300 and 1600. In the silk mills water-powered spindles twisted individual silk fibers into thread. By 1700 there were 100 silk mills in northeastern Italy alone. The large silk mill erected early in the 1700's by Thomas Lombe at Derby in England, powered by the River Derwent, was a multistoried structure with a work force of 300.

Between 1550 and 1750 water power was applied to other processes as well. It was harnessed to bore the barrels of cannons and muskets, to thresh grain (with rotary flails), to agitate mixtures of ore and water and to pulverize the raw materials of glassmaking. Edge rollers were applied to such new activities as the preparation of snuff, cement, potter's clay and gunpowder. By 1692 there were 22 gunpowder mills in France, some on a scale matching the British textile mills of the late 18th and early 19th centuries. By the middle of the 18th century water-actuated hammers had been applied to the crushing of bone for fertilizer and of chalk for whitewash, and complex water-driven transmission systems, including cranks, had mechanized glass polishing.

Just as the water-powered trip hammer had mechanized the hemp industry by the 12th century, so it had penetrated the linen industry before the middle of the 18th century. The making of linen had been completely dependent on manual labor. After the flax plants for the linen had been harvested the stems were put in water to rot. The stems were then beaten to separate their fibers. When the fibers had been spun into thread and the thread had been woven into cloth, the cloth was washed and then beaten with light wood hammers to toughen the weave and give the cloth a sheen.

Late in the 17th century and early in the 18th European technicians mechanized several of these steps. Water-powered scutching mills relied on wood blades, rather like fan blades, to separate the fibers from the rotted flax stems. Linen-washing mills harnessed the combination of a water wheel and a cam or a crank to drive scrubbing boards of corrugated wood, through which the wet linen was drawn. Beetling mills then used water-actuated wood hammers to toughen and give a sheen to the linen cloth as it was drawn over large wood rollers. In Ulster alone more than 200 water-powered linen plants were established between 1700 and 1760.

The traditional beginnings of the Industrial Revolution in the late 18th century are dated to the early English cotton-textile mills. It is true that no cotton-textile production had been mechanized with water power before the 1770's. Nevertheless, water power not only had

EDGE-ROLLER MILL differed from the mills that ground flour in that the top stone rolled over the bottom one instead of rubbing against it. Introduced in the 11th or 12th century, such mills were applied to crushing olives for the extraction of oil or pressing sugarcane for the extraction of sugar. Plate is from Vittorio Zonca's *Novo teatro di machine,* published in 1607.

LARGE UNDERSHOT WHEEL powers two gears that transform vertical rotation into horizontal rotation in this illustration of a 16th-century flour mill from Ramelli. The millstones are installed in the top story of the building; the flour falls into a bin below, beside the gears.

5. THE MEDIEVAL PERIOD

mechanized many nontextile industries but also had affected several processes in the production of textiles other than those of cotton. As we have seen, the fulling of wool, the spinning of silk and several stages of linen production had been taken over by water-powered machinery well before 1770.

By the same token, the cotton-textile mills of the late 18th century were not unique in replacing manual labor with powered machinery. Neither were they unique in the amount of power they concentrated in a single location. Most of the early mechanized cotton mills had available perhaps 10 to 20 horsepower. The replacement in these mills of water power by steam power, beginning in the 1790's, made little difference at first because until well into the 19th century the average power of the steam engines was less than 20 horsepower. Even as late as 1835 the average mechanized cotton mill had available no more than about 35 horsepower. Concentrations of that much energy were not at all unknown in water-powered mills between the ninth century and the middle of the 18th.

Precise data on the power output of water wheels do not exist before 1700. In the period between 1700 and 1800, however, before the traditional wood wheel was replaced by iron wheels, water turbines and the steam engine, widely scattered sources provide enough information to allow an approximate calculation of the power output of some of the traditional wheels. I have collected data on 40 wheels, of both the undershot and the overshot type, from scattered millwright manuals, engineering texts, encyclopedias and other sources. They indicate that the average power output at the shaft was between five and seven horsepower. Thus the concentration of three or four wheels of average size at a single site would represent a power concentration roughly equal to that of the mechanized English cotton mills.

Concentrations of this kind, although not commonplace, certainly existed. Monasteries provide some examples. For instance, as early as the ninth century the abbey of Corbie, near Amiens, had water mills with as many as six wheels. The monastery of Royaumont, near Paris, had a tunnel two and a half meters in diameter and 32 meters long in which there were mounted separate water wheels for grinding grain, tanning, fulling and working iron. In 1136 the abbey of Clairvaux, near Troyes, had wheels that ground grain, fulled cloth and tanned leather.

Similar concentrations of power existed elsewhere. In the 14th century the millers of Paris operated 13 water mills under the Grand Pont. Even earlier, late in the 12th century, the millers of Toulouse built three dams across the Garonne River; the largest of them, the Bazacle dam, was 400 meters long. These dams served 43 horizontal water mills. By the 13th century a division of capital and labor characteristic of the early British cotton mills had emerged at Toulouse: the mills were owned by investors and the millers were employees.

Elaborate water-power installations are also to be found in early modern Europe. For example, in the 1680's a Flemish engineer, Rennequin Sualem, designed and built for Louis XIV an elaborate water-powered complex at Marly-le-Roi on the Seine. There a dam diverted water to a set of 14 undershot wheels, each wheel 11 meters in diameter and 2.3 meters wide. The wheels drove 221 pumps at three levels by means of a complex linked set of cranks, rocking beams and connecting rods and lifted the river water 153 meters to an aqueduct a kilometer away. The transmission system was so cumbersome and inefficient, however, that the 14 wheels yielded only 150 horsepower.

Roughly contemporary with the Marly works was the Grand Rive mill, a paper plant in the Auvergne region with seven water wheels and 38 sets of hammers. In the 1720's Russian engineers built a large dam at Ekaterinburg in the Urals; an industrial complex powered

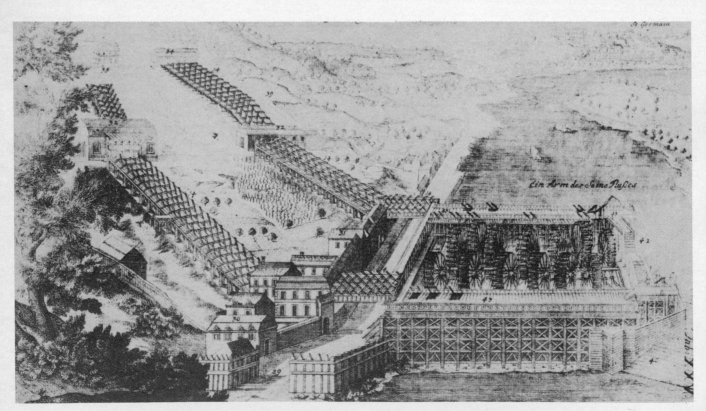

ARRAY OF 14 WHEELS on the Seine at Marly-le-Roi, 14 kilometers west of Paris, was erected in the 1680's. Developing from 300 to 500 horsepower at the shaft but only from 80 to 150 horsepower after losses in the pumps and the mechanical transmission are taken into account, the wheels pumped water to an aqueduct 153 meters above the river. It was carried to several of Louis XIV's palaces.

by water from the dam consisted of 50 water wheels that drove 22 hammers, 107 bellows and 10 wire-drawing mills. By 1760 the British Royal Gunpowder Factory at Faversham in Kent included 11 water wheels. At about the same time engineers in Cornwall built what was known as the tower engine; it had 10 overshot wheels, mounted one above the other, linked by connecting rods to two large mine pumps.

Some pre-1800 power concentrations were regional rather than confined to a single site. For example, in the Harz Mountain region of Germany mining engineers began constructing a complex network of dams, reservoirs and canals to turn wheels that powered mine pumps, wire-drawing engines, ore-wash-ing plants, ore-crushing mills and the bellows of furnaces and forges in about 1550. By 1800 this system included 60 dams and reservoirs, all within a four-kilometer radius of Clausthal, the center of the mining district. The largest dam in the system, the masonry Oder-teich dam, built between 1714 and 1721, was 145 meters long, 18 meters high and 47 meters thick at the base. The dams eventually fed water to 225 wheels through a network of 190 kilometers of canals. The aggregate power of the system almost certainly exceeded 1,000 horsepower.

Water power also spread to the New World. Near Potosí in the Bolivian Andes, Spanish engineers exploiting rich silver deposits began in 1573 to build a system of dams, reservoirs and canals to bring water to ore-crushing mills. By 1621 the system included 32 dams. A main canal five kilometers long carried water to 132 ore-crushing mills near the city. The system generated more than 600 horsepower.

Hence it is clear that the mechanized cotton mills of England in the late 18th and early 19th centuries represented no radical break with the past, either in the replacement of manual labor with machines or in the concentration of large amounts of power. The substitution of water-powered machinery for manpower and the concentration of water-powered industry were trends well under way before that time. The British textile mills were simply the culmination of an evolutionary process that had its origins in medieval Europe and even in the Classical Mediterranean.

Renaissance and Reformation

The departure from medieval patterns of life was first evident in Renaissance Italy. There the growth of capital and the development of distinctly urban economic and social organizations promoted a new culture dominated by townsmen whose tastes, abilities, and interests differed markedly from those of the medieval clergy and feudal nobility. Richard MacKenny's article on the guilds of Renaissance Venice demonstrates that the emergent economy was marked by continuity as well as change, while "How Jacques Coeur Made His Fortune" and "Bruges" explore early capitalism in France and northern Europe.

The emergent culture was limited to a small number of people, generally those who were well-to-do. But even in an increasingly materialistic culture it wasn't enough just to be wealthy. It was necessary to excel in the arts, literature, and learning, and to demonstrate skill in some profession. The ideal Renaissance man, as Robert Lopez observes, "came from a good, old family, improved upon his status through his own efforts, and justified status by his own intellectual accomplishments."

This new ideal owed something to the classical tradition. Renaissance man, wishing to break out of the otherworldly spirituality of the Middle Ages, turned back to the secular naturalism of the ancient world. Indeed, the Renaissance was, among other things, a heroic age of scholarship that restored classical learning to a place of honor. It was classical humanism in particular that caught the fancy of Renaissance man. In the new spirit of individualism, however, humanism was transformed. The classical version, "man is the measure of all things," became, in Alberti's modern version, "A man can do all things, if he will." And there was another Renaissance modification of the classical heritage—civic humanism. It involved a new philosophy of political engagement, a reinterpretation of Roman history from the vantage point of contemporary politics, and a recognition that moderns should not simply imitate the ancients but rival them. Of course, Renaissance humanism had its darker side, as Gene Mitchell's article about Pietro Arezzino attests.

Renaissance art and architecture reflected the new society and its attitudes. Successful businessmen were now as likely as saints to be the subjects of portraiture. Equestrian statues of warriors and statesmen glorified current heroes while evoking memories of the great days of Rome. Renaissance painters rediscovered nature (which generally had been ignored by medieval artists), often depicting it as an earthly paradise—the appropriate setting for man in his new image. In contrast to the great medieval cathedrals, which glorified God, Renaissance structures enhanced humanity.

Some of these developments in art and architecture indicate changes in the role of Christianity and the influence of the Church, which no longer determined the goals of Western man as they had during the medieval period. Increasingly civil authorities and their symbols competed with churchmen and their icons, while Machiavelli, according to Vincent Cronin, and other writers provided a secular rationale for a new political order. But most Europeans, including many humanists, retained a deep and abiding religious faith.

The Reformation, with its theological disputes and wars of religion, is a powerful reminder that secular concerns had not entirely replaced religious ones, especially in northern Europe. The great issues that divided Protestant and Catholic—the balance between individual piety and the authority of the Church, the true means of salvation—were essentially medieval in character. Indeed, in their perception of humankind, their preoccupation with salvation (and damnation), and their attacks upon the Church's conduct of its affairs, Luther, Calvin, Zwingli, and other Protestant leaders often echoed the views of medieval reformers as apparent in "Luther: Giant of His Time and Ours."

Taken together, then, the Renaissance and Reformation constituted a new compound of traditional elements (classical and medieval, secular and religious) along with elements of modernity. The era was a time of transition, or as Lynn D. White describes it, "This was a time of torrential flux, of fearful doubt, marking the transition from the relative certainties of the Middle Ages to the new certainties of the eighteenth and nineteenth centuries." An expression of such "fearful doubts" is chronicled in Midelfort's article, "Heartland of the Witchcraze."

Looking Ahead: Challenge Questions

Based on the career of Jacques Coeur, describe the basic elements of early capitalism.

Did secular humanism release humanity's darker side along with its creative impulses?

How did the guilds of Renaissance Venice retain their power in an age when guilds were weakening elsewhere?

What was the impact of overseas exploration upon Europe and the rest of the world?

How did politics change at the beginning of the modern era? What part did the ideas of Machiavelli play in the shift from medieval to modern politics?

How Jacques Coeur Made His Fortune

He made it none too scrupulously,
and lost it at the whim of a much wilier scoundrel than himself

Marshall B. Davidson

One should visit Bourges to see the curious house that Jacques Coeur built, wrote Jules Michelet a century or so ago in his gigantic history of France. It was, he added, "a house full of mysteries, as was Coeur's life." Then, in one of the picturesque asides that make his history such a treasury of unexpected discoveries, he went on to describe that house and the man who built it—the self-made man who played banker to King Charles VII of France, and who bailed out that monarch when his kingdom was at stake; the intrepid man of the world who traded privileges with Moslem sultans, Christian popes, and European princes; the implausibly rich parvenu who, within less than twenty years, parlayed a few counterfeit coins into the largest private fortune in France.

By 1443, when construction of his house started, Coeur was quite possibly the wealthiest man in the world. His new dwelling was to be a monument to his worldly success, and according to one contemporary it was "so richly ornamented, so spacious, and yet, withal, so magnificent, that neither princes of the blood, nor the king himself, had any residence comparable to it." That last point was not lost on Charles VII, as, in the end, Coeur had bitter cause to know.

The house still stands in the cathedral town of Bourges, a short drive south of Paris. It is a unique survival, a memorial as much to a time in history as to the man who built it, for Coeur's life spanned a critical period in the destiny of France. In the last decade of his life the agonizing internecine strife and the bloody slaughter that accompanied the Hundred Years' War were, with his substantial aid, finally brought to an end. The English were thrown back across the Channel, and the land was united as it had not been in living memory.

In the course of those protracted disorders the scrambled authority of feudalism gave way to the more orderly rule of national monarchy, the spirit of chivalry faded before the practical aims of an aspiring bourgeoisie, and the stultifying controls of medieval economy were turning into the growing pains of modern capitalism. To most contemporary eyes such vital changes appeared as a blurred image, like a dissolve in a movie. But Coeur's role in those transitions was so decisive, and he was so perfectly cast for the part he played, that he might well have written the script himself.

It could be said that in Coeur's time double-entry bookkeeping was proving

mightier than the sword, for without that instrument of precision and convenience (apparently a fourteenth-century invention), he could hardly have managed his complex affairs. To him, and other businessmen, time—and timekeeping—took on new importance. For time was money made or lost. The easy rhythm of the canonical hours was being replaced by the stern measure of mechanical clocks that counted out the cost of fleeting opportunities, pointed the way to quicker profits, and ticked off interest on loans. And Coeur pressed every advantage. He even used carrier pigeons to bring him advance notice of approaching cargoes so that he could improve his position in the local markets.

From the very beginning Coeur's enterprise was, for better and for worse, closely associated with the interests of his sovereign. Ironically, he first came to public notice in 1429, when, as an associate of the master of the Bourges mint, he was accused of striking coins of inferior alloy. Like so many other functions now considered the exclusive prerogative of government, minting money was then a private concession, albeit by privilege from the king, who took a substantial share of the milling toll as

 "How Jacques Coeur Made His Fortune," by Marshall Davidson, *Horizon,* Winter 1976. Reprinted by permission of the author.

seigniorage, at rates fixed by law. Since no practical system of taxation was yet in force, this was one of the few ways the king could raise money. To meet the demands of the moment, debasing the coinage was approved practice, and the royal "take" could be enhanced by secretly altering the rate of seigniorage —that is, by still further debasing the coinage without advising the public. If the counterfeit was detected, the royal accomplice could disavow the scheme and leave his concessionaires to face the music. And this is what happened to Coeur and his associates in 1429.

Desperate necessities drove Charles VII to practice such duplicity. When he inherited the throne in 1422, the Hundred Years' War was in its eighth grim decade and the fortunes of France were at their lowest ebb. This ill-omened, youthful heir, the tenth child of a madman who disinherited him and of a mother of loose morals who disowned him (it was widely reported that he was a bastard, no matter of shame at the time, but a shadow on his claim to the throne), was holed up in Bourges. An English king reigned in Paris, and English forces occupied all the land from the Channel to the Loire. Philip the Good, the powerful and autonomous duke of Burgundy, tolerated the foreign invader and was allied with him. And Brittany, ever mindful of its own independent traditions, wavered between allegiances.

The years that followed Charles's succession revolved in a murderous cycle of war and brigandage, pestilence and famine. The king could not afford a standing army, and his military leaders were independent contractors who, between battles with the enemy, roamed the land with their mercenaries, raping, stealing, burning, and killing. Under the circumstances, trade and commerce came to a standstill. Merchants took to the road only if they were armed to the teeth. The great international fairs of Champagne, once vital points of exchange for Europe's traffic, were abandoned as the north-south trade shifted to the sea routes between Flanders and the Mediterranean. France came close to ruin.

The winter of 1428–1429 brought a

turning point, or at least a promise of deliverance. The English had laid seige to Orléans, the principal city remaining in Charles's rump of a kingdom. Had Orléans fallen there would have been pitifully little left of that kingdom. The city became a symbol of resistance, while the timid young monarch vacillated in his provincial retreat barely sixty miles away. His mocking enemies dubbed him the "king of Bourges" and anticipated the fall of his petty realm. His treasury was empty; it is said he even borrowed money from his laundress. Only by a miracle could he keep his tottering crown.

The miracle materialized when, as if in direct response to the widely whispered prophecy that an armed virgin would appear and drive the English from the land, Joan of Arc was brought before the king at the château of Chinon where he was then holding court. After grilling the maid for three weeks, the king's counselors decided that she was, as she claimed, divinely appointed by "voices" she had heard to save her king and her country. Somehow, Charles found money to provide her with troops, and the siege of Orléans was lifted. Joan then persuaded her wavering monarch to be crowned at Reims, where Clovis had been baptized. By that ritual the stain of bastardy was automatically removed, and Charles was indisputably the true king of France. It took him eight more years to win Paris from the English, but when he did ride triumphantly into that city, after its sixteen years of foreign occupation, he came as the rightful Christian king.

It was hardly a coincidence that Coeur and his associates were charged with counterfeiting almost immediately after the "miracle" at Orléans, or that Coeur was pardoned of the crime. Charles had most likely met the payroll for Joan's troops with funds provided by the mint's illegal operations, and as party to the crime he saw that Coeur got off easily. At least there is no better explanation.

In any case, soon after his pardon Coeur set out to make his fortune. He formed a new partnership with his old

associates at the mint, this time to deal in "every class of merchandise, including that required by the King, Monseigneur the Dauphin, and other nobles, as well as other lines in which they [the partners] can make their profit."

For precedents in this new venture he looked abroad. The basis of Renaissance prosperity, already so conspicuous in Italy, was the carrying trade between East and West. For centuries Venice had fattened on this commerce, to the point where its successful and friendly business relations with Mongols and Moslems alike had encouraged those infidels to close in on the Christian world. Then, as European knighthood took the Cross to the Holy Land, Venetians supplied and equipped their fellow Christians and ferried them to the battle sites at exorbitant rates.

Venice also continued its flourishing trade in arms, armor, and diverse other goods with the Saracens of Egypt and Palestine. When Pope Benedict XII forbade unauthorized trade with the infidel, the merchants of Venice bought up papal authorizations wherever they could and used them as ordinary bills of exchange. With the Fourth Crusade, the "businessman's crusade," the merchants of Venice made a double killing. They dissuaded the debt-burdened knights from their proclaimed purpose of attacking Alexandria, one of Venice's richest markets, and persuaded them to sack the flourishing Christian capital of Constantinople.

Meanwhile, across the Apennines in Tuscany, enterprising merchants were swarming out of Florence into western Europe, collecting contributions to the Crusades as bankers to the Holy See, advancing money to land-poor feudal lords at fantastic interest rates, and with their ready cash buying up the privileges of the towns. During the Hundred Years' War the powerful Bardi and Peruzzi families equipped both French and English armies for the battlefields, prolonging the conflict and taking over the functions of state when it was necessary to secure their accounts. In return for helping Henry III of England with his running expenses, the Florentines asked for 120 per cent interest on advances and, when repayment was not prompt, added 60 per cent more. In such a company of greedy Christians, Shylock would have seemed hopelessly ingenuous.

During the most agonizing period of the Hundred Years' War, however, the Florentines had gradually abandoned their commercial colonies in France. Now that his time had come, Coeur moved to fill that vacuum with his own business and, with equal speed, to stake a claim among the markets of the East, so profitably exploited by Venice. His first try at emulating the Venetian merchants was a disaster. In 1432 he journeyed to Damascus, an awkward if not perilous place for Christians to be at the time, buying up spices and other exotic commodities for resale in the home markets of France. When his ship foundered off Corsica he lost literally everything but his shirt. He and his shipmates were stripped clean by the islanders.

He seems to have recovered promptly. He had centered his operations at Montpellier on the Mediterranean coast, the only French port authorized by the pope to deal with the infidel East. He threw himself with bounding determination into the development of the city's facilities, pressing the local authorities to improve its docks, dredge essential canals, construct adequate warehouses, and generally improve the advantages for commerce and navigation—even spending his own money when he had to. As he later wrote the king, he had plans for developing a vast maritime empire under the lily banner of France.

Almost from the moment Charles returned to Paris, Coeur's affairs started to move in a steady counterpoint to the affairs of state. Within a year or two he was installed as *argentier*, receiver of the revenues used to maintain the royal establishment. Since in his capacity as merchant he was also the principal purveyor to that establishment, his position was doubly advantageous—and ambiguous. And since for the most part the court could be accommodated only by long-term credit, both the advantage and the ambiguity were compounded. It

must have been quite easy for Coeur to convince himself that what was good for Jacques Coeur was good for France.

A reciprocal rhythm of commissions and benefits, responsibilities and opportunities, honors and profits, increased in tempo for more than a decade. The king may already have been in debt to Coeur even before the royal entry into Paris, and this relationship became more or less chronic thereafter. The Paris campaign had again exhausted the royal treasury. In an effort to tighten the leaking economy of the state, Charles, possibly advised by his *argentier*, forbade the export of money from his realm except by a special license, which he then granted, apparently exclusively, to Coeur.

In 1440 Charles further recognized Coeur's services by according him patents of nobility. The following year he appointed him *conseilleur du roi*, in effect minister of finance and, as such, adviser in the revision of the nation's tax structure. Charged with assessing and collecting regional taxes, Coeur sometimes received not only his due commissions but gratuities from local representatives who both respected his influence at court and feared his power as a merchant banker. The "states" of Languedoc, for example, of which Montpellier was the principal port, paid him handsomely for his good offices in the interest of their maritime prosperity—canceling his share of their taxes as a matter of course.

The king, meanwhile, with an unprecedented income from the revenues he received, reorganized his military forces into a paid standing army. He was no longer a mere feudal lord but a monarch able to make policy and enforce it, if need be, with cannon—cannon, cast at the foundries of bourgeois manufacturers, that could reduce the proudest knight's castle to rubble. In 1444 Charles arranged a temporary peace with the English, who still held Normandy and Guyenne. It was at the gay spring *pourparlers* on the banks of the Loire by which the peace was negotiated that Charles first spied the indescribably beautiful Agnes Sorel, "the fairest of the fair," whom he shortly afterward made his mistress. As the king's bedmate,

Agnes began to use her influence in matters of state, inaugurating a tradition in French history. As it later turned out, this was a fateful development in the life of Jacques Coeur. The immediate consequence of the truce arrangements, however, was that he could now move into the English-held markets in Rouen and Bordeaux as well as across the Channel.

Coeur's influence was already recognized far beyond the shores of France. In 1446 he served as negotiator between the Knights of Rhodes and the sultan of Egypt. Two years later, through the intercession of Coeur's agents, the sultan was persuaded to restore trading privileges to the Venetians, who had for a time been banned from the Arab world. At the same time, Coeur consolidated his own position in the Mediterranean and put a cap on his immense commercial structure. Pope Eugenius IV issued a bull authorizing Coeur to trade for five years in his own right, beyond the privileges enjoyed by the port of Montpellier, with the non-Christian world. With this special authority in his pocket, Coeur shifted the base of his maritime enterprise to Marseilles.

One important matter still needed mending. For all Coeur's good offices and his wide reputation, official relations between France and the Arab world were less cordial than suited his interests. In 1447 he persuaded Charles to agree to a formal pact with Abu-Said-Djacmac-el Daher, sultan of Egypt. The French ambassadors, traveling in Coeur's ships and at his expense, arrived in Egypt "in great state" bearing lavish gifts provided by Coeur in the name of the king. The sultan, in turn, arranged an extravagant reception. Coeur's diplomacy triumphed. Peace between the two lands was agreed upon, and French traders received "most favored nation" privileges in Arab ports.

Aided by the gratitude of the Venetians and the Knights of Rhodes, the friendship of the sultan, the favor of the pope, and the indulgence of his king, Coeur secured unassailable advantages at every important point in the world of his day. "All the Levant he visited with his ships," wrote the duke of

Coeur's mansion is adorned both inside and out with whimsical vignettes of daily life.

The trompe l'oeil *couple may represent servants watching for their master's return.*

Burgundy's chronicler some years later, "and there was not in the waters of the Orient a mast which was not decorated with the *fleur-de-lis*." The maritime empire he created remained for several centuries one of the principal bulwarks of French commerce. To carry on his far-flung, highly diversified operations— they had developed into a virtual monopoly of France's exclusive markets— Coeur employed some three hundred agents and maintained branch offices in Barcelona, Damascus, Beirut, Alexandria, and other strategic centers.

The inventories of his warehouses read like an exaggerated description of Ali Baba's caves. "All the perfumes of Arabia" were carried in stock, and spices and confections from the farthest shores; dyes and colors, cochineal and cinnabar, indigo and saffron—and henna to illuminate the king's manuscripts; materials of fabulous richness and variety, and gems supposedly from the navels of sacred Persian and Indian monkeys, which were mounted in precious metals and considered a universal antidote to human ills. He could provide for the court's most extraordinary or exquisite whim: a coat of mail covered with azure velvet for a Scottish archer of the king's bodyguard; a silver shoulder piece and Turkish buckler for Charles of Orleans; silks and sables for Margaret of Scotland; diamonds to set off the incomparable beauty of Agnes Sorel—

they were all to be had, including cold cash for the queen of France herself, who offered up her "great pearl" for security.

In order to put his surplus money to work and to spread his risk, Coeur joined associations that profited from the licensing of fairs (reborn since the temporary truce with England), from speculation in salt, and from the exploitation of copper and silver mines of the Lyonnais and Beaujolais. He had interests in paper and silk factories in Florence. He even invested in three-quarters of two English prisoners of war, each worth a handsome ransom.

The list of his varied enterprises is almost endless. Cash was still in short supply among the nobility, the long war had brought ruin to many lordly tenants, and Charles's fiscal reforms were reducing their income from traditional feudal dues. So Coeur accommodated some of the greatest families of the realm by buying up their manor houses and properties until he held more than thirty estates, some including whole villages and parishes within their grounds. All told, the complex structure of his myriad affairs, his control of the production, transport, and distribution of goods, his private banking resources, and his secure grasp on essential markets all suggest something like the first vertical trust in history.

So far, nothing belied the motto Coeur was then having chiseled into the

stones of his great town house at Bourges—*A vaillans cueurs riens inpossible*, nothing is impossible to the valiant. Coeur's star rose even higher in 1448 when he was sent to Rome by Charles with a select group of ambassadors to help end the "pestilential and horrible" papal schism that for long years had been a great trial to the Church. The French ambassadors entered Rome in a procession of splendor —their cortege included three hundred richly caparisoned and harnessed Arabian horses—and Pope Nicholas V wrote Charles that not even the oldest inhabitants could remember anything so magnificent.

Coeur promptly took center stage. Through his efforts, the rival pope, Amadeo VIII, duke of Savoy, was finally persuaded to renounce his claim to the papal throne and accept a position in the church hierarchy second only to that of Pope Nicholas V. As a reward, Coeur's privilege of dealing with the non-Christian world was extended indefinitely. He was also given a franchise to carry Christian pilgrims to the Holy Land.

There were some who complained of the outrageous cost of that papal mission from which Coeur gained such honor and profit. Coeur had no doubt paid the bills, but whether from his own purse or from the king's treasury would have been difficult to determine. Coeur's wealth was by now beyond imagining. It was reported that his horses were shod with silver. His table service was of gold and silver. Each year, it was said, his income was greater than that of all the other merchants of France combined. "The king does what he can; Jacques Coeur does what he pleases" was a repeated observation. He might even be in league with the devil, they began to say.

Jacques Coeur had indeed reached a singular, and perilous, eminence.

How rich Coeur really was and what resources he could command came out in the years immediately following. The time had come, Charles decided, to break the truce with the English and to push them out of France altogether. To launch and maintain the campaign, however, Charles needed more money than he could find in the royal coffers, and he turned to Coeur for help. Coeur responded by dredging every sou he could manage from the resources available to him and by stretching his almost inexhaustible credit to the limit. By one means or another, he turned over to the king, at the very minimum, two hundred thousand ecus, a sum equal to more than one-fifth of the kingdom's annual tax revenues.

He also took to the field at the king's side. In the victorious procession that entered Rouen on November 10, 1449, Coeur rode in the company of Charles; mounted on a white charger, he was clothed in velvet and ermine and wore a sword embellished with gold and precious stones.

Coeur was now about fifty-five years old. For some twenty years he had enjoyed increasing wealth and prestige. Then, suddenly, the wheel of fortune changed direction. Three months after the ceremonies at Rouen, Agnes Sorel died in childbirth, after having been delivered of the king's fourth child. Rumors spread that she had been poisoned. Almost automatically, a cabal of debtors formed to point a finger at the king's *argentier*, the "money

man" of almost magical faculties, who was known to be one of the executors of Agnes's will. To convict Coeur of murder would serve to disembarrass the king and every important member of the court from the claims of their common creditor.

Charles was quick to play his part. One week in July, 1451, he expressed his gratitude to Coeur for his many services; the next week he issued an order for his arrest. Supported by his most recent favorites, the king confronted Coeur with a long list of indictments, starting with the poisoning charge and going back over the years to the counterfeiting charge of 1429, set aside so long ago by the pleasure and the convenience of Charles VII.

No sooner were the dungeon doors closed behind Coeur than "the vultures of the court" started picking away at the estate he could no longer protect. The nobility of France swarmed about the tottering house of Jacques Coeur to redeem their own fortunes from his disgrace. The trial that followed was a mockery. With his enemies as both prosecutors and judges he never had a chance. Even though his accusers confessed that the charge of poisoning Agnes Sorel was false, and the pope pleaded for clemency and justice in the case, Coeur was shunted for several years from prison to prison.

Finally, in May, 1453, at Poitiers, when he was threatened with torture, he issued a statement that led his judges to condemn him, banish him, and confiscate his properties. By a remarkable coincidence, on the day of Coeur's sentence the sorely tried city of Constantinople fell, this time once and for all, to the Turks. It was the end of an era. Less than a week later, the convicted man made an *amende honorable*: kneeling, bareheaded, before a large crowd and holding a ten-pound wax torch in his hands, he begged mercy of God, king, and the courts.

One more adventure remained. For almost a year and a half after his trial, Coeur was kept imprisoned in France, in spite of his banishment, while most of his holdings were seized and sold off. Then, in the autumn of 1454, he managed to escape. Aided by several of his faithful agents, he crossed the Rhone out of France and fled to Rome, where the pope received him with honor. He never returned to France, nor to the house that was his pride.

But he did take to the sea one last time. He arrived in Rome at a crucial moment in the history of the Church and of Western civilization. All Christendom had been shaken by the fall of Constantinople less than two years earlier and felt threatened by further advances of the Ottoman hordes. In the summer of 1456, Coeur, sixty years old and "toiled with works of war," set forth in command of a fleet dispatched by Pope Calixtus III to help retake Constantinople. On the twenty-fifth of November, on the island of Chios, his *vaillant coeur* was stopped, possibly by wounds he suffered in battle.

As he lay dying, Coeur sent one last appeal to Charles, begging the king to show consideration for his children. At this point Charles could afford to be indulgent. In an act of royal compassion he conceded that since "the said Coeur was in great authority with us and rich and abounding in this world's goods and ennobled in his posterity and line ... it pleases us to have pity on [his children]," and ordained that what might be salvaged from their father's estate, including the house at Bourges, be returned to them.

It was, after all, little enough for him to do, and in the end Coeur had an ironic revenge. The thought of poisoning continued to haunt the king. Four years later, fearing he might be poisoned by his own son, he refused to eat, and died of starvation.

Bruges

A MEDIEVAL CENTRE OF COMMERCE

FAIR CITY OF FLANDERS

Paul Morren

PAUL MORREN, of Belgium, is State Inspector at the Ministry of Education and Dutch Culture in Belgium. He has been editor, since its inception in 1972, of the Dutch edition of the Unesco Courier. The author of many books, articles and radio and television scripts on human rights, he was awarded the 1979 Unesco Prize for the Teaching of Human Rights.

TOWARDS the end of the fifteenth century Duke Philip the Fair brought his young bride Joanna of Castile to his native city of Bruges. On her return from a walk in the city the future mother of the Emperor Charles V, surprised by the rich apparel of the patrician ladies, is said to have remarked: "I thought I was the only queen in this country, but I have seen many others!" The story may be apocryphal, but it says much for the opulence and splendour of what has been called "the Venice of the North". One might just as well speak of Venice as "the Bruges of the South" without in any way offending the prestige of the city of the Doges. Numerous canals crossed by picturesque bridges, imposing public buildings, rich patrician houses, winding old streets make up the charm of both cities—each of which, however, has its own special character and each of which was a nerve centre of trade in the Middle Ages.

The sea wind still blows in Bruges, although nowadays the city is about fifteen kilometres from the sandy beaches of the North Sea, to which it was connected in the Middle Ages by the estuary of the Zwin, which provided access to the city for vessels of every kind. Today the Zwin is a protected natural reserve where fauna and flora typical of the region continue to survive.

Although he never set foot in Flanders, in his *Purgatorio* Dante mentions the Flemish towns, which were amongst the most im-

Air view of Bruges, one of Europe's most flourishing commercial and artistic centres in medieval times. At centre is the Markt (the main square), with the governor's palace to the left. Above, the covered market, begun 1248 and altered in the 16th century, is surmounted by an 84-metre-high belfry, one of the finest in Belgium.

Reproduced from the *Unesco Courier*, June 1984, pp. 16-19.

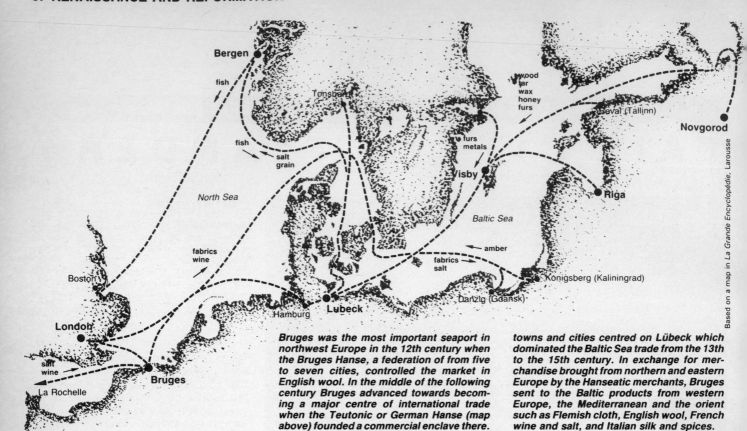

Bruges was the most important seaport in northwest Europe in the 12th century when the Bruges Hanse, a federation of from five to seven cities, controlled the market in English wool. In the middle of the following century Bruges advanced towards becoming a major centre of international trade when the Teutonic or German Hanse (map above) founded a commercial enclave there. The Teutonic Hanse was a confederation of towns and cities centred on Lübeck which dominated the Baltic Sea trade from the 13th to the 15th century. In exchange for merchandise brought from northern and eastern Europe by the Hanseatic merchants, Bruges sent to the Baltic products from western Europe, the Mediterranean and the orient such as Flemish cloth, English wool, French wine and salt, and Italian silk and spices.

Based on a map in *La Grande Encyclopédie,* Larousse

portant of his time. Bruges comes first on his list. These towns which developed very early in medieval Flanders were soon known all over the western world for the quality of their fabrics, manufacture of which was one of the chief industries in the Middle Ages.

Trade grew very rapidly. Initially it was conducted mainly during annual or bi-annual trade fairs, when merchants travelled from town to town according to a well-regulated calendar. Although a system of fixed trade centres came to be preferred to this arrangement, this did not mean that fairs ceased to exist, at least not immediately. It was at this time that the rise of Bruges began. Its growth was stimulated by a favourable geographical situation at the heart of busy, densely populated western Europe, where important countries and kingdoms met on the frontiers of two currents of civilization, the Germanic and Roman. The town was easily accessible by land and sea. When the silting-up of the Zwin estuary, by which Bruges was connected to the North Sea, later prevented vessels from entering the town itself they could still come within a short distance of it and moor in the outer harbour of Damme.

The people of Bruges were actively engaged in trade until the thirteenth century. They travelled to England and Scotland for their precious wool and they sailed along the Atlantic coasts, from which they brought back grain, wine and cheese. Bruges was a leading member of the Hanseatic League of Flemish towns.

A profound change took place in this economic pattern when the English merchant adventurers started to bring wool to the continent themselves. Bruges gave up active trade and concentrated on other activities. First it became an industrial town where the manufacture of cloth and clothing was stimulated and improved. Other textile-related industries also developed, as well as the manufacture of furniture, tapestries and other articles of interior decoration. Amber rosary beads were a highly esteemed speciality.

Above all, Bruges became a major international trading centre, the greatest market north of the Alps. Merchants came there to get supplies of the striped or single-coloured cloth from which the best clothes were made. This product was highly appreciated throughout Europe and even beyond. Thirteenth-century German poets sang the praises of Bruges breeches and in Russia the word *bryukish* was coined to describe Bruges cloth. Actually Bruges did not have a monopoly of this speciality but shared her skill in making it with a number of Flemish and Brabançon towns.

Those who frequented Bruges were sure of finding top quality goods at a reasonable price. But they were also sure of finding an outlet for the goods they brought with them, and of finding other interesting products brought there by their fellow-merchants from elsewhere. Henceforth, goods were no longer made for local consumption, but for international trade. It was this direct exchange of foreign products with all its attendant activities that brought great wealth to Bruges and enabled it to remain prosperous after the heavy cloth industry declined.

Towards the end of the thirteenth century the communal authorities issued a document which gives an idea of the products that could be procured in Bruges and of their countries of origin. It mentions no less than thirty-four different regions (in some cases, like the kingdom of Germany, the regions were grouped). All the regions of Europe were mentioned, from Sweden to Andalusia, from England to Russia. Also mentioned were Tunisia, Morocco, Constantinople, Jerusalem, Egypt, the Sudan, Armenia and Tartary. The document ended as follows: "From all these kingdoms and lands merchants and goods come to the land of Flanders, not counting those who come from the kingdom of France, from Poitou, Gascony... whose merchants come every year to Flanders, and from many other countries too. This is why no land can be compared with Flanders for merchandise".

The canals and monuments of Bruges form a magnificent urban landscape which today attracts large numbers of tourists. Bruges is linked by a canal to its seaport, Zeebrugge, 10 km away. Zeebrugge is Belgium's second most important port.

In the 15th century Bruges became the cradle of Flemish painting. Not all the artists who brought distinction to the city were natives of it. Hans Memling (c. 1433-1494) was a great master of the Flemish School. A painter of religious subjects and portraits, he worked in Bruges throughout his career. Above, Memling's The Virgin, St. John and Three Holy Women is the right hand panel of an altar diptych portraying the deposition from the Cross.

The béguinage, right, is one of the most famous sites in Bruges. A béguinage is an enclosed district which is the home of "Béguines", pious women who belong to a religious community although not under vow. The movement began in the 12th century and became particularly widespread in Belgium.

Five main routes ended in Bruges—from London; from Genoa and Venice by the Mediterranean and the Atlantic coast; from Hamburg, Lübeck and the Hanseatic towns; from Cologne along the Rhine; and from Genoa overland via the Rhône valley and Champagne.

Many foreigners settled in Bruges, where they organized themselves into groups and depended on what might be described as consulates. The most influential of these organizations was that of the Hanseatic cities (the great German Hanseatic League, not to be confused with the league of Flemish towns mentioned above). During a ducal visit in 1440 a procession of foreign residents included 136 members of the Hanseatic League, forty-eight Spaniards, forty Venetians, an equal number of Milanese, thirty-six Genoese, twenty-two

Florentines, twelve representatives of the town of Lucca and an unknown number of Portuguese and Catalans. For some reason the English, preponderant though they were in numbers, were absent that day.

In 1438, the Spanish chronicler Pedro Tafur set out on a journey "in search of adventure, and opportunities to prove my personal merit and that of my family and country". He had the excellent idea of keeping a diary of his journey in which he confides that he found Bruges to be superior to Venice, because it was a meeting-place for people from many countries, whereas on the shores of the Adriatic the natives attended to everything themselves. "I have been told that on certain days as many as 700 ships leave the port. The capital of Flanders is a very big town with pretty houses and fine streets. It

is densely populated and includes a great many craftsmen. The town is full of churches and convents as well as good inns. Everything, including the administration of justice, is organized in an exemplary manner. The inhabitants display boundless activity. Merchandise from all parts of the world is offered for sale in Bruges."

The comparison between Bruges and Venice does not end with their sites and economic activities. Here is the account of Leo von Rozmital, brother-in-law of the King of Bohemia, who in 1466 travelled through Germany, Belgium, England, France, Spain, Portugal and Italy, accompanied by a suite of forty gentlemen and servants. "In this country, but especially in Bruges, it is customary at the beginning of carnival for people of importance to disguise themselves, vying with each other to have the richest apparel. The colour chosen by the lord is also worn by his servants. But the wearing of masks prevents their being identified. Thus attired, they go wherever there are balls and other entertainments, accompanied by players of trumpets and drums."

In the fifteenth century the many feudal principalities which had arisen on what is

6. RENAISSANCE AND REFORMATION

today the territory of Belgium and the Netherlands were united under the sceptre of the Dukes of Burgundy. For several decades this extensive State was the richest and most powerful in western Europe. It had no fixed capital, but Bruges was one of the favourite places of residence of the Dukes and the Court. It was here that Charles the Bold and Margaret of York were married and that Philip the Good founded the Order of the Golden Fleece. It was at Bruges that much of the splendour of the Burgundian era was displayed. This included the development of music, the flowering of secular and ecclesiastical flamboyant Gothic and the fabulous school of painting which began with Jan Van Eyck and whose members have infelicitously been dubbed the Flemish Primitives, although this school was, in fact, one of the great achievements of plastic art.

For economic, social and political reasons the proud and valiant city of Bruges, which had even taken the liberty of imprisoning Maximilian I, then Regent of the Burgundian State, was obliged at the end of the fifteenth and the beginning of the sixteenth century to give ground to other cities, above all to Antwerp, which was to become the most important commercial and financial centre of the sixteenth century.

Foreign merchants abandoned Bruges which fell asleep and became a quiet provincial town, whose atmosphere was evoked by the novelist Georges Rodenbach in a book published in 1892 under the title *Bruges-la-Morte*. Today, thanks to its economic recovery and to the influx of tourists in search of beauty and the past, it is a dead town that has come to life again. It takes jealous care of its medieval character and the unity of its architectural style. For this it was awarded the European Prize for Urbanization in 1975.

Richard Mackenney

'IN PLACE OF STRIFE'

The Guilds and the Law in Renaissance Venice

FOR SOME TIME, GUILDS HAVE BEEN an unfashionable subject and tend to be identified with economic obsolescence and political passivity. They existed to protect those who practised a common trade, to maintain the standards of the craft and to express the solidarity of members through conviviality and the provision of support for guildsmen and their families. Such corporate organisations became increasingly common in the thirteenth century and were the products of economic growth in that period. By the sixteenth century, so the textbooks say, their exclusiveness and their monopolistic tendencies made them enemies of growth in an expanding economy. In England, guilds began to disappear by the end of the seventeenth century. Elsewhere, especially in France, their existence was artificially continued by governments which found them convenient for purposes of taxation.

On the face of it, the guilds of Venice would seem to embody economic introversion and political feebleness. As is well known, Venetian economic strength derived from

The trade guilds of Venice were organisations with a surprising amount of political and economic power in the patrician Renaissance city.

the commercial enterprise of the patriciate in overseas markets. The city's craft guilds had no part to play – except to build ships – in this branch of economic life: perhaps because of their distant markets and interests in maritime commerce, the merchants of Venice did not form corporations like the merchant guilds which existed elsewhere. Their economic interests were safeguarded by Venice's governmental institutions, which the merchants controlled, rendering other mercantile organisations superfluous.

The Venetian patriciate dominated

political life as they dominated the economy. The Venetian constitution – which came to be so admired – ensured the predominance of a tightly defined oligarchy whose composition was strictly fixed at the end of the thirteenth century. From that time onwards, only members of certain families could hold office and be members of the Great Council and the Senate, only they could become magistrates, only they could elect the nominal head of government, the Doge. The Venetian constitution gave noblemen a democracy amongst themselves: the common people were strictly excluded from political life. Ordinary folk were permitted to form guild organisations and the government found these useful in regulating economic life in the city itself. Despite their exclusion from politics, the people seem to have remained content. There was no popular uprising in Venice from the 'closing' of the Great Council to all except the adult males of certain families in 1297 to the fall of the Republic to Napoleon precisely five hundred years later.

This remarkable record of stability

From *History Today*, May 1984, pp. 17-22. Reproduced by kind permission of History Today, Ltd., 83-84 Berwick Street, London W1V 3PJ England.

*The Return of the Ambassador, by Carpaccio,
showing the rich civic life and fine
architecture of Renaissance Venice.*

was perhaps the main reason that the Venetian constitution became the envy of other states. But can we attribute half a millennium of stability solely to the wise government of the patricians? In the second half of the sixteenth century, the population of Venice stood at about 150,000: as few as 2,000 eligible for governmental office, as many as 120,000 either artisans or their dependents. One might have expected that at some point in a period of five hundred years, high food prices or military defeat would have spurred some guildsmen to riot or rebellion, yet they remain almost entirely anonymous in Venetian history.

In the early seventeenth century, there were about 120 guilds in the city. These represented an enormous range of trades in the state shipyards, in the textile and construction industries and, perhaps most important of all, in an ever-expanding retail sector. It is difficult to ignore altogether such large numbers of people engaged in such a substantial slice of a city's economic life and if we look a little more closely, we can see that the guilds played a more positive and active role in Venice than is usually imagined.

Certainly, their political position was a subordinate one. That subordination was effected in the later thirteenth century. Elsewhere in Italy, the 'little people' sought – and often won – political recognition from urban oligarchies. The Venetian experience was different. There was a flourish of popular celebration and an exuberant procession by the guilds when Lorenzo Tiepolo was elected Doge in 1268, but any suggestion that the guilds might have been on the verge of a political breakthrough had

A procession in the Piazza San Marco, circa 1500, by Gentile Bellini.

already been scotched. Laws which bound all guildsmen to the state by oath of allegiance had been formulated in 1265 and were hammered remorselessly into guild statutes in the 1270s. Everyone's workmate became a potential informer and guild officers, who in some cases were chosen by the magistrates and not by members, were clearly expected to represent the government in the guilds rather than vice versa.

There was not a murmur of protest from the corporations, even when the effectiveness of the city's constitutional arrangements was tested in the tempestuous fourteenth century. Indeed, during the abortive coup by the patrician Baiamonte Tiepolo in 1309, the painters rallied to the government cause and saw off an armed band of rebels on the Campo San Lucca. In 1355, the Arsenal workers who were supposed to be in league with the traitor-Doge Marin Falier never moved a muscle and the old

A Venetian trireme, from Cristoforo de Canale's 'Della Milizia Maritima', 1540.

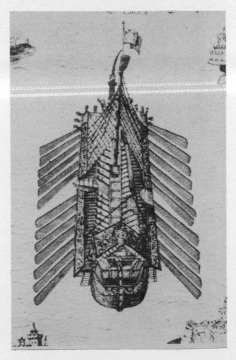

man was beheaded before most Venetians were aware he had been arrested.

Turning to guild economic life, we find, on the surface, the same picture of stability through government control. The Venetians were perhaps fortunate that there was no major woollen industry in the city in the middle ages for this may have avoided the kind of tensions between merchants and producers which erupted in Florence. In 1378, the Tuscan city was shaken to its foundations by an uprising of the lowest paid workers in the cloth industry – who were in fact denied the right to associate in guilds. Moreover, in Venice, the law of contract made it virutally impossible for guildsmen to take on more work than they could handle and supplies of raw materials were organised so that every master took a share. Within the Venetian guild system, it is difficult to see how a cartel of wealthy entrepreneurs could make a large number of

sion (as in Florence) between 'Greater' and 'Lesser' guilds and apparently no dependent proletariat who were outside the guilds altogether. The metropolitan economy of Venice was built on guilds of craftsmen and shopkeepers, not on entrepreneurs and wage labourers.

To summarise: medieval Venice had a large number of guilds whose economic status was roughly similar. The variety of their activities may have acted to fragment any sense of common interest in opposition to the patrician state which was able to render the corporations politically impotent. There was – and this is strange in a city so wary of individual assertiveness – an important compensation for guild members. Each guildsman pledged his loyalty to the state but there was a reciprocal arrangement, a species of social contract, in matters of justice.

The first Venetian artisan we know by name is almost certainly Giovanni Sagorino, a blacksmith mentioned in a chronicle of (probably) the twelfth century recording the events of the

Craftsmen of Venice carved on the columns of St Mark's Basilica. (Above left) barbers and coopers; (above right) blacksmiths; (below) boat builders.

workers dependent on their capital.

Significantly, this seems to have encouraged the development of a wide variety of guild organisations, characterised by very loose internal organisation, especially in a strikingly diverse and open-ended retail sector. The guilds of Venice were remarkable for the variety of their activities, many of which, as shown in the accompanying illustrations, were celebrated in the portals of St. Mark's and on the columns of the ducal palace. Virtually any activity, from sand carrying to mercery, from goldsmithery to dormouse skinning, was permitted a guild organisation. There was no divi-

year 1030. Giovanni had been told to carry out labour services for the Doge – as many artisans were required to do – at the ducal palace. He told the official who issued the order that the work could be done perfectly well in his shop. The dispute went to arbitration and the court found in favour of the artisan and, in effect, against the Doge.

The tradition continued even when the guild system was fully developed, though the right of appeal was more commonly exercised by an individual against the guild's officers than against the state. In the mid-fifteenth century, Pancrazio the baker was fined fifty ducats by his guild and took the case to three courts before he won his appeal and had the fine annulled. This was an important safeguard, especially when one remembers that the individual's right of appeal was authorised by the very statutes which rendered the corporations politically powerless. In Florence or Bologna, where the guilds were apparently more important in political life, such a right was specifically denied. Elsewhere the sentence of guild officers was final. In Venice, opportunities for appeal played a vital part in the history of the guilds.

In the course of the sixteenth and seventeenth centuries, there developed a 'myth of Venice' – the myth of a perfect constitution designed to avoid social discord. The way in which conflict was at the same time acknowledged and sublimated by the existence of channels through which protest might be expressed suggests that the myth had a certain grounding in everyday reality. Perhaps Shakespeare was not so wide of the mark when he chose to set the climax of *The Merchant of Venice* in a court-room. Even a patrician like Gasparo Contarini who spoke of the commonalty as 'the very scum of the people' acknowledged that the Venetian system of justice was characterised by collective judgements in a wide variety of courts. No magistrate, he wrote in 1524 'should bee an arbitrator without appeale in any thing'.

How did Venice's famed stability survive economic and political change? By the end of the sixteenth century, the city was declining relative to other states. The disruption of eastern markets by the Ottoman advance, the upheavals of the Italian wars which had brought France and Spain into the peninsula, and, though their impact was by no means sudden, the rise of economies which looked to the Atlantic rather than to Mediterranean routes, all threatened Venetian prosperity.

Those so-called enemies of progress, the guilds, played a crucial part in the process of adjustment and by 1600 it was clear that taxation, not guild obsolescence was hindering that process. Similar flexibility in the face of economic change has been brought to light in the construction industries of Renaissance Florence and indeed in the textile industries of Leyden and Lille in early modern times. What we know virtually nothing about – and where Venetian experience shows that guilds had a dynamism quite extraordinary in the pre-industrial world – is the history of shopping.

Today we take it for granted that the main street linking St. Mark's and Rialto is not dominated by banks or glass factories but by shops. Like the twentieth-century visitor, someone who went to Venice in the thirteenth century or the sixteenth would also have been besieged by people trying to sell him something – probably something he did not want – especially on the occasion of one of the city's great festivals, when Venice was packed with gullible outsiders. The street in question is the *Merceria* and it takes its name from the guild whose shops dominated the thoroughfare: the mercers.

In defiance of the rigid demarcation usually associated with guilds, Venetian mercers sold everything from amber to tin tacks, from buttons to perfume, from pots to brocade. In 1561, Antonio Valfredo set up at the *Città di Milano* as a seller of belts, mercery, purses and hats, Giacomo Morando, bell-maker at the St Anthony, took on the Falcon as a mercer in 1567.

There appears to have been something for everyone in the guild's activities. A series of tax assessments of 1568 records that Zilio da Ponte had about 60,000 ducats tied up in mercery while Marc'Antonio the capper 'has nothing he can call his own and struggles to stay alive'. The likes of Marc'Antonio never became dependent on the likes of Zilio, however. By 1594, we can identify between 350 and 400 independent mercers' businesses in the city and a membership of just under a thousand. There were clearly considerable opportunities for casual employment – perhaps as a shelf-stocker or even a window-dresser – and we might hazard the speculation that sixteenth-century Venice was the home of Europe's first corner shops and general stores. Their shop signs survive down to the present day, though the *Aquila Negra*, the *Città di Milano* and the *Madonna* are now smart restaurants, not mercers' shops.

The mercers stood at the centre of the city's economic life and of the guild network. In linking the worlds of international commerce and the corner shop, their activities provided the ligaments which enabled Venice to adjust to changed economic circumstances in the sixteenth century and to preserve the city's prosperity. The vitality of the retail sector and the wide variety of occupational opportunities within it helped ordinary Venetians to flourish even though there were some pointers to long-term decline.

A study of Venetian guilds shows that economic and political life within the corporations were inextricably linked. It is necessary, therefore, to consider the way in which the guilds' capacity for adjustment to change was hampered by the demands of the state. For, in the later sixteenth century, the government was forced to devote more and more of the city's resources to ever-increasing defence commitments. By this time, Venice stood in the shadow of two Mediterranean 'super-powers', the Ottoman Empire and Spain, and was trying to compete in a world in which the scale, duration and cost of warfare were all on the increase. The depredations of Turks and pirates forced the Venetians to double their reserve fleet in 1539, each of the hundred galleys requiring 156 oarsmen to produce its 19 horsepower. The crews were on more or less permanent stand-by, and the records suggest that tension was not relieved all that often by action at sea.

Men and money had to be found at regular intervals and the guilds were expected to help in supplying them. Men and money for wars which grew ever more expensive: the pattern of political necessity in republican Venice bears a striking resemblance to a state as remote in terms of size, geography and character as the France of Louis XIV.

The problem for the Venetians was that the war never reached a crisis point. For most of the sixteenth century, it was impossible to distinguish periods of declared war from periods of peaceful commerce. War was not a question of great victories and defeats, but a question of wearing the enemy down. The drain on Venetian resources was severe. The triumph of the Holy League at Lepanto in 1571 when Catholic Christendom routed the infidel fleet changed nothing. The campaign cost Venice about 700,000 ducats. By 1594, with the problem of piracy worsening all the time, the Republic had to find almost 600,000 ducats merely to keep the fleet in readiness. In 1582, the guilds alone were expected to supply 120,000 ducats for the fleet – about one quarter of the total capital resources of the mercers' guild around the time of Lepanto.

The guilds, not surprisingly, began to murmur. The burden on each member had worsened since the fearful plague of 1575-7 which had reduced the population of the city by about one-third. Such a loss could only be made good by immigration from the mainland, but by the end of the century potential replacements were deterred by the level of taxes and the possibility of having to serve in the galleys.

As the relations between guilds and government grew strained, the legal position of the former became increasingly important. Corporately, as we have seen, the guilds had little chance of political expression. No conscious decision is recorded, but by about 1585 what seems to begin to happen is a kind of pooling of individual rights within each guild. From about that date, there are complaints from the guilds to the magistrates that business is bad and taxes are making it worse. Demands for servicemen are too heavy and are starving the guilds of new members.

As early as 1578, some of the boatmen were grumbling about foreigners 'who can leave whenever there's a tax to pay' and the potters echoed the grievance. By 1611, the focal year of protest, some of the tanners had left the city 'running after work like birds after food', foreign workers among the goldsmiths and cabinet makers were also on the move and the bakers' journeymen had left the guild in the lurch since they were all 'northerners, Germans and outsiders who don't care where they are'.

Some of the wealthier guilds concentrated on the demeaning character of personal service at the oar. In 1594, merchants in the wool and silk guilds were exempted from personal service and were permitted to hire a substitute. Two years later the same privilege was extended to mercers and goldsmiths. The poor were expected to serve in person. The guilds never acted as one, but having moved away from the principle that all the corporations were equal before the law, the government found a tide of protest rising in waves from those who were expected to serve in person and those who felt that they should be exempted. In 1606, the leather merchants complained about being put on the same level as 'boatmen, odd-jobbers and other manual trades of no standing', the goldsellers 'have nothing to do with artisan workmen'.

There are dozens of complaints about the government's exactions. They reached a climax in 1611-2 after heavy impositions in 1610. The blacksmiths' records are instructive about the moment of crisis. In 1612, they complained that seven years earlier their quota of oarsmen had been cut from 147 to 100 when the guild numbered 131 able-bodied masters, now the demand was 120 from only 98. The smiths complained that business had dropped by 80 per cent in recent years, though they did not point out that their fuel bill had risen sharply. A steep rise in the price of charcoal began in 1572 when tax accounted for 16 *soldi* out of the 44 paid for each basket and the amount of tax continued to rise for the next half century. Perhaps it is not all that surprising that some members took matters into their own hands, as it were, at a meeting of 1612. The guild's records show that:

> having assembled as usual in the guild-hall, the officials took a seat at the tribunal with the holy cross and two lighted candles but there were some who had the audacity to go upstairs and with scant fear of God or our patron saint Also, they pissed over the tribunal and soaked it.

Along with many other guilds, the blacksmiths found debt an increasing problem (and one which their statutes were designed to obviate). By 1608, the smiths needed to raise 2,000 ducats to pay off one debt, another of 1,000 ducats taken out in 1592 remained unpaid in 1625 and another had to be taken out to meet it. In 1617, the bakers admitted debts of 1,100 ducats, the fruiterers were forced to borrow 2,000 in the same year.

Leonardo Loredan, Doge of Venice 1501-21; by Giovanni Bellini.

But by then the crisis had in many ways passed. The year of protest was 1611 with petitions from bakers, glass makers, coopers, water carriers, cheese sellers, woollen cloth shearers, bakers and tanners. The boatmen on the Padua route found a demand for 79 oarsmen from 79 members the last straw and there were similar complaints from many other boat stations.

Of special interest in this regard is that the crisis passed because the government backed down. In 1612, new impositions showed a reduction of more than 25 per cent on the 1610 figure (which was never approached again) with the discontents of 1611 lying in between. This may well represent a triumph for guild economics. By the early seventeenth century, a guild like the mercers was giving full membership to people being turned away by other sectors, particularly in manufactures. By 1660, Venice had as many mercers as boatmen and the guild was, by the end of the century, as large as any of those within the textile trades. Given the mercers' wide 'social catchment area', it made no sense to give them a legal privilege above other guilds. In 1639, perhaps in recognition of this, there was a return to legal equality. Galleys were to be manned in future by convicts, vagrants and odd volunteers. Any guild could collect money to pay for substitutes rather than finding its quota from its membership.

The guilds of Venice, constitutionally neutered and without the commercial interests and resources of the patricians, display in their history a surprising degree of economic vitality. By the early seventeenth century, through the exercise of a legal right afforded to each member, they found a new corporate strength within the 'normal channels' of political negotiation. In the case of the mercers, guild economics, characterised by diversity, flexibility and independent enterprise, outflanked an increasingly authoritarian government. The patricians, so often assumed to have manipulated Venice's constitutional machinery to maintain political stability, can be seen to have tampered with a process of economic adjustment and were forced to acknowledge a political defeat. When more is known about Venetian artisans – in terms of their material life and mentalities – it may be the case that the guilds' political articulacy and economic expertise drew on a resourceful cultural tradition. For the time being, we can conclude that the limits of aristocratic sovereignty in guild affairs in Renaissance Venice were set by the guilds themselves.

Thus, in the case of Venice, guilds displayed economic versatility and political resilience – characteristics not readily associated with the corporations of the pre-industrial era. The guilds were central to the economic life of the city in the middle ages. In the course of the sixteenth century, they acquired a new importance as taxable entities. By 1600, they began to show themselves capable of acting as the political representatives of a broad sector of Venetian society. As such they were able to check the excesses of a patrician state which had begun to look more like a collective absolutism than the defender of republican liberties.

FOR FURTHER READING:
F. C. Lane, *Venice: A Maritime Republic* (Johns Hopkins University Press: 1973); D. S. Chambers, *The Imperial Age of Venice* (Thames and Hudson: 1970); Brian Pullan, *Rich and Poor in Renaissance Venice* (Basil Blackwell: 1971); J. R. Hale, ed., *Renaissance Venice* (Faber: 1973); Brian Pullan, ed., *Crisis and Change in the Venetian Economy* (Methuen: 1968); Richard Rapp, *Industry and Economic Decline in 17th-century Venice* (Harvard University Press, 1976); A. Tenenti, *Piracy and the Decline of Venice, 1580-1615* (Longman: 1967); J. F. Guilmartin, *Gunpower and Galleys* (Cambridge University Press, 1974).

TO MECCA IN DISGUISE

JOHN H. WALLER

JOHN H. WALLER is the author of *Tibet: A Chronicle of Exploration* (pseudonym: John MacGregor) and *A History of Sino-Indian Relations: Hostile Co-Existence.* During World War II he served with the OSS in the Middle East.

Ludovico de Varthema of Bologna set out from Venice in 1500 determined to penetrate the East. He longed to investigate some small portion of "our terrestrial globe," and see with his own eyes "the situations of places, the qualities of peoples, the diversities of animals, the varieties of the fruit-bearing and odoriferous trees of Egypt, Syria, Arabia Deserta and Arabia Felix, Persia, India and Ethiopia." Because, as he phrased it, "the testimony of a one-eyed witness is worth more than ten hearsays," this Renaissance man shared his lively adventures with the reading public in a little-known book simply titled, *The Itinerary.* He hoped that his reading audience, "without discomfort or danger" would get pleasure from the "very great dangers and unsupportable fatigue" which he, himself, had endured.

Islam's most sacred city, Mecca, then as now, had been a cloistered shrine reserved for the faithful. An infidel commits blasphemy by intruding. Throughout history non-Moslem trespassers have been severely punished, often by forfeiting their heads. While Moslem pilgrims from all over the world make the *Haj,* as the pilgrimage is called, and ritually circle the holy Kaaba stone within the Great Mosque, woe be to the nonbeliever who tries to infiltrate their ranks. Ludovico de Varthema, disguised as a Mameluk—slave mercenary in the service of the Grand Sultan of Cairo—was probably the first European to travel to Mecca in a pilgrim caravan and perhaps the first to enter the spiritual heart of Islam. That he survived is a commentary on his native ingenuity and skill as a role-player. He left a lively description of contemporary Arabia and his own amazing adventures there, which is a tribute to his skill as a storyteller.

By the 15th century knowledge of the East accumulated in classical times was largely lost. Asia had become a legendary land, only dimly perceived in myth by Renaissance Europe. In earlier times commerce with the East through well-trod caravan routes was common. India was known to the ancients. Herodotus described it in the fifth century B.C. Alexander the Great's epic campaign to the borders of India brought to Greece a familiarity with the East. Geographers of ancient Greece such as Eratosthenes of Cyrene wrote voluminously of Asia, and Agatharchides, through his research at the famous Alexandrian library, identified the Sabeans of Southern Arabia as the medium of trade between Egypt and India. At the beginning of the Christian era, Pliny the Elder described India in his *Natural History,* and, of course, Claudius Ptolemy, the great astronomer and geographer of the second century, charted the East. As the third century ended, Rome was no longer able to trade directly with India since the Ethiopian Kingdom of Axum had forced Roman trading stations from the Red Sea. The division of the Roman Empire in the latter part of the fourth century also contributed to an isolation of the East from Europe.

Knowledge of Asia faded, soon to be forgotten. To Europe, Asia became a mysterious, frightening world, inhabited by fabulous beasts and barbarian warriors—Goths, Visigoths, Huns and Vandals—who swept into Christendom in successive waves of terror and pillage.

Suddenly in the seventh century a new force arose to challenge Christendom. An Arab bedouin named Mohammed from the Qoreish tribe of Mecca, inspired by heavenly visions, wrote his testament and teachings in what was to become one of the most influential documents the world has known, the Koran. Called by his followers "the Prophet," Mohammed rose in mid-life from obscurity to inspire his people and launch them on a missionary quest for conversion and power.

The calendar of Islam is reckoned from the Christian year 622 when Mohammed and his small band of original followers were forced to flee from Mecca to Medina by hostile tribes. The *Hegira,* or flight, ignited a religious movement which gained astonishing momentum. Mecca was taken in 630. As the Koran articulated the faith, the swords of the believers helped spread it until ultimately it reached from the borders of France in Europe to the Aral Sea in Central Asia. Yet Mecca, the sacred see of this incredible movement, was little known to Europe. No Christian claimed to have ever been there.

Centuries of religious Crusades to regain the Holy Land characterized Christendom's relationship with Islam. Even as Ludovico de Varthema entered Mecca in disguise, the Portuguese still cherished dreams of a new Crusade against Islam. Lisbon's envoy, Covilha, reached the Ethiopian Christian court of King Eskendar in 1493, his mission being to make him an ally of Portugal. For Portugal the humbling of Islam had long been a religious obligation as well as a commerical imperative. The discovery of a Christian monarch on the Arab's flank at last promised realization of one of Christendom's oldest hopes, a great Christian monarch in the East called Prester John, ready to save Christendom from Saracen harassment and finally rescue the Holy Lands.

Not long afterward, Albuquerque, then Portugal's Viceroy in the East Indies, sent two emissaries to Ethiopia's Regent-Queen, Elleni, to gain her support for a plan to seize the Red Sea port of Massawa and use it as a staging area for an invasion of Arabia. The occupation of Mecca would be the climax of Christendom's last Crusade. Without its heart, reasoned Albuquerque, Islam would die, never to challenge Europe again.

Varthema, travelling only for the sake of adventure and personal curiosity, was not interested in Portuguese imperial strategy or religious crusades. He was probably not overawed by the prospect of penetrating the citadel of Islam, nor was he excited by dreams of personal glory. What surely must have occurred to him, however, was his personal jeopardy. Traveling in the inhospitable Arabian desert was hazardous enough, but as an infidel in disguise his risks were very much greater.

O n April 18, 1503 Ludovico de Varthema joined a caravan bound for Mecca which was leaving Damascus. By befriending the caravan captain, a Mameluke, and generously crossing his palms with silver, Varthema became one of 60 Mameluke mercenaries hired to guard the pilgrims. The caravan consisted of some 40,000 pilgrims with 35,000 camels, who must walk for 40 days, mostly across brigand-infested desert, before reaching their destination.

The defense of the caravan was a serious responsibility for invariably when the long trains paused at watering places they were attacked by marauding bedouins seeking loot. Varthema described his fellow mercenaries as superb fighters; "for pagans, there are no better people with arms in their hands than are the Mamelukes." He saw one Mameluke soldier shoot a pomegranate from the head of his slave with an arrow at twelve paces. He described a horseshow in which a Mameluke rider at full gallop took off his saddle and placed it on his head, then returned it to its proper place without breaking stride.

Near the site of Sodom and Gomorrah, destroyed by an angry God for its wicked ways, the caravan was attacked by some 24,000 nomads, demanding payment for water. Besieged for two days, the caravan captain paid the marauders 1200 ducats of gold. But this did not satisfy them; the Mameluke guards were forced to fight a rear guard action so that the caravan could escape.

Varthema seemed to derive particular satisfaction in debunking a belief of the times that Mohammed's body was suspended in air over Mecca. At Medina, where Mohammed had fled in his escape from Mecca, Varthema visited the great Prophet's tomb. More than 400 columns made of burnt stone and lighted by 3000 lamps supported the arched roof of the mosque housing the sepulcher. Varthema was meticulous in describing Mohammed's resting place. The grave rested in an underground pit, flanked by the graves of his daughter, Fatema, her husband, Ali, and two disciples, Abu Bekr and Osman. He described a library of 25 books, chronicling the life and preaching of Mohammed and all the testaments of his disciples.

Varthema, acute to the sectarian schisms within Islam between the Sunnis and the Shias, was unable to conceal his contempt for such doctrinal squabbling. He commented: "These books treat about the followers of each of these captains (disciples); it is on this account that this rabble cut each other to pieces, for some wish to act according to the commandments of one, and some of another . . . and they kill each other like beasts about these heresies."

The captain of the caravan implored the keeper of the sacred mosque to reveal the coffin of the Prophet, offering him 3000 ducats of gold if he would do so. His offer was greeted by a bellow of rage: "How do those eyes of yours, which have seen so much evil in the world, desire to see Him for whom God has created the heavens and the earth?" That night, however, the caravan pilgrims were treated to a "miracle" of lights seeming to emanate from Mohammed's sepulcher. The Caravan captain, suspecting fraud, charged that the lights were caused by artificial fires. His doubts were attacked by a pious old man who ridiculed the Mamelukes as those not "well confirmed in the Truth," thus unable "to see celestial things."

Mecca lay beyond, across another stretch of arid desert whose bleached sand was "as fine as meal." Guided by the artful navigation of the Mameluke captain, the pilgrims found a "great quantity of water" just as they sorely needed it. (Local lore curiously attributed this remarkable well to a miracle once performed by God through the medium of the Christian disciple, Saint Mark.)

Only after twice beating off Arab brigands numbering some 50,000 did the weary travellers finally reach Mecca. Varthema's description is historically valuable because it was the earliest first-hand account of this holy citadel to reach Renaissance Europe.

W alled by the hills encircling it, Mecca was accessible by only four passes. Varthema estimated that some 6000 souls lived permanently in "well constructed" houses in the city. But the pilgrim population was huge; he commented: "Truly, I never saw so many people collected in one spot." Besides his own caravan from Damascus, a large caravan of pilgrims with 64,000 camels had just arrived from Cairo. Pilgrims from Ethiopia, India and Persia also thronged the narrow alleys of the city.

Mecca was an *entrepot* for trade as well as a shrine for pilgrims. In the bazaar jewels and spices from India, cloth goods from Bengal and incense from the African coast were traded. But religious devotion dominated the atmosphere. The pilgrims, many of whom had saved for this trip all their lives, earnestly sought salvation and absolution from their God. Varthema's 16th century description of the rite is not much different than it would be today.

"Within the courtyard of the Great Mosque and in the center is a tower, the size of which is about five or six paces on every side, about which there is a cloth of black silk. And there is a door all of silver. They say that the tower was the first house that Abraham built . . . On each side of the door there is a jar, which they say is full of balsam and which is shown on the day of Pentecost. On each side of the tower there is a large ring at the corner.''

Varthema also described the ritual: ''On the 24th of May all the people begin before daybreak to go seven times around the tower, always touching and kissing each corner. About ten or twelve paces from the tower there is a very beautiful well 70 fathoms deep . . . At this well there stand six or eight men appointed to draw water for the people. When the people have gone seven times around the first tower, they go to this well and place themselves with their backs toward the brink of the well, saying: 'In the name of God, the merciful, the compassionate, pardon us.' And those who draw the water throw three bucketfulls over each person . . . They say that their sins remain there after the washing.''

It is strange that Varthema makes no reference to the sacred Kaaba stone, housed in the black silk-covered tower, or house of Abraham. That rock, believed to have struck the earth as part of a meteorite, was an object of adoration from pre-Islamic times. Perhaps, at least this heart of Islam's most sacred shrine eluded Varthema's unwelcome prying.

In a later description of the pilgrimage to Mecca appearing in Hakluyt's well-known travel compendium, *The Principal Navigations, Voyages, Traffiques and Discoveries of the English Nation,* the House of Abraham, Islam's sacred shrine, is closely described. In this later 16th century account the Kaaba stone within the house ''fell downe from heaven, whereov was heard a voyce that wheresoever this stone fell, there should be built the house of God.'' According to Hakluyt's notices, the Kaaba is black because it ''hath been so oft kissed by sinners'' seeking absolution.

Varthema also makes mention of the ritual of sacrificing sheep. During his first days in Mecca he estimated that more than 30,000 sheep were slaughtered by having their throats sacrifically slit in the streets. The carcasses were then donated to the poor who ravenously consumed them, barely pausing to cook them. With con-

siderable cynicism, Varthema suggested that a large percentage of the pilgrims were, in reality, beggars who made the *Haj* only to live off the bounty of affluent pilgrims, moved to generosity by pious charity.

Vignettes of Mecca passed on by Varthema include his reference to the thousands of doves which fluttered over the streets. Local custom had it that they were descendants of the dove ''which spoke to Mohammed in the form of the Holy Spirit.'' Because of their miraculous forebear, the doves of Mecca were rigidly protected even though they were the bane of the grain dealers whose stocks were despoiled by them.

Varthema also referred to two ''unicorns in the temple of Mecca,'' which, he comments with casual understatement, ''are not very common in other places.'' The two ''very fierce'' specimens, presented to the Sultan of Mecca by a King of Ethiopia seeking a political alliance, are carefully described in Varthema's narrative. ''The oldest was much like a bay-colored colt of some 30 months except for a solitary horn protruding three yards out of his forehead. The creature's head resembled that of a stag, although his neck was short. The legs were slender, much like those of a goat, and the hoofs cloven. The smaller and younger specimen had a horn only four palms long.''

Varthema, while capable of telling an entertaining story, was not given to the invention of fact. This makes his passages on unicorns all the more astonishing. Even recognizing that unicorns figured prominently in the legends of the Renaissance, it is still difficult to reconcile Varthema's allegations with his otherwise objective reporting. What could he have seen?

Varthema's anguish can be imagined when one day he was accosted in the bazaar by a merchant who remembered him from the Damascus caravan and accused him of lying about his religion. ''By the head of Mohammed, I am a Moor,'' protested Varthema. The stranger insisted they go to his house to talk further. In the privacy of his rooms the accuser broke into Italian. Claiming to have lived in Genoa and Venice, he bragged that he could recognize an infidel Italian when he saw one.

Varthema admitted to having been a Roman Catholic from Bologna who

had lately become a Mameluke, but ingratiated himself with his accuser by claiming hostility toward the Portuguese. They found common cause in their hostility to the King of Portugal, now ''Lord of the Ocean Sea and of the Persian Gulf and Arabian Sea.'' Arab merchants and traders from the Italian city states alike were largely deprived of the once-lucrative overland commerce after Portugal found a sea route to India. Arab caravans no longer could reap rich profits by selling the products of the Indies to Venetian and Genoese merchants plying the Mediterranean. Speaking of Mecca, Varthema lamented: ''Where are the jewels and spices, and where are all the various kinds of merchandise which it was reported are brought here?'' The more Varthema maligned the Portuguese, the more the stranger warmed to him. He embraced Varthema, at last, saying, ''Mohammed be ever praised, who has sent us such a man to serve the Moors and God.''

Varthema's new-found friend also provided him with the means to escape from Mecca and continue on his way to the East. He concealed Varthema in his home and permitted him to remain there until the departure of a caravan bound for the coastal port of Jidda where he hoped to find passage to India. Varthema's benefactor, himself, had to rejoin the caravan for the return trip to Damascus, but the Italian appreciated the kindness of his friend's wife and her 15 year-old niece. In fact, when the time came to leave, they showed ''no small regret'' and ''made great lamentation.''

Varthema had spent a fortnight in Mecca, each day compounding the risk of discovery. His luck had held. Jidda, however, was no safer for an infidel. He found anonymity in a throng of 25,000 poor pilgrims who sought shelter in a mosque, and ventured forth only at night to buy food. Not before two weeks when he found ship to Aden could he breathe freely.

Ludovico de Varthema's troubles, however, were just beginning. Whatever security he felt as he sailed toward the mouth of the Red Sea, was soon dashed when the small ship put into Aden. This natural port, capital of that part of southern Arabia known then as *Arabia Felix*—Arabia the happy, or well-endowed—was a bustling crossroads where ships from all over the Indian Ocean, the Gulf, and the Red Sea met to exchange goods. The authorities of this cosmopolitan entrepot were, however, no more hospitable towards Christians than the guardians of Mecca. Varthema's luck gave out when a fellow passenger denounced him as a "Christian dog, son of a dog."

Accused of being a spy from Christendom, Varthema was jailed and shackled with 18-pound foot irons. Only narrowly did he avoid being put to death on the spot.

Some two months later Varthema was taken to an audience with the Sultan, an eight day march arcoss the desert to the city of Rhada. The place was packed with some 80,000 fighting men about to launch an attack against Sana, capital of what is known today as North Yemen. One can imagine that he was distracted when he received Varthema and probably in none too good temper. He did not believe Varthema's claim to be a good Moslem Mameluk from Cairo—particularly after the hapless prisoner proved unable to repeat the holy phrase, "Leila Illaala Mahometh Resullah" (*La illa ill' Alla Mohammed Resullala,* usually translated: "There are no gods but Allah and Mohammed is his Prophet"). Varthema was clapped into a dungeon where he was fed only two loaves of millet a day. While eventually permitted to shuffle around town in his leg shackles, his lot was a miserable one.

Varthema, resouceful as ever, hit upon an ingenious strategem. Realizing that Moslems are particularly indulgent toward madmen, he decided to pretend insanity. His description of this experiment reveals a consummate actor with a rare sense of humor.

"Truly, I never found myself so wearied or so exhausted as during the first three days that I feigned madness," wrote Varthema. He was constantly taunted by a retinue of 50 or 60 rock-throwing street urchins and mocked by local shopkeepers. Raving and babbling, he shuffled through the streets stark naked. This attracted the notice of the Sultan's Queen and her ladies-in-waiting. She "took the greatest delight in seeing me," recorded Varthema, "and would not let me leave her, and gave me good food to eat."

For the benefit of this new benefactress, he enlivened his act by accosting sheep and donkeys on the street, demanding that they prove themselves good Moslems by repeating the phrase, "Leila Illah Mahometh Resullah," as he had been asked to do. The Queen, clearly bored by her usual uneventful life in *purdah,* or veiled seclusion, found this hilarious and was moved to ever greater solicitude.

Two revered holy men were summoned to pass judgement as to whether Varthema was truly mad, or whether he was a holy man inspired to acts of apparent madness by holy design. They couldn't agree and argued fiercely for an hour as the Queen and her retinue of comely maidens watched from the palace balcony. Varthema wrote, "In order to get rid of the holy men, I raised my shirt and urinated over them both, whereupon they ran away, crying out, 'He is mad, he is mad.'" The Queen and her ladies exploded with laughter. Her Highness shouted gaily, "By the good God, by the head of Mohammed, this is the best fellow in the world," and sent for Varthema.

After hearing the Italian's story she concluded he was quite sane and, moreover, would make a welcome addition to the palace. Installed in a room without a door and still shackled, Varthema could nonetheless conclude that his lot was now somewhat better.

Soon the queen took to visiting Varthema nightly, bringing delicacies to pop into his mouth, and arranging scented baths to relax him. She now called him "Ludovico" and greeted him on a note of endearment as she entered his quarters. Varthema recalled an evening when she withheld the usual culinary delights she had brought him until he removed his nightshirt. He protested, "O Madam, I am not mad now."

The queen, smirking lasciviously, answered: "By God, I know well that thou never were mad; on the contrary, thou art the best witted man that ever was seen." She admired the naked Varthema for two hours. He remembered how "she contemplated me as though I had been a nymph and uttered a lamentation: O God, Thou has created this man white like the sun; would to God that this man were my husband." As she spoke, she continually "passed her hands over me," all the while promising that as soon as her husband returned from the battle she would have the heavy shackles removed.

Varthema had the wit to refuse her repeated offers to spend the nights with him. As he told her, "that would be quite enough to have my head cut off." He also realized "as soon as she had had me she would have given me gold and silver, horses and slaves. Then she would have given me ten black slaves who would have been a guard upon me so that I should never have been able to escape."

When at long last the Sultan returned, the Queen intervened in Varthema's behalf and had him pardoned. His shackles were removed and he was given the freedom of the city. The Queen took him to her chambers where, as he vividly recalled, "she kissed me more than a hundred times." She promised him a bright future, saying, "If thou wilt be good, though shalt be a lord."

Such enticements did not blind Varthema to the fact that he was now a kept man, a slave of the licentious Queen. His acute sense of survival warned him to concoct another strategem. While on a hunting trip with the Queen he feigned serious illness. She agreed to his entreaties that he be permitted to seek a cure from a well-known holy man in Aden, "who they said, performed miracles."

Once Varthema reached Aden, he found passage to Persia and India. But with a thoughtful touch, he wrote the Queen, praising God for his cure and saying, "since God has been so merciful to me, I wish to go and see the whole of your kingdom." He knew in time she would find a new object for her affections and thus think less unkindly of his defection.

Islam's forbidden see had been penetrated and the Sultan of Arabia Felix cuckolded by an infidel in disguise. That, however, was but the start of Ludovico de Varthema's remarkable odyssey in the East as an age of exploration burst upon Europe.

The Enigma of Aztec Sacrifice

*Human sacrifice was meant to appease
the appetites of the gods—and of the Aztecs themselves*

Michael Harner

On the morning of November 8, 1519, a small band of bearded, dirty, exhausted Spanish adventurers stood at the edge of a great inland lake in central Mexico, staring in disbelief at the sight before them. Rising from the center of the lake was a magnificent island city, shining chalk white in the early sun. Stretching over the lake were long causeways teeming with travelers to and from the metropolis, Tenochtitlán, the capital of the Aztec empire, now known as Mexico City.

The Spaniards, under the command of Hernán Cortés, were fresh from the wars of the Mediterranean and the conquest of the Caribbean. Tough and ruthless men, numbering fewer than four hundred, they had fought their way up from the eastern tropical coast of Mexico. Many had been wounded or killed in battles with hostile Indians on the long march. Possibly all would have died but for their minuscule cavalry of fifteen horses—which terrified the Indians, who thought the animals were gods—and the aid of a small army of Indian allies, enemies of the Aztecs.

The panorama of the Aztec citadel across the water seemed to promise the Spaniards the riches that had eluded them all their lives. One of them, Bernal Díaz del Castillo, later wrote: "To many of us it appeared doubtful whether we were asleep or awake . . . never yet did man see, hear, or dream of anything equal to our eyes this day." For the Spaniards, it was a vision of heaven.

Slightly more than a year and half later, in the early summer of 1521, it was a glimpse of hell. Again the Spaniards found themselves on the lakeshore, looking toward the great capital. But this time they had just been driven back from the city by the Aztec army. Sixty-two of their companions had been captured, and Cortés and the other survivors helplessly watched a pageant being enacted a mile away across the water on one of the major temple-pyramids of the city. As Bernal Díaz later described it,

The dismal drum of Huichilobos sounded again, accompanied by conches, horns, and trumpetlike instruments. It was a terrifying sound, and when we looked at the tall *cue* [temple-pyramid] from which it came we saw our comrades who had been captured in Cortés' defeat being dragged up the steps to be sacrificed. When they had hauled them up to a small platform in front of the shrine where they kept their accursed idols we saw them put plumes on the heads of many of them; and then they made them dance with a sort of fan in front of Huichilobos. Then after they had danced the *papas* [Aztec priests] laid them down on their backs on some narrow stones of sacrifice and, cutting open their chests, drew out their palpitating hearts which they offered to the idols before them.

Cortés and his men were the only Europeans to see the human sacrifices of the Aztecs, for the practice ended shortly after the successful Spanish conquest of the Aztec empire. But since the sixteenth century, Aztec sacrifice has persisted in puzzling scholars. No human society known to history approached that of the Aztecs in the quantities of people offered as religious sacrifices: 20,000 a year is a common estimate.

A typical anthropological explanation is that the religion of the Aztecs required human sacrifices; that their gods demanded these extravagant, frequent offerings. This explanation fails to suggest why that particular form of religion should have evolved when and where it did. I suggest that the Aztec sacrifices, and the cultural patterns surrounding them, were a natural result of distinctive ecological circumstances.

Some of the Aztecs' ecological circumstances were common to ancient civilizations in general. Recent theoretical work in anthropology indicates that the rise of early civilizations was a consequence of the pressures that growing populations brought to bear on natural resources. As human populations slowly multiplied, even before the development of plant and animal domestication, they gradually reduced the wild flora and fauna available for food and disrupted the ecological equilibriums of their environments. The earliest strong evidence of humans causing environmental damage was the extinction of many big game species in Europe by about 10,000 B.C., and in America north of Mexico by about 9,000 B.C. Simultaneously, human populations in broad regions of the Old and New Worlds had to shift increasingly to marine food resources and small-game hunting. Finally, declining quantities of wild game and food plants made domestication of plants and animals essential in most regions of the planet.

In the Old World, domestication of herbivorous mammals, such as cattle, sheep, and pigs, proceeded apace with that of food plants. By about 7,200 B.C. in the New World, however, ancient hunters had completely eliminated herbivores suitable for domestication from the area anthropologists call Mesoamerica, the region of the future high civilizations of Mexico and Guatemala. Only in the Andean region and southern South America did some camel-related species, especially the llama and the alpaca, manage to survive hunters' onslaughts, and thus could be domesticated later, along with another important local herbivore, the guinea pig. In Mesoamerica, the guinea pig was not available, and the Camelidae species became extinct several thousand years before domesticated food production had to be

seriously undertaken. Dogs, such as the Mexican hairless, and wildfowl, such as the turkey, had to be bred for protein. The dog, however, was a far from satisfactory solution because, as a carnivore, it competed with its breeders for animal protein.

The need for intensified domesticated food production was felt early, as anthropologist Robert Carneiro has pointed out, by growing populations in fertile localities circumscribed by terrain poorly suited to farming. In such cases, plants always became domesticated, climate and environment permitting, but herbivorous mammals apparently could not, unless appropriate species existed. In Mesoamerica, the Valley of Mexico, with its fertile and well-watered bottomlands surrounded by mountains, fits well Carneiro's environmental model. In this confined area, population was increasing up to the time of the Spanish conquest, and the supply of wild game was declining. Deer were nearly gone from the Valley by the Aztec period.

The Aztecs responded to their increasing problems of food supply by intensifying agricultural production with a variety of ingenious techniques, including the reclamation of soil from marsh and lake bottoms in the chinampa, or floating garden, method. Unfortunately, their ingenuity could not correct their lack of a suitable domesticable herbivore that could provide animal protein and fats. Hence, the ecological situation of the Aztecs and their Mesoamerican neighbors was unique among the world's major civilizations. I have recently proposed the theory that large-scale cannibalism, disguised as sacrifice, was the natural consequence of these ecological circumstances.

The contrast between Mesoamerica and the Andes, in terms of the existence of domesticated herbivores, was also reflected in the numbers of human victims sacrificed in the two areas. In the huge Andean Inca empire, the other major political entity in the New World at the time of the conquest, annual human sacrifices apparently amounted to a few hundred at most. Among the Aztecs,

the numbers were incomparably greater. The commonly mentioned figure of 20,000, however, is unreliable. For example, one sixteenth-century account states that 20,000 were sacrificed yearly in the capital city alone, another reports this as 20,000 infants, and a third claims the same number as being slaughtered throughout the Aztec empire on a single particular day. The most famous specific sacrifice took place in 1487 at the dedication of the main pyramid in Tenochtitlán. Here, too, figures vary: one source states 20,000, another 72,344, and several give 80,400.

In 1946 Sherburne Cook, a demographer specializing in American Indian populations, estimated an overall annual mean of 15,000 victims in a central Mexican population reckoned at two million. Later, however, he and his colleague Woodrow Borah revised his estimate of the total central Mexican population upward to 25 million. Recently, Borah, possibly the leading authority on the demography of Mexico at the time of the conquest, has also revised the estimated number of persons sacrificed in central Mexico in the fifteenth century to 250,000 per year, equivalent to one percent of the total population. According to Borah, this figure is consistent with the sacrifice of an estimated 1,000 to 3,000 persons yearly at the largest of the thousands of temples scattered throughout the Aztec Triple Alliance. The numbers, of course, were fewer at the lesser temples, and may have shaded down to zero at the smallest.

These enormous numbers call for consideration of what the Aztecs did with the bodies after the sacrifices. Evidence of Aztec cannibalism has been largely ignored or consciously or unconsciously covered up. For example, the major twentieth-century books on the Aztecs barely mention it; others bypass the subject completely. Probably some modern Mexicans and anthropologists have been embarrassed by the topic: the former partly for nationalistic reasons; the latter partly out of a desire to portray native peoples in the best possible light. Ironically, both these attitudes may represent European ethnocentrism regarding cannibalism—a viewpoint to be expected from a culture that has had relatively abundant livestock for meat and milk.

A search of the sixteenth-century literature, however, leaves no doubt as to the prevalence of cannibalism among the central Mexicans. The Spanish conquistadores wrote amply about it, as did several Spanish priests who engaged in ethnological research on Aztec culture shortly after the conquest. Among the latter, Bernardino de Sahagún is of particular interest because his informants were former Aztec nobles, who supplied dictated or written information in the Aztec language, Nahuatl.

According to these early accounts, some sacrificial victims were not eaten, such as children offered by drowning to the rain god, Tlaloc, or persons suffering skin diseases. But the overwhelming majority of the sacrificed captives apparently were consumed. A principal—and sometimes only—objective of Aztec war expeditions was to capture prisoners for sacrifice. While some might be sacrificed and eaten on the field of battle, most were taken to home communities or to the capital, where they were kept in wooden cages to be fattened until sacrificed by the priests at the temple-pyramids. Most of the sacrifices involved tearing out the heart, offering it to the sun and, with some blood, also to the idols. The corpse was then tumbled down the steps of the pyramid and carried off to be butchered. The head went on the local skull rack, displayed in central plazas alongside the temple-pyramids. At least three of the limbs were the property of the captor if he had seized the prisoner without assistance in battle. Later, at a feast given at the captor's quarters, the central dish was a stew of tomatoes, peppers, and the limbs of his victim. The remaining torso, in Tenochtitlán at least, went to the royal zoo where it was used to feed carnivorous mammals, birds, and snakes.

Recent archeological research lends support to conquistadores' and in-

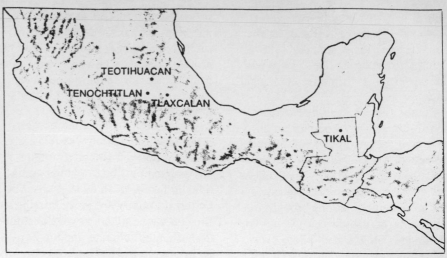

formants' vivid and detailed accounts of Aztec cannibalism. Mexican archeologists excavating at an Aztec sacrificial site in the Tlatelolco section of Mexico City between 1960 and 1969 uncovered headless human rib cages completely lacking the limb bones. Associated with these remains were some razorlike obsidian blades, which the archeologists believe were used in the butchering. Nearby they also discovered piles of human skulls, which apparently had been broken open to obtain the brains, possibly a choice delicacy reserved for the priesthood, and to mount the skulls on a ceremonial rack.

Through cannibalism, the Aztecs appear to have been attempting to reduce very particular nutritional deficiencies. Under the conditions of high population pressure and class stratification that characterized the Aztec state, commoners or lower-class persons rarely had the opportunity to eat any game, even the domesticated turkey, except on great occasions. They often had to content themselves with such creatures as worms and snakes and an edible lake-surface scum called "stone dung," which may have been algae fostered by pollution from Tenochtitlán. Preliminary research seems to indicate that although fish and waterfowl were taken from the lakes, most of the Aztec poor did not have significant access to this protein source and were forced to be near-vegetarians, subsisting mainly on domesticated plant foods such as maize and beans.

The commoners theoretically could get the eight essential amino acids necessary for building body tissues from maize and beans. (A combination of the two foods complement each other in their essential amino acid components.) However, recent nutritional research indicates that in order to assure that their bodies would use the eight essential amino acids to rebuild body tissues, and not simply siphon off the dietary protein as energy, the Aztec commoners would have had to consume large quantities of maize and beans simultaneously or nearly simultaneously year-round. But crop failures and famines were common. According to Durán, a sixteenth-century chronicler, poor people often could not obtain maize and beans in the same season, and hence could not rely upon these plants as a source of the essential amino acids. How did the Aztecs know they needed the essential amino acids? Like other organisms perfected under natural selection, the human body is a homeostatic system that, under conditions of nutritional stress, tends to seek out the dietary elements in which it is deficient. Without this innate capacity, living organisms could not survive.

Another Aztec dietary problem was the paucity of fats, which were so scarce in central Mexico that the Spaniards resorted to boiling down the bodies of Indians killed in battle in order to obtain fat for dressing wounds and tallow for caulking boats. While the exact amount of fatty acids required by the human body remains a subject of uncertainty among nutritionists, they agree that fats, due to their slower rate of metabolism, provide a longer-lasting energy source than carbohydrates. Fatty meat, by providing not only fat, which the body will use as energy, but also essential proteins, assures the utilization of the essential amino acids for tissue building. Interestingly, prisoners confined by the Aztecs in wooden cages prior to sacrifice could be fed purely on carbohydrates to build up fat.

In contrast to the commoners, the Aztec elite normally had a diet enriched by wild game imported from the far reaches of the empire where species had not been so depleted. But even nobles could suffer from famines and sometimes had to sell their children into slavery in order to survive. Not surprisingly, the Aztec elite apparently reserved for themselves the right to eat human flesh, and conveniently, times of famine meant that the gods demanded appeasement through many human sacrifices.

At first glance, this prohibition against commoners eating human flesh casts doubt on cannibalism's potential to mobilize the masses of Aztec society to engage in wars for prisoners. Actually, the prohibition was, if anything, a goad to the lower class to participate in these wars since those who single-handedly took captives several times gained the right to eat human flesh. Successful warriors became members of the Aztec elite and their descendants shared their privileges. Through the reward of flesh-eating rights to the group most in need of them, the Aztec rulers assured themselves an aggressive war machine and were able to motivate the bulk of the population, the poor, to contribute to state and upper-class maintenance through active participation in offen-

sive military operations. Underlying the war machine's victories, and the resultant sacrifices, were the ecological extremities of the Valley of Mexico.

With an understanding of the importance of cannibalism in Aztec culture, and of the ecological reasons for its existence, some of the Aztecs' more distinctive institutions begin to make anthropological sense. For example, the old question of whether the Aztecs' political structure was or was not an "empire" can be reexamined. One part of this problem is that the Aztecs frequently withdrew from conquered territory without establishing administrative centers or garrisons. This "failure" to consolidate conquest in the Old World fashion puzzled Cortés, who asked Moctezuma to explain why he allowed the surrounded Tlaxcalans to maintain their independence. Moctezuma reportedly replied that his people could thus obtain captives for sacrifice. Since the Aztecs did not normally eat people of their own polity, which would have been socially and politically disruptive, they needed nearby "enemy" populations on whom they could prey for captives. This behavior makes sense in terms of Aztec cannibalism: from the Aztec point of view, the Tlaxcalan state was preserved as a stockyard. The Aztecs were unique among the world's states in having a cannibal empire. Understandably, they did not conform to Old World concepts of empire, based on economies with domesticated herbivores providing meat or milk.

The ecological situation of the Aztecs was probably an extreme case of problems general to the high population pressure societies of Mesoamerica. Cannibalism encouraged the definition of the gods as eaters of human flesh and led almost inevitably to emphasis on fierce, ravenous, and carnivorous deities, such as the jaguar

and the serpent, which are characteristic of Mesoamerican pantheons. Pre-Columbian populations could, in turn, rationalize the more grisly aspects of large-scale cannibalism as consequences of the gods' demands. Mesoamerican cannibalism, disguised as propitiation of the gods, bequeathed to the world some of its most distinctive art and architecture. The temple-pyramids of the Maya and the Toltecs, and of the pre-Aztec site at Teotihuacán in the valley of Mexico, resemble those of the Aztecs in appearance and probably had similar uses. Even small touches, such as the steepness of the steps on pyramids in Aztec and other Mesoamerican ruins, become understandable given the need for efficiently tumbling the bodies from the sacrificial altars to the multitudes below. Perhaps those prehistoric scenes were not too dissimilar from that which Bernal Díaz described when his companions were sacrificed before his eyes in Tenochtitlán:

Then they kicked the bodies down the steps, and the Indian butchers who were waiting below cut off their arms and legs and flayed their faces, which they afterwards prepared like glove leather, with their beards on, and kept for their drunken festivals. Then they ate their flesh with a sauce of peppers and tomatoes.

Gruesome as these practices may seem, an ecological perspective and population pressure theory render the Aztec emphasis on human sacrifice acceptable as a natural and rational response to the material conditions of their existence. In *Tristes Tropiques*, the French anthropologist Claude Levi-Strauss described the Aztecs as suffering from "a maniacal obsession with blood and torture." A materialist ecological approach reveals the Aztecs to be neither irrational nor mentally ill, but merely human beings who, faced with unusual survival problems, responded with unusual behavior.

Our Man from Arezzo

GENE MITCHELL

*He is the symbol of the dark side
of the Renaissance, the "can of worms"
that is inseparable from the works of genius.
In other words, if you want the Sistine Chapel,
you'll also have to take Pietro Aretino.*

If we would think of the Renaissance as a coin with a bright side symbolizing the tremendous works of art produced, and a dark side representing the "can of worms" that was the social and political reality, we probably could understand the dark side best by studying the career of that Pietro from Arezzo who took his surname, Aretino, from the town as, in the same manner, did a certain Leonardo from the town of Vinci.

There are men prominent in history whose main claim to fame is their ability to survive. Pietro Aretino was a classic survivor who met his end undramatically in his bedchamber when it seemed certain that he was bound to wind up in a dark alley with a tastefully designed dagger in his back.

Pietro Aretino was born in Arezzo in April, 1492. As any schoolboy knows, it was the year that Columbus discovered America for the Europeans (the Indians had already discovered it for themselves) and it was the year that Lorenzo the Magnificent died. If one needs an arbitrary separation between the modern and the old, Pietro Aretino's timing was perfect.

His father was a cobbler known only by his given name of Luca. Various last names have been suggested such as Bonamici, de Bura, or Camaiani, but the evidence is tenuous.

Tina, his mother, was also of the urban poor. She must have been pretty because she one time sat as a model for the Madonna for a painter named Matteo Lappoli. Aretino was immensely proud of his mother's fleeting fame and at one time he had Vasari make him a copy of the Lappoli work. (Like many men who hop from bed to bed, Aretino was always constant to his mother.)

It we believe Aretino (which is not the ideal way to understand him), his father was a nobleman named Luigi Bacci who made hay while Luca cobbled. To combine an old expression with a current one, Aretino knew it was better to be born on the wrong side of the blanket than on the wrong side of the tracks. In other words, Aretino loved his mother but he was willing to surrender her virtue for a little noble blood. In any event, being a bastard was no drawback at that time. Cesare Borgia was a bastard and when Aretino reached middle age, a bastard attained the papacy itself. But what evidence we have is all in favor of Luca, the shoemaker, being the chap who impregnated Tina, the Madonna. Aretino's claim to being a bastard will have to rest on the modern use of the word and, in that sense, no one can gainsay him.

Aretino always showed a great affection for his native Arezzo and for all fellow Aretines. Any Aretine who came to him in distress could always expect succor. The only thing he asked of his hometown is that he not be exected to live there and share in its provincial glories at first hand. At the age of fourteen he left Arezzo and returned only for extremely short visits thereafter.

He went to Perugia to study art but he left hurriedly after adding his own touches to a painting of Christ and Mary Magdalen. Rome was his next stop where he worked in various households. He was fired from one iob for stealing the silver, and lost out in another when his master died. Back on the road again, he bobbed up in Vicenza as a street singer. Next he played at being a wandering friar and, then, worked successively as a moneylender, a tax collector, a mule driver, and a hangman's assistant.

For some obscure indiscretion, he served time at an oar on a galley in the Mediterranean and survived the brutal ordeal. Back on land again, he passed rapidly through another succession of lowly jobs including pimping. Fortune took him to Venice where he entered the literary lists with a first book. It was a piece of pastiche, modeled closely on the work of Serofino Aquilano, a flashy but inconsequential poet. Finally, he entered a monastery at Ravenna. They put him to binding books. He soon discovered that unholy practices and women steal into the best regulated monasteries. He was never one to lead in reform so he followed his natural bent and was dismissed for lechery.

His education was complete. He was ready for Rome. He was a man of the Renaissance—ready to condone treachery and murder to attain a goal. He had been through the great university of Renaissance villainy, been graduated with honors and was ready for post-graduate work. He was possibly the greatest authority on low life that the world had ever known. He was 24 and bursting with animal vitality. He went to Rome.

The Eternal City was made to order for Aretino's ambitions. It was the quintessence of the Renaissance—brilliant, worldly and corrupt. A man who had his eye on the main chance and who was not weighed down with scruples could go a long way, provided he could present a moving target to the ambushes that lay on all sides.

Aretino started climbing the Roman ladder from the lowest rung. He entered the lavish household of Agostino Chigi as a servant. Agostino Chigi was the papal treasurer, which was like being Secretary of the Treasury in the United States. He was an international banker of tremendous power and it is one of the ironies of history that the fledgling writer who entered his service as a lackey is better known to posterity than Chigi. Aretino was put to work lighting candles, cleaning privies, polishing chamberpots, and sweeping out bedrooms. Aretino continued his writing career by handing out witty verses to the parade of the famous who supped and slept at Chigi's palace.

The reigning Pope was Leo X, formerly Cardinal Giovanni de' Medici, and son of Lorenzo the Magnificent. Leo was rich, fat and fun-loving. He surrounded himself with buffoons. The post of papal privy seal which had once been held by Bramante was bestowed on an ex-barber and, then, on one Fra Mariano whose outstanding achievement was that he once ate twenty capons at a sitting.

It was the easygoing Leo who gave Martin Luther sufficient provocation to nail his 95 theses to the door of the church in Wittemburg and to write his fiery letter of denunciation of the papacy.

In 1514 King Manuel of Portugal presented an elephant to Leo. The huge creature, on its presentation to the Pope, filled its trunk with water and hosed down the papal courtiers. Leo, who enjoyed nothing better than low farce, was enchanted. The elephant had definitely joined the papal "in" crowd. But the beast had a short tenure. In the unsalubrious air of Rome it sickened and died. Leo was plunged into gloom and summoned Raphael to do a portrait of the elephant so that it would never be forgotten.

The stage was set for Aretino. A pamphlet appeared in the streets of Rome entitled "The Last Will and Testament of the Elephant." Written by Aretino, this burlesque of a legal will gave with a heavy-handed but savage wit the possessions of

the elephant and portions of its body to various princes of the church. As an indication of the level of subtlety of the lampoon, Cardinal Grassi, the outstanding womanizer of the curia, was bequeathed a rather obvious member of the dead elephant's equipment. Laughter swept through Rome and Aretino rode on the crest of it. The Pope, more amused than anyone, asked Chigi to release Aretino to the papal service. In Rome for only two years, he had progressed from lackey to papal laureate. Aretino had arrived.

Aretino's newly found security lasted only five years. In 1521 Leo caught a chill which progressed into pneumonia, and he went to join the big fisherman. The cardinals descended on Rome and the scramble for the papacy began. The cardinals were locked in the Sistine Chapel for their deliberations with a strong guard to insure against information going in or coming out. Pietro Aretino stepped into the vacuum that had been created by issuing his own news bulletins.

In the Piazza Navona, which was a marketplace, stood an ancient statue which was popularly called Pasquino for reasons that are lost in time. It had become the custom to plaster Pasquino with scurrilous and libelous witticisms which naturally became known as "pasquinades." Aretino decided this custom was an excellent vehicle to bring to the public his own interpretations of the conference to choose a new pope.

And so, he covered the deliberations with his own Pasquinades. Before the final choice was made on the successor to Leo, Aretino was well on his way to the goal he had set for himself: to be the most dangerous tongue in Europe. Just a brief sample will give one an idea of his acid humor:

Valle'll give up his children, Cesarini his whore,
And Trani his mamma, who loves him sore
Cortona, his plots, and more.

Inside the Sistine Chapel events were taking a turn that boded no good for Aretino's future. Cardinal Guilio de' Medici was the favored choice for Pope but could not secure the necessary majority of votes for election. Three months went by with no break in the deadlock. For his own immediate political concerns, Cardinal Guilio de' Medici could not remain locked up in the Sistine Chapel. He decided on a bold stroke. He would put in nomination a dark horse who would be so dark that in all likelihood the nomination would act as a catalyst to break the deadlock and, finally, bring the choice back to him. Medici nominated Adrian of Utrecht, a good and sincere Dutch prelate, who had not even bothered to come to Rome for the election. To Medici's consternation, Adrian was elected Pope on the first ballot after the nomination.

Aretino's future in Rome was dependent upon a worldly papal court. The unsophisticated Dutchman known to history as Adrian VI who took his Christianity seriously would not be likely to encourage Aretino. Worse, he would probably throw the impudent Aretine in jail. Aretino put his chagrin into verse:

O villain college, who has betrayed Christ's name;
And given over His earthly heritage,
The Vatican, to vile Teutonic rage,
Do not your hearts split open wide with shame?

As Adrian journeyed toward Rome, Aretino moved again to watch events from the safety of Bologna.

Bologna bored Aretino. In Rome he had been famous, in Bologna he was nobody. Giulio de' Medici, having lost the papacy, had retired to his native Florence to see which way Adrian would bounce. He had delivered the papacy to the simple Dutchman, but Adrian did not realize that one becomes Pope through political intrigue so he was not properly grateful to Medici. In his Pasquino period, Aretino had thrown a few darts at Giulio de' Medici but basically had supported him for Pope. Now he went to him in Florence to be closer to the action.

Giulio de' Medici was not exactly bowled over to see the self-exiled satirist. He was trying to gain the favor of Adrian and Aretino surely could not help him with that. But Medici reasoned that the Aretine had a way with words and he might come in handy some day.

He sent Aretino with a letter of introduction to Federigo Gonzaga, the Marquis of Mantua. The Marquis was a great admirer of Aretino's work and he was overjoyed to have him for a guest. Darkly handsome, the Marquis had been painted by Raphael and would later be painted by Titian. He was an avid sensualist and therefore an ideal companion for Aretino. They had lusty times together. But the pleasant backwater palled on Aretino as had Bologna. He returned to Florence to seek something better from Giulio de' Medici. The Cardinal sent him north to his kinsman, Giovanni de' Medici who was known as Giovanni delle Bande Nere. A swashbuckling captain, Giovanni de' Medici guarded Italy against invasions from the north. He had an intuitive military sense in a time when military commanders were more likely to be masters of intrigue than tacticians. Even more to Aretino's delight, Giovanni was a good companion in drinking and wenching. Aretino had found his only hero.

Pope Adrian lasted less than two years. Apparently, he really tried to reform the church—and nothing would do one in more quickly. His death was the cause for celebrations in Rome—the Romans were free of this fool who took his religion seriously. Moving with sure political dispatch, Cardinal Giulio de' Medici became Pope Clement VII.

From Milan Aretino hailed with glee the turn of events. With characteristic caution, he moved south but stopped short of Rome at Reggio. There he lived with a cook so that the delights of the kitchen would keep him from being bored by the games of the bedchamber. Of course, it wasn't food or fun that made him choose Reggio; it was the struggle for power in the Vatican that kept him on the sidelines until he could pick the winning team. When he did join the game, he blundered. He joined the opposition to Giovanmatteo Giberti, who held the office of Papal Datary, a post of great power in the Holy See. With typical impudence, Aretino turned his bitter pen against the Datary. Giovanmatteo Giberti was not a man to suffer with the Christian patience that befitted his calling. He sent an assassin to rid himself of this troublesome literary blackmailer. The assassin came close to fulfilling his mission. He stabbed Aretino twice in the chest and Aretino lay near death for several weeks. But he recovered and clamored for justice. Everyone of power, inclding Clement, turned a deaf ear. Aretino had to be content with an artist's revenge. He put all his powerful enemies in his first satiric comedy, *La Cortegiana*. Then he returned to his old haven in Mantua.

As usual, the charms of provincial Mantua could not sustain Aretino for long. He was not cut out to be a backwater courtier or, for that matter, a courtier at all. War snatched him from boredom. Venice, Milan, and the Papal States had made common cause with Francis I of France against Charles V, the Holy Roman Emperor. Charles V invaded Italy and a motley army assembled to block his passage south. The papal troops were commanded by Aretino's hero, Giovanni delle Bande Nere. Aretino rode out to join Giovanni.

The battle was joined at the small town of Governolo near Mantua. The German troops of Charles V had four excellent cannons made for them in the factory of Alfonso d' Este, Duke of Ferrara. A neat profit meant more to the Duke than Italy; he sold his cannons to the invading Germans.

It was an Italian ball fired from an Italian cannon that killed Giovanni delle Bande Nere, the only Italian that could have saved Rome and Italy from the foreigner. Aretino, genuinely grief-stricken for the first time in his life, wrote a moving tribute to his dead captain. It was December 10, 1526.

He chose Mantua again as the sanctuary from which to solicit forgiveness from Clement and the Datary. But no forgiveness was forthcoming and Aretino lashed out against Pope, Datary, and all the cardinals. In a note to the Marquis of Mantua, the Pope suggested that Mantua be denied to Aretino as a fort from which to assail his enemies. The Marquis counted out one hundred gold crowns and suggested Venice. On March 27, 1527, Aretino arrived in Venice. He was almost 35 and lucky to be alive.

Venice had passed the peak of her glory. The states of Italy were ringed around her like hounds around a stag. On the water, the rising power of the Turk had pushed her back to her inland sea, thereby striking a terrible blow at the trade which had made her great. The explorers had pushed around Africa to reach the Indies. This new route would soon challenge seriously the position of Venice as the gateway to the riches of the Orient. None of this decline was visible on Aretino's arrival; Venice was still rich and played the role to the hilt.

Aretino had found his home at last. It seems one can go home if the ideal which is in one's mind is found on earth. Aretino had discovered his mighty fortress, beside which Mantua was only the most puny of refuges, from which to send out his literary sallies.

Two years after his arrival Aretino was established in a splendid palace on the corner of the Grand Canal and the Rio San Giovanni Crisostomo. Jacopo Tintoretto dropped in to adorn a ceiling with two paintings. On the walls there were paintings by Titian including a portrait of Giovanni delle Bande Nere. Scattered around the palace were sculptures by Sansovino and medallions by Lione Lioni and Alessandro Vittoria. At the entrance, on a pedestal, there was a marble bust of a virile, bearded man. Of course, it was Aretino.

To wind up with a palace in Venice two years after arriving with a pittance is a neat trick. The explanation is not a complicated one. Aretino was confident of his position in Italy. He demanded support from those he thought should be his patrons and, surprisingly enough, he got it.

He badgered his old host from Mantua, Federigo Gonzaga, for support and although he did not receive what he thought was his just due, Aretino did not plead in vain except in one instance. He dedicated a long poem to Federigo which he called the *Marfisa*. It was slight work ground out for money. The Marquis expressed his appreciation in glowing terms—which made him either a poor critic or a liar—but he refused to pay for it except in praise. Aretino offered it to several young noblemen (the poem being a kind of all-purpose epic in which anybody could play the hero.) He finally marketed it with the Marquis of Vasto in 1532. The Marquis of Vasto had long been the butt of some of Aretino's most scurrilous slams, so one may be astonished that he sponsored the *Marfisa*. It was really not out of character. The Marquis of Vasto anticipated modern celebrities by one time saying in effect to Aretino: "I don't care what you say about me so long as you mention my name."

While Aretino was tapping Federigo Gonzago for funds he did not forget his friends, Titian and Sansovino. He peddled their works to the Marquis in the form of gifts. As a true patron of the arts, Federigo had to respond with suitably lavish thanks.

A list of Aretino's patrons would look like a who's who of the sixteenth century in Europe. Why did they all send him money? Possibly because they knew he could dip his words in honey or poison. Honey was just more expensive.

The Casa Aretino soon became the haunt of women of all classes who sought Aretino's favors. There were street-walkers, famous courtesans, middle-class spouses, and noble-women. They came to cook his food, and arrange his possessions, and sleep with him. Three stand out from all the rest for special consideration.

There was Caterina Sandella who was married to a dissolute nobleman who made the mistake of bringing his wife to the Casa Aretino. She became friendly with Aretino and sought his advice concerning her husband's inveterate infidelity. He consoled her with such success that she became his mistress and bore him two children.

Perina Riccia was a delicate creature whose husband brought her to the palace and then left suddenly with some of Aretino's gold and one of the more fetching girls from the kitchen. Perina, left behind, fell sick and had to be nursed back to health by Aretino. As soon as he had her back in shape, he made her his mistress. She tired of Aretino and, taking a cue from her agile husband, left with a young man who was a guest. She, also, helped herself to the funds. She returned briefly to be forgiven by Aretino and to die in Venice.

The third was a woman by the unlikely name of Angela Serena who accomplished the almost impossible feat of maintaining a platonic relationship with Aretino. One feels that she was only saved from continuing her relationship in bed by her husband and family who removed her from Aretino's influence. The abortive affair rankled with Aretino who boasted in print that both Angela Serena and her husband would only be remembered in history because they had known Aretino.

The husband, Giovanni Serena, struck back at Aretino. He brought charges of blasphemy in the Venetian courts and dropped a dark hint that charges of sodomy would follow. The first offense, if proved, called for beheading and if one were guilty of sodomy, the punishment was to be exhibited in a cage in a public place, and left to die. One feels that if the second charge had been pressed in Venice, the law enforcers would have run out of cages. However, the charge of homosexuality against Aretino may have had some foundation. There are references to it by his enemies in the venomous pamphlets written against him. Even discounting malice, a man so overflowing with sensuality must have considered all variations of sexual experience. Certainly, if a man in his position had desire, he had access.

In any event, Aretino decided to take no chances with the block or the cage; he fled to a villa he had purchased in Gamberare. His exile was short. He was back in his beloved Venice in two weeks when the Duke of Urbino intervened and had the charges withdrawn. It was no consolation for Aretino to learn that besides Giovanni Serena one of his own secretaries, Niccolo Franco, had conspired against him. Franco was later to write a muckraking biography of Aretino which is the source of many of the disreputable things we believe of him.

A retino had all the Renaissance vices, but he had one Renaissance virtue: his love of art and his consideration for artists. Jacopo Tatti, known as Sansovino, was such a close friend of Aretino that when he wrought the bronze doors to the sacristy of St. Mark's cathedral, he included the bearded face of Aretino in the guise of an evangelist. It was Sansovino who introduced Aretino to Titian. The painter and the writer became the closest of friends.

In his extravagant way, Pietro Aretino said that Titian was another version of himself. The comparison is flattering to Aretino only. Titian was a genius; Aretino was a minor talent with a great flair for self-promotion. Titian painted Aretino and the magnificent portrait hangs in the Frick Gallery in New York City. Titian caught the coarseness, the exuberance, and the essential ruthlessness of the Aretine.

As we all know, there is no accounting for friendships. The most dissimilar persons find things in each other that attract. Particularly, it seems that people like to experience low life vicariously by being friendly with scoundrels. This may be what drew Titian to Aretino. Whatever the reason, they shared every interest including the details of their households.

Aretino takes considerable credit for promoting Titian. It is a disputable claim. Titian was well on his way to greatness before he met the Aretine. And although some of the commissions of Titian are traceable to Aretino, it does not follow that those commissions are that critical in the final analysis of Titian's genius. To give Aretino his due, his pen helped rather than hindered Titian.

There is another side of the picture. Based on Aretino's letters, there is good reason to believe that Titian made Aretino less of a ruffian.

If Aretino cannot be classed as a genius, just where does he rank in the world of letters when one forgets his ebullient personality?

If it were only a matter of productivity, he would rank with Shakespeare. He spewed out an unending stream of comedies, poems, biographies, and letters. But quantity is not quality; many earnest literary journeymen are well forgotten. Aretino is remembered because he belonged to his own age, was aware of it, and wrote as one who was aware of it. His language is the language of his time. In him there is not, as there were in so many of his day, simpering imitation of Petrarch and Boccaccio. The essence of any artist worth his salt is that what he sees constantly and firmly is his private and special vision of the world. Aretino's world was Italy of the Renaissance; a mixture of farce and tragedy—a living theater of the absurd. He is reported to have said: "Men live in a different fashion in modern Rome than they did in ancient Athens." He also said: "It is better to drink out of one's own wooden platter than another's golden goblet."

His work was read all over Europe. It had a lot to do with the Italianizing influence that permeated the Elizabethan dramatists, particularly Shakespeare. His plays, which are not acted at all today, were widely performed in his time. They were social comedies influenced by Terence with assists by Boccaccio. Essentially, however, they were his very own, the world viewed through the eyes of Aretino: lusty, lewd, violent and vivid.

Today his work is largely forgotten. If one would say his name aloud at a cocktail party it would not draw any more response than if one said "Joseph Hergesheimer" (who was a vogue in the United States in the 1930's). It is ironic to realize that only two hundred years ago Joseph Addison doubted if there was a single man then living who did not know who Aretino was.

T o return to Aretino's career, he reached the pinnacle of his fame and influence in the great struggle for power between Charles V, the Holy Roman Emperor, and Francis I, the King of France.

He had long sought the favor of Francis, who was a rather gallant figure if one has a turn for romanticism. Francis had smiled on Aretino but had never rewarded him with more than a gold necklace. On the other hand, Charles had sacked Rome, which had caused him to be showered with the verbal slings and arrows of an outraged Aretino. The ill will of Aretino was no mean thing. As Ariosto said:

> Behold the scourge
> Of Princes, mighty Pietro Aretino!

Now it was Charles who sought Aretino's support. He sent his courtiers to offer him two hundred gold crowns a year as a pension with no services asked. Aretino graciously accepted the pension and gave his writing services free.

Francis, in his desperate struggle with Charles, turned to an ally outside Europe, the dreaded Ottoman Emperor, Suleiman the Magnificent. One must understand the times to realize what panic swept through Europe on the heels of the French move. A rough analogy would be the reaction in the United States today if the United Kingdom entered into a military alliance with the Soviet Union. The Turkish threat had been lapping on the shores of Southern Europe. With French support it could strike at the heart of Europe. The French alliance with the Turk gave Aretino his opportunity to pay back Charles for his pension by merely writing two letters.

Both of the letters were addressed to Francis; both were as public as an editorial in the *New York Times;* both cried shame on Francis for consorting with the enemy of Christendom and Europe. Across the continent millions of voices roared their assent to Aretino's words. There is no doubt it was the crest of his wave; a common writer had dared to call a king to account for his politics. Francis sent couriers to offer Aretino double the amount of the pension if he could learn to see things differently. One cannot be certain if Aretino really believed in the Turkish threat or if he decided that two hundred crowns in hand were worth four hundred in French promises; but he refused the offer from Francis. His refusal was couched in such a fashion that if Charles did welsh, Francis could still have hopes. As we say, he left the door open.

No account of Aretino's life would be complete without mentioning his clash with Michelangelo. When he heard of the project for the Sistine Chapel, he wrote to Michelangelo, describing in detail how the subject matter should be treated. Some modern critics have upbraided Aretino for his presumption in this matter, which shows that they do not understand the age. It was quite common for a man of letters to sketch out with words a proposed painting. It was just that Michelangelo felt no need for help. He replied to Aretino praising his conception in words that actually dismissed Aretino and his views.

Aretino was not easily put off. He returned to the correspondence with a different end in view. He wanted a gift of one of Michelangelo's drawings. For eight years he kept up the campaign for a free drawing, but the stubborn Buonarroti was not to be coerced into surrendering one. In 1545 Aretino decided the time was ripe for him to strike at Michelangelo in reprisal for his refusal. In a letter to Michelangelo, Aretino managed to praise Raphael as a better artist, attack the work in the Sistine Chapel for being both irreligious and licentious, and imply that Michelangelo was a homosexual. One can only dismiss the letter as the spiteful attack of a man of small character. How droll a role it was for Aretino to pose as the shocked puritan. If one would measure Aretino for meanness, the encounter with Michelangelo would provide the best rule. Michelangelo's response was simply to paint the portrait of Aretino on the head of Saint Bartholomew in the enormous fresco. As a final mocking note, the angry Aretino is holding a flayed skin which has a caricatured face of Michelangelo.

Illogically enough, one of the worldly Aretino's ambitions was to be made a cardinal of the church. During one of his peaceful periods with Clement, an emissary of the Pope had hinted that Aretino was in line for the honor. But Clement never got around to it, and it is very unlikely that he ever had any serious thought to make Aretino a prince of the church. Pope Paul III who followed Clement was even more adamant in dismissing the suggestion as ridiculous. Aretino had a typical reaction to Paul's refusal: he castigated the Pope in gutter language.

In 1549 Paul died and was succeeded by Julius III who was from Arezzo. Aretino was so certain that his fellow Aretine would honor him with a red hat that he broke a vow he had made to himself never to leave his adopted home and left Venice in April of 1554 to journey to Rome to be ready for the honor. When he reached Rome he found that most of his old enemies and friends were dead. But there were new friends, friends on the basis of his reputation as the most dangerous tongue in Europe. They thronged around him and he felt like the conquering hero come home.

But the summer came and there was no mention of the hat. Finally dreadful August came. August in Rome in the sixteenth century was no festival. Heat lay heavy in the streets. The stench of sewage, dead dogs, and human excrement pervaded the air. It came to Aretino in that oppressive setting that he would never be a cardinal. With sudden decision and without recrimination he packed and went home to his beloved Venice.

But all was not well in paradise. The landlord of the Casa Aretino had taken advantage of his absence to evict him. The landlord had not been paid in twenty years except for a published eulogy that Aretino had dashed off. Aretino took the setback in stride and moved to a large apartment. There were still enough patrons left to keep him in style.

The year 1556 came and Aretino realized that all the great princes that he had known were dead. Only Charles V was still alive and he had abdicated as Emperor to go to the lonely monastery of Yuste in Spain. Aretino had survived only in spirit. He was racked by erysipelas, epilepsy, syphilis, and palsy. He only had time for one epic donnybrook.

Anton Francesco Doni, who has been called the father of modern journalism, probably because he was completely mad, had been living off Aretino's charity. While cadging from Aretino, he had been stealing his host's patrons. Aretino discovered his duplicity and roasted him in one of his public letters of the kind that had disposed of so many enemies. Doni replied in kind but added the prediction that Aretino would not last out the year.

Aretino almost made a liar of him because he got all the way to October. On the night of October 21, 1566, while drinking heavily, at a riotous gathering in a tavern, he suffered a cerebral hemorrhage and died in his bed a few hours later. Rumor has it that he was telling bawdy stories about his sisters when the seizure came.

There is little to add by way of conclusion except to say that if you want the Sistine Chapel, you'll have to take Aretino too.

MACHIAVELLI

Would you buy a used car from this man?

VINCENT CRONIN

Machiavelli—the most hated man who ever lived: charged, down the centuries, with being the sole poisonous source of political monkey business, of the mocking manipulation of men, of malfeasance, misanthropy, mendacity, murder, and massacre; the evil genius of tyrants and dictators, worse than Judas, for no salvation resulted from *his* betrayal; guilty of the sin against the Holy Ghost, knowing Christianity to be true, but resisting the truth; not a man at all, but Antichrist in apish flesh, the Devil incarnate, Old Nick, with the whiff of sulphur on his breath and a tail hidden under his scarlet Florentine gown.

Machiavelli is the one Italian of the Renaissance we all think we know, partly because his name has passed into our language as a synonym for unscrupulous schemer. But Niccolò Machiavelli of Florence was a more complex and fascinating figure than his namesake of the English dictionary, and unless we ourselves wish to earn the epithet Machiavellian, it is only fair to look at the historical Machiavelli in the context of his age.

He was born in 1469 of an impoverished noble family whose coat of arms featured four keys. Niccolò's father was a retired lawyer who owned two small farms and an inn, his mother a churchgoer who wrote hymns to the Blessed Virgin. Niccolò was one of four children; the younger son, Totto, became a priest, and the idea of a con-

fessional occupied by a Father Machiavelli is one that has caused Niccolò's enemies some wry laughter.

Niccolò attended the Studio, Florence's university, where he studied the prestigious newly-discovered authors of Greece and Rome. Like all his generation, he idolized the Athenians and the Romans of the Republic, and was to make them his models in life. This was one important influence. The other was the fact that Florence was then enjoying, under the Medici, a period of peace. For centuries the city had been torn by war and faction; but now all was serene, and the Florentines were producing their greatest achievements in philosophy, poetry, history, and the fine arts.

This point is important, for too often we imagine the Italian Renaissance as a period of thug-like *condottieri* and cruel despots forever locked in war. We must not be deceived by the artists. Uccello and Michelangelo painted bloody battles, but they were battles that had taken place many years before. If we are to understand Machiavelli, we must picture his youth as a happy period of civilization and peace: for the first time in centuries swords rusted, muscles grew flabby, fortress walls became overgrown with ivy.

In 1494, when Machiavelli was twenty-five, this happiness was shattered. King Charles VIII of France invaded Italy to seize the kingdom of Naples; Florence lay on his route. In

the Middle Ages the Florentines had fought bravely against aggressors, but now, grown slack and effete, they were afraid of Charles's veterans and his forty cannon. Instead of manning their walls, they and their leading citizen, Pietro de' Medici, meekly allowed the French king to march in; they even paid him gold not to harm their country.

This debacle led to internal wars, to economic decline, in which Niccolò's father went bankrupt, to much heart-searching, and to a puritanical revolution. Savonarola the Dominican came to rule from the pulpit. Thundering that the French invasion was punishment for a pagan way of life, he burned classical books and nude pictures and urged a regeneration of Florence through fasting and prayer. The French just laughed at Savonarola; he lost the confidence of his fellow citizens and was burned at the stake in 1498.

In that same year, Machiavelli became an employee of the Florentine Republic, which he was to serve ably as diplomat and administrator. Machiavelli scorned Savonarola's idea of political regeneration through Christianity; instead, he persuaded the Florentines to form a citizen militia, as was done in Republican Rome. In 1512 Florence's big test came. Spain had succeeded France as Italy's oppressor, and now, at the instigation of the Medici, who had been exiled from Florence in 1494 and wished to return, a Spanish army of five thousand marched against Tuscany. Four thousand of Machiavelli's militia were defending the strong Florentine town of Prato. The Spaniards, ill-fed and unpaid, launched a halfhearted attack. The Florentines, instead of resisting, took to their heels. Prato was sacked, and a few days later Florence surrendered without a fight. The Medici returned, the Republic came to an end, Machiavelli lost his job and was tortured and exiled to his farm. For the second time in eighteen years he had witnessed a defeat that was both traumatic and humiliating.

In the following year an out-of-work Machiavelli began to write his great book *The Prince*. It is an attempt to answer the question implicit in Florence's two terrible defeats: what had gone wrong? Machiavelli's answer is this: for all their classical buildings and pictures, for all the Ciceronian Latin and readings from Plato, the Florentines had never really revived the essence of classical life—that military vigor and patriotism unto death that distinguished the Greeks and Romans. What then is the remedy? Italy must be regenerated—not by Savonarola's brand of puritanism, but by a soldier-prince. This prince must subordinate every aim to military efficiency. He must personally command a citizen army and keep it disciplined by a reputation for cruelty.

But even this, Machiavelli fears, will not be enough to keep at bay the strong new nation-states, France and Spain. So, in a crescendo of patriotism, Machiavelli urges his prince to disregard the accepted rules of politics, to hit below the belt. Let him lie, if need be, let him violate treaties: "Men must be either pampered or crushed, because they can get revenge for small injuries but not for fatal ones"; "A prudent ruler cannot, and should not, honor his word when it places him at a disadvantage and when the reasons for which he made his promise no longer exist"; "If a prince wants to maintain his rule he must learn how not to be virtuous."

Machiavelli develops his concept of a soldier-prince with a couple of portraits. The first, that of the emperor Alexander Severus, is an example of how a prince should not behave. Al-

exander Severus, who reigned in the third century, was a man of such goodness it is said that during his fourteen years of power he never put anyone to death without a trial. Nevertheless, as he was thought effeminate, and a man who let himself be ruled by his mother, he came to be scorned, and the army conspired against him and killed him. Machiavelli scorns him also: "Whenever that class of men on which you believe your continued rule depends is corrupt, whether it be the populace, or soldiers, or nobles, you have to satisfy it by adopting the same disposition; and then *good deeds are your enemies*."

Machiavelli's second portrait is of Cesare Borgia, son of Pope Alexander VI, who carved out a dukedom for himself and then brought it to heel by appointing a tough governor, Ramiro. Later, says Machiavelli, Cesare discovered that "the recent harshness had aroused some hatred against him, and wishing to purge the minds of the people and win them over . . . he had this official [Ramiro] cut in two pieces one morning and exposed on the public square . . . This ferocious spectacle left the people at once *content and horrified*."

The words I have italicized show Machiavelli's peculiar cast of mind. He grows excited when goodness comes to a sticky end and when a dastardly deed is perpetrated under a cloak of justice. He seems to enjoy shocking traditional morality, and there can be little doubt that he is subconsciously revenging himself on the Establishment responsible for those two profound military defeats.

Machiavelli wrote *The Prince* for Giuliano de' Medici. He hoped that by applying the lessons in his book, Giuliano would become tough enough to unite Italy and drive out the foreigner. But Giuliano, the youngest son of Lorenzo the Magnificent, was a tubercular young man with gentle blue eyes and long sensitive fingers, the friend of poets and himself a sonneteer. He was so soft that his brother Pope Leo had to relieve him of his post as ruler of Florence after less than a year. Preparations for war against France taxed his feeble constitution; at the age of thirty-seven he fell ill and died. Machiavelli's notion of turning Giuliano

into a second Cesare Borgia was about as fantastic as trying to turn John Keats into a James Bond.

This fantastic element has been overlooked in most accounts of Machiavelli, but it seems to me important. Consider the *Life of Castruccio Castracani*, which Machiavelli wrote seven years after *The Prince*. It purports to be a straight biography of a famous fourteenth-century ruler of Lucca, but in fact only the outline of the book is historically true. Finding the real Castruccio insufficiently tough to embody his ideals, Machiavelli introduces wholly fictitious episodes borrowed from Diodorus Siculus's life of a tyrant who really was unscrupulous: Agathocles. As captain of the Syracusans, Agathocles had collected a great army, then summoned the heads of the Council of Six Hundred under the pretext of asking their advice, and put them all to death.

Machiavelli in his book has Castruccio perform a similar stratagem. Just as in *The Prince* the second-rate Cesare Borgia passes through the crucible of Machiavelli's imagination to emerge as a modern Julius Caesar, so here a mildly villainous lord is dressed up as the perfect amoral autocrat. In both books Machiavelli is so concerned to preach his doctrine of salvation through a strong soldier-prince that he leaves Italy as it really was for a world of fantasy.

Machiavelli had a second purpose in dedicating *The Prince* to Giuliano de' Medici (and when Giuliano died, to his almost equally effete nephew Lorenzo). He wished to regain favor with the Medici, notably with Pope Leo. This also was a fantastic plan. Machiavelli had plotted hand over fist against the Medici for no less than fourteen years and was known to be a staunch republican, opposed to one-family rule in Florence. Pope Leo, moreover, was a gentle man who loved Raphael's smooth paintings and singing to the lute; he would not be interested in a book counseling cruelty and terror.

How could a man like Machiavelli, who spent his early life in the down-to-earth world of Italian politics, have yielded to such unrealistic, such fantastic hopes? The answer, I think, lies in the fact that he was also an imaginative artist—a playwright obsessed with extreme dramatic situations. Indeed, Machiavelli was best known in Florence as the author of *Mandragola*. In that brilliant comedy, a bold and tricky adventurer, aided by the profligacy of a parasite, and the avarice of a friar, achieves the triumph of making a gulled husband bring his own unwitting but too yielding wife to shame. It is an error to regard Machiavelli as primarily a political theorist, taking a cool look at facts. *The Prince* is, in one sense, the plot of a fantastic play for turning the tables on the French and Spaniards.

What, too, of Machiavelli's doctrine that it is sometimes wise for a prince to break his word and to violate treaties? It is usually said that this teaching originated with Machiavelli. If so, it would be very surprising, for the vast majority of so-called original inventions during the Italian Renaissance are now known to have been borrowed from classical texts. The Florentines valued wisdom as Edwardian English gentlemen valued port—the older the better.

In 1504 Machiavelli wrote a play, which has been lost, called *Masks*. It was in imitation of Aristophanes' *Clouds*, the subject of which is the Sophists, those men who claimed to teach "virtue" in a special sense, namely, efficiency in the conduct of life. The Sophists emphasized material success and the ability to argue from any point of view, irrespective of its truth. At worst, they encouraged a cynical disbelief in all moral restraints on the pursuit of selfish, personal ambition. Florentines during their golden age had paid little attention to the Sophists, preferring Plato, who accorded so well with Christianity and an aesthetic approach to life; but after the collapse in 1494 it would have been natural for a man like Machiavelli to dig out other, harder-headed philosophers.

The source for his doctrine of political unscrupulousness may well have been the Sophists as presented in Aristophanes' play. The following sentence from one of Machiavelli's letters in 1521 is close to many lines in *The Clouds*: "For that small matter of lies," writes Machiavelli, "I am a doctor and hold my degrees. Life has taught me to confound false and true, till no man knows either." In *The Prince* this personal confession becomes a general rule: "One must know how to color one's actions and to be a great liar and deceiver."

How was it that an undisputably civilized man like Machiavelli could advise a ruler to be cruel and deceitful and to strike terror? The answer lies in the last chapter of *The Prince*, entitled "Exhortation to liberate Italy from the barbarians." Often neglected, it is, in fact, the most deeply felt chapter of all and gives meaning to the rest. "See how Italy," Machiavelli writes, "beseeches God to send someone to save her from those barbarous cruelties and outrages"—he means the outrages perpetrated by foreign troops in Italy, a land, he goes on, that is "leaderless, lawless, crushed, despoiled, torn, overrun; she has had to endure every kind of desolation."

Machiavelli is a patriot writing in mental torment. He seldom mentions the deity, but in this chapter the name of God occurs six times on one page, as an endorsement for this new kind of ruler. Machiavelli really believes that his deceitful prince will be as much an instrument of God as Moses was, and this for two reasons. First, Italy is an occupied country, and her survival is at stake; and just as moral theologians argued that theft becomes legitimate when committed by a starving man, so Machiavelli implies that deceit, cruelty, and so on become legitimate when they are the only means to national survival.

Secondly, Machiavelli had seen honest means tried and fail. Savonarola had hoped to silence cannon by singing hymns; Machiavelli himself had sent conscripts against the Spaniards. But the Italians had been then—and still were—bantams pitted against heavyweights. They could not win according to the rules, only with kidney punches. And since they had to win or cease to be themselves—that is, a civilized people as compared with foreign "barbarians"—Machiavelli argues that it is not only right but the will of God that they should use immoral means.

We must remember that *The Prince* is an extreme book that grew out of an extreme situation and that its maxims must be seen against the charred, smoking ruins of devastated Italy. The nearest modern parallel is occupied France. In the early 1940's cultivated men like Camus joined the Resistance, committing themselves to blowing up German posts by night and to other sinister techniques of *maquis* warfare. Like Machiavelli, they saw these as the only way to free their beloved country.

But the most original and neglected aspect of Machiavelli is his method. Before Machiavelli's time, historians had been the slaves of chronology. They started with the Creation, or the founding of their city, and worked forward, year by year, decade by decade, chronicling plague, war, and civil strife. Sometimes they detected a pattern, but even when they succeeded in doing so, the pattern was *sui generis*, not applicable elsewhere. Machiavelli was the first modern historian to pool historical facts from a variety of authors, not necessarily of the same period, and to use these facts to draw general conclusions or to answer pertinent questions.

He applies this method notably in his *Discourses on Livy*, and among the questions he answers are these: "What causes commonly give rise to wars between different powers?" "What kind of reputation or gossip or opinion causes the populace to begin to favor a particular citizen?" "Whether the safeguarding of liberty can be more safely entrusted to the populace or to the upper class; and which has the stronger reason for creating disturbances, the 'have-nots' or the 'haves'?"

Machiavelli does not wholly break free from a cyclical reading of history —the term Renaissance is itself a statement of the conviction that the golden age of Greece and Rome had returned. Nor did he break free from a belief in Fortune—what we would now call force of circumstance—and he calculated that men were at the mercy of Fortune five times out of ten. Nevertheless, he does mark an enormous advance over previous historical thinkers, since he discovered the method whereby man can learn from his past.

Having invented this method, Machiavelli proceeded to apply it imperfectly. He virtually ignored the Middle Ages, probably because medieval chronicles were deficient in those dramatic human twists, reversals, and paradoxes that were what really interested him. This neglect of the Middle Ages marred his study of how to deal with foreign invaders. Over a period of a thousand years Italy had constantly suffered invasion from the north; the lessons implicit in these instances would have helped Machiavelli to resolve his main problem much better than the more remote happenings he chose to draw from Livy. For example, at the Battle of Legnano, near Milan, in 1176, a league of north Italian cities won a crushing victory over Frederick Barbarossa's crack German knights. The Italians didn't employ duplicity or dramatic acts of terrorism, just courage and a united command.

So much for Machiavelli's teaching and discoveries. It remains to consider his influence. In his own lifetime he was considered a failure. Certainly, no soldier-prince arose to liberate Italy. After his death, however, it was otherwise. In 1552 the Vatican placed Machiavelli's works on the Index of Prohibited Books, because they teach men "to appear good for their own advantage in this world—a doctrine worse than heresy." Despite this ban, Machiavelli's books were widely read and his political teaching became influential. It would probably have confirmed him in his pessimistic view of human nature had he known that most statesmen and thinkers would seize on the elements of repression and guile in his teachings to the exclusion of the civic sense and patriotism he equally taught.

In France several kings studied Machiavelli as a means of increasing their absolutism, though it cannot be said that he did them much good. Henry III and Henry IV were murdered, and in each case on their blood-soaked person was found a well-thumbed copy of *The Prince*. Louis XIII was following Machiavelli when he caused his most powerful subject, the Italian-born adventurer Concini, to be treacherously killed. Richelieu affirmed that France could not be governed without the right of arbitrary arrest and exile, and that in case of danger to the state it may be well that a hundred innocent men should perish. This was *raison d'état*, an exaggerated version of certain elements in *The Prince*, to which Machiavelli might well not have subscribed.

In England Machiavelli had little direct influence. England had never been defeated as Florence had been, and Englishmen could not understand the kind of desperate situation that demanded unscrupulous political methods. The political diseases Machiavelli had first studied scientifically were in England called after his name, rather as a physical disease—say Parkinson's—is called not after the man who is suffering from it but after the doctor who discovers it. Machiavelli thus became saddled with a lot of things he had never advocated, including atheism and any treacherous way of killing, generally by poison. Hence Flamineo in Webster's *White Devil*:

O the rare tricks of a Machivillian!
Hee doth not come like a grosse plodding
  slave
And buffet you to death: no, my quaint
  knave—
Hee tickles you to death; makes you die
  laughing,
As if you had swallow'd a pound of saffron.

The eighteenth century, with its strong belief in man's good nature and reason, tended to scoff at Machiavelli. Hume wrote: "There is scarcely any maxim in *The Prince* which subsequent experience has not entirely refuted. The errors of this politician proceed, in a great measure, from his having lived in too early an age of the world to be a good judge of political truth." With Hume's judgment Frederick the Great of Prussia would, in early life, have agreed. As a young man Frederick wrote an *Anti-Machiavel*, in which he stated that a ruler is the first servant of his people. He rejected the idea of breaking treaties, "for one has only to make one deception of this kind, and one loses the confidence of every ruler." But Frederick did follow Machiavelli's advice to rule personally, to act as his own commander in the field, and to despise flatterers.

Later, Frederick began to wonder whether honesty really was the best policy. "One sees oneself continually in danger of being betrayed by one's allies, forsaken by one's friends, brought low by envy and jealousy; and ultimately one finds oneself obliged to choose between the terrible alternatives of sacrificing one's people or one's word of honor." In old age, Frederick became a confirmed Machiavellian, writing in 1775: "Rulers must always be guided by the interests of the state. They are slaves of their resources, the interest of the state is their law, and this law may not be infringed."

During the nineteenth century Germany and Italy both sought to achieve national unity, with the result that writers now began to play up Machiavelli's other side, his call for regeneration. Young Hegel hails the author of *The Prince* for having "grasped with a cool circumspection the necessary idea that Italy should be saved by being combined into one state." He and Fichte go a stage further than Machiavelli: they assert that the conflict between the individual and the state no longer exists, since they consider liberty and law identical. The necessity of evil in political action becomes a superior ethics that has no connection with the morals of an individual. The state swallows up evil.

In Italy Machiavelli's ideal of a regenerated national state was not perverted in this way and proved an important influence on the *risorgimento*. In 1859 the provisional government of Tuscany, on the eve of national independence, published a decree stating that a complete edition of Machiavelli's works would be printed at government expense. It had taken more than three hundred years for "a man to arise to redeem Italy," and in the event the man turned out to be two men, Cavour and Garibaldi. Both, incidentally, were quite unlike the Prince: Cavour, peering through steel-rimmed spectacles, was a moderate statesman of the center, and Garibaldi a blunt, humane, rather quixotic soldier.

Bismarck was a close student of Machiavelli, but Marx and Engels did not pay much attention to him, and the Florentine's books have never exerted great influence in Russia. In contemporary history Machiavelli's main impact has been on Benito Mussolini. In 1924 Mussolini wrote a thesis on *The*

Prince, which he described as the statesman's essential vade mecum. The Fascist leader deliberately set himself to implement Petrarch's call quoted on the last page of *The Prince*:

Che l'antico valore
Nell' italici cor non è ancor morto.

Let Italians, as they did of old,
Prove that their courage has not grown cold.

After a course of muscle building, Mussolini sent the Italian army into Ethiopia to found a new Roman Empire. He joined Hitler's war in 1940, only to find that he had failed to impart to modern Italians the martial qualities of Caesar's legions. The final irony occurred in 1944, when the Nazis were obliged to occupy northern Italy as the only means of stopping an Allied walkover, and Italy again experienced the trauma of 1494 and 1512. Mussolini's failures discredit, at least for our generation, Machiavelli's theory that it is possible for one man to effect a heart transplant on a whole people.

What is Machiavelli's significance today? His policy of political duplicity has been found wanting in the past and is probably no longer practicable in an age of democracy and television. His policy of nationalism is also beginning to date as we move into an era of ideological blocs. His insistence on the need for military preparedness has proved of more durable value and is likely to remain one of the West's key beliefs. His technique for solving political problems through a study of the past is practiced to some extent by every self-respecting foreign minister of our time.

Was Machiavelli, finally, an evil man? He made an ethic of patriotism. In normal times that is a poisonous equation, but defensible, I believe, in the context of sixteenth-century Italy. Machiavelli wrote on the edge of an abyss: he could hear the thud of enemy boots, had seen pillage, profanation, and rape by foreign troops. Imaginative as he was, he could sense horrors ahead: the ending of political liberty and of freedom of the press, which put the lights out in Italy for 250 years. He taught that it is civilized man's first duty to save civilization—at all costs. Doubtless he was mistaken. But it is not, I think, the mistake of an evil man.

Luther: Giant of His Time and Ours

Half a millennium after his birth, the first Protestant is still a towering force

It was a back-room deal, little different from many others struck at the time, but it triggered an upheaval that altered irrevocably the history of the Western world. Albrecht of Brandenburg, a German nobleman who had previously acquired a dispensation from the Vatican to become a priest while underage and to head two dioceses at the same time, wanted yet another favor from the Pope: the powerful archbishop's chair in Mainz. Pope Leo X, a profligate spender who needed money to build St. Peter's Basilica, granted the appointment—for 24,000 gold pieces, roughly equal to the annual imperial revenues in Germany. It was worth it. Besides being a rich source of income, the Mainz post brought Albrecht a vote for the next Holy Roman Emperor, which could be sold to the highest bidder.

In return, Albrecht agreed to initiate the sale of indulgences in Mainz. Granted for good works, indulgences were papally controlled dispensations drawn from an eternal "treasury of merits" built up by Christ and the saints; the church taught that they would help pay the debt of "temporal punishment" due in purgatory for sins committed by either the penitent or any deceased person. The Pope received half the proceeds of the Mainz indulgence sale, while the other half

went to repay the bankers who had lent the new archbishop gold.

Enter Martin Luther, a 33-year-old priest and professor at Wittenberg University. Disgusted not only with

the traffic in indulgences but with its doctrinal underpinnings, he forcefully protested to Albrecht—never expecting that his action would provoke a sweeping uprising against a corrupt church.

RUDI FREY

A statue of the reformer stares defiantly across Eisenach, East Germany

To some Catholic scholars, he has even become a "father in the faith."

Luther's challenge culminated in the Protestant Reformation and the rending of Western Christendom, and made him a towering figure in European history. In this 500th anniversary year of his birth (Nov. 10, 1483), the rebel of Wittenberg remains the subject of persistent study. It is said that more books have been written about him than anyone else in history, save his own master, Jesus Christ. The renaissance in Luther scholarship surrounding this year's anniversary serves as a reminder that his impact on modern life is profound, even for those who know little about the doctrinal feuds that brought him unsought fame. From the distance of half a millennium, the man who, as Historian Hans Hillerbrand of Southern Methodist University in Dallas says, brought Christianity from lofty theological dogma to a clearer and more personal belief is still able to stimulate more heated debate than all but a handful of historical figures.

Indeed, as the reformer who fractured Christianity, Luther has latterly become a key to reuniting it. With the approval of the Vatican, and with Americans taking the lead, Roman Catholic theologians are working with Lutherans and other Protestants to sift through the 16th century disputes and see whether the Protestant-Catholic split can some day be overcome. In a remarkable turnabout, Catholic scholars today express growing appreciation of Luther as a "father in the faith" and are willing to play down his excesses. According to a growing consensus, the great division need never have happened at all.

Beyond his importance as a religious leader, Luther had a profound effect on Western culture. He is, paradoxically, the last medieval man and the first modern one, a political conservative and a spiritual revolutionary. His impact is most marked, of course, in Germany, where he laid the cultural foundations for what later became a united German nation.

When Luther attacked the indulgence business in 1517, he was not only the most popular teacher at Wittenberg but also vicar provincial in charge of eleven houses of the Hermits

The room where Luther translated the New Testament; title page of his Bible

of St. Augustine. He was brilliant, tireless and a judicious administrator, though given to bouts of spiritual depression. To make his point on indulgences, Luther dashed off 95 theses condemning the system ("They preach human folly who pretend that as soon as money in the coffer rings, a soul from purgatory springs") and sent them to Archbishop Albrecht and a number of theologians.*

*Despite colorful legend, it is not certain he ever nailed them to the door of the Castle Church.

The response was harsh: the Pope eventually rejected Luther's protest and demanded capitulation. It was then that Luther began asking questions about other aspects of the church, including the papacy itself. In 1520 he charged in an open letter to the Pope, "The Roman Church, once the holiest of all, has become the most licentious den of thieves, the most shameless of brothels, the kingdom of sin, death and hell." Leo called Luther "the wild boar which has invaded the Lord's vineyard."

The following year Luther was summoned to recant his writings before the Diet of Worms, a council of princes convened by the young Holy Roman Emperor Charles V. In his closing defense, Luther proclaimed defiantly: "Unless I am convinced by testimony from Holy Scriptures and clear proofs based on reason—because, since it is notorious that they have erred and contradicted themselves, I cannot believe either the Pope or the council alone—I am bound by conscience and the Word of God. Therefore I can and will recant nothing, because to act against one's conscience is neither safe nor salutary. So help me God." (Experts today think that he did not actually speak the famous words, "Here I stand. I can do no other.")

This was hardly the cry of a skeptic, but it was ample grounds for the Emperor to put Luther under sentence of death as a heretic. Instead of being executed, Luther lived for another 25 years, became a major author and composer of hymns, father of a bustling household and a secular figure who opposed rebellion—in all, a commanding force in European affairs. In the years beyond, the abiding split in Western Christendom developed, including a large component of specifically "Lutheran" churches that today have 69 million adherents in 85 nations.

The enormous presence of the Wittenberg rebel, the sheer force of his personality, still broods over all Christendom, not just Lutheranism. Although Luther declared that the Roman Pontiffs were the "Antichrist," today's Pope, in an anniversary tip of the zucchetto, mildly speaks of Luther as "the reformer." Ecumenical-minded Catholic theologians have come to rank Luther in importance with Augustine and Aquinas. "No one who came after Luther could match him," says

Father Peter Manns, a Catholic theologian in Mainz. "On the question of truth, Luther is a lifesaver for Christians." While Western Protestants still express embarrassment over Luther's anti-Jewish rantings or his skepticism about political clergy, Communist East Germany has turned him into a secular saint because of his influence on German culture. Party Boss Erich Honecker, head of the regime's *Lutherjahr* committee, is willing to downplay Luther's antirevolutionary ideas, using the giant figure to bolster national pride.

Said West German President Karl Carstens, as he opened one of the hundreds of events commemorating Luther this year: "Luther has become a symbol of the unity of all Germany. We are all Luther's heirs."

After five centuries, scholars still have difficulty coming to terms with the contradictions of a tempestuous man. He was often inexcusably vicious in his writings (he wrote, for instance, that one princely foe was a "faint-hearted wretch and fearful sissy" who should "do nothing but stand like a eunuch, that is, a harem guard, in a fool's cap with a fly swatter"). Yet he was kindly in person and so generous to the needy that his wife despaired of balancing the household budget. When the plague struck Wittenberg and others fled, he stayed behind to minister to the dying. He was a powerful spiritual author, yet his words on other occasions were so scatological that no Lutheran periodical would print them today. His writing was hardly systematic, and his output runs to more than 100 volumes. On the average, Luther wrote a major tract or treatise every two weeks throughout his life.

The scope of Luther's work has made him the subject of endless reinterpretation. The Enlightenment treated him as the father of free thought, conveniently omitting his belief in a sovereign God who inspired an authoritative Bible. During the era of Otto von Bismarck a century ago, Luther was fashioned into a nationalistic symbol; 70 years later, Nazi propagandists claimed him as one of their own by citing his anti-Jewish polemics.

All scholars agree on Luther's importance for German culture, surpassing even that of Shakespeare on the English-speaking world. Luther's masterpiece was his translation of the New Testament from Greek into German, largely completed in ten weeks while he was in hiding after the Worms confrontation, and of the Old Testament, published in 1534 with the assistance of Hebrew experts. The Luther Bible sold massively in his lifetime and remains today the authorized German Protestant version. Before Luther's Bible was published, there was no standard German, just a profusion of dialects. "It was Luther," said Johann Gottfried von Herder, one of Goethe's mentors, "who has awakened and let loose the giant: the German language."

Only a generation ago, Catholics were trained to consider Luther the arch-heretic. Now no less than the Vatican's specialist on Lutheranism, Monsignor Aloys Klein, says that "Martin Luther's action was beneficial to the Catholic Church." Like many other Catholics, Klein thinks that if Luther were living today there would be no split. Klein's colleague in the Vatican's Secretariat for Promoting Christian Unity, Father Pierre Duprey, suggests that with the Second Vatican Council (1962–65) Luther "got the council he asked for, but 450 years too late." Vatican II accepted his contention that, in a sense, all believers are priests; while the council left the Roman church's hierarchy intact, it enhanced the role of the laity. More important, the council moved the Bible to the center of Catholic life, urged continual reform and instituted worship in local languages rather than Latin.

One of the key elements in the Reformation was the question of "justification," the role of faith in relation to good works in justifying a sinner in the eyes of God. Actually, Catholicism had never officially taught that salvation could be attained only through pious works, but the popular perception held otherwise. Luther recognized, as University of Chicago Historian Martin Marty explains, that everything "in the system of Catholic teaching seemed aimed toward appeasing God. Luther was led to the idea of God not as an angry judge but as a forgiving father. It is a position that gives the individual a great sense of freedom and security." In effect, says U.S. Historian Roland Bainton, Luther destroyed the implication that men could "bargain with God."

Father George Tavard, a French Catholic expert on Protestantism who teaches in Ohio and has this month published *Justification: an Ecumenical Study* (Paulist; $7.95), notes that "today many Catholic scholars think Luther was right and the 16th century Catholic polemicists did not understand what he meant. Both Lutherans and Catholics agree that good works by Christian believers are the result of their faith and the working of divine grace in them, not their personal contributions to their own salvation. Christ is the only Savior. One does not save oneself." An international Lutheran-Catholic commission, exploring the basis for possible reunion, made a joint statement along these lines in 1980. Last month a parallel panel in the U.S. issued a significant 21,000-word paper on justification that affirms much of Luther's thinking, though with some careful hedging from the Catholic theologians.

There is doubt, of course, about the degree to which Protestants and Catholics can, in the end, overcome their differences. Catholics may now be permitted to sing Luther's *A Mighty Fortress Is Our God* or worship in their native languages, but a wide gulf clearly remains on issues like the status of Protestant ministers and, most crucially, papal authority.

During the futile Protestant-Catholic reunion negotiations in 1530 at the Diet of Augsburg, the issue of priestly celibacy was as big an obstacle as the faith *vs.* good works controversy. Luther had married a nun, to the disgust of his Catholic contemporaries. From the start, the marriage of clergy was a sharply defined difference between Protestantism and Catholicism, and it remains a key barrier today. By discarding the concept of the moral superiority of celibacy, Luther established sexuality as a gift from God. In general, he was a lover of the simple

pleasures, and would have had little patience with the later Puritans. He spoke offhandedly about sex, enjoyed good-natured joshing, beer drinking and food ("If our Lord is permitted to create nice large pike and good Rhine wine, presumably I may be allowed to eat and drink"). For his time, he also had an elevated opinion of women. He cherished his wife and enjoyed fatherhood, siring six children and rearing eleven orphaned nieces and nephews as well.

But if Luther's views on the Catholic Church have come to be accepted even by many Catholics, his anti-Semitic views remain a problem for even his most devoted supporters. Says New York City Rabbi Marc Tanenbaum: "The anniversary will be marred by the haunting specter of Luther's devil theory of the Jews."

Luther assailed the Jews on doctrinal grounds, just as he excoriated "papists" and Turkish "infidels." But his work titled *On the Jews and Their Lies* (1543) went so far as to advocate that their synagogues, schools and homes should be destroyed and their prayer books and Talmudic volumes taken away. Jews were to be relieved of their savings and put to work as agricultural laborers or expelled outright.

Fortunately, the Protestant princes ignored such savage recommendations, and the Lutheran Church quickly forgot about them. But the words were there to be gleefully picked up by the Nazis, who removed them from the fold of religious polemics and used them to buttress their 20th century racism. For a good Lutheran, of course, the Bible is the sole authority, not Luther's writings, and the thoroughly Lutheran Scandinavia vigorously opposed Hitler's racist madness. In the anniversary year, all sectors of Lutheranism have apologized for their founder's views.

Whatever the impact of Luther's anti-Jewish tracts, there is no doubt that his political philosophy, which tended to make church people submit to state authority, was crucial in weakening opposition by German Lutherans to the Nazis. Probably no aspect of Luther's teaching is the

subject of more agonizing Protestant scrutiny in West Germany today.

Luther sought to declericalize society and to free people from economic burdens imposed by the church. But he was soon forced, if reluctantly, to deliver considerable control of the new Protestant church into the hands of secular rulers who alone could ensure the survival of the Reformation. Luther spoke of "two kingdoms," the spiritual and the secular, and his writings provided strong theological support for authoritarian government and Christian docility.

The Lutheran wing of the Reformation was democratic, but only in terms of the church itself, teaching that a plowman did God's work as much as a priest, encouraging lay leadership and seeking to educate one and all. But it was Calvin, not Luther, who created a theology for the democratic state. A related aspect of Luther's politics, controversial then and now, was his opposition to the bloody Peasants' War of 1525. The insurgents thought they were applying Luther's ideas, but he urged rulers to crush the revolt: "Let whoever can, stab, strike, kill." Support of the rulers was vital for the Reformation, but Luther loathed violent rebellion and anarchy in any case.

Today Luther's law-and-order approach is at odds with the revolutionary romanticism and liberation theology that are popular in some theology schools. In contrast with modern European Protestantism's social gospel, Munich Historian Thomas Nipperdey says, Luther "would not accept modern attempts to build a utopia and would argue, on the contrary, that we as mortal sinners are incapable of developing a paradise on earth."

Meanwhile, the internal state of the Lutheran Church raises other questions about the lasting power of Luther's vision. Lutheranism in the U.S., with 8.5 million adherents, is stable and healthy. The church is also growing in Third World strongholds like racially torn Namibia, where black Lutherans predominate. But in Lutheranism's historic heartland, the two Germanys and Scandinavia, there are deep problems. In East Germany, Lutherans are under pressure from the Communist regime. In West Germany, the Evangelical Church in Germany (E.K.D.), a church federation that includes some non-Lutherans, is wealthy (annual income: $3 billion), but membership is shrinking and attendance at Sunday services is feeble indeed. Only 6% of West Germans—or, for that matter, Scandinavians—worship regularly.

What seems to be lacking in the old European churches is the passion for God and his truth that so characterizes Luther. He retains the potential to shake people out of religious complacency. Given Christianity's need, on all sides, for a good jolt, eminent

Historian Heiko Oberman muses, "I wonder if the time of Luther isn't ahead of us."

The boldest assertion about Luther for modern believers is made by Protestants who claim that the reformer did nothing less than enable Christianity to survive. In the Middle Ages, too many Popes and bishops were little more than corrupt, luxury-loving politicians, neglecting the teaching of the love of God and using the fear of God to enhance their power and wealth. George Lindbeck, the Lutheran co-chairman of the international Lutheran-Catholic commission, believes that without Luther "religion would

have been much less important during the next 400 to 500 years. And since medieval religion was falling apart, secularization would have marched on, unimpeded."

A provocative thesis, and a debatable one. But with secularization still marching on, almost unimpeded, Protestants and Catholics have much to reflect upon as they scan the five centuries after Luther and the shared future of their still divided churches.

—By Richard N. Ostling. Reported by Roland Flamini and Wanda Menke-Glückert/Bonn, with other bureaus.

Heartland of the Witchcraze:

Central and Northern Europe

More witches were executed in the German-speaking territories than in any other part of Europe. Why was the German witch-hunt so assiduously and successfully prosecuted?

H. C. Erik Midelfort

MAXIMILIAN I, HOLY ROMAN EMPEROR and the 'last knight of the Middle Ages' kept a magician, Johannes Trithemius, Abbot of Sponheim, at his court. On one occasion, the Emperor asked him to settle empirically the rival claims of the pagan and biblical worthies by bringing them back to earth. We do not know what the famous humanist abbot made of this imperial request; nor can we tell what spectacles and illusions he produced to entertain the court at Innsbruck. What we do know is that Trithemius had a reputation as a learned necromancer.

But was his art witchcraft, a demonic gift made possible only by a pact with the devil? No one in the early sixteenth century seems to have thought so. Indeed, Germany was alive with learned magicians in those years, men whose neo-Platonic convictions led them to harness the magical forces of the cosmos. Henry Cornelius Agrippa of Nettesheim and Theophrastus Bombastus von Hohenheim, known more simply as Paracelsus, flourished in the early sixteenth century and tried to bring magic to the aid of philosophy and medicine. Dr. Johann Faust may even have given himself to the devil before his death in 1540, thereby engendering a myth that has firmly linked Germany and the devil together ever

since. And yet it is worth noting that none of these magicians was ever even prosecuted for witchcraft. Theologically, they all deviated from Christian orthodoxy, but even dabbling with demons did not endanger their lives. Later in the century, David Leipzig might actually sign a pact with the devil and receive a punishment no more severe than expulsion from his university.

In a court of law all of these men might have been convicted of witchcraft, but the interesting point is that no-one thought of bringing charges against them. In 1563, in his famous *De Praestigiis Daemonum*, Johann Weyer complained bitterly that these *magi infames* got off scot free while deluded old women were convicted and executed by the hundreds. Weyer's sense of outrage illustrates the important point that, regardless of what the theologians and jurists might say, witchcraft in Germany was not simply a crime of mental or spiritual deviation; it was not primarily heresy or apostasy or learned diabolism. Rather, witchcraft was mainly a social offence: the use of harmful magic by a secret conspiracy of women. The German prosecutors who assumed the task of rooting out the godless witches knew whom they were looking for. And they were so successful that they made the German-speaking territories the classic land of the witch-hunt. It is certain that the Holy Roman Empire and Switzerland executed far more witches than any other

parts of Europe. How can we account for this?

Recent studies have illuminated the important extent to which witchcraft trials remained popular in inspiration or became subject to learned influence and interference. It has become clear that down to 1550, and probably much later, the common folk of the village feared witchcraft not as a demonic conspiracy but as a practical threat to the fertility of their fields, flocks and families. Witches were popularly imagined as solitary sorcerers, practicing their malific magic through the manipulation of cursing tablets, ointments, charms, and all the mysterious rubbish that could be combined in a *Hexentopf*. Their baneful poisons could cause hailstorms and untimely frosts; sickness in man and beast; impotence, miscarriage and death. These were everyday threats to country life, and it is not surprising that common people accused the local crone of enviously casting evil spells. Indeed it is probable enough that some of the locally accused were guilty as charged of at least *trying* to harm a neighbour or secure his affection with love magic. Throughout the centuries of the witch-hunt these locally inspired and locally controlled sorcery trials continued to be common. They usually ended as abruptly as they had begun, with the execution or banishment of one or two witches. There was nothing

From *History Today*, February 1981. History Today, 83-84 Berwick Street, London W1V 3PJ. Reprinted by permission.

peculiarly German in this procedure and nothing to cause the panic that the great witch-hunt inspired. But the true panic did not remain rooted in these rural concerns and did not rest content with the extermination of one or two geriatric outcasts.

To have some understanding of the difference we may look with profit at some of the frightful trials that became characteristic of Germany, especially in the prince-bishoprics and ecclesiastical states of central Germany. Between 1587 and 1593 the Archbishop-Elector of Trier sponsored a witch-hunt that burned 368 witches from just twenty-two villages. So horrible was this hunt that two villages in 1585 were left with only one female inhabitant apiece. In the lands of the Convent of Quedlinburg, some 133 witches were executed on just one day in 1589. At the Abbey of Fulda, Prince Abbot Balthasar von Dernbach conducted a reign of terror in the first decade of the seventeenth century: his minister Balthasar Ross boasted of having sent over 700 witches to the stake, no less than 205 of them in the years 1603–05 alone. At the *Fürstprobstei* of Ellwangen, ecclesiastical officials saw to the burning of some 390 persons between 1611 and 1618, while the Teutonic Order at Mergentheim executed some 124 in the years 1628–30. The Prince Bishopric of Würzburg endured a frightful panic during the 1620s: in just eight years Bishop Philipp Adolf von Ehrenberg executed some 900 persons including his own nephew, nineteen Catholic priests, and several small children. In the Prince Bishopric of Eichstätt some 274 witches were executed in 1629. At Bonn, the Archbishop Elector of Cologne supervised the execution of his own Chancellor, his wife and his secretary's wife. The worst ecclesiastical excesses may well have occurred in the Bishopric of Bamberg, where Bishop Johann Georg II Fuchs von Dornheim is said to have eliminated 600 witches during his reign of ten years (1623–33), including his own Chancellor and one of the burgermeisters of Bamberg, Johann Junius.

Although these ecclesiastical territories were the most ferocious exterminators of witches, secular territories were not always far behind them in their zeal to purge the commonwealth. The tiny county of Helfenstein killed sixty-three witches in 1562–63. The Duchy of Braunschweig-Wolfenbüttel executed fifty-three between 1590 and 1620, while Duke August of Braunschweig-Lüneberg elimi-

nated seventy between 1610 and 1615 in the tiny district of Hitzacker. The County of Lippe tried 221 witches between 1550 and 1686 and another 209 in the town of Lemgo. All told the Duchy of Bavaria probably executed close to 2,000 witches, and the secular territories of south-western Germany very likely accounted for another 1,000. Even the imperial cities hunted witches in sizeable numbers, both among their own burghers and among the peasants of their outlying hinterlands.

When we ask who these witches were, the German evidence agrees closely with that from most of the rest of Europe: they were women, usually old and poor, often widows. Overall, some 80 to 90 per cent of the accused were female, and one cannot begin to understand the European witch-hunt without recognising that it displayed a burst of misogyny without parallel in Western history. Scholars are still far from agreement as to the sources of this hatred and fear of women, but it is clear that the major trials sprang from fears that were no longer rooted merely in the vagaries of peasant misfortune. The thousands executed in these chain-reaction trials may have had to confess to harmful magic, but their chief crime was one of which peasants were generally unaware: the obscene worship of the devil. Where and how had this idea penetrated the German-speaking lands?

The first massive persecutions in Germany are inseparably connected to the author of the famous *Malleus Maleficarum*, the Hammer of Witches, published in 1487: Heinrich Institoris, OP. In 1484 Institoris obtained from Pope Innocent VIII a bull (*Summis desiderantes*) urging German secular and ecclesiastical officials to co-operate with Institoris and his associate, Jacob Sprenger, OP, in the hunting of witches. Theologically, this bull contained nothing that previous popes had not said; but the bull had considerable importance because it seemed to sanction the subsequent activities of these two Dominican inquisitors. Reprinted with every edition of their *Malleus*, the bull seemed to bestow papal approval on their inquisitorial theories as well. So successful was this stroke of advertising strategy that the authors hardly even needed the approval of the Cologne University theologians, but just for good measure Institoris forged a document granting their apparently unanimous approbation. Armed with the bull, Institoris began a campaign in the diocese of Constance and executed forty-eight witches between 1481 and 1486. Although these efforts

finally ran into the effective opposition of the bishop of Bressanone, Institoris assembled enough practical experience to enliven the manual he and Sprenger composed in 1486.

The *Malleus Maleficarum* is a remarkable treatise that actually reveals how far Germany still was from a full-fledged witch-hunting panic. True enough, the two Dominicans injected so much misogynist venom into their pages as to construe witchcraft almost exclusively as a crime of female lust. True, too, the *Malleus* recommends a degree of judicial terror and deception that helps us understand why those accused of witchcraft often found that they had no real chance to defend themselves. But it is also true that the *Malleus* repeatedly mentions popular incredulity. In the late fifteenth century Germans were still far from unanimous in their acceptance of the fine points of demonology. In fact, the *Malleus* itself is innocent of the most important detail of late medieval witchcraft theory: the witches' dance or sabbath. Institoris and Sprenger spent so much time working out the way that witches co-operated with the devil that they neglected to spend any attention on the single feature that made massive, chain-reaction trials possible. Indeed it was another 75 to 100 years before the orgiastic ritual of the sabbath had worked its way into the obsessions of the learned and the imagery of the artists. It is noteworthy that German artistic representations of witchcraft in the late fifteenth century agree with the *Malleus* in portraying a basically solitary crime. The famous prints of Hans Baldung Grien and Albrecht Dürer enliven the theme with visual jokes, playing changes on the theme of the classical muses, but their figures are still far from the lusting, turbulent, populous scenes of the late sixteenth and seventeenth centuries.

The *Malleus*, for all its wealth of corrupt and confused argument, cannot be viewed as the final synthesis of witchcraft theory. In its own day it was never accorded the unquestioned authority that modern scholars have sometimes given it. Theologians and jurists respected it as one among many informative books; its peculiarly savage misogyny and its obsession with impotence were never fully accepted. Emperor Charles V promulgated a criminal code for the Empire in 1532 (the *Carolina*) with a witchcraft clause that was still far from reflecting the spirit of the *Malleus*. Article 10 read simply:

When someone harms people or brings them trouble by witchcraft, one should punish him with death, and one should use the punishment of death by fire. When, however, someone uses witchcraft and yet does no one any harm with it, he should be punished otherwise, according to the custom of the case; and the judges should take counsel as is described later regarding legal consultations.

This article preserved intact the Roman legal distinction between harmful and harmless magic, a distinction that appeared impious to the authors of the *Malleus*. As long as courts insisted that witchcraft prosecutions be closely tied to actual cases of harm and loss, there was little chance of a chain reaction trial breaking out.

Unfortunately, the witchcraft article of the *Carolina* did not make full theological sense, for it seemed to permit a more lenient treatment of the most diabolical magic so long as it harmed no one. Through the middle and late decades of the sixteenth century in Germany, one can mark the advance of two notions, both fateful for the development of the German panic trial; gradually, the witches' sabbath became a common obsession among the ruling élite; and, just as gradually, territorial laws were altered to allow for the execution of witches whose only crime was association with the devil, regardless of harm (*maleficium*) to anyone. In 1572 the Criminal Constitutions of Electoral Saxony declared, for example, that 'if anyone, forgetting his Christian faith, sets up a pact with the devil or has anything to do with him, regardless of whether he has harmed anyone by magic, he should be condemned to death by fire'. With a law such as this, one could proceed to torture a suspect until one had not only an admission of guilt but a list of the names of others seen at the witches' dance. These persons could then in turn be examined and tortured if necessary. A panic might be under way.

To return to our earlier question, it seems clear that the German holocaust of witches depended both on torture and on the learned obsession with the sabbath. But where had local courts and the petty princes of Germany obtained their notions of the sabbath? And let us make no mistake that it was an illusion: no careful researcher has discovered even a trace of a true witch-cult with sabbaths, orgies, black masses and devil worship. So how did this inquisitor's nightmare become part of the secular law of hundreds of German jurisdictions? Here the notion of the peculiarly German reception of Roman Law is useful again. For as Roman procedures replaced traditional ones in the sixteenth century, local judges were frequently at a loss as to how to proceed. Roman procedure dictated the rational device of seeking learned counsel, as we have seen in the witchcraft article of the *Carolina*; and, beginning in the mid-sixteenth century and with regularity in the seventeenth century, local districts turned to the juridical faculties of the German universities. In this way local procedures all across the Holy Roman Empire were tied to the Roman legal theories of the professors – but, just as fatefully, local witchcraft theory was now dependent as never before on the demonological illusions of learned jurists. In requiring ignorant petty judges to take counsel, the *Carolina* in effect undercut its own prudent Roman witchcraft doctrine, and opened the door to the possibility that the panic about the witches' sabbath could spread beyond the learned studies where it had first taken root.

The Holy Roman Empire thus became the classic land of the witch-hunt, not so much because of the 'German temperament' as because of the German legal system, a system that allowed bishops and other ecclesiastics an unparalleled degree of influence in their territories, and permitted university professors to become full members of the judicial mechanism. Episcopal and professorial fantasies still need close investigation, but at least it seems clear now where we need to look in order to understand how popular and peasant notions of merely harmful magic were perverted into the witchcraft delusion. We may find that the full panoply of demonology never became deeply rooted in the villages, that local accusations almost always stemmed from some local misfortune. At any rate it appears that small-scale witch-trials could survive long after the chain reaction panics had disappeared. Across the Empire the mass trials proliferated between *c.* 1570 and *c.* 1630. Some regions had flare-ups again in the 1670s, but by 1630 in most places the worst was over.

How shall we understand this decline? A common answer has been that the magistrates and learned élites of Europe finally gave up their belief in witchcraft. Without their support, trials were no longer possible. This may help explain why even the small, local trials withered away in the eighteenth century; but by then the large, chain trials had been dead for a generation or more.

One reason for the disappearance of large trials is that during the seventeenth century they came increasingly to involve children. Most of the huge trials after 1625 featured children as accusers and even as the accused. In several cases it was finally recognised, if not by learned university jurists then at least by local officials, that the testimony of minors was simply not credible. Critics of witchcraft trials, from Johann Weyer in the sixteenth century to Friedrich von Spee in the seventeenth, had long maintained that tortured evidence was equally unreliable. Slowly but surely the territories of the Holy Roman Empire put on the brakes, becoming much more cautious in the use of torture than they had been. Already in 1603 the Protestant Archbishop of Bremen, Johann Friedrich, published an *Edict Concerning Witchcraft* that made continuation of the trials almost impossible. In 1649 Queen Christina of Sweden put an end to witchcraft trials in Verden, which was controlled by her country after the end of the Thirty Years' War. Bishop Johann Philipp von Schönborn ordered the end to trials in Würzburg in 1642 and carried this caution to Mainz when he became Elector and Archbishop there in 1647. Similarly Prince Bishop Christoph Bernhard von Galen, put a stop to trials in Münster. By the 1670s the legal faculties of Tübingen and Helmstedt were urging extraordinary caution in the application of torture. Although the enlightened Professor Christian Thomasius of Halle won renown for his dissertation *De Crimine Magiae* (1701) and for his other attacks on the witchcraft theory and demonology of the learned, by then the true age of witchcraft trials was over.

A glance at witchcraft in Denmark can serve as a comparative check on the picture presented here of the Holy Roman Empire. The Lutheran Bishop of Sealand, Peder Palladius, urged vigorous prosecution of witches in 1544 and reported that successful trials were uncovering 'swarms' of witches in Malmø, Køge, and Jutland, and that at Als and in the nearby islands a chain reaction trial had sent fifty-two witches to the stake as 'one of them betrays another'. But all of these trials dealt with specific cases of *maleficium*, and in general the Danish trials never developed the fascination with the devil and the sabbath that one finds just to the south. The main reason for this surprisingly

209

'backward' condition (one much like that of England) was the promulgation of two laws in 1547. The first forbade the use of testimony from those convicted of infamous crimes, such as theft, treason, and sorcery, against others. The second held that 'no person shall be interrogated under torture before he is sentenced'. These two rules effectively cut off the spread of massive chain trials like those of 1544. It was no longer possible to torture suspects into confessing their horrible misdeeds or into naming those whom they had seen at the witches' dance. From beginnings that seem similar to those in Germany, Danish trials were thus steered into an English path. Even without ideas of the sabbath, the best recent estimate suggests that the Danes tried some 2,000 persons and executed something less than 1,000. A further reason for the Danish 'mildness' is that after 1576 all death sentences had to be appealed to the high court (*Landsting*), which often proved more cautious than the local courts. After 1650 cases dropped off dramatically to just a few per annum. As in the Holy Roman Empire, however, the popular fear of *maleficium* survived long after the élite had put an end to actual witchcraft trials.

In the rest of Scandinavia, however, the picture was somewhat different. In Norway, where the records of about 750 trials survive between 1560 and 1710, torture was seldom used and only one-quarter of those accused (mostly those convicted of causing the death of a person or an animal) were executed. But in Sweden, although the use of torture was infrequent in the sixteenth century, church leaders convinced the government that all found guilty of making a pact with the Devil should be sentenced to death. From 1668 until 1676 a major witch panic gripped northern Sweden (with repercussions in Finland until 1684): thousands were accused, interrogated and tortured; over 200 were executed. After 1672, persons accused by several witnesses were executed even if they did not confess. The panic only abated in 1676 when several child-witnesses involved in a major Stockholm trial admitted that their stories of Sabbaths and Covens were entirely false.

These Scandinavian trials all serve to point up the extremely pernicious effects of legalised torture and the idea of the sabbath. Wherever the testimony of witches and the possessed could be excluded, trials remained small and manageable; but whenever these restraints were relaxed, the Scandinavians rapidly imitated the legal excesses of the prince-bishops of central Germany. Local suspicions of *maleficium* seem to have flourished throughout northern Europe for centuries, certainly surviving long into the nineteenth century, and even into our own. By themselves, however, these suspicions never led to more than a few trials or lynchings. It was the fateful intervention of learned and thoughtful lawyers and theologians with their panicstricken demonology that sent thousands of women to their deaths. It is a legacy for the learned to ponder.

NOTES ON FURTHER READING
K. Baschwitz, *Hexen und Hexenprozesse. Die Geschichte eines Massenwahns* (Munich, 1963); H. C. E. Midelfort, *Witch Hunting in Southwestern Germany, 1562–1684. The Social and Intellectual Foundations*, Stanford University Press (Stanford, USA, 1972); G. Schormann, *Hexenprozesse in Nordwestdeutschland* (Hildesheim, 1977).

Credits/ Acknowledgments

Cover design by Charles Vitelli

1. Pre-History and the Earliest Civilizations
Facing overview—York Archaeological Trust. 23—Mansell Collection. 24—Cairo Museum. Photograph: Roger Wood. 25—(top) Courtesy of the Victoria & Albert Museum; (left bottom) Louvre Service Photographique; (right bottom) HT Archives. 26—(top) Mansell Collection; (bottom) Courtesy of the Musee des Plan Reliefs. 27—Mansell Collection. 28—(top) Mansell Collection; (bottom) Courtesy of the Imperial War Museum.
2. Greece and Rome
Facing overview—"Compendium of Illustrations in The Public Domain," Compiled by Harold H. Hart, Hart Publishing Co. 69—Mansell-Graudon. 71—Michael Holford. 72—Courtesy of the Trustees of the British Museum. 73—Mansell-Alinari. 74—(top) Mansell-Alinari; (bottom) National Museum of Naples. 75—Mansell-Alinari.

3. The Judeo-Christian Heritage
Facing overview—United Nations/Chen.
4. Moslems and Byzantines
Facing overview—Dover Publications, Inc.
5. The Medieval Period
Facing overview—WHO Photo. 137—Courtesy of the author. 138—HT Map by Ken Wass. 139—Courtesy of the National Building Record. 140—Courtesy of the Treasurer & Masters of the Bench of the Inner Temple. 141—Victoria & Albert Museum. 142—Warburg Institute.
6. Renaissance and Reformation
Facing overview—WHO photo.

We Want Your Advice

ANNUAL EDITIONS:
WESTERN CIVILIZATION, VOLUME I
Article Rating Form

Here is an opportunity for you to have direct input into the next revision of this volume. We would like you to rate each of the 39 articles listed below, using the following scale:

1. **Excellent: should definitely be retained**
2. **Above average: should probably be retained**
3. **Below average: should probably be deleted**
4. **Poor: should definitely be deleted**

Your ratings will play a vital part in the next revision. So please mail this prepaid form to us just as soon as you complete it.
Thanks for your help!

Annual Editions revisions depend on two major opinion sources: one is our Advisory Board, listed in the front of this volume, which works with us in scanning the thousands of articles published in the public press each year; the other is you—the person actually using the book. Please help us and the users of the next edition by completing the prepaid article rating form on this page and returning it to us. Thank you.

Rating	Article	Rating	Article
	1. The Cosmic Calendar		22. Understanding Islam
	2. How Man Invented Cities		23. The Natural History of Medieval Women
	3. Potlatch Politics and Kings' Castles		24. The Viking Saga
	4. Where Nations Began		25. Student Power in the Middle Ages
	5. War and Man's Past		26. Wandering for the Love of God
	6. The First Olympics: Competing "for the Greater Glory of Zeus"		27. Murder and Justice, Medieval Style
	7. Love and Death in Ancient Greece		28. Robin Hood Revisited
	8. Life with Father, Life with Socrates		29. The Social Influence of the Motte-and-Bailey Castle
	9. The Two Thousand Years' War		30. Medieval Roots of the Industrial Revolution
	10. Charting the Unknown		31. How Jacques Coeur Made His Fortune
	11. Maritime Trade in Antiquity		32. Bruges: Fair City of Flanders
	12. The Silent Women of Rome		33. In Place of Strife: The Guilds of Renaissance Venice
	13. Nero, Unmaligned		34. To Mecca in Disguise
	14. Murderous Games		35. The Enigma of Aztec Sacrifice
	15. Jews and Judaism in the Ancient World		36. Our Man from Arezzo
	16. New Finds Cast Fresh Light on the Bible		37. Machiavelli
	17. Who Was Jesus?		38. Luther: Giant of His Time and Ours
	18. Who Was St. Peter?		39. Heartland of the Witchcraze: Central and Northern Europe
	19. The Contest for Men's Souls		
	20. The Byzantine Greeks' Heritage from the Hellenic Greeks		
	21. The World of Islam		

(cont. on next page)

ABOUT YOU

Name _____ Date _____

Are you a teacher? ☐   Or student? ☐

Your School Name _____

Department _____

Address _____

City _____ State _____ Zip _____

School Telephone # _____

YOUR COMMENTS ARE IMPORTANT TO US!

Please fill in the following information:

For which course did you use this book? _____

Did you use a text with this Annual Edition?   ☐ yes   ☐ no

The title of the text: _____

What are your general reactions to the Annual Editions concept?

Have you read any particular articles recently that you think should be included in the next edition?

Are there any articles you feel should be replaced in the next edition? Why?

Are there other areas that you feel would utilize an Annual Edition?

May we contact you for editorial input?

May we quote you from above?

WESTERN CIVILIZATION, VOLUME I

BUSINESS REPLY MAIL

First Class   Permit No. 84   Guilford, CT

Postage will be paid by addressee

The Dushkin Publishing Group, Inc.
Sluice Dock
Guilford, Connecticut 06437